GERARD MURRAY
JONATHAN TONGE

Sinn Féin and the SDLP

From Alienation to Participation

HURST & COMPANY, LONDON

First published in the United Kingdom by
C. Hurst & Co. (Publishers) Ltd,
41 Great Russell Street, London WC1B 3PD
© 2005 by Gerard Murray and Jonathan Tonge
All rights reserved.

The right of Gerard Murray and Jonathan Tonge to be
identified as the authors of this publication has been
asserted by them in accordance with the Copyright,
Designs and Patents Act 1988.

A catalogue record for this book is available
from the British Library.

ISBNs
1–85065–649–5 *casebound*
1–85065–648–7 *paperback*

CONTENTS

Preface and Acknowledgements   *page* ix

Chapters
1. The Development of Nationalist Politics
   in Northern Ireland   1
   The National Democratic Party   7
   The birth of the SDLP   10
   Developments within Republicanism: the IRA Border
   Campaign, 1956–62   13
   Republican politics in the 1960s   16
   Republican split   20

2. Collapsing Stormont: Politics and Rebellion
   in the early 1970s   25
   Constitutional nationalism   25
   The Official and Provisional IRAs   29
   Provisional politics   33
   Provisional policy: Éire Nua   36
   The revival of 'armed struggle', 1970–2   39

3. The Sunningdale Experiment   43
   The attempt to create power-sharing   43
   SDLP ingredients and reaction   46
   The aftermath of Sunningdale   49
   The Constitutional Convention   51
   Political irritation: the debate on independence   54
   Internal ruptures and reappraisal of SDLP strategy   58
   The exit of Gerry Fitt   62

4. Marginalisation, Exclusion and Rebirth: Republicanism,
   1972–9   67
   Unreconstructed militarism? The Provisionals' offensive   67

The Whitelaw talks   69
Rejecting Sunningdale   73
Ceasefire   74
The descent into sectarianism: 'dealing' with Loyalists   77
From criminalisation to reorganisation   80

5. Ending Political Inertia: Internationalisation
   of the Northern Ireland conflict   83
   Traditional Irish-American attitudes   83
   John Hume in America   85
   Hume and Irish government   90
   The SDLP and Europe   93
   Guns not government: Republicans and international solidarity   99

6. The Republican Second Front: Hunger Strikes
   and Ballot Boxes   101
   Legitimising a long war   101
   Developing Republicanism as a political force   104
   Shaping coalitions   106
   The election of Sands and Carron   110
   Impacts North and South   112
   The new electoralism of Sinn Féin   114

7. Rescuing the SDLP: the New Ireland Forum   118
   The rolling devolution cul-de-sac   118
   Developing nationalist consensus   121
   SDLP policy positions: the New Ireland Forum   124
   Sinn Féin: rejecting federalism and the Forum   127
   Margaret Thatcher's dismissal of the New Ireland Forum   132

8. The Anglo-Irish Agreement   136
   The importance of the SDLP analysis   138
   SDLP gains   141
   SDLP disappointments   144
   Sinn Féin's double-edged response   147
   The balance-sheet for nationalists   150

9. Republican Reappraisal: the Initiatives of Gerry Adams   153
   Electoral gains and plateaus   153
   *Goodbye fundamnentalism, hello pragmatism: the end
   of abstentionism*   156

The 1986 Republican split 159
The road to Hume-Adams 162
SDLP-Sinn Féin dialogue 166
The SDLP and Unionists 170

10. Towards Peace, Pan-Nationalism and Co-Determination 175
The Brooke talks: creating a basis for change 175
Self-determination, co-determination and persuasion 178
The 1993 Downing Street Declaration 183
Republican reaction to the Downing Street Declaration 184
Ceasefire 187
The US conundrum 190
Temporary fracture 192

11. The Good Friday Agreement: SDLP Triumph? 196
The contents of the Agreement 196
An SDLP analysis of the Agreement 200
The SDLP membership 203
Nationalists and policing 205
The impact of the Agreement: electoral problems? 208

12. Triumph or Sell-Out? Sinn Féin and Constitutional
Republicanism 213
Republican politics and the Good Friday Agreement? 213
Conflict resolution measures 215
Selling the Agreement: the maintenance of Republican unity 217
Keeping the flame burning 219
Decommissioning physical force Republicanism 223
Sinn Féin overtakes the SDLP 227
The electoral squeezing of the SDLP: irreversible gains
for Sinn Féin? 230
Progress or sell-out? Theorising Republican change 233

13. New Agendas? Nationalist Social and Economic
Policies 240
Developing other political agendas 240
A radical approach to education policy 241
Local government 243
Health and housing 244
Employment and the economy 246

The European agenda 248
Moral agendas 250

Conclusion 255
Whither the SDLP? 256
Selling a 'partitionist' settlement 260
Post-Republicanism? 263
Post-nationalism? 266

Notes 271
Index 297

TABLES

11.1. Identification of the SDLP by party members 203
11.2. Constitutional preferences of SDLP members 204
11.3. SDLP-Sinn Féin electoral competition, 1982–2003 209

PREFACE AND ACKNOWLEDGEMENTS

The peace process and the 1998 Good Friday Agreement fundamentally altered the political landscape in Northern Ireland, despite the various problems associated with the process and the deal. Both nationalist parties in Northern Ireland are committed to full implementation of the Agreement, which offers the prospect of a more peaceful future. The extent of nationalist unity in support of the Agreement contrasts with the division evident among Unionists since it was signed. Historically, however, Irish nationalism has endured greater division, between the constitutional form evident for most of the previous century and more episodic, but periodically strong, militant Republicanism, prepared to countenance 'armed struggle' to end British rule in any part of Ireland. The formation of a more vibrant constitutional nationalist organisation, the Social Democratic and Labour Party (SDLP), in 1970 occurred as militant Republicanism underwent its most significant and enduring revival since 1918. This revival was translated into support for the Irish Republican Army (IRA) and, from the 1980s onwards, Sinn Féin, both organisations having been relaunched under Provisional (PIRA and PSF) labels in 1970. The contest for the support of nationalists in Northern Ireland after 1970 was often bitter, but, by the early years of the twenty-first century, differences in politics between the SDLP and Sinn Féin were less readily apparent.

This book traces the evolution of the policies of the SDLP and Sinn Féin since their foundation in 1970. It assesses the reasons for the birth of both organisations, analysing the relationship of each to traditional forms of Irish nationalism. The degree to which the SDLP offered a more participatory model of politics is explored, whilst earlier portrayals of the Provisional IRA and Sinn Féin as, variously, Northern defenders, Catholic sectarians, romantic nationalists or Marxists are all subject to critical analysis. The roles of John Hume and Gerry Adams in shaping the Northern Ireland peace process are assessed, as is the extent to which the process fostered intra-nationalist convergence. Three key questions are addressed in the assessment of the peace and political processes. To what extent did either party shape the Good Friday Agreement? Did the Agreement reflect the political outlook of either party? How accurate is it to describe the SDLP as the political winner, but the electoral loser, in the intranationalist competition in Northern Ireland?

A basic argument within the book is that political winners have become electoral losers. Sinn Féin was obliged to travel much further in supporting the Good Friday Agreement, a deal which recognised Northern Ireland, kept it within the United Kingdom and asked Republicans to assist in the governance of a political entity they fought to destroy. In contrast, the SDLP's analysis for resolving the Northern Ireland conflict was based upon ideas of partnership government with moderate Unionists in Northern Ireland, accompanied by a significant Irish dimension. Implementation of a deal based upon this analysis has, however, been followed by electoral triumph for Sinn Féin, as Republicanism has overtaken nationalism as the majority preference of Catholics in Northern Ireland. The extent of change within republican politics (assuming we can still use the term in respect of the offerings of Sinn Féin) requires detailed scrutiny. To what extent were the changes in Sinn Féin a product of persuasion from the SDLP via Hume-Adams? Alternatively, as Moloney suggests, were Sinn Féin's 'ideological somersaults' part of an Adams-inspired determination to separate the movement from its historical baggage, which predated any dialogue with the SDLP?[1]

The structure of the book is chronological, with events described and reasons assessed within each chapter. The opening chapter explores the formation of both parties and their doctrines. For Sinn Féin, British withdrawal and the establishment of an independent 32-county Irish Republic were for many years a non-negotiable demand. Whilst Sinn Féin was eventually required to undergo political transformation, the SDLP was not immune from policy changes from those outlined at formation. The party's first leader, Gerry Fitt, argued that primacy of SDLP policy should have been given to power sharing with Unionists, instead of trying to also incorporate an Irish dimension. This was an error in Fitt's judgement based on two factors. If the SDLP had adopted such a strategy there was little to differentiate it from the Alliance Party, also established in 1970, which was basically a Unionist party with a small 'u'. Furthermore, the strong opposition from unionists to the 1974 power sharing experiment demonstrated that community's reluctance to share power with Northern Ireland's Catholics. For Sinn Féin, *any* internal settlement was unacceptable. The 1970s was a period in which the party was subordinate to the IRA. Chapter 2, however, questions the orthodoxy that there were no politics, only militarism, during this period, suggesting that ideological 'purity', lack of realism and dominance by the republican movement's military wing did not mean that the movement lacked political strategies. The political stances of the Republican movement were nonetheless non-negotiable and overshadowed by armed struggle, with the result that the vision of a new Ireland attracted little interest from core supporters.

Following the collapse of Sunningdale in 1974, discussed in chapter 3, it was impossible to bridge the gap between Unionist aspirations for a return to majority rule as an internal settlement and constitutional nationalist demands for power sharing and a role for the Irish government. SDLP strategists reached the conclusion that further negotiations with Unionists for partnership government within the Province were futile. John Hume took over from Gerry Fitt as SDLP leader in 1979. Hume's impatience with Unionists can perhaps be traced to his experience of the Ulster Workers' Council strike that eventually brought down the ill-fated 1974 Power-Sharing Executive. Hume had already been introduced to senior American diplomats by Edward Kennedy by the time he took over the party leadership from Gerry Fitt in 1979. Earlier that year he had been elected as a MEP to the European Parliament at Strasbourg. Thus the new SDLP leader was well placed to internationalise the Northern Ireland conflict to the detriment of Unionists, as analysed in chapter 5.

By the end of the 1970s the SDLP argued that negotiation with the other Northern Ireland political parties was a futile exercise. The chief obstacles to the two constitutional nationalist demands of power sharing and an Irish dimension were, firstly, the refusal of Unionists to acknowledge that the *status quo* was totally unacceptable to Northern nationalists: for constitutional nationalists, unionists failed to recognise the legitimate political aspirations, and sense of identity, of the minority community. Secondly, the SDLP blamed the British government for bolstering the unionist position by its unwillingness to take a responsible role in resolving the conflict in an impartial manner which addressed nationalist interests in the Province. The British government, by continually upholding the Unionist guarantee, was in effect governing Northern Ireland in a partisan manner. To continue governing Northern Ireland simply as another region of the United Kingdom was to ignore the causes of the conflict.

For Republicans the late 1970s was also a period of reappraisal, explored in chapters 4 and 6. Having effectively brought down the Stormont government in 1972, the IRA believed it was on the verge of victory. The collapse of power-sharing in 1974, although precipitated by Loyalists, also offered encouragement since it indicated that a devolved parliament, governing Northern Ireland within the United Kingdom, would not easily be reconstituted. By 1977, however, it was evident that the British government was content to retain sovereignty over Northern Ireland and maintain direct rule. The IRA settled down to a long war, but the desire to legitimise that war led, more by chance than design, to electoral politics. The demand of Republican prisoners for political status led to a hunger strike, which resulted in the deaths of ten hunger strikers but mobilised support among Northern Ireland's Catholics. Electoralism was born within the movement, as Sinn Féin rapidly emerged during the early 1980s as a party capable of challenging SDLP electoral hegemony.

As outlined in chapter 7, the rise of Sinn Féin was a problem for the SDLP, but Hume's party was able to make the British government address the issue through the 1985 Anglo-Irish Agreement. The Agreement is discussed in detail in chapter 8. After Sunningdale and prior to the signing of the Anglo-Irish Agreement, the British government refrained from any attempt to become involved in addressing the core dimensions of the Northern Ireland conflict. By exercising a policy of containment in Northern Ireland, the British government upheld Unionist interests. At the start of the 1980s, the SDLP had begun campaigning for an Anglo-Irish framework as the proper formula to resolve the Northern Ireland conflict. Despite the Anglo-Irish process being in tatters by the middle of 1982, the SDLP and John Hume in particular were the main catalyst behind the publication of the New Ireland Forum Report in May 1984. Although the British Prime Minister appeared dismissive of the Report, the Anglo-

Irish Agreement was signed eighteen months later. From a republican point of view, the Anglo-Irish Agreement was created to shore up the SDLP's weakening electoral position. The Agreement was predominantly a counter-insurgency measure planned for some time and hastened as a result of the IRA's bombing of the Conservative Party Conference in Brighton in 1984. The Anglo-Irish Agreement of November 1985 signified a major coup for the SDLP over the Republican movement. Henceforth it was the SDLP's analysis of the Northern Ireland conflict that was accepted by the British and Irish governments along with the White House. By 1992 the SDLP was polling well ahead of Sinn Féin, and in the 1998 Assembly elections it obtained its highest vote ever. Yet three years later, at the 2001 general election, Sinn Féin overtook it as the larger nationalist party.

By the early 1990s Sinn Féin's leadership sought an end to a conflict that could not be won through military or 'armalite and ballot box' approaches. Sinn Féin's electoral support, though substantial, was stagnant, with the IRA's 'armed struggle' apparently the main barrier to a serious challenge to the SDLP. This electoral plateau is assessed in chapter 9. The Hume-Adams dialogue, begun in 1988, allowed Sinn Féin to move through a succession of policy changes. Most fundamentally, calls for 'Brits out' were displaced by demands that the British government act as persuader to Unionists for Irish unity. Republicans might claim that the Good Friday Agreement creates an institutional logic for unity, through its all-Ireland dimension. The moves towards a common nationalist approach to conflict resolution are discussed in chapter 10.

From the outset, the SDLP were the protagonists of British civil rights for the nationalist community in Northern Ireland. This was in essence about persuading the British government to adopt an agenda to promote an inclusive equality agenda for the nationalist community in Northern Ireland. The SDLP's input to the Good Friday Agreement is examined in chapter 11. The questions begged are to what extent has Sinn Féin adopted a political approach centred upon nationalist civil rights, and to what degree can equality within the North complement a continuing declared commitment to Republican objectives? Can the republican movement legitimately claim to have forced concessions from the British government and can some of these be viewed as transitional to Irish unity? Alternatively, has the

movement 'sold out', abandoning fundamental Republican principles? These questions are addressed in chapter 12. The institutions of
the Good Friday Agreement can be traced to the SDLP's first policy
documents, outlining the party's political strategic options for resolving the Northern Ireland conflict. The Good Friday Agreement was
based on a SDLP analysis, but the SDLP failed to reap electoral benefit. Chapter 13 notes how the two parties share a common outlook on
many social and economic policies, with these aspects of party policy
likely to develop greater importance in coming years. The book con-
cludes by assessing why Sinn Féin, despite the apparent rejection of
its earlier political strategy, is entrusted by the nationalist electorate as
the superior custodian of the Agreement.

Over the duration of the Northern Ireland troubles there have
been several publications dealing with the nationalist community in
Northern Ireland, but none providing a head-to-head comparison of
its two main political representatives. A pre-modern Troubles account
is offered in Eamonn Phoenix's *Northern Nationalism: Nationalist Politics, Partition and the Catholic Minority in Northern Ireland, 1890–1940*,
which traces the sense of alienation of border nationalists and Belfast
nationalists. His work illustrates the discriminatory actions of unionists during the early years of devolved government. Enda Staunton's
The Nationalists of Northern Ireland, 1918–1973 is also a detailed study
of the minority community in Northern Ireland.

As a consequence of the Nationalist Party's non-participatory role
at Stormont the Catholic Church played an important role in giving a
voice to a marginalised minority in the years following the establishment of Northern Ireland. The Church played a substantial role particularly in the area of education. This is clearly demonstrated in
Michael McGrath's *The Catholic Church and Catholic Schools in Northern
Ireland: The Price of Faith*. Other works have attempted to trace the
historical and religious dimensions of the Catholic community in
Northern Ireland. Marianne Elliott's comprehensive work *The Catholics of Ulster* addresses the problems faced by Catholics before and after partition, as does Oliver Rafferty in his work *Catholicism in Ulster,
1603–1983*. These books also offer some wider discussion of Northern nationalism and republicanism, but the main strident condemnation of the treatment of Catholic nationalists under the unionist
regime remains Michael Farrell's *Northern Ireland: the Orange State*.

Economic discrimination is highlighted in the work of Harris, *Regional Economic Policy in Northern Ireland, 1948–1988*, which shows that the Unionist industrial development programme to replace indigenous industries with large scale multinational companies did not lead to the allocation of new factories in many areas of high Catholic unemployment. Up to 1963, 75 per cent of all new factories opened in Northern Ireland were in the predominantly Protestant north-east of the country. The areas of nationalist majorities were neglected in this industrial boom.

The current conflict and the post-ceasefire period have seen abundant written material examining the evolution of the Republican movement in Ireland from armed struggle to democratic politics. Many of these works concentrate upon military aspects of the Republican struggle, whilst not neglecting its politics outright. Two of many examples are Bishop and Mallie's *The Provisional IRA* and M. L. R. Smith's *Fighting for Ireland*. The most authoritative study of the IRA, in terms of information concerning its internal deliberations and the control of the movement by its leadership, is Ed Moloney's *A Secret History of the IRA*. The most judicious work is Richard English's *Armed Struggle*, which provides a realistic analysis of the reasons why the Provisional IRA was born and the political basis to its violence, whilst debunking historical myths concerning the value of the organisation's self-ascribed defender role. Brian Feeney's *Sinn Féin: a Hundred Turbulent Years* traces the party's mainly marginal position in Irish politics until its entry into the current peace process.

In contrast, there has been a dearth of published sources examining developments within the constitutional nationalist Social Democratic and Labour Party (SDLP). Ian McAllister's important volume on the party (1977) is now out of date.[2] More than two decades elapsed before a further account of the SDLP's political development emerged.[3] Some of the themes in that 1998 work, concerning the consistent three-stranded approach to conflict resolution offered by the SDLP, the neglect of party organisation and the internal tensions within the SDLP, are revisited and updated within this work.

This book provides a political balance sheet for the two nationalist parties in Northern Ireland and assesses the extent to which it is realistic to speak of nationalist unity, or pan-nationalism. It examines how the Republican leadership persuaded the party rank and file of the merits of the Good Friday Agreement, a deal which contained the essence of SDLP strategy for the last twenty-eight years. Since formation in 1970 the SDLP sought to create partnership government in Northern Ireland with moderate Unionists. The concept of cross-border co-operation through a Ministerial Council of Ireland and the principle of power-sharing between Unionists and nationalists were set out in unpublished SDLP documents in 1971. The SDLP argued in these discussion documents for almost exactly the same principles that were set out in the Good Friday Agreement.

The book ends with consideration of the irony of how two long-established political arch-enemies are now singing from the one hymn sheet. Nationalists and republicans who still aspire to a united Ireland acknowledge that this cannot be achieved by coercion. Both parties, but particularly Sinn Féin, have revised their thinking regarding unionists. The authors consider why Sinn Féin settled for terms falling a long way short of their original objective of British withdrawal. Unionist consent is still required for the foreseeable future for any change in Northern Ireland's position within the UK. Yet any victory for the SDLP in political terms is counterbalanced by a seemingly unstoppable shift of electoral support to its more vigorous, greener rival.

Acknowledgements

A large number of debts have been incurred in the production of this book. In particular we wish to thank Gerry Cosgrove and Tim Attwood at SDLP HQ for facilitating the research in to the SDLP; likewise Dawn Doyle at Sinn Féin HQ and the Sinn Féin Ard Chomhairle for approving cooperation with the project. Whilst we are sure that both parties will disagree with aspects of our findings, we hope that what follows is a fair-minded, objective study. We divided the research, Gerry undertaking the SDLP material, Jon researching Sinn Féin. Gerry wishes to thank all those SDLP members who agreed to be interviewed; likewise Jon thanks Sinn Féin members who gave their time in being interviewed. These include Mitchell McLaughlin, Pat Doherty, Alex Maskey, Rita O'Hare, Joan O'Connor, Michelle Gildernew, Sean Crowe, Bobby Lavery, Eoin O'Broin, Michael Brown, Mary Nelis, Micheál McDonnacha, Lyn Fleming, Robbie Smyth, Peter Anderson and Seán Brady.

We acknowledge with special thanks initial funding for this research from the Nuffield Foundation and the University of Salford and full funding from the Economic and Social Research Council (New Nationalism in Northern Ireland, R000222668). Jon is also grateful to St John's College, Oxford University, for a Visiting Scholarship in 2003. We are both grateful for the considerable assistance of Dr Jocelyn Evans. In addition to particular gratitude to both our families, Gerry wishes to thank Professor Alice Brown and Professor Dave McCrone of Edinburgh University, Rosy Addison, Catherine Butler, Therese Fitzgerald, Theo Dijkman, Dr Dominic Bryan, Director of the Institute of Irish Studies, Queen's University Belfast, Peter Randall SJ, June Wilkinson, and in particular Martin Gilroy. Jon wishes to thank Kevin Bean, Dr Anthony McIntyre, Professor James McAuley, Dr Chris Gilligan, Dr Peter Shirlow, Dr Catherine McGlynn and the ever-helpful Yvonne Murphy and her staff in the treasure-trove that is the Political Collection in the Linen Hall Library, Belfast. Personal special thanks are due to Anita and Conaill. Jon dedicates his parts of the book to Maria.

Belfast, Salford and Edinburgh 2004   G. M.
                                                         J. T.

1

THE DEVELOPMENT OF NATIONALIST POLITICS IN NORTHERN IRELAND

The partition of Ireland in 1920 left nationalists in the newly created statelet of Northern Ireland feeling isolated and vulnerable. The Government of Ireland Act received the royal assent on 23 December 1920, dividing Ireland into two separate and mainly self-governing areas. In the North, a new, devolved parliament in Belfast would be dominated by a Protestant Unionist majority. The localised ethnic majoritarianism which created the borders of the artificial new statelet would be extended to its internal arrangements, with a distrusted Catholic, mainly nationalist, minority excluded from power and influence for the next 50 years. In the South the twenty-six counties became the Irish Free State and from 1949 the Republic of Ireland. The contempt of the twenty-six-county state for Northern Orangeism and British rule in Northern Ireland was matched by a willingness to allow the Roman Catholic Church to become *the* symbol of Irishness within its own borders. Relationships between two antagonistic embryonic statelets became frozen. Ironically, a Council of Ireland had been set up by the 1920 Act, designed to involve Belfast and Dublin in seeking what it called 'harmonious action between the parliaments and governments of Southern Ireland and Northern Ireland'. It was hoped the Council would lead to the eventual reunification of the island.

Nationalists insisted that the creation of Northern Ireland was a denial of democracy, enshrining a Unionist veto over political arrangements. Even allowing for caveats to the election result, such as uncontested seats and the lack of a Republican majority in the North, the claim had a strong resonance. Unionist rejection of the aggregate Republican victory in the 1918 general election, when Sinn Féin won

1

a landslide victory over the Home Rule Party and Northern unionists, ensured that Northern Ireland would be seen by nationalists as an undemocratic, illegitimate state, based more upon the loyalist threat of force than upon democratic principle. The first meeting of the post-1918 Irish parliament, the Dáil Éireann, was held on 21 January 1919 with Éamon De Valera, one of the survivors of the Irish republican 1916 Easter Rising against British rule, elected president of the new parliament.[1] The manifesto of Sinn Féin at the 1918 election was unambiguous; the party wanted to break all links with Britain, and would not accept Home Rule within the Empire. However, on 7 January 1922 the Anglo-Irish Treaty, dividing the island into Northern and Southern countries, the former in the United Kingdom and the latter within the Empire, was approved in the Irish Parliament by sixty-four votes to fifty-seven. Under the 1921 treaty, signed under duress by the Sinn Féin delegation, the twenty-six Southern counties were to be known as the Free State. It was to have its own government, parliament and army whilst remaining within the British Empire. Members of the parliament would have to swear an oath of allegiance to the King.

The 1921 Anglo-Irish Treaty split Sinn Féin over the implications of the Free State remaining within the British Empire and the requirement of members of Dáil Éireann to make an oath of allegiance to a British King. De Valera resigned as head of the original government. Arthur Griffith replaced De Valera, and prepared for a British withdrawal from the Free State. Civil war broke out in the South between the pro-Treaty Irish Free State forces and anti-Treaty republicans. The war lasted from June 1922 until May 1923, ending in defeat for exhausted anti-Treaty forces. The civil war came to shape Irish politics for generations, with political contests frozen between anti-Treaty Fianna Fáil and pro-Treaty Fine Gael. Following his release from prison after the civil war in the South, Éamon De Valera formed Fianna Fáil and the new party entered the Irish Parliament, waiting for an opportunity to obtain power. In the 1932 Free State election Fianna Fáil was indeed elected. In the subsequent years De Valera quickly dismantled British interests in the Free State with the introduction of a new Constitution in 1937. Article 44 recognised the special position of Catholicism within the state. Article 2 referred to the national territory of Ireland consisting of the whole island; and article 3 outlined that the laws passed by the Southern government would only apply to the twenty-six counties until Ireland was reunified. As a result Northern nationalists looked to De Valera as the source of their support from Southern Ireland.[2] Whilst De Valera renounced violence as a means of achieving reunification, his Constitution legitimised the claims of republicans and nationalists that Britain's claim to Northern Ireland was illegal.

In 1921 Northern Ireland came into existence with James Craig becoming the country's first Prime Minister. Unionists accepted that a Home Rule Parliament in Belfast was the only realistic way of preserving the union with Britain. Northern Ireland evolved politically in a manner that exacerbated the historic divisions between its nationalist and unionist traditions. The new political institutions gave the majority community, Unionists, who were mainly Protestant, total control of the new devolved Belfast legislature. Northern nationalists had reason to feel estranged from the rest of their Unionist political foes and their nationalist counterparts in Southern Ireland. The manner in which partition was applied in terms of self-determination was improper, with the new statelet having no geographical basis. Part of the Southern state, in Donegal, lay further north than 'Northern' Ireland. Two of the six counties of Northern Ireland contained nationalist majorities, undermining the notion that self-determination was awarded on a county basis. Instead, Northern Ireland appeared an arbitrary entity, manufactured to yield a sufficiently safe, Unionist-British-Protestant majority. For nationalists, a country was divided owing to the concentration of rejectionists within a small part of the island, who had, as settler colonials over earlier centuries, displaced the native Irish population. Additional populace and territory could have been awarded to the Irish Free State in the 1920s either through the 1921 Anglo-Irish Treaty or as a recommendation of the Boundary Commission,[3] but boundaries remained unchanged. Northern nationalists hoped that Boundary Commission recommendations might ultimately lead to the dissolution of Northern Ireland state. The Commission was to report to the governments in London, Dublin and Belfast at the end of 1925. Both heads of government in Ireland felt that subsequent changes to the border might lead to further violent clashes

In order to consolidate Unionist unity and discourage party fragmentation, the Unionist government abolished proportional representation (PR) for local government on 5 July 1922. Allied to the gerrymandering of electoral boundaries, the move also inhibited nationalist representation on local councils, which, falling under nationalist control, had threatened to secede from Northern Ireland. A similar move was made in respect of elections to the Northern Ireland parliament in 1929. In 1922, the Special Powers Act was introduced by the Northern government. It gave the police unlimited powers to stop, search and arrest anyone suspected of threatening the security of Northern Ireland. These measures further alienated nationalists, who felt second-class citizens within the Northern state.

Despite the extent of hostility among nationalists to the Northern state, the IRA in the North was not strong. Cut off from its southern roots, the organisation struggled to maintain itself as a properly armed force. The IRA was also pressured by the Special Powers Act, whilst criticism from the Catholic Church, anti-partition and certainly anti-Orange, but also anti-violence, inhibited development within the Catholic community. Conventional politics were also lacking among nationalists. The anti-partition Nationalist Party in Northern Ireland did not have a proper organisational structure, with much of its existence being locally based through strong clerical influence. It did not attend the Northern Ireland Parliament until 1927 and participated due to pressure from the Catholic authorities, which sought improved funding conditions for their schools. The Nationalist Party Parliamentarians were reduced to acting as 'ombudsmen' for their constituents and paid little attention to the 'legislative process'. Their only successful piece of legislation was the Wild Birds Act of 1931.[4]

The nationalist politician Joe Devlin engaged in 'active politics' in Northern Ireland, and sought election by campaigning for the restoration of PR for local elections.[5] Devlin failed to gain office, but nevertheless tried to give the nationalist minority in the north a mechanism to bring about reform by instituting the National League of the North in 1928. The National League of the North was, according to Phoenix, a direct consequence and response to unionists 'altering the electoral system and the renewal of the Special Powers Act' for a further five-year span in May 1928.[6] However, at an inaugural meeting in Belfast on 28 May 1928, the National League received a notable setback when De Valera turned down an invitation to attend.[7]

The National League of the North, although committed to Irish unity, had a broad set of objectives. It sought 'justice for Nationalists and other bodies', 'conciliation ... amongst all creeds and classes' and wished 'to co-operate with and assist every practical movement within or without the six counties, having for its object the economic and social betterment of the people'.[8] However, Phoenix has noted that Devlin became disillusioned with the religious associations in the league, and 'with its exclusivist Catholic character'. In poor health, he was unable to 'transform it into the broader populist alliance, which he regarded as the only prospect of a serious challenge of Unionism.'[9] The Unionist government became more hardline in upholding the interests of unionism. The 'temporary' 1922 Special Powers Act became permanent in 1933, reflecting the unionist government's distrust of Catholics in Northern Ireland because of their nationalist aspirations. The Agriculture Minister, Basil Brooke in March 1934 urged loyalists not to employ Roman Catholics, '99 per cent of whom are disloyal'. The Northern Ireland Prime Minister, James Craig, later Lord Craigavon, fully endorsed Brooke's remarks. He referred to the Northern Ireland parliament as 'a Protestant Parliament for a Protestant people'.

The Irish Free State, meanwhile, became a largely Catholic state for a Catholic people, even if discrimination against the Protestant population was less overt or state-sponsored than that undertaken by Unionists against Catholics in the North. With the Free State, whatever its anti-partitionist rhetoric, having abandoned the Catholic community in the North, Northern nationalists were marginalised. Devlin's attempts to distance himself from claims that he led a Catholic party fell on deaf ears. The National League came to an end after the 1929 general election. Following Fianna Fáil's electoral success in the 1932 Free State elections, and the resurgence of militant republicanism, Devlin reverted to a hardline nationalist position, prior to his death in 1934. In Belfast, the Irish Union Association was established in 1936 largely to bring together disparate nationalist interests. Its constitution promoted a traditional nationalist agenda, guaranteeing 'that no final settlement with Britain is made by the Irish people which will permit the present system of a partitioned Ireland to be continued'.[10]

The outbreak of the Second World War consolidated differences between Northern Ireland and Éire, as the Free State later became known.[11] Éire declared its neutrality in the war, De Valera using the opportunity as a timely way of demonstrating his country's independence from Britain. He rejected Winston Churchill's offer of post-war Irish unity for a variety of reasons; Britain was not guaranteed to win the war at the time of the offer; De Valera did not trust Churchill to deliver and, despite his earlier commitment to physical force Republicanism, the reality of office had cooled De Valera's enthusiasm for inheriting one million Unionist dissidents. Northern Ireland played an important role in British wartime defence. The war helped to emphasise Northern Ireland's Britishness, reflected in the 1949 Ireland Act, which enshrined Northern Ireland's place in the United Kingdom, subject to the will of the devolved parliament at Stormont.

Following the end of the war a new Labour government came into power at Westminster with a crusade for radical health and education reform. Although the Stormont government was not overly impressed with these sweeping changes, Northern Ireland benefited from the new reforms. There were benefits for both communities arising from the changes. Although they were still underachieving in education and jobs compared to their Protestant counterparts, the introduction of grammar schools and the (crude) meritocracy of educational selection at the age of eleven did open third level education to a new generation of Catholics in Northern Ireland who were traditionally prevented from accessing university education.

Politically, however, there was no progress for Catholics within Northern Ireland. Although it received little support from a demoralised urban nationalist population, which opposed violence or feared a Unionist backlash from any armed rebellion, the IRA border campaign of 1956–62 nonetheless embarrassed the Nationalist Party. To help improve community relations, Eddie McAteer (deputy leader in 1958, and leader in 1964) held meetings between the Ancient Order of Hibernians and the Orange Order from October 1962 to early 1963 with no tangible outcome.[12] The Nationalist Party sought real changes in 1964 when a delegation from the party met 'with British party leaders on the issue of discrimination'. According to Arthur, there was a 'tacit acknowledgement … that Britain had a right and a duty to interfere in Northern Ireland affairs'.[13] In February 1965 McAteer brought his party into Stormont as the official opposition. Lynn has argued that although McAteer wanted to modernise the Nationalist Party, his tenure as leader was marked by caution over party reorganisation and a sceptical attitude to the Civil Rights move-ment.[14] Any attempts by members of the Nationalist Party to take part in active politics in Northern Ireland were cosmetic and did not signify any deeper commitment to move away from the status quo.

The Nationalist Party power-base eroded over the course of the February 1969 election. Clashes between Civil Rights campaigners and militant Unionists 'disrupted the traditional pattern of political leadership in the Catholic community'.[15] From this point onwards, the extinction of the Nationalist Party was 'the price paid for lapsing into a too easy acceptance of the Northern status quo'.[16] This was a turn-ing point in the history of the province in terms of northern nation-alist willingness to operate as a political force within the existing constitutional framework.

The National Democratic Party

By the 1960s the Catholic community in Northern Ireland was be-coming more conciliatory. This conciliatory attitude was attributable, largely, to potential reform measures presented by Terence O'Neill, Prime Minister from 1963 until 1969. Educational changes also played a major part in developing a new tier of middle-class Catholics. The pragmatism of this new generation of Northern Catholics mar-ked a new willingness in the Catholic community to give at least *de facto* recognition to Northern Ireland. Prior to the formation of the National Democratic Party (NDP) in 1965 there was no structured or coherent party organisation among Catholics in Northern Ireland.

The Catholic community, disappointed by the futile role played by the Nationalist Party, welcomed new initiatives by an organisation known as 'National Unity' in December 1959. National Unity was a think-tank whose aim was to encourage debate among disparate po-litical Catholic opposition groups in Northern Ireland.[17] Significantly, National Unity wanted to move away from the sterile traditional na-tionalist ideology. The group sought to develop new ideas through its magazine *The New Nation*. The group was encouraged by a speech from the Taoiseach, Seán Lemass, delivered to the Oxford Union in October 1959, which offered a federal solution to the Northern Ireland problem.[18] This speech had far-reaching implications: first, it gave *de facto* recognition to Northern Ireland from a Southern viewpoint; secondly, both the Social Democratic and Labour Party

(SDLP) and the Republican movement resumed the theme of federal political organisation for Northern Ireland in the early 1970s. Ian McAllister has discussed the objective nature of National Unity, and has argued that '[its] main aim was to produce a more constructive belief in politics as an end in itself, and not merely as a means towards attaining reunification.'[19]

The Maghery Convention in April 1964 was the first opportunity for Nationalist parliamentary members to debate the philosophy of National Unity. However, the Nationalist leader, Eddie McAteer and his parliamentary colleagues were highly conservative in their reaction to the new mood for active politics in Northern Ireland. As a consequence, the champions for reform in the Catholic community formed a new party in Belfast, originally called the National Party. Subsequently, at a conference in 1965, the National Party renamed itself the National Democratic Party and members of the Protestant community were encouraged to join.

The NDP held six conferences during its lifespan between 1965 and 1970. In sharp contrast to the absence of formal political organisation in the Nationalist Party, the NDP epitomised a well-run party-political machine. It ran strictly according to legislative requirements: constitution, central council, executive and local associations. The NDP constitution was modelled on those of the two major political parties in the South. By 1967 the NDP had ten local associations 'covering Belfast, Antrim and parts of Down, Armagh and Tyrone, with an association also established in Queen's University, Belfast'.[20] The function of each local association was to maintain electoral organisation and to serve as a point for recruitment to the NDP. In the Stormont election of 1965 the NDP secured the election of one MP, while the Nationalist Party held nine seats. The NDP struck an alliance with the Nationalist Party, by not putting forward candidates where the Nationalist Party had an elected representative. Significantly, the NDP did put up candidates in traditionally uncontested Protestant areas of Northern Ireland.

The NDP attempted 'to form a strong, united, democratic alternative to the Unionists', with the objective of becoming the government of Northern Ireland.[21] In practical terms it had the potential to operate as a successful opposition in the British political system. However, the nature of majority rule politics in Northern Ireland,

and in particular the Province's parochialism made the NDP's task of creating a socialist, rather than a pan-Catholic, party virtually impossible.[22] Most crucially of all, given the rejectionism of Northern nationalism, the NDP also introduced the consent principle into the nationalist debate by stating it 'would negotiate for re-unification only if the majority of the people in the North wanted it.[23]

From the outset the NDP rejected Nationalist Party resistance to Northern Ireland's separate identity, and faced up to the reality that the island of Ireland was partitioned. What was articulated through NDP policy was an active political voice that demanded a democratic role in Northern Ireland society. The NDP represented new approaches to nationalism. The party argued that partition was not imposed by the British, but grew out of the divisions in Ireland. In a statement of party policy, Patrick Ritchie, NDP Secretary for Lisburn, wrote: 'We are ready to sacrifice our separate identity, and the political ambitions of our members, to establish a left-of-centre radical party capable of leading Northern Ireland into the 70s.'[24] The earliest SDLP drafts of the constitutional issue can be traced back to elements of NDP policy. The NDP asserted: 'The eventual negotiated unity of our island in a European context will serve the best interests of the people. Real nationalism, such as has never been tried in Northern Ireland, expressed in a concern for the people who are the nation, is a necessary ingredient of internationalism.'[25] The statement can be seen as a forerunner to the commitment of John Hume to European co-operation and integration.

In its election manifesto for the 1970 general election the NDP set out five key points, which were debated by the SDLP in 1971. These key points were proposed:

— A Council of Ireland, with representatives from both Dublin and Belfast, to promote harmonious cross-border relations and economic development between North and South.
— A Bill of Rights guaranteeing basic civil rights for all in Northern Ireland.
— Repeal of the Special Powers Act and other repressive laws.
— Proportional representation in all elections—including local government.

The manifesto also insisted that '... the only long-term solution to Ireland's troubles is the creation—by consent—of a thirty-two County

Republic. The united and prosperous Ireland of the future could also take its place proudly beside Britain in helping to build a united Europe and a better world'.[26]

The NDP soon lost the one seat it had gained in the 1969 Stormont election. NDP interest in opposing Gerry Fitt, then a member of the Republican Labour Party, in West Belfast produced internal divisions before the 1969 Stormont elections. During the course of its five-year existence the NDP produced policy documents concentrating on socio-economic issues, in an attempt to offer the Northern Ireland electorate an alternative to one-party Unionist politics still dominated by constitutional issues. However, the socio-economic emphasis of politics in the 1960s was 'superseded by a more strident and uniform demand for Civil Rights'.[27]

The NDP tried to co-operate with the Nationalist Party, but such efforts had few results. The SDLP then attempted to supersede both the Nationalist Party and the NDP, a goal eventually achieved in August 1970.[28] Once the SDLP was established, the NDP dissolved itself by consent at a special party conference in October 1970. A resolution was passed that NDP members should join the newly formed SDLP. The NDP may appear to have been a failure, but for former members, such as John Duffy, it formed 'a psychological, organisational and political link between the unorganised, single-issue Nationalists and the modern party organisation of the SDLP, with its wide range of policy aims'.[29]

The birth of the SDLP

The 1969 Stormont elections marked the beginning of the end of the Nationalist Party. Ivan Cooper took Thomas Gormley's seat in Mid-Tyrone; John Hume took the Foyle constituency seat previously held by Nationalist Party leader, Eddie McAteer; Paddy O'Hanlon took Eddie Richardson's seat in South Armagh. The origins of the SDLP lay specifically in the Civil Rights movement, and the party was established by members who were already Stormont MPs.

In May 1970 the six MPs—Ivan Cooper, Austin Currie, Paddy Devlin, Gerry Fitt, John Hume and Paddy O'Hanlon—accompanied by Senator Paddy Wilson, met in Bunbeg, Donegal to draw up the principles for a new party. John Hume and Austin Currie drew up the general principles, which were used at the official launch of the party in August 1970. At a meeting in Tomebridge, Antrim, Hume and Currie wanted the party to be named the Social Democratic Party. However, Fitt and Devlin insisted on Labour being included in the title to reflect their socialist credentials. As a consequence the party was finally named the Social Democratic and Labour Party of Northern Ireland.

Having reached agreement on the aims and name of the new party, a decision still had to be taken on who was to become leader. Paddy Devlin has claimed that John Hume held meetings with former NDP members to try and 'revitalise the old Nationalist Party'. To stop him, an announcement was made by Austin Currie that a new party would start with Gerry Fitt as leader.[30] During an RTE interview in August 1970 Austin Currie was asked if there were difficulties with the choice of leader for the new party. During the interview Currie claimed: 'The only one with sufficient experience, ability and acceptability was Gerry Fitt.'[31] Hume agreed to be deputy leader. In a hastily arranged press conference at the Grand Central Hotel in Belfast, an official launch party took place on 21 August 1970. The 'elected' leader of the SDLP was indeed the Westminster MP for West Belfast, Gerry Fitt. Despite the misgivings Hume and other members had about Fitt's leadership, the SDLP might not have been as popular or as successful in its early years without Fitt. The leader had played a major role promoting the principles of the Civil Rights movement at Westminster because of his links with the British Labour Party. This was a vital platform for the newly-created SDLP to promote its policies in Britain.

The first SDLP policy document, drawn up by John Hume and Austin Currie, was signed by the six founding MPs at the launch of the party. The document committed the party to broad socialist principles in relation to economic and social issues including 'the provision of a minimum wage'. The original statement of principles supported the introduction of familiar policies: 'proportional representation'; 'co-operation in all fields between North and South' and 'to promote co-operation, friendship and understanding between North and South with the view to the eventual re-unification of Ireland through the consent of the majority of the people in the North and in the South'.[32] In essence there was nothing novel in party aims or general principles; they echoed what had already been set out in earlier NDP documentation. Although Irish reunification was desired, it was subject to the consent of a majority in Northern Ireland, tacit nationalist recognition of what had in previous decades been seen as an illegitimate statelet.

Austin Currie has recalled: 'At the time of the formation of the SDLP … nationalism was being put on a back burner…There was recognition that we had to live within Northern Ireland for a considerable period of time…we had to make the best of that situation, but that we were entitled to an equal spot in the sun—that was our determination and commitment.'[33] A founder member, Ben Caraher, has pointed out that one of the earliest debates within the SDLP was over the basic question: '…would the unity of Ireland be a formal aim or would that formal aim be left out? There was no question of the unity of Ireland being the primary aim of the party. Their primary preoccupations were Civil Rights in Northern Ireland, and social and economic matters in Northern Ireland.'[34]

Ben Caraher has expressed the political optimism of the early days of the SDLP, by noting, 'Your dream would have been to share power with liberal unionists.'[35] This assertion has been supported by the backing of Gerry Fitt for 'the maintenance of Stormont at the present time as it is the only institution which can bring about the stated reforms we desire'.[36] From the outset the SDLP believed that Irish unity could only be achieved in two major ways. First, unity required the political co-operation of unionists at Stormont, even though there was not the slightest prospect of assistance. Secondly, unity depended on building up trust between the two traditions in Northern Ireland through active politics, which, over time, might eradicate unionist suspicions and prejudices towards Catholics. From the beginning, the SDLP was ultimately focused on reform in Northern Ireland. The constitutional issue was a much lower priority.

Although the party had been launched officially it was still 'merely at steering committee stage, being without constituency branches or constitution'.[37] For a year the party appeared similar in organisational terms to the Nationalist Party. Not until the SDLP held its first annual conference at Strabane in 1971 did the party set up the mechanisms of a modern political party with a written constitution and an executive committee. John Duffy has suggested that of the first 300–400 new members who joined the SDLP, not less than eighty per cent would have been current NDP members or else would have been part of the NDP membership over the course of the previous five years.[38]

The ethos of the NDP informed SDLP ideology, philosophy and political policy to a large extent.

Developments within Republicanism: the IRA Border Campaign, 1956–62

Whilst nationalist politics became more nuanced during the 1960s, republican politics also underwent reappraisal. The political development of Sinn Féin and the IRA was influenced by the failure of the IRA's 1956–62 Border Campaign, the latest of the IRA's episodic attempts to revive the physical force tradition within republicanism. The 1956–62 armed insurrection, Operation Harvest, by the IRA against British rule in Northern Ireland began with a considerable amount of activity in border areas, but soon petered out and, owing partly to a leadership decision, barely registered in Belfast. The lack of success of the campaign led to a reappraisal of the use of physical force as the primary tactic of the republican movement. Subsequent downgrading of 'armed struggle' in favour of more political strategies split the movement by the early 1970s, and this led to the formation of the Provisional IRA and Provisional Sinn Féin. Failure in the 1956–62 campaign also prompted a re-examination of the need to engage the nationalist population of Northern Ireland in support for the nationalist 'struggle'. The IRA statement terminating the campaign in 1962 blamed the 'attitude of the general public whose minds have been deliberately distracted from the supreme issue facing the Irish people—the unity and freedom of Ireland'. At this abject conclusion, the IRA was 'a husk—its strength eroded, its purpose lost, its future unclear'.[39] Within ten years, however, a substantial section of the disinterested Northern population of 1962 had developed a new sympathy for the ambitions, even the methods, of armed republicanism.

Despite its ultimate political and military failure, the Border Campaign had nonetheless been founded on promising developments. As early as 1951 the IRA leadership had taken the decision to launch an armed campaign confined to the Six Counties of Northern Ireland. By 1955 the secret decision appeared timely because the Northern nationalist population did appear to be concerned with the national question, as indicated by a good performance by Sinn Féin in the Westminster elections that year. Two of the party's candidates were elected on an abstentionist platform. Both candidates maintained their commitment to IRA activity and were removed from their seats. In the subsequent by-election in mid-Ulster, Sinn Féin candidate Tom Mitchell trebled his majority, before finally losing the seat in a further by-election. Electoral success was repeated one month later in local elections in the South. These triumphs were interpreted by republican leaders as a mandate for the resumption of armed struggle. After all, Sinn Féin was unequivocal in its support for the IRA. Its Northern electoral candidates were usually IRA prisoners. Although parity of importance of armed and political struggles was claimed by the Vice-President of Sinn Féin, Criostoir O Néill, at the Bodenstown Wolfe Tone commemoration in 1949, the IRA asserted tighter control over Sinn Féin during the 1950s.[40]

During the first year of the Border Campaign, it appeared that Sinn Féin might benefit from IRA military activity in the North. In Fianna Fáil's 1957 general election victory, Sinn Féin had four of its 19 candidates elected to Dáil Éireann, again on an abstentionist platform. A wave of Republican sympathy had swept Ireland after the death of Seán South and Feargal O'Hanlon in an attack on the Royal Ulster Constabulary (RUC) station at Brookeborough six months earlier. Nonetheless, the electoral success of Sinn Féin was largely a mirage. The absence of any rival nationalist candidate facilitated the party's Westminster election successes in 1955. The stance of Sinn Féin allowed nationalists to register a united cry of frustration at the discriminatory Unionist regime in Northern Ireland, while fostering the illusion that the population might support the armed overthrow of the Unionist government. When a rival nationalist candidate did intervene, as in the second by-election in Mid-Ulster in 1955, Sinn Féin could not achieve success.

Furthermore, any slender hopes that the Fianna Fáil election victory in the South might lead to a 'blind eye' being turned to the IRA Northern campaign evaporated almost immediately. The De Valera government introduced internment. With one exception, the entire membership of the Sinn Féin Ard Chomhairle (ruling executive) was detained, along with many senior IRA members. Given De Valera's antipathy to erstwhile Republican colleagues after first taking office in 1932, the clampdown was unsurprising. Sinn Féin and the IRA remained uncompromising in their challenge to partitionist institutions in the twenty-six counties of the South and the six counties of the North. Nonetheless, debates in Sinn Féin ranks over attitudes towards the Dáil Éireann did occur. Sinn Féin argued that the examples of Fianna Fáil in the 1920s and Clann na Poblachta led by Sean Mac-Bride in the 1940s indicated that there was no alternative to 'purist' abstentionist Republicanism. Since Fianna Fáil and Clann na Po-blachta had taken their seats in the Dáil Éireann, both had, according to Sinn Féin, become little more than 'verbal Republicans', engaging in anti-partition rhetoric which made little impact. During the 1950s, the ideological 'purists' maintained the upper hand and took action against dissenters. In 1951, the IRA expelled Liam Kelly for conduct-ing an unauthorised operation. Kelly, a popular figure elected as (abstentionist) MP for mid-Tyrone, formed Saor Uladh (Free Ulster) backed by a political organisation Fianna Uladh (Soldiers of Ulster). Saor Uladh was a six-county organisation which viewed the contin-ued refusal to recognise the political institutions of the twenty-six counties as pointless, given that the citizens of the twenty-six counties were now clearly loyal to such bodies, whilst continuing to reject the Northern state. Saor Uladh indicated that Republicans should con-centrate on bringing about the demise of Northern Ireland, without dwelling on abstract principles concerning the twenty-six-county state, a political position adopted in recent times by the Provisional IRA and Sinn Féin post-1986 and by the tiny 32-County Sovereignty Com-mittee, a breakaway from Sinn Féin.

Although the IRA's General Order No. 8 forbade actions against the police or military in the twenty-six-county state, continuing oppo-sition to political institutions by the IRA provided one pretext for the reintroduction of internment, a measure also applied in Northern Ireland. By the time internment was introduced North and South of the border, in 1957, however, the IRA campaign was already heading for defeat. The campaign could not be sustained by flying columns from the twenty-six counties. Significant numbers of personnel had been trained in the North, including over one hundred men in Derry, but they played little part in the campaign.[41] By 1959 the IRA contem-plated whether to extend the campaign to Belfast, hitherto ignored. Elements in the movement thought that an escalation of sectarian tensions in the city arising from IRA activity might be beneficial.[42]

More cautious counsel prevailed partly because of the weakness of the republican movement, both militarily and politically, in the city.

Aimed at the British forces of occupation, Operation Harvest caused no fatalities among British Army personnel. Six RUC members were killed, half the losses of Republicans. From 341 incidents in 1957, the campaign dwindled to 26 in 1960. At most an irritant, Operation Harvest had become almost irrelevant. Political gains of the mid-1950s were also reversed. The Sinn Féin votes cast in Northern Ireland in the 1959 Westminster election were half the 1955 figure. In the 1961 general election in the Irish Republic, 36,393 first-preference votes cast for Sinn Féin amounted to only three per cent of total votes cast. Fourteen of the twenty-one Sinn Féin candidates lost their deposits.[43] The IRA statement calling off the campaign emphasised the primacy of the national question. Nonetheless, having failed to inspire the nationalist population in the 1950s, a section of the small number remaining in the Republican movement preferred the linkage of constitutional issues to economic and social questions.

Republican politics in the 1960s

The period from 1962 to 1969 involved the most intense reviews of strategy undertaken by the republican movement since its foundation. Given the lack of earlier strategic thinking, this might be seen as a small advance. Linking the IRA approach to a period of 'militant Catholic anti-communism', Michael Farrell has argued that the 1956–62 campaign took place in 'possibly the most unpolitical phase' of IRA history.[44] His comment represents one interpretation of IRA political opinion, but unbridled anti-partitionism, not left-wing politics, has been the *raison d'être* of the IRA for most of its existence. The extent of change in Republicanism following the Border Campaign has been disputed. Bishop and Mallie have emphasised that there was unrest among traditionalists who were angered by substantial shifts towards socialism and atheism.[45] Broadly supporting their perspective, Tim Pat Coogan acknowledged that the programme of re-education in the Republican journal *The United Irishman* carried a 'medley of Fenian and Marxist airs'.[46]

In separate accounts Henry Patterson, M. L. R. Smith and Pat Walsh have been less convinced that a substantial shift towards the left really occurred. Patterson's argument has been contained in a wider theme of the irreconcilability of militarist nationalism and gen-uine socialism. Any reassessment by the republican movement was only partial. The IRA began to see itself as 'armed guarantor of the social and political gains of a revolutionary popular movement'.[47] Yet this represented a substantial shift from the traditional 'ourselves alone' belief of Republicans. Like Patterson, M. L. R. Smith has noted that Republicans did not seem able to adopt serious thinking on the role of unionists.[48] Perceptions of the conflict as a war against British imperialism ensured that a traditional absence of Republican thought on the possible autonomy of unionist action remained. Pat Walsh has emphasised that the intellectual bankruptcy of the movement and its attendant military crisis provided, as usual, a base for social republi-canism.[49] Yet the roots of leftist Republicanism remained shallow in the movement. The social and economic programme adopted by the party at its 1964 Ard Fheis (annual conference) was unquestionably a move to the left, offering garrison, nation state socialism and support-ing local cooperatives.[50] The new ideological outlook, however, was abandoned by some at the first opportunity, in favour of a revival of militarism.

Unquestionably there were substantial changes in the Republican movement between 1962 and 1969. Although the movement did not adopt a clear or decisive theoretical position during this period, it be-gan to theorise, shifting substantially towards the left. Economic the-ory became particularly prominent, with analyses of imperialism central to strategic development. Militarism was downgraded in favour of politics. The position of the IRA as the 'sole liberator' of the Irish people was abandoned in favour of strategies for coalition. For all the rhetoric about the need to engage with the Irish people, the net result of this republican theoretical introspection was to make the move-ment even less popular and more marginal to Irish politics than at any period in its history. If the Northern population was uninterested in armed struggle to overthrow Unionism, its apathy was nothing com-pared to Southern lack of interest in 'strategies of anti-imperialism'. Furthermore, the attempt to develop Catholic and Protestant anti-imperialist unity in the North was, predictably, an abject failure. By 1967 Cathal Goulding, the Chief of Staff of the IRA, lamented that 'units of the IRA and the cumann of Sinn Féin had become almost non-existent'.[51] This account has been contradicted by intelligence sources, possibly to justify their existence.[52] The main think-tank of the Republican movement during this period was the Wolfe Tone Society. Prominent authors such as Anthony Coughlan and Roy Johnston, who had worked in the Connolly Society in England, joined the review processes of the society. Although Republicans of all hues perennially invoke the name of Connolly as justification for their views, the English-based Connolly Society, and its links to the Communist Party, invoked a certain suspicion from Republican traditionalists. Sinn Féin played little role in these strategic reviews. Its ranks contained mainly those 'exhausted' from earlier campaigns.[53]

With the encouragement of Goulding in particular, the leadership of the Republican movement discussed the development of a more independent role for Sinn Féin, rather than one in which it came directly under the orders of the Army Convention.[54] It was also hoped that Sinn Féin would begin to look outwards. The political strategy developed by the leadership centred on the development of a broad coalition of anti-imperialist activity. This would involve Republican engagement with other agencies, including trade unions, housing groups and small farmers. Sinn Féin argued that a variety of ingredients for revolution were necessary: working-class mobilisation; political and theoretical development; imperialist crises and military activity.[55] In this context of a coalition engagement against imperialism, the IRA enthusiastically endorsed the development of the Civil Rights campaign in the North, involving itself in the umbrella organisation, the Northern Ireland Civil Rights Association (NICRA). This support was based on an optimistic, 'stageist' analysis of political progression in the North. As early as 1963 the Connolly Association had advocated a Civil Rights campaign.[56] By the mid-1960s, the IRA believed that divisions emerging in Unionism created a sufficiently promising arena. Prime Minister O'Neill's limited programme of reform and modernisation was fracturing unionism, as hardliners, led by Ian Paisley, opposed change. The Republican leadership took an optimistic view of the decline of Unionist deference, believing the Civil Rights campaign possessed sufficient potential to expose divisions in unionism. According to this view, as sections of the Protestant working class also demanded an increase in Civil Rights, old discriminatory Orangeism, for which the British government now had less use, would fade. A Civil Rights campaign based on issues such as jobs and housing would help sweep away sectarian division and provide a basis for working-class, anti-imperialist unity. Catholics and Protestants would combine to sweep away the old regimes in North and South and establish Irish unity. This political fantasy was outlined by the President of Sinn Féin, Thomas MacGiolla, at the party Ard Fheis in 1967, when he spoke of the 'welcome evidence of change amongst the Protestant community in the North...no-one will be more receptive than they to Republican principles.'[57]

Although Goulding claimed that 'the Army Council set up NICRA' this exaggerated the IRA's role.[58] The main input from Republicans into NICRA came from the presence of two members of the Wolfe Tone Society on its committee.[59] Members of the IRA acted as stewards at marches, but in an individual capacity. Sinn Féin, banned in the North, operated under the guise of Republican Clubs. However, in 1967, Republican Clubs was also banned and the organisation had only one official representative on the committee. The presence of the IRA, no matter how tendentious, nonetheless impacted upon perceptions of the Civil Rights movement. Already limited, any Unionist sympathy for NICRA was eroded and the inaccurate view of NICRA as merely a Republican front persisted. According to David Trimble, elected leader of the Ulster Unionist Party in 1995, 'the behaviour and tactics of the Civil Rights movement soon clarified the matter...this was really just the Republican movement in another guise.'[60] The increased hostility to NICRA dealt a fatal blow to ultimate republican hopes of working-class unity among Catholics and Protestants, as loyalists sided with the militant brand of unionism offered by Ian Paisley.

By 1969 the obsession with 'economistic' politics among members of the republican movement reached its climax. The policy document *Ireland Today* conceived the twenty-six counties as 'the area where the greatest anti-imperialist unity is possible'.[61] To a conservative electorate, lacking a large urban proletariat and still rooted in the post-civil-war politics of Fianna Fáil and Fine Gael, such an assertion would have come as a surprise. To the Unionists of the North, the belief of the Republican leadership that a shared agenda on jobs and housing might reshape Unionist identity and lead them towards a socialist Irish Republic appeared incredible. Whatever the unrealism of unreconstructed militarists within the Republican movement, they were amateur fantasists when contrasted with dedicated 'anti-imperialists'.

Meanwhile, as reform proved problematic for Unionists, the notion of reform troubled traditionalists in the Republican movement.

Republican split

The increasingly political direction of the Republican movement after 1962 upset elements of a movement based upon the centrality of physical force. From 1962 until 1965, these elements were at their quietest, demoralised by the Border Campaign. Some, such as Joe Cahill, resigned:

> I had a feeling that ultra-left politics were taking over. As far as I was concerned, the main purpose of the IRA and Sinn Féin was to break the connection with and get rid of the 'Brits' from Ireland. They'd gone completely political and the military side of things was being run down. The Republican Movement was being led off the true path of republicanism.[62]

Others shared Cahill's linkage of purist Republicanism with the physical force tradition. The main focus of dissent towards politicisation was the Committee for Revolutionary Action.[63] Using the journal *An Phoblacht*, this group had four main grievances in the mid-1960s. Firstly, it opposed the downgrading of military action. Secondly, it saw most political activity as pointless. With some prescience, it feared that the political route would adopt parliamentarianism as a tactic. Thirdly, this loose grouping of dissidents loathed the links held by members of the Republican leadership, particularly those with Communist organisations. Finally, some of the militarists regarded with contempt the atheistic leanings of sections of the leadership. Roy Johnston criticised Catholic practices, such as the reciting of decades of the rosary, at Republican commemorations.[64] Johnston may have been 'testing the water' regarding the extent to which the movement might change. He was left in no doubt as to the unacceptability of his comments; protest letters sent to the *United Irishman* were censored by the editor.[65] One of the most vocal critics, Seán McStiofáin, had already attempted to expel Johnston from the Army Council, citing his Communist allegiances. Now, McStiofáin declined to circulate the *United Irishman* and received a six-month suspension.[66] Other dissidents were expelled, including the entire Sinn Féin membership in North Kerry, a traditionalist stronghold.

Grievances over strategy might have been dismissed by the Johnston, Coughlan, Goulding and MacGiolla leadership axis had it not been for the changing situation in the North. The leftward shift and emphasis on social Republicanism could be contrasted with the theoretical and intellectual bankruptcy of opponents, still haunted by 1956–62. Furthermore, MacGiolla reassured the Sinn Féin faithful that the socialism of the new republican era was rooted in Republican traditions and 'had nothing to do with either atheism or totalitarianism, as is evident from even a superficial reading of Connolly'.[67] The leadership had not entirely discounted the idea of an armed campaign, and Goulding feared a split were militarism to be publicly abandoned.[68] His message on its role was often unclear, although his speech at the Sinn Féin Ard Fheis in 1967 clearly downgraded the role of armed struggle in the furtherance of Republican aims. By the late 1960s, the use of the policy of armed struggle was primarily in the realm of anti-imperialist activism, and foreign-owned businesses were attacked. Whatever the fears of some that the movement was subservient to international Communism, the politics of verbal attacks on the European Economic Community and physical attacks on external investors offered a narrower, inward-looking nationalism. The changes in Republicanism were later partly ascribed to 'the worldwide development of socialist revolutionary movements and imperialist struggle'.[69] While there is some truth in this, the Republican socialism of the 1960s was largely home-grown. Moreover, 'new' republicanism was largely unchanged in its (lack of) thinking concerning Northern Protestants. New Republicans saw the need for working-class unity across the religious divide, but adopted a view of Unionists as imperial dupes, who ought to realise their true Irish identity. For all its contempt for the dominant party of the South, the left-wing Sinn Féin offered a view of Northern Unionists indistinguishable from that held by Fianna Fáil. To such a group, nationalists throughout Ireland 'could only emphasise the short-lived Presbyterian radical/nationalists of 1798, or dangle the figures of Wolfe Tone and John Mitchel before their unsympathetic eyes.'[70]

In 1966, the fiftieth anniversary of the Easter Rising allowed 'a greater uncritical receptivity to the message of physical force nationalism'.[71] Despite the resurgence of interest in Republicanism, developments in Loyalism had greater impact. The rebirth of the Ulster

Volunteer Force and its sectarian assassination of two Belfast Catholics revived minority community vulnerability. If the Dublin leadership regarded the Belfast IRA as unfortunate Catholic sectarians, the contempt was heartily reciprocated. In 1968–9 attacks upon Civil Rights marches in Derry and elsewhere heightened tensions, but the IRA in the North was woefully short of weapons, a situation that the Goulding axis appeared unwilling to rectify. Dissident Southern elements in the IRA had continued to be attacked by the dominant wing of the movement, being dismissed as 'mealy mouthed sentimentalists … saddling the next generation with useless tools and tactics'.[72] With events moving quickly in the North, however, the armed wing of the movement eventually found an outlet for old-fashioned Republicanism. Later, such dissidents claimed to have read the situation in the North correctly, arguing that the Loyalist backlash against the Civil Rights campaign was inevitable.[73] The response to attacks by Loyalist mobs in Derry was mainly an act of citizens' defence, which the few remaining IRA personnel helped organise. The IRA in Belfast engaged directly with the encroaching Loyalist activity where possible, blaming Dublin for insufficient support for their run-down organisation. With nationalist areas largely defenceless, the IRA endured the humiliation of the arrival of the British Army as the force charged with the protection of Catholics. In Ardoyne in North Belfast, a particular repository of 'Catholic defenderism', the limited weaponry held by the IRA had been moved into a central pool in the west of the city. According to Martin Meehan, later to become a leading Belfast Provisional, the 'seeds for the split, which gave rise to the Provisionals, were partly sown in North Belfast'.[74]

Such unsatisfactory local decisions have often made as much impact as ideological dissent in fostering a split. The sectarian geography of 1969 was, arguably, as important as the politics of 1916 in dividing the IRA. Nonetheless, there were clear ideological fault-lines, reinforced by growing sectarian conflict in the North. In the Republican movement, the principle of abstention had been under discussion for some years. Following the Sinn Féin Ard Fheis of 1968, a joint Sinn Féin-IRA committee was established to examine whether abstentionism should be abandoned.[75] The Army Council recommended the wholesale abandonment of abstention. Recognition of the Leinster House, Stormont and Westminster parliaments was a drastic step, certain to enrage traditionalists. The Army Council also supported the establishment of a National Liberation Front of leftist groups. By the end of 1969, the Army Convention had ratified the changes. The Belfast IRA had declined to send delegates.[76] Shortly after the Convention, a Provisional Army Council was formed. The split was publicly confirmed at a chaotic Sinn Féin Ard Fheis in January 1970. The two-thirds majority required to change the party constitution to allow participation in 'partitionist' parliaments was not forthcoming, emphasising that the Goulding axis was not entirely dominant. A subsequent vote of confidence in the Goulding leadership was then (successfully) proposed, ensuring that Sinn Féin was, in effect, obliged to follow the Army Convention's strategy. Led by Seán McStiofáin, a group of delegates left the conference to state their allegiance to the '32-County Irish Republic proclaimed in 1916 and established by Dáil Éireann in 1919'. The Provisional IRA, along with a very weak political sidekick, Provisional Sinn Féin, was born.

For nationalists in Northern Ireland, the period from 1921 until 1970 was an unhappy one, during which they felt trapped within a statelet to which they did not belong. Many nationalists did not feel a great sense of loyalty to the Dublin government either, having felt abandoned by the twenty-six-county state to the South. Nonetheless, considerable welfare reform and some gradual improvements in material wellbeing as a consequence of measures introduced by Westminster governments failed to induce a sense of Britishness. Instead Northern nationalism adopted distinctive but heterogeneous forms. For some republicans, British control of Northern Ireland was part of a wider imperial strategy. Northern Unionists were settler colonials, existing to prop up the remnants of empire. Other Northern nationalists were more concerned with the petty sectarianism of the Unionist and Orange regime, which eliminated nationalists from political influence and reinforced the idea of Northern Ireland as a Protestant and Unionist homeland. This Unionist triumphalism was to have disastrous consequences as nationalists demanded change by the late 1960s. Moderate nationalists challenged the inequities of Unionist governance, whilst physical force republicanism was re-ignited through the grafting of hostility to Orange sectarianism onto more traditional Republican anti-imperial orthodoxies. The 1960s witnessed considerable debate within nationalist and Republican politics in Northern

Ireland. The political representatives of both tendencies attempted to develop a more participatory form of politics. Whilst many nationalists endorsed this development and were prepared to support the embryonic SDLP, a section of the disaffected Catholic working class, disillusioned by political marginalisation, sectarian discrimination and the lack of change, was to prefer armed rebellion, designed to overthrow a state from which it felt utterly alienated.

2

COLLAPSING STORMONT
POLITICS AND REBELLION IN THE EARLY 1970s

During the early 1970s nationalists and Republicans opposed the political structures of Northern Ireland. The SDLP wished to fundamentally revise its parliament, as a precursor to the establishment of a united Ireland. Although many within the party had participatory leanings, the inability of the unionist regime to reform itself meant that the SDLP engaged in episodic civil disobedience. Republicans, increasingly confident of turning the disaffection of the nationalist population into rebellion, moved rapidly towards armed insurrection. This movement tended to sweep many of those opposed to an armed campaign, as the Official IRA, from 1970 until 1972, participated in actions not dissimilar from those undertaken by the growing Provisional IRA (PIRA). Feeding on a combination of economic and political discontent, religious sectarianism and 'moral' outrage at the excesses of poorly organised and 'biased' security forces, the PIRA found fertile recruiting grounds among Northern urban working-class Catholics. Provisionalism developed as a response to the failures and excesses of Unionism, rather than from a deeply rooted ideological commitment to armed rebellion as the mode of Irish 'liberation'.

Constitutional nationalism

Apart from a few months of calm when British troops first arrived in Belfast in August 1969, the security situation in Northern Ireland had been deteriorating since 1968. Division within unionism over how to respond to political protest had not been matched in scale among nationalists, but nonetheless significant movement was occurring. A moderate, but more left-wing nationalist party was emerging in the form of the SDLP, but concurrently, the IRA was reviving as

25

nationalist disaffection with British security forces quickly became evident. Three days of rioting in Derry in July 1971 saw two unarmed youths shot by the British army. Under pressure from a nationalist community denied normal institutional redress and from a revitalised IRA, the SDLP was prepared to veer from its avowedly constitutional course. John Hume was the main instigator in leading the SDLP parliamentary party out of Stormont in July 1971, despite strong reservations by Gerry Fitt and Paddy Devlin on this course of action. The Fitt wing of the party wished to test Brian Faulkner's offer of accommodation to the minority community through his proposed committee system at Stormont. However, Faulkner's tone of moderation was somewhat undermined after members of his cabinet and himself met representatives of the Orange Order to discuss the issue of Orange parades and indicated little sensitivity towards nationalist opposition.[1]

The SDLP held a press conference on 17 July 1971 formally announcing its withdrawal as official opposition at Stormont. The party's statement criticised the Conservative government for not consulting it and for buttressing the Unionist administration at Stormont. Under pressure from the wider Republican community, the SDLP had to take this action with the objective of bringing down Stormont. The SDLP withdrew elected representatives at Stormont, and at local level. This was an outward manifestation of constitutional nationalism withdrawing consent from the system of government in Northern Ireland. Hume declared: 'We are prepared to accept in the short term the charges of creating polarisation, in order to remove the real roots of sectarian discord, with all its consequent evils—the system of government created by the Government of Ireland Act 1920.'[2] Hume strongly believed that the first phase in bringing about a solution was for Westminster to acknowledge the ineffectiveness of the system of government in Northern Ireland and prepare its abolition. The SDLP promoted a civil disobedience campaign, comprising the non-payment of rents and rates, following the commencement of internment in August 1971.

The protest campaign involved the SDLP in high profile activity, which offered succour to nationalists desirous of non-violent direct action, whilst doing little to staunch the flow of nationalists into the Provisional IRA. Any SDLP aspirations of capturing Protestant support evaporated, although such hopes were always the product of unbridled optimism rather than reality. Later in August 1971, John Hume and his fellow Stormont MP Ivan Cooper, along with others including senior SDLP members Michael Canavan and Hugh Logue, were taking part in an anti-internment demonstration in Derry. They participated along with hundreds of other Derry people in a sit down protest against internment, and against the decision of the British Army to remove barricades.[3] The five men were arrested by the British Army, and formally charged under the Special Powers Act. Hume and Cooper successfully challenged the legality of the British Army's actions in the High Court (R (Hume and others) v. Londonderry Justices, 1972).[4] On 23 February 1972 the three judges of the Northern Ireland Court of Appeal accepted that the Army had no legal basis to act under the Special Powers Act. In effect, much of the Army's actions in the last two and a half years had been found to be unlawful. At this time the Northern Ireland Act 1972 was rushed through Westminster in a day and night sitting to plug this legislative gap.[5]

In the autumn of 1971 the SDLP formed the Assembly of the Northern Irish people, the unofficial 'Dungiven Parliament'. Whilst the creation of the Parliament was a futile exercise, privately the party think-tank was setting out its position on the constitutional question in a number of internal discussion documents between September 1971 and January 1972. The first detailed internal unpublished SDLP paper, dated September 1971, argued that a solution to the Northern Ireland conflict would not be viable unless it recognised the interdependence of both parts of the island. In its attack on unionist intransigence the paper argued: 'We do not suggest that the Unionists do not have a right to equal consideration where the future of this country is concerned. What is challenged is the right of the Unionist Party to claim more than equality.' This was less a critique of the Unionist 'constitutional veto' than a denunciation of the sectarian tendencies of the Unionist government. The paper put the blame for the outbreak of violence in Northern Ireland on the British government and the Unionist Party. It pointed to the poor standing of the British government in the wider international domain by 'propping up a discredited, unjust and corrupt post-colonial regime'. The language of colonialism is interesting and suggests commonalities with the historical overview of Sinn Féin. The SDLP gave no indication as to when the conflict had moved from being colonial to 'post-colonial' in nature.

Instant reunification was not the solution, however, as this would exacerbate the problem. The SDLP's analysis was grounded in pragmatism rather than advanced political thinking, although it contained the broad outline of the 'two traditions' approach which came to dominate party thought. Nonetheless, reiterating former NDP constitutional policy, the paper declared that the SDLP would 'ultimately wish to seek a socialist 32-County Republic enjoying a harmonious relationship with Britain and other countries.'

The paper set out detailed proposals on the fundamental premise that Stormont was to be suspended forthwith. As an interim measure the former powers of Stormont, with the exception of the judiciary, police and security, were to pass to a 100 member Commission. The Commission was to elect an executive committee by proportional representation, along with a chairman and vice-chairman. It was suggested that security should be transferred to a neutral body selected by the two governments, the unionists and the SDLP. After consulting with the Irish government the British government should enact the following legislation:

– a Bill of Rights guaranteeing equality before the law for all Northern Ireland citizens;
– an Anti-Discrimination Act dealing with all aspects of discriminatory action in employment, and creating an effective mechanism to deal with individual cases of alleged discrimination.[6]

The document recommended that the two governments should pass legislation establishing a Supreme Council of Ireland composed of members from the Northern Ireland Commission and from the Republic. The Supreme Council should have the power to analyse legislation in Northern Ireland and the Republic. Its other main role would be to identify cross-border programmes for economic development and other areas of co-operation between both parts of the island. Every ten years there should be a review of the totality of relationships between both parts of Ireland, and between both parts of Ireland and Britain. The overall objective was to review the harmonisation of the legal and other systems on both sides of the border and to prepare a new constitution for the whole island. Meanwhile, the paper indicated, the Republic of Ireland should re-examine its Constitution along with the Supreme Council of Ireland, and make necessary amendments to any parts seen as offensive to 'any section of the

Irish people', namely the unionists. The Irish government, along with the Northern Ireland Council, 'should make arrangements for voters in Northern Ireland to participate in future elections of the President of Ireland'. In charting an immediate way forward, the SDLP document recommended elections by proportional representation in Northern Ireland, to be held no later than the middle of 1973, to elect an 80-seat council in Northern Ireland. Once elected, the council should choose from within its numbers a chairman, vice-chairman and executive committee. Significantly, the British government was asked to declare 'that she has no interest in perpetuating the partition of Ireland, but that she actively desires re-unification whenever this can be achieved on such terms as will win the consent of the majority of people in N. Ireland'.[7]

There are a number of important principles arising from this paper. First, it is clear that the SDLP, having withdrawn from Stormont in July 1971, now wanted to see the end of the Stormont regime. Second, although a traditional unitary state is the party's ultimate goal, the party accepted this was not a short-term option, and this early document details an interim solution without a specific timescale. Third, as part of these interim measures, unionist interests must be fully protected at any negotiations—a formal acknowledgement of the consent principle. Fourth, the main aspects of the interim measures are through harmonisation of a wide range of cross-border issues, which has the subtlety of implementing an evolving mechanism towards Irish unity. Fifth, for the first time Britain's role as a persuader for Irish unity is set out. Sixth, the Republic's government is challenged to make necessary changes to the Irish Constitution seen as offensive to the Unionist community in Northern Ireland. Lastly, voters in Northern Ireland should be able to participate in future elections for the President of Ireland.

The Official and Provisional IRAs

As the SDLP established a clear nationalist identity and a way forward for addressing the realities of partition, Republicans recovered from the split of early 1970. At the time, the split was irrelevant to most nationalists, but, as significant numbers of Catholics demonstrated a willingness to engage in armed conflict, the division of the IRA assumed greater salience. It would be a caricature to describe the split

between the 'Official' and the 'Provisional
theory versus practice; politics versus milita
Socialism, or atheism versus Catholicism. I
an account would be based upon vestig
visionals were justifiably dismissive of thei
(the 'Stickies') as 'men without politics',
'tools of Fianna Fáil' or even 'fascists'.[8] Indeed much of the literature offered by the Provisionals was devoted to attacks upon the
institutions they were alleged to support. The Catholic Church hierarchy was regularly condemned; there were frequent denunciations of
sectarianism; Jack Lynch's Fianna Fáil government and the twenty-
six-county state were the targets of sustained abuse and the Provisional leadership, at some length, discussed politics. The *form* of politics offered may have been basic and little political education was
undertaken, but compared to the utopian Republican political fanta-
sies of 1962–9, Provisional politics were no more inadequate than
those previously on offer. To dismiss the Provisional leadership as
unthinking militarists, or as mere Catholic defenders, is inaccurate.

The Provisionals used the organs of *An Phoblacht* and *Republican
News*, launched in February and June 1970 respectively, to justify their
breakaway in some detail. Five criticisms were offered of what became known as the 'Official IRA': its recognition of 'partitionist' parliaments at Leinster House and Stormont, plus that at Westminster;
extreme socialism; the internal methods of organisation within the
movement; the 'let down' of the North; and the Officials' support for
Stormont as a potentially progressive institution.[9] The end of
abstentionism was seen as a gross infringement of the IRA's constitution. The declaration of Tom Maguire, the last surviving member of
the original Dáil Éireann, that the IRA leadership had 'neither the
right nor the authority' to end abstentionism was cited.[10] Maguire was
later to criticise the Provisionals for taking similar steps in respect of
Leinster House in 1986, on their route towards constitutionalism.
The Provisionals also pointed out that there was not a clear majority
for the end of abstentionism within the IRA and Sinn Féin. Given
that, for the Provisionals, participation in partitionist parliaments was
'illegal', their discussion of whether a majority in favour actually existed appeared to be an irrelevance. The Officials were seen as worse
than other parties on the question of abstentionism. 'It is possible

e are at least some people in Fianna Fáil and the Irish Labour who would be opposed to sitting in Westminster and Stor-nt,' argued *Republican News*.[11]

The Officials were not accused of abandoning armed struggle. Such a claim would have been difficult to justify given that at the time of the split, the Officials' newspaper, the *United Irishman*, declared that 'those who think that political means alone are sufficient for the re-conquest of Ireland are closing their minds to the lessons of history'.[12] Furthermore, the Officials were to engage in some of the most sig-nificant acts of violence until calling a ceasefire in 1972. Although the ceasefire moved the Officials to a position of defence and retaliatory action only, the Officials still had almost one hundred prisoners aris-ing from their armed campaign at the end of 1974.[13] Nonetheless, the Officials persistently dismissed the military campaign of the Provi-sionals as 'counter-revolutionary', maintaining their own delusion that the 'potential for revolution which existed up to late 1970 in both North and South, has been smashed'.[14] The main criticisms of the Officials upon which the Provisionals focused were, first, the down-grading of military action in favour of abstract theorising, reflected in the unwillingness to supply arms to the North, and secondly the end of abstentionism, which was tantamount to acceptance of partition. 'Purist' republicanism was thus fused with Northern defenderism, with differences of emphasis at different levels. Elements of the local Provisional membership were, for a short time at least, more inter-ested in community defence, which quickly converted into a 'hitting back at the Brits' 'strategy'. The lack of political sophistication of some of the Provisionals' local membership earned distaste from the Officials, who believed the PIRA units comprised youngsters who 'were in it just to fight Prods'.[15] This contempt extended beyond the circles of the Official IRA. Bishop and Mallie cite a West Belfast businessman:

> 'When you heard who the new officer commanding the Provision-als in our district was you had to laugh. Many of them were the scum of the area. They had the political awareness of Glasgow Celtic football fans… The Officials were sharper, more decent, a better type of person.'[16]

Nonetheless, the same account highlights other examples of dedica-ted local Provisional leaders with long membership of the Republican movement. Undoubtedly sectarian motivations prompted some to join the Provisionals. Furthermore, some local Provisional leaders in Belfast, such as Billy McKee, offered a comforting religious piety, which did no harm in offering reassurance to the local population that the PIRA was an organisation worthy of support. Yet when membership of both IRAs increased hugely from 1970 to 1972, the decision over which organisation to join was often shaped by the nature of the local leaders, the state of either organisation in the locality, or family ties, as much as political nuance. Some joined the Provisionals because, although sympathetic to the ultimate aspirations of the Officials, they rejected their theoretical and practical inflexibility, exemplified by the failure to respond to events in the North.[17] This dereliction encouraged even some of those otherwise sympathetic to the Officials, such as Gerry Adams, to side with the Provisionals. Others were unconcerned with or unaware of differences. Alex Maskey, later to become a member of Sinn Féin's executive and the Northern Ireland Assembly, claimed he had 'no awareness of the split' when he joined the Provisional IRA.[18]

Although exclusively sectarian attacks by the Provisionals were comparatively rare (although some saw all its activity as sectarian) the Officials continued to accuse the Provisionals of being a 'religious-sectarian organisation' engaged in a 'mad-dog' campaign.[19] Sympathy for the Catholic defender aspect of the Provisionals' work was offered via the *Voice of the North* newspaper, which first appeared in October 1969. Designed to 'expose the propaganda of the Unionist regime', it concentrated mainly upon criticism of the Orange Northern state and Loyalist attacks upon Catholics.[20] Funded by the 'green wing' of Fianna Fáil, including the future leader Charles Haughey, *Voice of the North* was one example of assistance for Northern Provisionals from the South. Overall, however, help for the Provisionals from Fianna Fáil was extremely limited. The Irish government did discuss intervention in the North, but ruled out such a prospect on practical grounds. Despite the links between *Voice of the North* and elements within Fianna Fáil, the party leader was strongly criticised for failing to support Northern Defence Committees.[21] The paper also offered occasional support for the purist Republicanism of the Provisionals. The January 1970 edition dismissed 'separate nations' arguments in favour of partition, reproducing a *Handbook of the Ulster*

Question first produced in 1923.[22] The tone was anti-pluralist, rejecting a separate non-Irish unionist identity. It was also dismissive of alternative forms of nationalism within Northern Ireland. The SDLP was dismissed as a pro-British, 'Redmondite' party, located within the tradition of the compromisers of the Irish Parliamentary Party nearly a century earlier.[23]

The other forms of help from elements of Fianna Fáil were financial aid and arms supply. In both these cases the amounts were small and, despite Fianna Fáil's obvious preference for anti-Communist, green nationalist Provisionals, some aid also reached the Officials. The Officials were anxious to portray the Provisionals as dupes of Fianna Fáil. There remains dispute over the extent and impact of Fianna Fáil assistance to the Provisionals. Patterson's account suggests that elements within Fianna Fáil were indeed important in the establishment of the Provisionals in the early days, but this contention is rejected in the works of Bishop and Mallie, Coogan and Bowyer-Bell.[24] A balanced account is offered by Richard English, who stresses the symbolic value of support from a section of the Southern establishment to the Provisionals in reawakening the national question, whilst emphasising that the PIRA would have developed regardless of the view of Fianna Fáil, green wing or otherwise.[25] Aid from the South appeared to be of marginal significance in the establishment of the Provisionals. That it arrived at all indicated residual sympathy for the aims of traditional Republicanism and the plight of Northern Catholics amongst some members of Fianna Fáil, especially among those located in the party's Northern sub-committee. Such support as this was of very limited value to the Provisionals, who wished for greater practical assistance.

Provisional politics

Given that they had been formed as part of a critique of the over-politicisation of the Republican movement, it was inevitable that the Provisionals appeared to favour militarism over political education. Gerry Adams lamented the split for over-militarising the Republican movement, a regret expressed in words that would not have looked out of place in the Officials' *United Irishman*:

> [The split] ensured that the reinvigorated republican struggle which emerged then was an inadequate one, because the only republican

organisation which arose from the ashes was a military one: it had little or no proper educational process, no formal politicisation courses, and there was scant regard paid by the leadership to such needs.[26]

Unquestionably, the Provisionals' political thinking was basic. The leadership relied upon the Republican shibboleth that 'the war is morally justified and that the Army is the direct representative of the 1918 Dáil Éireann parliament'.[27] Political structures were extremely weak. The very early politics of the Provisionals were mainly justifications of the split. A virulent anti-Communism was linked to the promotion of the virtues of 'purist' nationalism. The Officials were accused of political failure by attempting to link the liberation of Ireland to support for a Marxist Socialist republic. Collaboration with Communists and the presence of 'reds under the umbrella of the National Liberation Movement' were viewed as contrary to Army rules.[28] Nonetheless, politics did matter to some in the movement. The political impotence and subordinate position of Sinn Féin were acknowledged in *Republican News* in 1971:

> When the Sinn Féin Ard Fheis is held later this month a much needed opportunity will be afforded for radical change in that organisation. Here in Belfast, Sinn Féin appears to be its own worst enemy. Instead of being seen as an efficient and effective machine providing the political leadership, it seems content to sit and bask in the reflected glory of the military wing of the movement... No party can be a success without the support of a solid grass roots organisation. To this end full-time, paid organisers should be appointed by the Ard Chomhairle and the criterion for their appointment should be ability and efficiency—not their length of service in the Republican Movement or the fact that they have served long sentences in gaol.[29]

The article criticised Sinn Féin's 'holier than thou' attitude, prohibiting membership of the political (but not military) wing of the movement to those who had taken any form of allegiance to the British or Stormont governments. This barred entry to the legal, teaching or nursing professions, in addition to public sector employment. Although it was claimed that such a barrier 'drastically reduces the talent available', few were being turned away from Sinn Féin.[30] Within Republican working-class constituencies, there was a greater interest in paramilitary activity, although this was accentuated by the dismal state of Provisional Sinn Féin as an organisation. The problem lay less in the Provisionals' neglect of political attitudes than in convincing the 'grass-roots' in areas such as Ardoyne and the Falls of the need for political education. Such needs were seen as irrelevant in the context of events such as the imposition of the Falls curfew by the British Army and the developing 'ad hocery' of the IRA's military campaign. The main value of the public criticism of Sinn Féin was to open an embryonic debate over the organisation of politics within the movement. Belfast Sinn Féin responded by insisting that it had always advocated that job-enforced declarations of allegiance to the Northern Ireland state should not be a barrier to party membership. Yet the party within the city was itself the subject of criticism in the republican press:

> At present, Sinn Féin in Belfast is not a political force. There are many reasons for this. Here are a few:
> 1 lack of effective spokesmen;
> 2 lack of trained personnel;
> 3 lack of discipline and dedication;
> 4 lack of appreciation among many republicans of the need for political action.[31]

Each reason was indeed valid, but little was done to rectify matters during the early years of the Provisional movement. There were calls in the Republican press for Sinn Féin members to 'assert themselves and not to allow themselves to be treated as second class members of the Republican movement'.[32] Most Republicans, however, had yet to discover the value of 'armed propaganda'. As the actions of the British Army, operating in a political vacuum, alienated the local population, such propaganda as existed concentrated upon warnings not to 'fraternise' with the enemy.[33] Problems concerning Army activity in a particular locality were linked, if any wider connections were made, to national rather than social questions. The Provisionals reinstated the importance of the 'national question' as the supreme issue. Somewhat contradictorily, the Provisionals denied that nationalism was more important than socialism, whilst arguing that socialism could not be attained without the promotion of nationalism. Social liberation as viewed as consequential upon national liberation. Nationalism and socialism were seen as separate entities, with nationalism the precursor for social change.

Provisional policy: Éire Núa[34]

The differences between the Provisionals and Officials were, to a considerable extent, matters of strategy, sequencing and tactics. The Officials argued for social struggle, based upon constitutional politics, but backed, if absolutely necessary, by an armed campaign. The Protestant working class could, and must, be won over to such a campaign. The Provisionals argued for national struggle, backed, where necessary, by social struggle. Constitutional politics would merely ensure that Republicans 'get absorbed into the imperial system'.[35] Support from the Protestant working class would, of course, be desirable, but pending this, nationalist areas must be 'defended'. Both organisations believed the struggle to be anti-colonial and anti-imperialist. Each claimed to believe in socialism of the James Connolly variety. Placing the appeals of the Officials to Protestants within the (unlikely) context of post-Vatican II Catholicism, the (far-left) account of Pat Walsh even claims that the 'outlook of both sets of Republicans was Catholic-nationalist'.[36] Although some aspects of green nationalism continued to linger within the Officials, this exaggerates this impact of Church teaching upon their leadership. Some Church teaching did influence the Provisionals and contributed to political differences between them and the Officials. Their strongly anti-Communist stance was justified not merely as in keeping with the true flame of Republicanism, but as a Christian, anti-materialistic view. Where Walsh is correct is in asserting that the promotion of green, Catholic nationalism by the Provisionals was not a right-wing deviation, but an attempted return to mainstream Republicanism.[37] This was true even though the 'street politics' of 1969 were more important than the Republican vision of 1916 to many participants.

The manner in which the Provisionals had emerged as a largely reactive force in their early days meant that it took a little time to develop a political strategy. When one emerged, it offered the same basic analysis of Unionism and Unionists as the Officials, whilst providing greater institutional autonomy. *An Phoblacht* and *Republican News* devoted much of the first three years of their existence to considerations of unionist identity, each reaching the conclusion that they were of course Irish. The second edition of *Republican News* appealed 'to our Protestant Irishmen' to make common cause.[38] *An Phoblacht* asked 'Is the Orangeman British?' before, to the surprise of no-one, rejecting the idea.[39] Sinn Féin's policy was based upon ethno-geographical determinism. The island of Ireland constituted a clearly defined territorial entity, within which lay a distinct Irish people. The people were the nation. There was a clear congruence between nation and state. In Republican eyes, unionists offered a distinctive *Irish* tradition, to be accommodated through the construction of a decentralised, federal Ireland. *Éire Núa* was published as draft Sinn Féin policy in January 1971 and ratified at the 1972 *Ard Fheis*, not merely as policy, but as part of the constitution, having acquired the necessary two-thirds majority among delegates.[40] Ironically, given the hostility to the leftward shift of the movement, the plan was loosely based upon the thinking of a Stalinist intellectual, Seán Cronin.[41] Whatever its origins, *Éire Núa* was presented as a democratic socialist plan. It amounted to a romanticised vision of a co-operative, democratic socialist, agrarian Ireland. The plan envisaged the establishment of four parliaments in Ireland, controlling the affairs of the ancient provinces of Ulster, Leinster, Connacht and Munster. As such, it offered the prospect of limited constitutional autonomy to Unionists in the North-East. This guarantee was repeated regularly by the President of Sinn Féin, Ruairí Ó Brádaigh:

> 'We do not wish to submerge the Unionists of the North-east in an All-Ireland state; we offer them very real powers in majority control of a greater Ulster through the Dáil Uladh plan; incorporation of all nine counties will give a healthier balance of population with a credible opposition—something the Six County state of Northern Ireland has always lacked. We would never ask you to join the 26-County state—we are trying to escape from it ourselves!'[42]

For republicans, the concession of a parliament in Ulster, Dáil Uladh, possibly controlled by Unionists, was the most that could ever be offered, even if such concessions met with the obvious contempt of Northern Protestants. Notwithstanding potential gravitation of power to the federal government, a genuinely federalist structure offered limited autonomy protection of Unionist identity, although given the importance of Britishness to that identity, it was unclear what such protection entailed. The Provisionals were repeatedly critical of the desire of the Officials to retain the Stormont parliament, dismissing it as a colonial, British institution. The Provisionals were offering a heavily modified variant, a potentially Unionist parliament, without the Union. In the political worldview of the Provisionals, this was not a problem, as the Unionists were not British and thus did not need the Union. The Provisionals would not have demurred from the proposition offered in the *United Irishman* in respect of Stormont that 'are not all those who are members of it Irishmen, even the right-wing Unionists?'[43]

Éire Núa's federalism was accompanied by a rigid socialism. This opposed private ownership other than that of basic, non-exploitative concerns, mainly small farmholdings, often owned by Republicans; advocated nationalisation of land and business, and promised the replacement of capitalism with farming and worker co-operatives. The 54-page social and economic programme promised redistribution of wealth and prohibition of land ownership by foreigners. There was much concentration upon farming issues and little indication of how a strategy of industrial modernisation was to be undertaken. The favouring of socialism in one country was reflected in Sinn Féin's bitter, unsuccessful opposition to EEC entry in the Republic's 1972 referendum. Membership was supported by over 80 per cent of the Republic's voters. *Éire Núa* contained tensions between the bureaucratic statism required in the extent of proposed socialist controls, which could not have been effected by local co-operatives and its insistence on decentralised political structures. The federal parliament would be confined to foreign affairs, defence and overall financing, but such a limited role would inevitably expand because of the amount of regulation required. The Sinn Féin President promised a 'community of communities' throughout Ireland, through *Éire Núa's* strong district councils covering populations of 10,000–40,000, grouped into fifteen regional bodies.[44] Federalism, regionalism and localism would not merely solve the problems of the North, but also cure the poverty of the West.[45]

The existence of *Éire Núa* indicated that political thinking did take place within the Provisional IRA/Sinn Féin leadership. The desire to create a new Ireland was genuine, exemplified in Ó Brádaigh address to Sinn Féin's Dublin *Cumann* (branch) in 1972. 'The term United

Ireland means nothing but the incorporation of the Six Counties in the 26 County system of over-centralised economic imperialism. Sinn Féin has long ceased to advocate merely a 'united Ireland' because of what it has come to mean in the public mind.'[46]

Ó Brádaigh regularly cited respectable sales of *Éire Núa* as evidence of how it had captured the public imagination.[47] The truth was less encouraging. Outside the Republican movement interest was only slight, and non-existent among Unionists. Within the movement, there was disinterest amongst the urban supporters in Belfast and Derry, for whom *Éire Núa's* worthy pronouncements on farming co-operatives were of minimal relevance. Criticism of the Provisional movement's lack of policies was unjustified, as the movement had abundant politics. More justified was the criticism of the lack of a vibrant or *relevant* politics. *Éire Núa* did not engage the Northern republican population. It lacked a set of interim demands around which Sinn Féin could campaign in the North. As such, when Northern Republicans finally developed an interest in *Éire Núa*, it was merely to enact its abandonment.

The revival of 'armed struggle', 1970–2

By 1970, it was evident that the reformism of the Unionist Prime Minister, Terence O'Neill, had run aground. A programme of reforms had been announced as early as 1968, including changes in the voting franchise in local government, through the abolition of the business vote; introduction of a points system of allocation in housing; the establishment of an Ombudsman. The changes were regarded as too little, too late by Civil Rights campaigners and derided as a sellout of unionism by the growing number of hardline detractors. On security issues, O'Neill promised only a review of the Special Powers Act, rather than the removal of the B Specials, the 100 per cent Protestant police force, seen by many nationalists as sectarian and partisan. O'Neill's replacement in April 1969, James Chichester-Clark, offered little succour to the Officials' view that Stormont could be converted into a progressive institution. Although, like O'Neill, a relatively moderate patrician, Chichester-Clark did little to enhance the reform programme, as it was swept aside by pressing security issues. By February 1971, he announced that 'Northern Ireland is at war with the Irish Republican Army Provisionals'.[48]

The Provisionals and Officials both recruited rapidly after their split. Given the Provisionals' lack of inhibition over the centrality of violence to their struggle, it was unsurprising that they were the first to engage in an armed campaign. The Provisionals recruited heavily after the first major public souring of relations between the British Army and the local populace, in Ballymurphy in April 1970. An Orange parade had been permitted through the area. As the Army used CS gas against protestors, the perception of the British Army as an oppressor began to grow. A bombing campaign against Unionist-owned businesses began early in the summer of 1970. The Officials in Belfast were not averse to engaging with the British Army. Strong in parts of the city, they gained renewed respect after entering into a gun battle with the British Army after it imposed a curfew on the Lower Falls in June 1970. As in Derry, the Officials engaged in military activity to maintain credence in nationalist communities. Accordingly, there was 'little to choose in tactics or intentions' between them and the Provisionals between 1970 and 1972.[49] Both recruited through emotionalism, rather than from considered study of their particular brands of politics by recruits. The Belfast Provisionals underwent several changes of leadership. Billy McKee was replaced by Joe Cahill, in turn replaced by Seamus Twomey.[50] It was later claimed that McKee's replacements would 'feel politically at home on the extreme right of the Tory party'.[51] Although the claim was essentially extravagant nonsense, McKee and Twomey were ardent militarists, who fused Catholic nationalism with a core republicanism. McKee regarded more left-wing elements within the movement with suspicion, a concern that partly explained his hostility to Gerry Adams.[52]

With their greater visibility, partly through participation in the Civil Rights campaign, the Officials suffered more through the introduction of internment in 1971, although the Provisionals were affected later in strongholds such as Ardoyne. The first killing of a British soldier by the Provisionals occurred in February 1971. As the Provisionals stepped up their campaign, the Officials' insistence that it did not intend to engage in a purely military campaign began to look threadbare. Increased militarism even within the Officials led to the departure of the main original architect of their political approach, Roy Johnston, in 1972.[53] The Officials blamed the 'sectarian bombing campaign' of the Provisionals for their own escalation of violence.[54]

Both organisations needed to engage in violence to maintain interest and recruitment. The Provisionals engaged in some disastrous actions, not least a car bomb that killed six civilians in Belfast in 1972. Within the Officials, similar incompetence provoked greater debate over the validity of armed struggle. Their attempt at avenging Bloody Sunday was botched, killing civilians and a priest. The attempted assassination of the Unionist MP and former Northern Ireland Home Office Minister, John Taylor, appeared the type of sectarian action which would have yielded vociferous condemnation had it been an operation of the Provisionals. Finally, the killing of a British soldier, William Best, at home on leave in Derry in May 1972 prompted a local backlash. For all the optimism of the Officials concerning the prospect of breaking through to the Protestant working class, their own community was less than impressed by their performance. As a consequence, the Officials called a conditional ceasefire following the Best killing. Fearing a further loss of potential recruits to the Provisionals, the Officials in Belfast opposed the ceasefire, their dissent supported by Southern figures such as Seamus Costello. The ceasefire was sold on the basis that it would lead to the release of the Officials' internees and need not be permanent.[55] The ceasefire soon split the Officials and led to the formation of the Irish National Liberation Army (INLA), an organisation attempting to fuse armed rebellion with a neo-Marxist political agenda.

The remarkable rise of the IRA (or IRAs) from 1970 to 1972 owed much to the inadequacies and excesses of the security forces, ill-equipped to deal with a growing anti-colonial campaign in urban areas. Equally, the illegitimacy of state institutions was exposed by the SDLP's campaign of civil disobedience. The period was characterised by disinterest in purely constitutional routes to change among nationalists. Although a number of Catholics joined the innately Unionist Alliance Party, formed in 1970, most Catholics expressed dissatisfaction with the Northern state and its institutions through mild or virulent forms of extra-constitutional politics. The milder version offered by the SDLP produced a 'greenprint' for Irish unity and had little interest in participation in Unionist institutions. Both IRAs sought the overthrow of the state, although their political strategies were clearly distinctive and the Officials believed that existing institutions could be 'captured' and turned into progressive vehicles of change.

Unsurprisingly, the suspension of Stormont in 1972 was hailed as a victory by the Provisionals. The collapse of the Unionist government was seen as the removal of a major barrier to the establishment of a new unitary state. The Provisionals' primary short-term goal had been to render Northern Ireland ungovernable. An ever-expanding campaign of bombings and shootings achieved this by March 1972. With Unionists divided over the most appropriate security response and the British government distrustful of Brian Faulkner's ability to manage change as head of the Unionist regime, collapse became inevitable. On 24 March 1972 the British government announced that Stormont was prorogued for one year, to be replaced by direct rule from London, under the Secretary of State, William Whitelaw. Successful instigation of the collapse of the state was not, however, to lead to the fulfilment of Republican aspirations. The Provisionals' belief in the imminence of victory was to prove sorely misplaced.

3

THE SUNNINGDALE EXPERIMENT

With a growing IRA campaign, civil disobedience from even moderate nationalists and a strong Unionist backlash, Northern Ireland had become ungovernable by 1972. The suspension of Stormont in 1972 was readily interpreted by the Provisional IRA as a vindication of its strategy, amounting to the removal of the first barrier to a united, independent Ireland. Yet in introducing direct rule from Westminster, the British government had not abandoned the idea of devolved government for Northern Ireland. What would be required, however, was a new form of devolution, based upon the principle of power-sharing between Unionists and nationalists, with an attached Irish dimension.

The attempt to create power-sharing

The British government attempted to broker a consociational deal among constitutional politicians, in which there would be power sharing via a grand coalition between Unionists and nationalists (and the centre Alliance Party); proportionality in government; mutual veto rights for the political representatives of Unionism and nationalism, and limited community autonomy. The key theoretical exponent of consociationalism, Arend Lijphart, was sceptical of prospects for his own favoured type of solution in the mid-1970s, however, believing that Unionists were still too wedded to majoritarianism to share power with nationalists.[1] The British government, whilst far from sanguine concerning prospects for a deal, nonetheless believed that a reformed Northern Ireland, with recognition of the Irishness of the minority, could offer a solution to the crisis. Such a solution would offer challenges of a different order to the SDLP, involved in the formation of such an accord, and Republicans, whom the agreement attempted to marginalise.

Attended by British and Irish government officials, plus the Ulster Unionist Party, SDLP and Alliance Party, the Sunningdale Conference took place on 6–9 December 1973. Agreement had already been reached three weeks earlier between the three political parties on the formation of a Power-Sharing Executive in which representatives of each would hold posts. Power-sharing arrangements had been favoured in the British government's 1973 White Paper, *Northern Ireland Constitutional Proposals*.[2] The Sunningdale Conference attempted to clarify the roles of this executive and place it in a wider political framework of Anglo-Irish co-operation. In this context Sunningdale formalised plans not merely for the Executive, but also for a Council of Ireland. Internal power sharing arrangements were controversial enough, rejected by many unionists and all republicans for different reasons. The plans for a Council of Ireland enraged even many moderate unionists, who believed such a structure gave unwarranted Irish interference in the affairs of Northern Ireland. During the Sunningdale Conference there was much evidence that Faulkner's Unionist Party was divided on the acceptability of the Council.[3] Republicans viewed any deal short of Irish unity as unacceptable.

Sunningdale had the attraction to moderate unionists of the return of devolved government for the first time since Stormont had been prorogued in March 1972. It offered an institutional means of rapprochement between mainstream Unionism and nationalism for the first time ever in Northern Ireland. Concurrently, the Council of Ireland could enable North-South and indeed East-West (that is, London-Dublin) relations to become more congenial. The proposed Council contained two levels. Its upper level comprised seven ministers from the Irish Republic and seven from the Northern Ireland executive, making unanimous decisions. The remit of the Council was somewhat vague. It was designed to study areas of cross-border co-operation in line with European Community (EC) initiatives; agricultural and industrial resources; tourism; transport; health, sport and culture. With the exception of the EC element, these forms of North-South co-operation had been mooted since the talks between Terence O'Neill and Seán Lemass, Prime Ministers of the North and South respectively, in 1965. The extent to which the Council would adopt consultative, harmonising or executive functions in these areas was unclear, and this led to sharp differences in its perceived role and potential. One of the few items of clarity displeased Unionists: the Council would be consulted on policing appointments. A Consultative Assembly was to form the lower tier of the Council, comprising thirty members from Dáil Éireann and thirty from the Northern Ireland Assembly. Assembly members would be elected by their own parliament.

Constitutional declarations accompanied the Sunningdale Agreement. The Irish government fully accepted and solemnly declared that there could be no change in the constitutional status of Northern Ireland without the support of a majority in Northern Ireland for change. Although Fine Gael held power in the South, far less wedded to the rhetorical Republicanism of the Soldiers of Destiny (Fianna Fáil), the Irish government pointedly declined to state that Northern Ireland was part of the United Kingdom. Despite this, the acceptance of the *status quo* in Northern Ireland under Article 5 of the Agreement was still far too much even for those whose Republicanism was constitutional. In an attempt to render the Sunningdale Agreement unconstitutional, Kevin Boland, a staunchly Republican former Fianna Fáil Minister, claimed that Article 5 of the agreement infringed Article 2 of the 1937 Constitution of the Irish Republic, laying claim to the entire island. The Irish Courts rejected the claim, but made clear that if Article 5 had gone further than a mere *de facto* recognition of existing political realities in Northern Ireland, Sunningdale would have been declared unconstitutional. The insistence of the Irish Attorney General that 'Any person living on this island could not possibly construe the declaration as meaning we did not lay claim over the Six Counties' scarcely offered succour to Unionists either.[4] For its part, the British government reiterated its claim to sovereignty over Northern Ireland and solemnly declared that it supported the wishes of the majority of the Northern Ireland population in their constitutional preference. It would support the transfer of Northern Ireland into the Irish Republic in the unlikely event of that becoming the wish of the majority of the North.

Elections to the new Northern Ireland Assembly, held in June 1973, yielded a slight majority of anti-power-sharing Unionists. While the Ulster Unionist Party (UUP) continued to support power-sharing, there was still slight hope for its development. The power-sharing Executive was formally established at the beginning of January 1974, although, during the same month, the Ulster Unionist Council declined to support the concept of the Council of Ireland outlined at Sunningdale. Meanwhile the British Prime Minister Edward Heath was beset by deteriorating industrial relations elsewhere in Britain, which led to an unexpected general election in February 1974. The election was a major turning-point in the eventual demise of the Power-Sharing Executive. Brian Faulkner attempted to prolong its life by resigning from the Ulster Unionist Party, with pro-Sunningdale party members campaigning on a Unionist 'Pro-Assembly' label. The 'new' organisation failed miserably, gaining only thirteen per cent of the vote in the February 1974 general election, compared to 51 per cent of the total vote for anti-Sunningdale Unionists. Arguing that the agreement was a huge gain for republicanism, even though republicans viewed the deal with contempt, the 'antis' provided eleven of the twelve MPs returned to Westminster.[5]

The executive finally collapsed after the loyalist Ulster Workers' Council strike in May 1974, although lack of political support, rather than physical intimidation which accompanied the strike, has been held as the primary factor in the demise of power-sharing arrangements.[6] The collapse of Sunningdale had considerable political ramifications, in terms of attitudes to power sharing and an all-Ireland dimension. Its consociational, cross-border and intergovernmental themes were to be revisited almost a quarter of a century later. Sunningdale's only legacy in terms of actual policy implementation, however, was the establishment of a Joint Law Commission. This led to reciprocal legislation under which suspected paramilitaries could be brought to trial on whichever side of the border they were arrested.

SDLP ingredients and reaction

The 1973 Northern Ireland Constitution Act included enough SDLP policy for the party to support the British government's legislation. The main principles leading to the 1973 Northern Ireland Constitution Act appeared in parts of unpublished documents of the SDLP. The party supported the ideas that were to be formalised at Sunningdale, believing that any new arrangements in Northern Ireland had to offer guarantees to the Catholic community 'against further repression', whilst simultaneously assuring Protestants they were not being subsumed 'into an all Ireland Republic'.[7] The SDLP document suggested necessary changes might emerge from a conference that addressed the genuine fears of both communities. The four interested parties to the discussions were to be the majority and minority communities in Northern Ireland, and crucially, the British and Irish governments. The Conference was to examine a range of factors: a Bill of Rights; a Fair Practices Act; introduction of proportional representation for elections; and dropping the Westminster model of government for 'a system in which the members of the Government are elected by Proportional Representation and they in turn elect the Prime Minister from among their own numbers'.[8] To underpin all these recommendations proposals had to include a Council of Ireland dealing with cross-border economic and social matters. Also, the Council of Ireland was to provide the mechanism to form a joint security authority responsible for suitable border policing.

In another internal document, written just before the publication of the final version of *Towards a New Ireland* in 1972, the SDLP argued that the main obstacle to Irish unity was 'not British imperialism but rather the strength of the fears of the Protestant/Majority community'.[9] The paper again advocated an interim settlement aimed at creating an immediate peace in Northern Ireland and set a possible time-scale of 15 years with the principle of consent for unity to take place.[10] Other more controversial aspects of the paper included the call for an 'amnesty for all those convicted of or charged with "political" offences since 13th August 1969'.[11] The SDLP promised to participate in discussions over the future of Northern Ireland when internment was ended. The party argued that the only solution to the Northern Ireland question was 'a totally new Ireland' necessitating a 'new constitution for the whole island'.[12] The SDLP document proposed a wide range of reform measures for the purposes of building up community relations in Northern Ireland, accompanied by the continuation of direct rule and encouraged 'increasing co-operation between Northern Ireland and the Republic of Ireland in economic and cultural affairs'.[13]

The Northern Ireland Constitution Act (1973) was far from the stated aim of the SDLP to commit both governments to declare their new arrangements as the commencement of 'organic political institutions for Ireland'.[14] Power sharing with an all-island dimension was a dilution of the SDLP's condominium, or joint sovereignty proposals. Nevertheless the Act demonstrated a notable move away from the former majority rule system of government. Establishing a Council of Ireland was an acknowledgment that cross-border institutions were required to take account of the Irish identity. Consequently, the SDLP was bitter and somewhat humiliated at the collapse of the Power-Sharing Executive. Recriminations about who was to blame for the downfall of the Executive came from all sides of the Party. Gerry Fitt claimed that the Council of Ireland tainted the successful operation of the power-sharing experiment. However, John Hume, Minister of Commerce in the Executive, contended that Sunningdale failed because of the weakness of the British government. He argued that Westminster should have stood its ground against Loyalist opposition to the power-sharing experiment. Hume later contrasted the response of the British government to the loyalist strikes which broke Sunningdale to the way in which government stood up to Unionists over the implementation of the Anglo-Irish Agreement in November 1985.[15] Eddie McGrady, former Minister for Executive Planning and Co-Ordination in the Executive, also shared this view: the power-sharing government was brought down by failings at Stormont and Westminster, rather than the workers' strike. McGrady argued: 'Of course there was treason also upstairs—Stormont'.[16]

The Minister for Health in the Executive, Paddy Devlin, claimed that the decision to undermine the Power-Sharing Executive was taken in October 1973 at a meeting between William Craig and the electricity workers based at Ballylumford Power Station in Larne. The electricity workers played a key role during the Ulster Workers' Council strike in May 1974, by bringing Northern Ireland to a standstill. At this stage of political developments in Northern Ireland, the concept of a Council of Ireland had not been discussed between the political parties and two governments, and only the power-sharing dimension had been negotiated. Devlin, unlike other SDLP colleagues, expressed the view that 'the decision was taken against Catholics coming into power'.[17] His view was reiterated by Austin Currie, who insisted: 'The real reason why unionists did not accept Sunningdale related to power-sharing. Not only did they [Unionists] not want nationalists in government, but also they didn't want Catholics in government. That is as far as their thinking got at that particular time.'[18] The strongest rebuke for what happened at Stormont has been expressed by Eddie McGrady. He has said: 'We agreed to participate in a Stormont institution in return for unionists agreeing to participate in an all-Ireland institution. That was the *quid pro quo*. One would not have happened without the other. The first pro happened, i.e. the formation of the executive, but the quid didn't, which was then termed the Council of Ireland. People have forgotten since then that the *quid pro quo* still exists. Whatever solution there is cannot be a solution unless it has those components.'[19] Perhaps with hindsight, John Duffy has identified the main problem: 'The mistake of Sunningdale was not simply about power sharing, or the Council of Ireland: but because everything was not hammered out at Sunningdale.'[20]

The aftermath of Sunningdale

In September 1974 the SDLP repeated its policy that 'Northern Ireland is not an economic, social, cultural, or geographical unit' and they confirmed that any system of government in Northern Ireland must first address the realities of the conflict: divisions in Northern Ireland; conflicting national identities; and Northern Ireland's special relationship with Britain and the Republic of Ireland.[21]

The party's statement confirmed its view that negotiations for the actual institutional arrangements must be based on the principle of 'power sharing in government and an Irish dimension expressed through North/South institutions'.[22] The SDLP was seriously concerned by the British government's new approach, which, instead of adherence to these core principles, gave political representatives in Northern Ireland free rein to draw up recommendations for an acceptable system of government in Northern Ireland. The British government would then determine which proposal was likely to command the greatest support in a Northern Ireland Constitutional Convention. The SDLP called on the British and Irish governments to declare in public that the two principles, of power-sharing and an Irish dimension, were 'non-negotiable' before the Convention took place. The party called on the British government to declare a new basis for its policy and to affirm that it would remain in Northern Ireland only until such time as agreed institutions of government were established which would allow the people of Ireland, North and South, to live together in harmony, peace and independence. The SDLP did not

advocate 'indefinite direct rule', but proposed that the British government should work in union with the Irish government and the Northern Ireland people to bring about this change.[23] The SDLP moved
away from using the term 'united Ireland' to 'agreed Ireland'. They
defined an agreed Ireland as meaning that North and South would
reach agreement on new institutions. The party sought a withdrawal
of the British Army presence in Northern Ireland in parallel with a
political settlement.[24]

Initially the SDLP was unsure what strategy to adopt for the Convention elections. John Hume told the Assembly party on 13 November 1974 that the SDLP should privately tell the government that it
would not take part in the election unless there was 'legislative commitment to power sharing and an Irish dimension', and that all those
taking part in the election should be 'compelled to accept this position'.[25] If the government did not accept this private ultimatum,
Hume suggested the party should boycott the Convention elections
and publicly declare its position. Hume believed the government
would not proceed with the election without the participation of the
SDLP. Hume accurately predicted that in the forthcoming election
there would be a Unionist majority that sought to return to the Stormont regime and its committee system for minority representation.
Hume believed that rather than surrender the minority community to
that position, it would be better if the party abstained if the principles
of power-sharing and an Irish dimension were not accepted as the basis for the elections. However, other arguments inside the party suggested that not taking part in the elections would mark the end of the
SDLP. Significantly, the SDLP paper outlining strategy on the Convention election argued that in boycotting the elections, the SDLP
might leave itself open to Republican opportunism. The absence of
the SDLP might enable republicans to 'announce their desire to have
talks with the Loyalist people and use the Election as a means of
electing their leaders for such talks'.[26]

Calling for a rejection of these proposals by Hume, and suggesting
alternative tactics, the SDLP review strategy paper on the Convention
election also suggested that the SDLP form an association with Brian
Faulkner's Unionist Party of Northern Ireland, which had emerged as
the pro-power-sharing section of Unionism, and the Alliance Party,
with the objective of uniting participants in the ill-fated Power-

Sharing Executive around a joint programme to present to the electorate. The proviso was that the SDLP would have to be content before the election took place that the British government would not accept any recommendations from the Convention that did not include power sharing and an Irish dimension. The SDLP drew up a list of undertakings for the British government to implement before agreeing to form a government, and in the event of attaining a majority in the election. These included the ending of internment; agreement on a police service; an amnesty for short-term prisoners and a review of long-term sentences; gradual withdrawal of the British Army to barracks; an amnesty for illegal guns; and abolition of political prisoner status. The SDLP wished the Irish dimension to any settlement to be clearly defined in terms of full recognition for Irish aspirations and culture. The display of flags and emblems was to be allowed to enable the expression of Irish identity. There was a shift in party aspirations in terms of the Council of Ireland as originally set out at Sunningdale and an acceptance that establishment of a Council of Ministers was the summit of immediate aspirations. The party did not insist on linking police policy to a Council of Ireland, instead believing it was better to 'get a new Police Authority with equal representation from both communities'.[27]

Meanwhile the SDLP, although performing well in elections, acknowledged that it was enduring difficulty in making itself relevant among sections of the Catholic working class. This problem would be more acute if a political solution was impossible to attain, as the SDLP would lack the visibility accruing to a presence in political institutions. To improve party membership, it was argued within the party that the SDLP should be at the forefront of community relations and take initiatives in helping prisoners' dependents, assisting family visits to Long Kesh, Magilligan and Crumlin Road jails.

The Constitutional Convention

The Constitutional Convention was established under the Northern Ireland Act of July 1974. The ethos behind its creation was based on talks conducted by the Secretary of State, Merlyn Rees, with political leaders and interest groups in Northern Ireland, following the collapse of the power-sharing administration. Following these discussions, Rees determined that the formation of a Convention would

test whether political leaders in Northern Ireland would be able to resolve problems among themselves. The legislation for the Constitutional Convention was therefore 'to consider what provisions for the
government of Northern Ireland would be likely to command the
most widespread acceptance throughout the community'.[28] The conclusions reached by the parties were to be presented before the Westminster parliament. The importance of the Irish dimension was
recognised, the British government stating: 'Northern Ireland, unlike
the rest of the United Kingdom, shares a common land frontier and a
special relationship with another country, the Republic of Ireland.
Any political arrangements must recognise and provide for this special relationship. There is an Irish dimension.'[29]

The Convention was not a legislative assembly, but a forum strictly
for elected representatives in Northern Ireland. From the outset the
British government established that it would not be part of the proceedings, which were chaired by Sir Robert Lowry, Lord Chief Justice
of Northern Ireland.[30] The 78 members of the Convention were
elected by proportional representation from twelve parliamentary
constituencies in Northern Ireland, on a similar basis to that of the
Earlier Power-Sharing Executive. The United Ulster Unionist Council (UUUC)[31] held 47 of the convention seats, an indication that any
power-sharing solution among the local parties was far from certain.
The SDLP won seventeen seats with 156,049 first-preference votes,
23.7 per cent of the poll. The results demonstrated a loss of two seats
and 3,724 first preference votes for the SDLP.

The Convention Report was delivered in November 1975. There
were a number of broad-based proposals, which overall reflected
UUUC political thinking. These included: an increase in the number
of Northern Ireland MPs at Westminster; a return to devolved government for Northern Ireland based on the former powers of the 1920
Government of Ireland Act; opposition participation to be equally
included in departmental committees; and a Bill of Rights securing
the rights of individual citizens.[32] Significantly, the main body of the
Convention report stated that 'good-neighbourly relations should be
welcome, but that imposed institutionalised associations with the Republic of Ireland should be rejected'.[33]

The SDLP input into the Convention discussions were set out in
one of the appendices of the Report. The party reiterated its position

that: 'Every person in Northern Ireland should be made fully to understand that the SDLP does not wish to force him [*sic*] into a United Ireland against his will.'[34] Nevertheless the SDLP argued that 'membership of the United Kingdom has its duties as well as its rights. It implies accepting the will of Parliament and the rights of all other citizens of the United Kingdom including those of the minority in Northern Ireland'.[35] The SDLP referred to paragraph 78 of the October 1972 Northern Ireland White Paper, declaring 'that any new arrangements for Northern Ireland should, whilst meeting the wishes of Northern Ireland and Great Britain, be, so far as possible, acceptable to and accepted by the Republic of Ireland'.[36] Once new institutions could be agreed to the satisfaction of both communities in Northern Ireland, the SDLP believed, 'the Oireachtas should be requested to offer the people in the Republic an opportunity to endorse the new institutions in a Referendum in the Republic'.[37]

The Northern Ireland White Paper of October 1972 stated at paragraph 78 'if institutions of Government acceptable to the majority and minority traditions in Northern Ireland can be devised… the authority of all the people of Ireland could be thrown behind the institutions of Government North and South.' For the first time the people of Ireland would be united on how they wished Ireland to be governed—North and South. The SDLP submission to the Convention included suggestions for the reform of the Royal Ulster Constabulary (RUC). Measures included proposals for the civilianisation of the RUC, accompanied by the establishment of a new image and written guidelines to ensure a professional service. The party's submission on policing repeated the SDLP argument that a successful police force was dependent on society's consent at large, and on institutions which had the support of the majority.[38] However, the lukewarm SDLP support for the RUC was one of the major reasons why the UUUC stated in the main body of the Convention Report that it was not in a position to accept power-sharing government with the SDLP.[39]

An unexpected development during the Convention talks was overtures put forward by William Craig in relation to the idea of a voluntary coalition. The concept was presented to the SDLP during a process of bilateral talks under the formal procedure of subcommittees. Craig had a hypothesis of forming a coalition executive that was not unlike the Churchill coalition of 1940–5. Craig proposed that the UUUC could 'join with the SDLP in a temporary or emergency coalition to run Northern Ireland for a four or five-year parliamentary term until the security situation improved and the political deadlock was resolved.'[40]

When it came to a vote on a voluntary coalition, only one unionist, Craig himself, voted for it. Most unionist activists were clearly not open to power sharing. Any hope of a temporary coalition was soon abandoned. The coalition talks were the nearest the SDLP ever came to accepting internal arrangements for Northern Ireland.

Political irritation: the debate on independence

The collapse of the Constitutional Convention meant that from 7 May 1976, SDLP members of the Convention were, in effect, no longer salaried politicians. This was a crucial period for the party, and one in which the SDLP had the potential of drifting out of politics. There was a period of confusion in the party concerning the most appropriate political strategy. In the aftermath of the Constitutional Convention, the SDLP felt frustrated at what it perceived as Unionist and Loyalist intransigence. Unionist critics of the SDLP questioned the party's allegiance to the Northern Ireland state and were concerned over the SDLP's seeming ambiguity over whether it supported the security services. In a futile attempt to alleviate unionist fears, the SDLP placed an advertisement in the predominantly Protestant-read *Newsletter*, reiterating the party's position on constitutional issues and on policing. The consent principle was reiterated; a united Ireland could only come about with the agreement of the majority in Northern Ireland. The open letter stated: 'Our objective is to work in the best interests of all the people in Northern Ireland.'[41] In relation to policing, the SDLP consistently argued that a political settlement must come first, and then full support for policing services would follow. However, it is important to stress that although the SDLP did not take up seats on the Policing Authority, the party did support the RUC in upholding law and order and in tackling paramilitary violence.

In the aftermath of the failed Sunningdale experiment and Constitutional Convention, the British government did not believe that a political solution was attainable in the foreseeable future. The resumption of direct rule led to a shift by the government from a political to a security focus on Northern Ireland. Following the failure of the inter-party talks between the SDLP and the Official Unionists to explore power sharing proposals it was clear that there was no significant shift from the Unionist policy of majority rule. The talks originated from the closing days of the Convention, when the SDLP was approached by the UUP's Reverend Martin Smyth about the possibility of holding talks to achieve devolution. A joint statement on the talks indicated that both parties were committed to the return of devolved power in Northern Ireland with greater powers than the former Northern Ireland Assembly and a dilution in the powers of the Secretary of State. No agreement was reached on the principle of power sharing in a future Northern Ireland government. In context, the areas of agreement set out in the joint statement had previously existed during the Constitutional Convention. The talks, which commenced in March 1976, did not resume again after July 1976.

The SDLP reappraised its power sharing demands as set out in the Northern Ireland Constitution Act of 1973, because Unionists and the British government failed to develop the proposals. The British government belief that a political solution in Northern Ireland was unattainable in the foreseeable future frustrated members of the SDLP. Partly because of the party's disappointment in the outcome of the Act, the independence issue came to the fore during the mid-seventies. The political vacuum of the mid-1970s inclined the SDLP to pursue a more hardline policy, opposing British sovereignty over Northern Ireland. At the 1976 Annual Conference, controversial motions on negotiated independence for Northern Ireland and demands for a British withdrawal were debated. Unionists were branding the SDLP as nationalists who were 'green' and saying that the party as a whole was showing its true colour. In addition to criticising the British government for a lack of political ambition, the SDLP was persistently critical of Irish government indifference to the issues in Northern Ireland for the remainder of the 1970s.

The British government put more emphasis on security than on a political initiative. As Secretary of State for Northern Ireland, Merlyn Rees had used the IRA's 1975 ceasefire and truce as the basis of an Ulsterisation strategy.[42] Following the collapse of the Constitutional Convention, this strategy was further endorsed by the government, on the basis of the 1975 Gardiner Report. The strategy rested upon the gradual substitution of the Army by the RUC and Ulster Defence Regiment (UDR). It was government policy to try and 'normalise' Northern Ireland society. The government ended internment and special category status for prisoners convicted of terrorist crimes before 1 March 1976. Members of paramilitary groups convicted after this date were to be treated as common criminals, sentenced under the 'normal' processes of the law. However, the area of criminal justice was controversial, given that many normal processes had been suspended. Diplock Courts, conducting trials without a jury, were held in Northern Ireland as a means of dealing with suspects associated with terrorist offences.

Roy Mason, who succeeded Merlyn Rees as Northern Ireland Secretary of State in September 1976, focused not only on security, but also on the economy as an integral dimension of his normalisation strategy. The highlight, but ultimately the white elephant, of this strategy was the De Lorean car project in West Belfast. Mason adopted a strategy which was 'to combine a tough security policy designed to wipe out the Provisionals, with a massive programme of overseas investment designed to provide jobs and wean the young away from violence'.[43] However, harsh security measures, and ill-treatment of terrorist suspects by the RUC during the remainder of the 1970s ensured continued hostility towards the security forces among the nationalist community in Northern Ireland. The Compton Report (1971), the European Court of Human Rights in 1976 and the Bennett Report (1979) found the government responsible for permitting inhuman and degrading treatment of suspects. In particular, the Bennett Report expressed concern as to the RUC interview techniques, which were inappropriate: the SDLP leader Gerry Fitt called for Mason to resign over the findings of the report.[44]

The theme of withdrawal had been falsely developed by the British government in its negotiations to obtain the Provisional IRA ceasefire in 1975. The failure of the parties to the Constitutional Convention to reach agreement as to the future government of Northern Ireland also added to the uncertainty of British government strategy for Northern Ireland. Among loyalists, the idea of an independent Northern Ireland had gained some ground.[45] At the 1976 SDLP annual conference a motion calling for British withdrawal from Northern Ireland was defeated by 153 votes to 111. The debate was a reflection of the political uncertainty hanging over the Province. The strong support in the SDLP for British withdrawal from Northern Ireland echoed a similar line taken by Provisional Sinn Féin, and the Fianna Fáil parliamentary opposition in the South. Gerry Fitt, John Hume and Austin Currie were opposed to the motion for British intent to withdraw. Paddy Devlin, Seamus Mallon, Ivan Cooper and Paddy Duffy in Mid-Ulster were among the advocates of the motion. This pro-withdrawal group was willing to meet representatives of the Ulster Loyalist Central Coordinating Committee to discuss negotiated independence for Northern Ireland. Devlin believed that serious consideration should be given to negotiated independence 'as a temporary preposition if not as an ideal solution'.[46] Even the moderate Eddie McGrady argued that the British would have to withdraw in order to allow meaningful dialogue between the representatives of the two communities.

Independence indicated a constitutional change surely incompatible with the party constitution which declared an aim to promote Irish unity, based on consent. Significantly, the 1976 SDLP annual conference generated a challenge in party ranks as to whether members should continue to support the majority consent principle. Also, the hardline motion that the Irish government should exercise its constitutional claim to Northern Ireland to break the stalemate was defeated by a close 26–24 vote. The problem for the SDLP for the remainder of the 1970s was the unwillingness of the Unionist community to address what the Northern Ireland conflict was about. Unionists, like the British government, focused on resolving the conflict purely in security terms. The government and Unionist leaders were reluctant to acknowledge the separate identity of the substantial minority community within the Northern Ireland. By the time of the 1977 SDLP annual conference, however, the SDLP membership demonstrated a lack of enthusiasm for independence as debated one year earlier.

The SDLP operated against a background of opposition not only from loyalists, but also from Provisional IRA activity. Early in 1976 Gerry Fitt, Austin Currie, Paddy Devlin and John Hume were informed by the RUC that they were at the top of the Provisional IRA's assassination list.[47] The Provisional IRA campaign against the SDLP during the 1970s is often overlooked in terms of some of the difficulties facing the party. The SDLP were considered a threat to Republicans, who viewed the party as made up of Quislings, and a buttress to the Union through participation in political institutions at Westminster and, when functioning, in Northern Ireland. Throughout the 70s, prominent SDLP figures were targeted by Loyalists and Republicans. Senior members of the SDLP including Seamus Mallon, Austin Currie, Bríd Rogers and Denis Haughey were among members of the party attacked by Republicans when attempting to revitalise the SDLP's Ardoyne branch in Belfast in September 1978.

Internal ruptures and reappraisal of SDLP strategy

Power sharing seemed impracticable in the aftermath of the Constitutional Convention. By mid-June 1977 the SDLP took a more radical position by moving away from power-sharing to emphasise an all-Ireland political framework. This was in reaction to feeling betrayed and abandoned by the British Labour government because it accommodated Unionists at Westminster. The hardening position of the SDLP was also a direct response to what were seen as government moves towards a more integrationist position. The opposition also demonstrated a movement away from its former power sharing stance. The Conservative Northern Ireland spokesman, Airey Neave, announced that while devolution was still his party's aim, it was nevertheless more realistic to concentrate on a new tier of local government, and improved methods of dealing with Northern Ireland legislation.[48]

The SDLP attempted to overcome a lingering supremacist attitude among some Unionists. Party policies at this time were also about placing pressure on the British government to grasp the concept that the root of the Northern Ireland problem lay in the fundamental issue of identity. The 'Ulsterisation' policy of the government, and the political vacuum existent for the remainder of the Labour government's period in office until 1979, contributed to a process of re-alienation of the minority community in the Province. The British government, by taking short-sighted views, failed to grasp the significance of the far-reaching shift in attitudes by the Northern Ireland minority community, demonstrated through the existence of the SDLP. As a result, the SDLP viewed power sharing as an unattainable short-term goal, and placed greater attention on the Irish dimension.

The government was seen as giving preference to the unionist tradition over that of the minority. The 1977 SDLP document *Facing Reality* focused on the need for the two governments to agree a form of governance for Northern Ireland incorporating stronger cross-border economic co-operation. It was a policy document that directed attention to a form of joint sovereignty for Northern Ireland. By 1977 the party had reached the painful realisation that the unionist community did not wish to embrace the concept of partnership with the minority community in Northern Ireland, and the party responded with a 'greener', more nationalist political outlook. Until this point, the SDLP promoted a policy for constitutional change in Northern Ireland which recognised the equal validity of the two communities in the Province and accepted the 'consent principle'. After what the party perceived as unionist rejection of its partnership strategy, the SDLP reassessed its policy in 1977 to take account of what the party discerned as lack of unionist goodwill.

Meanwhile, the arguments over strategy within the SDLP had become personal. Paddy Devlin was subject to public censure by his party, which eventually led to his departure from it. Devlin felt bitter at his exclusion from the main policy think-tank. He was scathing in his criticism of John Hume in particular, who he felt was an opportunist in seeking influence among Irish-American circles. Another bone of contention for Devlin was that he felt frustrated that the party would not promote him as its main European candidate for the forthcoming elections to the European Parliament. More objectively, however, one reason he gave in explaining his resignation was that the SDLP ignored the possibility of seeking a negotiated independence in its overall policy strategy in 1977, even though it had been committed to this policy at the party conference in November 1976. Loyalists, under the partial leadership of Ian Paisley, almost brought Northern Ireland to a standstill in May 1977, as in 1974. Devlin believed that the commitment of the British government to defeating this second Loyalist strike, allied to lack of Unionist interest, was evidence of the dawning of a new political dispensation. However, Roy Mason in his memoirs recalled that anonymous sources provided his ministerial team with evidence that Loyalist paramilitaries involved in the strike were intent on implementing 'ethnic cleansing' against the Catholic community in the Province.[49] In the local government elections later that month, support for Paisley amounted to 12.7 per cent of the vote, approximately one-third of the Unionist electorate, an indication perhaps that the initial optimism Devlin had held in relation to unionist voting patterns was exaggerated. When Devlin left the SDLP, his departure caused only minor damage to the party. There was no 'Devlin wing' in the overall organisation and his biggest failure had been his reluctance to build up the SDLP party machine in Belfast.

Speculation that when Devlin left the SDLP there would be splits in the party led to an enthusiastic launch of the Irish Independence Party (IIP) on 7 October 1977. Frank McManus, a former Unity MP for Fermanagh-South Tyrone, and Fergus McAteer, a Derry Nationalist, were among its leaders. The only immediate policy of the IIP was to obtain a British withdrawal from Northern Ireland. The IIP announced that it would be contesting the next Westminster election, and forthcoming election to the European Parliament. At the outset the SDLP feared that bad publicity surrounding the Devlin controversy might enable the IIP to supersede it as the main electoral voice of the nationalist community in Northern Ireland. It has been suggested that the IIP did contribute to SDLP moves to a greener, more nationalistic position.[50] However, the overall hardline position in the SDLP is perhaps better seen in the context both of British inertia and of unionist reluctance to accept the principle of a power-sharing government in Northern Ireland.

The 1978 SDLP Annual Conference passed a motion that declared that British disengagement was 'inevitable and desirable'. As a consequence, the gap between Unionists and the SDLP hardened. There were nevertheless tensions in the SDLP as to whether the British should make a declaration to withdraw. Those who supported this strategy had to consider what necessary conditions were required prior to withdrawal. Delegates at the conference gave the leadership a mandate to enter into dialogue with the Secretary of State, Roy Mason, who planned a new series of talks. Mason supported talks on interim devolution, and he intended to devolve powers not on a legislative basis, but rather on a local government or administrative foundation. The new leader of the Ulster Unionist Party, James Molyneaux, refused to take his party into the talks because Mason ruled out Unionist demands for an upper tier of local government as an acceptable short-term political solution for the Province. Mason was insistent that devolution was the basis for the way forward. Although the SDLP accepted the offer of talks on interim devolution, it was sceptical as to the possibility of their success.

The SDLP opposed any increase in Northern Ireland seats at Westminster. The party feared that any increase in seats would lead to unionists feeling in a stronger position to press ahead for integration. The party also opposed local government reform, fearing that unionists would abuse local powers, given the legacy of Unionist-controlled authorities in the years of the Stormont regime. The SDLP thought that granting extra Northern Ireland parliamentary seats at the request of the UUP and added moves towards strengthening local government powers would simply consolidate Unionist supremacy in Northern Ireland. The SDLP was horrified at the suggestion from Airey Neave, the Conservative Northern Ireland spokesman, that power-sharing should be abandoned in favour of proceeding with greater changes to local government. Relations between the SDLP and the Secretary of State, Roy Mason, and Airey Neave were at a low ebb by the end of the 1970s. By the end of 1978 the extent of nationalist 'greening' in the party was apparent. Put in its overall context, this greening process was one outcome of the tremendous frustration experienced by the party at the lack of political movement. British uncertainty over long-term policy in Northern Ireland led to speculation that the government was moving towards integration. Against this background the SDLP felt it was better to campaign for the end of the British link with Northern Ireland because it was convinced that Britain only reinforced unconditional guarantees to the Unionist community. The SDLP plot was less of a green 'Brits out' campaign and more of an expression of exasperation in the party at the failure of the government to grasp what the party viewed as the essence of the Northern Ireland conflict: namely the existence of two distinct communities in the Province, one of which attempted to veto political change.

By abstaining from participation in the events of the Jubilee visit of Queen Elizabeth II to Northern Ireland in August 1977, the SDLP gave the impression to the Protestant community that the party was moving towards the policies of Sinn Féin. However, in contrast to the abstentionist stance taken by the party for the Queen's visit, SDLP councillors, in a break with precedent, attended a special commemoration of the Battle of the Somme in Belfast City Hall in July 1978.

The 1978 SDLP Annual Conference also marked confusion as to where the SDLP stood on the issue of Irish unity. The party position at this time could be interpreted as one that abandoned the consent principle for constitutional change in Northern Ireland. At the 1978 SDLP annual conference, Seamus Mallon stated, 'This party does want to see Britain out as part of a long-term solution. It is as simple as that, no matter what form of words we dress it up in.'[51] The party was drifting back to the original concept of nationalism. The SDLP wanted a stronger Irish dimension in the political framework.

The concept of federalism became an issue of debate in the party in 1978. The focus on a federal option in 1978 was not so much an expression of a serious desire for such a system as an attempt to examine all available options. During 1978 John Hume and other senior members of the SDLP called on political parties in the Republic to spell out what they meant by unity. Hume has said that a large percentage of his party favoured a federal system of government with a regional parliament in Northern Ireland.[52] Fianna Fáil, Fine Gael and Irish Labour had set up study-groups on North-South relations, all of which favoured a federal solution, as did Sinn Féin with its *Éire Núa* policy. Therefore, the federal debate was an all-island one by the end of the seventies.[53]

The exit of Gerry Fitt

When the Labour MP Gerry Fitt abstained from a crucial vote of confidence in the Callaghan administration, his abstention ironically led to the collapse of the Labour government in March 1979 and its replacement by a Conservative administration under Margaret Thatcher two months later.[54] The fierce contest for the Fermanagh-South Tyrone Westminster seat that made the international headlines in the early 1980s was already creating tensions in the SDLP in the 1979 general election. The party decided that it would not put forward a candidate against the independent Fermanagh-South Tyrone, MP, Frank Maguire. Despite this, Austin Currie, Chief Whip of the SDLP, handed in his nomination as an SDLP Independent candidate. Currie received support from the local SDLP Constituency Association and received strong backing from the party leader, Gerry Fitt, plus other senior figures such as Paddy O'Hanlon. However, others, such as Seamus Mallon and Paddy Duffy, were upset by Currie's candidacy, feeling it would adversely affect their own respective electoral performances in Armagh and Mid-Ulster, by highlighting divisions within the SDLP and, more generally, within non-violent nationalist politics. This independent action by Austin Currie destroyed his political career in the SDLP and left him somewhat demoralised. He survived only as an ordinary rank-and-file member in the party. His demotion in the SDLP was a considerable blow to Gerry Fitt, who had in effect viewed him as one of his lieutenants.

The Conservative Northern Ireland Secretary of State, Humphrey Atkins, appointed in 1979, announced that the government wanted to set up a conference comprising local political parties in Northern Ireland to discuss the restoration of local powers in Northern Ireland, but ruled out discussion of the Irish dimension or a return to the Sunningdale proposals. The government's Working Paper for a Conference was published on 21 November 1979, to be followed by talks two days later. The government mistakenly believed that the SDLP was more malleable than anticipated over the resumption of local powers in Northern Ireland. The government was led to believe that the SDLP would do what it wanted because of positive signals coming from the party leader, Gerry Fitt, regarding Atkins' forthcoming talks. The SDLP initially rejected the government's proposals because the White Paper ruled out discussions over the Irish dimension. Before the SDLP collectively considered the proposals, Fitt broke an agreement not to give a reaction on the paper until the party met, claiming that the SDLP welcomed the document.[55] The party rejected the working paper because it ruled out discussion of an Irish dimension. The sharp difference of opinion between Fitt and the rest of the party over the White Paper demonstrated Fitt's independent and individualistic style. The SDLP would not participate in the conference unless the parameters were extended to include the aspirations of the minority community.

Fitt unexpectedly resigned from the SDLP on 22 November 1979, allegedly over the party's refusal to attend the imminent conference organised by Atkins. His career continued at Westminster, where he was granted a peerage. He never recovered psychologically from the collapse of Sunningdale, and in a sense its downfall marked the beginning of the end of his career as a leading Northern Ireland politician. Fitt was a firm opponent of Republican violence and was never afraid to speak out against the IRA. In August 1976 fifty Republican demonstrators broke into his home threatening him, his wife and one of their daughters.[56] Hume later criticised Fitt for heightening anti-SDLP sentiment in West Belfast, where 'Fitt the Brit' was a commonly used derogatory slogan. Hume argued that Fitt failed to bring his former Republican Labour Party colleagues into the SDLP, allowing Sinn Féin to dominate nationalist *and* socialist politics in west Belfast.[57]

   Towards the end of his tenure as SDLP leader, Fitt adopted the line taken by the Taoiseach, Jack Lynch, who, never committed to the republicanism that motivated some within Fianna Fáil, increasingly supported an internal Northern Ireland settlement. Lynch believed it was unhelpful to lay emphasis on unity while attempts where being made by the British government to secure a settlement which would be acceptable to both sections of the community.[58] When Fitt parted company with the SDLP, the party was thought to be moving towards hardline nationalism. In his resignation speech, Fitt stated that the SDLP was in total conflict with his own ideology. He noticed a 're-publican element' emerging in the party, particularly in the absence of any political initiative.[59] Yet even Fitt flirted with undiluted nationalist politics. At the 1978 SDLP conference, he told delegates that British withdrawal was in line with the thinking of party founders and insisted that 'the SDLP stands for the reunification of this country'.[60] These contradictory approaches highlight Fitt's inconsistencies, but also indicate broader tensions between the SDLP's commitments to internal social democratic politics within Northern Ireland and support for Irish nationalist politics designed to end the British connection. Sinn Féin, in contrast, offered a simple, often beguiling message: nothing less than British withdrawal would suffice, with all internal settlements doomed to failure. Given the abject collapse of political initiatives during the 1970s, the republican message had resonance.

   The SDLP power-sharing strategy in the Sunningdale Agreement and as the basis for the Constitutional Convention was no longer sustainable in the political vacuum in Northern Ireland of the late 1970s. There was insufficient unionist electoral support for a partnership government with Catholics in Northern Ireland. Any form of increased local powers, or 'super assembly', for Northern Ireland would not be sufficiently attractive to the minority community to ensure electoral support for the SDLP. Such moves would, according to the minority mindset, be seen to continue unionist supremacy in the Province. By the end of the 1970s, the SDLP had given up trying to make political progress through the local Northern Ireland political parties. Despite firm criticism of successive Irish governments' lack of willingness to earnestly address the Northern Ireland conflict, the SDLP knew it needed the Dublin government as an ally to implement policies of power sharing and a meaningful Irish dimension. The SDLP now wished to move the focus of the Northern Ireland problem from a purely British context to a British-Irish framework. Political progress might no longer be blocked by Unionist opposition, or the use of their veto. Instead, as internal unpublished SDLP documents of the 1970s illustrate, what was required was a political process that could not be boycotted and that Unionists were unable to dismantle.[61] The party was also aware that without an Irish dimension that was absolutely clear to the minority electorate, democratic politics would be overshadowed by militant Republicanism. Politically the late 1970s in Northern Ireland were overshadowed by the failure of Sunningdale.

Aside from the unforeseen departure of Gerry Fitt from the SDLP, 1979 was an important year for strategic developments in the party. The SDLP detected the indifference of the Republic towards the Northern Ireland conflict, but was now actively seeking Irish government participation with the British in conflict resolution. Seamus Mallon, at the 1979 Annual Conference, attacked the Irish government for making it 'easy' for the British government to drop the Irish dimension in any future Northern Ireland arrangement. He called for joint action, adding, 'Both governments are increasing unionist fears by treating unity as a divisive concept'.[62] The attitude of the SDLP to British and Irish governments throughout the late 1970s was epitomised by one of the founding members of the party, Paddy O'Hanlon in 1976. He stated: 'We have not yet learned the art of compromise in Northern Ireland and we have not yet awakened to the reality that we are political lepers rejected by both the British and Irish Governments.'[63] The core of SDLP philosophy in 1979 can be summed up in the party document *Towards a New Ireland*, which became the bedrock of party strategy from the beginning of the 1980s onwards. This SDLP policy paper set out three major proposals:

— the problems of Northern Ireland should only be solved by joint Anglo-Irish action taken as part of a clearly agreed programme between both governments;
— the British government should drop its unconditional guarantee to the Unionist population; and
— the Irish government should spell out what it meant in practical terms by Irish unity in terms of social and economic changes.

Significantly, an emergency motion at the 1979 annual conference pressing for talks with the IRA was defeated by a three-to-one show of hands. The strong opposition to the IRA talks within the SDLP reflected bitter hostility, based on a belief that politics must remain constitutional and non-violent, untainted by association with Republican armed struggle. Such contempt was heartily reciprocated by republicans, fearful of a stabilising of British rule in Northern Ireland through moderate nationalism whilst envious of the SDLP's electoral support.

4

MARGINALISATION, EXCLUSION AND REBIRTH

REPUBLICANISM, 1972–9

After the initial 'defence and retaliation' phase, the Provisional IRA launched its campaign against the British Army, Royal Ulster Constabulary and Ulster Defence Regiment in 1971. The short-term aim of the Provisionals was to render Northern Ireland so ungovernable as to collapse Stormont. Absurdly, but in keeping with their 'perception' of loyalism as a form of Irishness, the Officials argued that republicans 'must welcome' Protestant resistance to the demise of Stormont.[1] More realistically, the Provisionals welcomed the collapse of Stormont as the end of a sectarian 'Protestant parliament for a Protestant people'. The suspension of Stormont in March 1972 led to direct rule by the British government. A straightforward confrontation between the British forces and the IRA would, according to the Provisionals, result in victory for the latter, as the human and economic cost of remaining in Ireland would become too great for the British. The period from 1971–7 is often seen as one of unreconstructed militarism. Initially, however, the *political* strategy of the Provisionals, from which stemmed the belief in militarism, appeared justified. Even critics of the movement recognised that this strategy was based upon a serious analysis of British colonial involvement in countries such as Palestine and Cyprus.[2]

Unreconstructed militarism? The Provisionals' offensive

Following the suspension of Stormont, the Provisionals' strategy may have appeared realistic. The organisation was recruiting rapidly, protected by the existence of no-go areas in Belfast and Derry and fuelled by resentment against the British Army, particularly after the introduction of internment in 1971 and the killing of thirteen civilians by the British Army on 'Bloody Sunday' in Derry in January 1972. Levels of violence were substantial, exceptionally so in 1972. During that year, there were 10,628 shooting incidents, more than double the figure of any other year of the conflict. The death toll of 467 nearly doubled that of any other year. A sense of perspective is offered by the observation that deaths from car accidents in the province between 1969 and 1972 remained substantially higher than those caused by terrorist violence during the same period.[3] Nonetheless, the sheer level of violence created ungovernability. Arguably, 1972 was the year when the scale of violence was such that the label 'low intensity conflict' could not be used. This was a situation created largely by PIRA violence, even allowing that Stormont was 'an anachronism waiting for its own downfall'.[4]

Unsurprisingly, the collapse of Stormont fuelled the Provisionals' belief that victory was imminent. Despite a lack of evidence of British withdrawal, Republican propaganda insisted that 1972 would be the 'Year of Victory'.[5] If such optimism was justified at the time, its repetition two years later was mystifying. 'Brits get ready to pull out' trumpeted *An Phoblacht* in April 1974.[6] The Provisionals believed a short, sharp war would be sufficient to sicken the British government into withdrawal from Northern Ireland. The British government had, after all, demonstrated a lack of interest in Northern Ireland since partition.[7] The province had never been an integral part of the United Kingdom and, with the exception of a brief period after the Second World War, there was little warmth between the Westminster and Stormont governments.[8] There was little to convince the Provisionals, therefore, that Britain's willingness to remain in Northern Ireland would prove any stronger than in the other colonies already abandoned. Even the belief of the Provisionals (shared with the Officials) that Protestants could be weaned from their imperial masters had some grounding in reality. Unionist homogeneity could be exaggerated. The Northern Ireland Labour Party had often polled respectably amongst the Unionist working class. There was a tradition of support for radical, non-Unionist Party candidates amongst Shankill Loyalists. This notwithstanding, the Republican analysis was flawed in two respects. It underestimated the willingness of the British government to remain in Northern Ireland, despite the growing subvention and the lack of political advantage in staying. Domestic political disadvantage was minimised by bipartisanship at Westminster. This persisted despite almost continuous majorities for withdrawal among the British public throughout the Troubles.[9] Furthermore, the Provisionals mistakenly supposed that occasional dissent shown by Unionists towards their 'imperial masters' was somehow convertible to support for Irish unity.

The Whitelaw talks

The belief that the demise of Stormont represented phase one of victory for the Provisionals was understandable. It resulted, as they predicted, in direct engagement with the British government. In July 1972, the Provisionals entered into secret talks with the British government. A delegation comprising Gerry Adams, Ivor Bell, Dáithí Ó Conaill, Seán Mac Stiofáin, Martin McGuinness, Myles Shelvin and Seamus Twomey met the Home Secretary, William Whitelaw. The IRA called a truce before the talks, a longer cessation than the previous affair in March, designed to show that the Provisional leadership could exert discipline. Sinn Féin's role in the talks was minimal. Myles Shelvin represented the party, but mainly as an observer and as the delegation's note-taker.[10] The party president, Ruairí Ó Brádaigh, arguably the movement's main political thinker, did not join the delegation. The main role of Gerry Adams was also observational. The significance of the talks was huge; for the first time since 1921, the British government was engaged in direct talks with the IRA. Moreover, the recognition by the British government of the Provisionals confirmed what they had claimed since the split: they were *the* IRA.

The five demands of the IRA delegation were straightforward: acceptance by the British government of the principle of Irish self-determination; a declaration of British intent to withdraw from Northern Ireland, withdrawal to be completed by the end of 1974 (although the delegation insisted that the timing was negotiable); immediate return to barracks of British troops; an amnesty for political prisoners; and an end to internment. The clarity of the IRA's demands was matched by their impracticality, at least in the short-term. There was a lack of cognisance of the machinery of British government. Whitelaw could not act unilaterally to remove Britain's claim to sovereignty embedded in the Government of Ireland Act. Further-more, the British government would need to liaise with the Irish Re-public. The naivety of the delegation was matched by Whitelaw. He dismissed the 'absurd ultimatums' of the IRA, whilst failing to ac-knowledge or even discuss historical responsibility for the problem.[11] The meetings *could* have been constructive examinations of historical perceptions of the conflict; the role of loyalists; the position of the Irish government, and interim settlements. Instead a 'damn your con-cessions' approach from Mac Stiofáin's PIRA delegation and virtual ignorance of the Irish question on Whitelaw's behalf ensured the opportunity was wasted.

Soon after the talks, the truce collapsed, against the IRA leader-ship's wishes, following sectarian conflict on the Lenadoon Estate in Belfast. The Provisionals stepped up their campaign of violence, which reached a nadir on 'Bloody Friday' in July, when nine civilians were killed as a result of twenty-two PIRA bombs in Belfast city cen-tre. Although support for the Provisionals was threatened by earlier 'accidents', such as the Abercorn and Lower Donegall Street bombs, which killed a total of eight civilians, Bloody Friday was seen as far worse, not least because of the graphic television coverage. After Whitelaw's dismissive rejection of their demands, the Provisionals be-lieved that the best method of achieving serious negotiations was to wage 'total war'. This failed to take account of the need to retain sup-port and ignored the overwhelming superiority of British forces. It also ignored the risk of a Loyalist backlash, which duly emerged via the Ulster Defence Association (UDA). The UDA's random sectarian assassinations of Catholics soon threatened to suck the Provisionals into a futile sectarian war. Shortly after Bloody Friday, the 'no-go' areas of Belfast and Derry were removed. There were no longer any relatively safe havens in which the PIRA could operate. Although still high, the level of Republican paramilitary activity dropped. In March 1973, the IRA took its war to London. Although this was a new de-parture, there is considerable evidence that British intelligence knew of the arrival of the London bombers. As early as 1973, the IRA had high level informers within its ranks, a problem that was to plague the organisation for the remainder of its campaign.[12] Those arrested dur-ing the initial London bombing campaign included Gerry Kelly, later to become Sinn Féin's 'law and order' spokesman, and the Price sisters, Marian and Dolours, bitter critics of the Provisional Republican movement's later entry into constitutional politics.

Sinn Féin's response to the crises of support engendered by 'accidents', sectarianism and an uncompromising British attitude was irrelevant, centred upon the 'visionary' type of Ireland created after British withdrawal. The main problem for the Republican movement was *not*, however, its lack of politics between 1970 and 1972. The emphasis during that period was inevitably upon developing an armed campaign. Arguably, Sinn Féin did as much as possible in that context in at least producing a 'greenprint' for Irish federal unity via *Éire Núa*. The weakness lay in the relative lack of politics when needed in the mid-1970s, when the armed campaign had clearly failed to dislodge the British. Incredibly, given the main issues at the time, the main policy documents produced by Sinn Féin in 1973 and 1974 concerned themselves with issues such as consumer protection, the environment, advertising and mining.[13]

The extent of Northern grassroots disinterest in such politics was emphasised by the threat of suspension issued to the Sinn Féin *Cumainn* in Andersonstown by the Belfast Comhairle Ceanntair, for failing to send sufficient delegates to the party's Ard Fheis in 1975.[14] The Andersonstown *Cumann* was run by two of Sinn Féin's most senior figures, Máire and Jimmy Drumm. Sinn Féin's leadership continued to propagate the myth that British withdrawal was imminent. It could also point to increased overall attendances at the Ard Fheis by 1975.[15] Interim politics were seen as unnecessary, or even a distraction. Protests against internment or the increasingly draconian legislation used to deal with suspected terrorists were thus not translated into political campaigns. The armed struggle, followed by British withdrawal, would take care of such matters. For the Republican leadership, the problem of the membership's lack of interest in politics did not lie at the centre. Lamenting Sinn Féin's performance in the Republic's 1974 local elections, even though its 26 seats represented a 100 per cent increase, *An Phoblacht* insisted:

> If we are genuine revolutionaries we need to know what we are fighting for and to believe it. If we do not agree with every proposal, changes may be made by general consent. That work starts in the *Cumann* and is finalised at the *Ard Fheis*. Our *Ard Fheiseanna* (annual conferences) have been singularly lacking in such work. The blame does not lie with the *Ard Chomhairle* but with the local *Cumann*.[16]

In the Republic, Sinn Féin's very limited support was largely a product of residual nationalist sentiment in the border counties, rather than of the value of its campaigning. The counties of Donegal, Leitrim, Cavan and Monaghan yielded 12 of its 26 seats. Of course, the party could take refuge in its electoral failure by insisting that it had no intention of:

> playing the sort of role in Irish politics which the Communist Party has been playing in France or Italy—as a 'revolutionary party' firmly anchored in the system it is supposed to overthrow…I believe Sinn Féin is not interested in this kind of political future. Its aim is not to enter the present political system and become a part—even a major part—of its machinery. Indeed its aim is not to win an overall majority and to control the present political system, even if this meant bringing about a united Ireland.[17]

Sinn Féin's confidential document to members, *A Broader Base*, issued in 1974, urged members to 'become more active in trade unions, language organisation, co-operatives, credit unions etc'.[18] According to the document, however, the primary purpose of such activity appeared to be to sell *Éire Núa* to an uninterested workforce or co-operative. Beyond this, the aims of such involvement were unclear, other than to promote the Irish language in sympathetic societies. *A Broader Base* also made an undeveloped point concerning the need to 'break Fianna Fáil', arguing that the 'weak link in Fianna Fáil are their nationally minded Irish speaking supporters'.[19] Whilst some sympathy might indeed be expected from that quarter for the PIRA, it was far from clear how it was to be harnessed by Sinn Féin's activities. Sinn Féin's lack of specific policies was justified on the grounds that *Éire Núa* offered the prospect of self-governing communities. The party declined to engage in policy debates on, for example, future policing arrangements, exemplified by this statement from Derry Sinn Féin:

> Sinn Féin does not insist on a specific draft plan for a new police force, because Sinn Féin does not insist on a specific blueprint for a new state. No political party at this stage has the right to insist on any predetermined from and details of that state which must be created.[20]

It was argued by others that *Éire Núa* offered a 'rough outline' of the new state, with 'republicans expected to fill in the details'.[21] Although some republicans did attempt this, *Éire Núa* did not develop beyond a broad set of federal principles.

Rejecting Sunningdale

Predictably Sinn Féin was dismissive of the Sunningdale experiment. Some form of Power-Sharing Executive had been indicated as the likely form of future British policy since 1972. For the Provisionals Sunningdale represented an unacceptable internal settlement, which institutionalised sectarianism. Particular opprobrium was reserved for the SDLP's willingness to participate in the Power-Sharing Executive. In *An Phoblacht*, 'Freeman' summarised this contempt:

> …the SDLP is not a nationalist party and has never seriously pretended to be. No nationalist party, even a bourgeois nationalist one, would declare itself willing to recognise the RIGHT of the Ulster separatists to keep Ireland partitioned indefinitely, as the SDLP has so often done. Nor would a nationalist party of any hue avoid all reference to the Irish nation, or describe the nation's rights in Ireland by that sickening English term 'the Irish dimension'.[22]

The Provisionals' loathing of Sunningdale was genuine enough. Much republican propaganda emphasised the inadequacies of the 'Free State'. Its 'gain' of an All Ireland Council, with vague powers, meant little to republicans still believing in imminent victory. Sunningdale offered virtually nothing to militant Republicans, the pledge to review internment of little consolation to those convicted republicans whose cases had been processed by the courts. In political terms, however, Sunningdale was seen as a dangerous attempt to marginalise republicans. The potential bolstering of support for the SDLP, backers of the Agreement, was of considerable concern, threatening inroads into the Republican constituency. It was to be a further two decades before the process of policy learning ensured that the British government attempted solutions based upon the inclusion of this constituency, rather than futile attempts at isolation.

There was never any prospect of republican interest in the Sunningdale Agreement. It revived Stormont, albeit on a fundamentally different basis, and abstention from partitionist institutions remained a basic Republican principle. The Republican movement did discuss whether to contest elections, an idea supported by the president of

Sinn Féin, but rejected by the party.[23] The idea was dropped, partly for reasons of expense. Another fear was electoral embarrassment, unwelcome even if an enduring mandate from 1918 was claimed. The major reason offered by opponents was that electioneering would prove a considerable distraction from the war effort for scant tangible reward.

A further reason why the Provisionals were so contemptuous of Sunningdale was that they felt better placed to engage in working relations with the Protestant population than the constitutional parties, or the British and Irish governments. Such optimism led to bizarre political stances. The defiance of Loyalists in resisting British attempts to enforce Sunningdale, expressed in the Ulster Workers' Council strike of May 1974, was welcomed as a positive development by republicans. Loyalists were seen as heroically resisting their British imperialist oppressor. Support from Republicans had two dimensions. Firstly, such resistance to the shoring-up of the state via the consociational power-sharing of Sunningdale was seen as useful. Secondly, the Provisionals argued that there was a strong class dimension to the Loyalist action. That the loyalists were engaging in opposition to even a nudge towards Irish unity was overlooked.

Ceasefire

The announcement by the PIRA leadership of a ceasefire at Christmas 1974, which became indefinite in February 1975, did not please everyone within the movement, even though it followed the disaster of the Birmingham pub bombings in November 1974, in which nineteen people were killed. The ceasefire came as a relief to most IRA members operating in urban locations, where the security forces had applied considerable pressure. A shortage of arms was also apparent in Belfast.[24] A British declaration of intent to withdraw, the avowed minimum for a prolonged ceasefire, had not preceded the PIRA's cessation announcement, which was opposed by the IRA's two Northern representatives on its Army Council.[25] The ceasefire was called following a meeting between the republican leadership and Protestant clergymen at Feakle in December 1974, an event disrupted by the arrival of the Irish police. The clergy conveyed their report of the meeting to the British government. A representative of the government subsequently contacted the President of Sinn Féin, Ruairí Ó

Brádaigh, insisting that the British wished to 'devise structures of withdrawal' or 'disengagement' from Northern Ireland.[26]

The suspicion of the sceptics was well-founded. The British government had no intention of withdrawing from Northern Ireland. Instead, 'obfuscation was central to state policy', designed to confuse and disorient republicans.[27] The temptation to see the Provisionals as simple victims of an elaborate con should be resisted. As early as April 1975 republicans declared their awareness of the risks of 'British trickery'.[28] The problem was finding a viable alternative, given that the armed campaign had stagnated and Republican politics were largely intertwined with that campaign. The Provisionals wanted to believe that the British government was serious, because Republicans did not have any alternative to the unpalatable truth. The IRA's truce was monitored by incident centres, staffed by members of Sinn Féin. This was an important development, as for the first time it gave Sinn Féin a prominent role in the Republican movement and represented the first shift towards formalised community politics.[29] During the previous year, the British government had lifted the ban on Sinn Féin in the hope of persuading Republicans into political activity. Within the republican movement, there were those who argued that Sinn Féin should switch from its seeming disdain of immediate issues as 'reformist' politics and develop greater community politics in the 'context of the truce'.[30] Indeed as the truce approached final collapse, Sinn Féin insisted its truce incident centres would continue as advice centres.[31] They also functioned as bases for the Provisionals' 'community policing', with warnings to 'hooligans' that their conduct had been 'reported to the Sinn Féin Advice and Complaint Centres'.[32]

In 1975 embryonic local politics were developing within Sinn Féin around issues not necessarily related to the armed struggle. Since its foundation, the Provisional Republican movement had not rejected politics. Such a perception rests upon a reductionist view of politics, associating political activity with parliamentary and institutional politics. As an IRA member of the period, Tommy McKearney, later commented, the boycotting of elections and staging of anti-internment elections were 'highly "political" decisions'.[33] The concentration thus far had been upon constitutional issues, an area in which it was believed that military action was the superior vehicle of initial change, to be followed by the implementation of the federal structures of

Éire Núa. From the mid-1970s onward, promotion of these beliefs needed to be accompanied by community politics. The need for broad political support for the 'struggle', developed through community political involvement, was increasingly aired. Under the pseudonym 'Brownie', Gerry Adams stressed the need to ensure that the IRA operated with the broadest community support base, to prevent it being reduced to mere 'nuisance value'.[34] The idea was not new, but had received little attention in the immediacies of a huge military campaign in the 1970s. Adams pointed to Sinn Féin's inability to mobilise support in the twenty-six Counties as the reason why successive Free State governments had been able to isolate and stifle the movement.[35] Elsewhere within the broader Republican movement, the Official IRA retreated further into Marxist theorising, to the chagrin of its few more military-inclined members. The organisation's feud with the Provisionals led to 11 deaths in 1975. Demanding an end to the conflict, Official Sinn Féin fared poorly standing as Republican Clubs, as Republicans deserted the party and the Official IRA. The disaffected within the Official IRA formed the Irish National Liberation Army (INLA) by 1975, preceded by the formation of a political organisation, the Irish Republican Socialist Party (IRSP), comprising a variety of leftist elements. Although the IRSP attempted to interest the population in 'anti-imperialist' politics, military means of action were often preferred, to the extent that it was claimed that INLA membership trebled that of the IRSP in Belfast in the mid-1970s.[36]

The 1975 IRA ceasefire allowed the security forces space to gather intelligence on republicans. Walsh suggests that the truce was useful for the IRA.[37] Already hard-pressed, the organisation used the concessions offered by Rees to free many members from jail, partly through the ending of internment. A more general view, shared by many republicans, is that the ceasefire was a disaster for the IRA, in which the security forces 'probably came nearer…to defeating the republican struggle than at any time'.[38] Sinn Féin's lack of involvement in local politics, the absence of short-term demands (other than the release of prisoners) and the use of *Éire Núa* as a mantra rather than an evolving policy, ensured that the republican struggle stagnated during the ceasefire, producing little more than what Gerry Adams described as 'spectator politics'.[39] For Adams the demoralisation of

the ceasefire was useful in helping him eventually to oust the leadership of the movement, which he regarded as overly conservative and
militaristic. Publicly Adams offered unswerving loyalty to the cause.

The contraints of 'war' discouraged debate, delegates to the 1975
Ard Fheis being helpfully informed that there 'can be no room for
dissidents and those at variance with the leadership'.[40] The main debate of that Ard Fheis concerned recognition of 'partitionist' institutions, with the pragmatic value of recognition of the courts under
contest. A motion that 'Sinn Féin members who recognise the courts
in the six and twenty-six counties be suspended from the organisation' was defeated. A critic of the motion argued that the membership
should accept that 'recognition or non-recognition of courts is a tactic not a principle'.[41] The tactic-principle debate was extended to more
fundamental aspects of republican politics in due course. With the
imprisonment of Provisionals continuing unchecked, arguments in
favour of tactical recognition of the courts, even allowing for slim
prospects of acquittal in Diplock Courts, found widespread favour.
The opponent of the Ard Fheis motion emphasised the lack of
worth of Sinn Féin *Cumainn* in insisting that it would be 'wiser to
leave strategy and tactics to the leadership of the Republican Movement instead of wasting time.'[42]

The responsibility for the limitations to politics did not rest solely
with the Provisionals. The poverty of the thinking of the British government was exemplified by its plans for a Northern Ireland Constitutional Convention, in effect power-sharing without the Irish
dimension. The Provisionals aptly described the Convention as a
'foregone failure', although the simultaneous claim that the British
government 'continued to negotiate with representatives of the Republican Movement about the wording of a declaration of intent to
withdraw and how the withdrawal should be ordered' indicated that
neither side had a monopoly on political delusion.[43]

The descent into sectarianism: 'dealing' with Loyalists

Aside from unreconstructed militarism, the other main charge against
the Provisionals was that of sectarianism. A preference for Catholicism over atheism had been a factor, albeit not a decisive one, in the
split with the Officials. As the Provisionals developed, the fomenting
of sectarian unrest was undoubtedly useful in building the organisation

and rendering the state of Northern Ireland ungovernable. When the Provisionals engaged in action after rioting, which frequently followed Orange parades near nationalist areas, their standing within the community increased. For example, gun battles after riots in Ardoyne and the Short Strand in June 1970 led to the deaths of six Protestants due to PIRA actions.[44]

Yet outright sectarian killings by the Provisional IRA, if defined as killings due to religion rather than the wearing of a police or army uniform, were not the norm and largely disappeared after 1976. Many within the Protestant community, understandably feeling under siege, did not make such subtle distinctions, seeing an attack on, for example, a UDR member who happened to be a Protestant in the Orange Order as sectarian. Yet the victim's Orange Order membership was of no interest to the Provisionals. In their early years, the Provisionals oscillated between attacks upon commercial property and security force personnel. The latter were mainly Protestant. This has led even an otherwise excellent account of the development of the Provisionals to assert erroneously: 'Many in the Provisionals' ranks believed that because PIRA's attacks, particularly those against the security forces, often resulted in the deaths of Protestants, they were at war with the Protestant community.'[45] There is little evidence for such a sweeping claim and, in any case, such numbers would be impossible to quantify. Sectarianism may have been a motivation for joining and, undoubtedly, there were those within the Provisionals' ranks who loathed Protestants. Indeed such contempt was associated with the Provisionals' Chief of Staff, Seán Mac Stiofáin, who allegedly described Protestants as 'all bigots'.[46] For the Provisionals to believe they were 'at war with the Protestant community', however, would have required a much broader range of 'legitimate' sectarian targets, such as the Orange Order. Mac Stiofáin had no interest in the broadening of targets. Even the lowest ranks of the Provisionals would soon have gleaned that the movement's main targets were security personnel, not the Protestant community and that a 'political war, not a sectarian war', was being fought.[47] Those acts labelled as sectarian sometimes had a deeper remit, allowing them to be justified to the Republican constituency. The attack on the Bayardo Bar on the Shankill Road, killing five, was justified by the Provisionals on the grounds that the Ulster Volunteer Force met in the pub. Indeed it was later claimed that a UVF meeting had only just concluded.[48] There was sufficient unease over the extent of sectarian action for one member to decline leadership of the Belfast Brigade.[49] Given the UVF's sectarian assassinations of Catholics and the position of loyalism as the last barrier to a united Ireland (assuming British disinterest) the attacks upon paramilitary loyalism may have possessed a certain logic. Equally, however, the IRA's actions of the period demonstrated how the British loyalist presence in Ireland, as opposed to the British government, was the organisation's real problem. The theoretical position of the Provisionals was clear and crude regarding Protestants. 'These are our people' insisted Dáithí Ó Conaill.[50] Ó Conaill persistently expressed his belief in the virtues of a Protestant majority in the new federal parliament in Ulster, under the *Éire Núa* proposals.[51]

The period of the PIRA's truce in the mid-1970s provided the catalyst for the bulk of the incidents labelled as sectarian. As Bishop and Mallie assert, the ceasefire 'marked the Provisional IRA's darkest hours since its inception' as it descended into sectarianism, feuding and near-defeat.[52] It was a period in which the IRA, in the words of one of its former members, later to become a prominent Republican fundraiser in the United States and an 'on-the-run' from the British government, 'did some terrible things'.[53] The UVF routinely carried out random killings of Catholics from 1972 onwards. In 1974 and 1975, the scale and geography of these attacks extended, to include attacks in the Irish Republic and further afield from Belfast. The massacre of the Miami Showband, a pop group returning to the Republic after a concert in the North, sparked an upsurge in sectarian conflict. Towards the border Republicans declined to accept the PIRA ceasefire, operating semi-autonomously. The South Armagh Republican Action Force, a thin cover for the PIRA, killed ten Protestant workmen at Kingsmills in January 1976 in retaliation for the killing of five Catholics the previous day. It was argued that 'from the Provisionals' point of view, the truce made less sense in South Armagh than anywhere else. Here, after all, they were winning.'[54] Even the blatantly sectarian act at Kingsmills, a massacre prompting much disquiet within the movement, was justified by one Republican on the grounds that 'it stopped any more Catholics being killed'.[55] Before the ceasefire there had been no sectarian killings in the area. With uncertainty over the state of the truce in respect of 'Crown forces', some PIRA units found alternative targets. Even 'efficient' units of the IRA killed more civilians than 'Crown forces' during much of the 1970s. In the northern districts of South Armagh, for example, nineteen Protestant civilians were killed by the IRA from 1972 to 1978, compared to fifteen members of the security forces.[56]

During this period, the Catholic basis of support for the Provisionals was openly acknowledged. In *An Phoblacht* 'Freeman' boasted that Sinn Féin was ... 'the only body proclaiming Catholic social principles and committed to their implementation. And if you take the view that "political Protestantism" does not really represent Catholic social principles at all, then it can be said that Sinn Féin is alone in Ireland in its commitment to *Christian* social principles *tout court*.'[57]

From criminalisation to reorganisation

With recruitment in decline and arrests of volunteers mounting, the PIRA endured a crisis during the mid-1970s. The organisation also suffered from a changed British policy approach. Having effectively treated paramilitary prisoners as 'prisoners of war' since their strike in Belfast in 1972, the British government embarked upon a new strategy of criminalisation. Depoliticisation of the conflict was now viewed as a vital tool of British counter-insurgency strategy, diminishing the perception that the IRA was fighting an anti-colonial war. Although special provisions were in place for the processing of cases, with non-jury Diplock Courts presiding over a high rate of convictions, convicted defendants were to be treated as ordinary criminals. The privileges accorded to 'political' prisoners (the term was never officially used) serving sentences exceeding nine months included housing in compounds in some locations, extra visits and parcels, dispensation to wear non-prison clothing and exemption from prison work. By the end of 1974, 1,116 prisoners were covered by special category status, rising to over 1,500 by the end of 1976, the year of announcement of abolition.[58] Although the gradual phasing out of special category status ensured that there remained some prisoners in jail under its terms until 1991, most new admissions were treated as common criminals, a denial of the political basis of Republican or Loyalist actions.

The decision to end special category status was followed by a toughening of the security regime under the Secretary of State, Roy

Mason, appointed in 1976. Mason pledged to squeeze the IRA 'like a tube of toothpaste' and, although not eschewing politics entirely, rejected dialogue with terrorists, preferring robust physical force measures.[59] This tougher security was matched in the Irish Republic. There, the election of a Fine Gael/Labour government in 1973, under Liam Cosgrave, a virulent critic of continuing 'anti-Treatyism', led to the introduction of emergency powers of arrest and detention, used mainly against the IRA. The IRA's bombing campaign in Britain, including the disastrous Birmingham pub bombings, led to the enactment of similar legislation by the Westminster government. Actions from these quarters further impinged upon the organisation's military activities, but the campaign of violence had been in decline since 1972, even before the onset of such legislation. Pressure upon the IRA did not stem merely from top-down initiatives. The formation of the Peace People in 1976 briefly challenged the Provisionals' claim to represent 'the people' by offering a cross-community and cross-class challenge. A combination of the limitations of an apolitical approach and internal disputes, rather than any effective counter-strategy from the Provisionals, led to the eventual decline of the first major grassroots challenge to violent Republicanism.

The counter-insurgency measures of the British government led to the restructuring of the IRA into smaller cells, following the widespread infiltration of the larger brigades and battalions by British Army agents. The 1977 Staff Report demanded that the IRA adopt greater secrecy and improve its counter-interrogation techniques. In effect the movement was preparing to bed down for the long war. Plans for the development of Sinn Féin as an outlet in that war remained vague and there was still no hint of electoralism. The IRA was to exert direct control over the organisation at all levels and Sinn Féin was to play a 'big role' in publicity and propaganda campaigns, while campaigning on social and economic issues.[60] Although recruitment to the IRA had slowed, the calibre of volunteers drew some admiration from the British Army, a leaked 1978 intelligence document, *Northern Ireland: Future Terrorist Trends*, asserting that 'evidence of the calibre of rank-and-file terrorists does not support the view that they are merely mindless hooligans'. The Provisionals moved leftwards during the 1970s. Although the concentration on economic targets was not new, the attacks on major businessmen offered a novel development. This new range of targets was 'softer' than the security forces and was justified as part of an emphasis upon the need for socialist revolutionary politics found in republican rhetoric during this period.

By the end of the 1970s the Provisionals had bedded down for a long war. A revival of activity in 1979—with the killing of eighteen soldiers in two bomb attacks at Warrenpoint, the murder of Lord Mountbatten and the Irish National Liberation Army's killing of Airey Neave, the Conservative Northern Ireland spokesman—indicated the limits of 'Masonism' as a security-oriented strategy to defeat armed republicans. Yet the advent of a Conservative government in 1979 under Margaret Thatcher was hardly likely to lighten security policy, particularly after the Neave killing at the outset of the election campaign. Without the development of a coherent political and electoral strategy, however, the Provisionals could barely articulate their objectives, let alone advance their cause.

5

ENDING POLITICAL INERTIA
INTERNATIONALISATION OF THE
NORTHERN IRELAND CONFLICT

Traditional Irish-American attitudes

The Irish Famine of 1845 led many Irish emigrants to take refuge in America. Irish immigration reached its peak between 1840 and 1880, when almost 2.5 million people (mainly Catholics) arrived in America.[1] The resentment towards Britain for the cause of one of the worst disasters in Irish history remained in the forefront of the psyche of Irish-Americans into the 1960s. The outbreak of the Northern Ireland troubles in 1969 reactivated the hostility of some Irish Americans to Britain, and initially the main beneficiary of Irish-American militancy against Britain was the Provisional IRA.

For the Irish government, emigration of its citizens to the United States was unwelcome and relations between the Irish-American lobby and successive Irish governments were not particularly close. Seán Lemass, Minister for Foreign Affairs in the De Valera government, believed that unless Irish emigration was restricted, the Republic would be unable to develop an economic infrastructure. Irish-Americans had expected the Irish government to lobby for a greater allocation of United States entry visas for Irish citizens rather than adopting entirely the opposite position, especially at a time when the United States encouraged Hispanic immigration and wished to increase the growing self-confidence of the black population in America.

There were fractures in the relationship between Irish-America and Ireland. This became increasingly evident after the partition of Ireland and led to increasing discrepancies of opinion between the two countries. Of the recent generations of Irish descendants in America, many were well-educated and fully integrated into American society. Many developed into wealthy middle-class American citizens and abandoned parochial Irish nationalism. The dormant nature of nationalist politics in Northern Ireland (discussed in chapter 1) meant in turn that there were no foundations for constitutional nationalism in America.

The semi-independent Ireland formed after the Anglo-Irish civil war of 1921–2 developed into a nation state based on De Valera's ideals of self-sufficiency in a largely rural Irish society, a Gaelic culture and a conservative Catholic ethos. This romantic vision was somewhat distant from the Irish diaspora in America as its society became increasingly less religious and more secular. After the partition of Ireland, much of American society became a pluralistic, mixed population. Irish-Americans were playing a significant role in the corporate and financial sectors of the American economy and were less interested in political quarrels back in Ireland. Irish-Americans did not share the ideology of De Valera. They considered Irish-Ireland as provincial, reactionary and an anachronism. As a consequence the Catholic education system in America started to promote an English and Continental history and literature curriculum that eliminated Irish history.[2]

During the Second World War relations between America and Britain became close as both countries joined as allies in the war against Hitler and the Nazi regime. The policy of De Valera's Irish government of neutrality further eroded relations between Ireland and America. Three American military bases were built in Northern Ireland in 1941 without any diplomatic consultation with the Irish government. The absence of consultation with the neutral South tended to reinforce the idea of Northern Ireland as part of the United Kingdom.

In postwar years, the State Department distanced itself from Irish nationalism and preferred to deal with Irish matters directly through Britain. Irish-American awareness of discrimination against Catholics during fifty years of Unionist rule in Northern Ireland was virtually non-existent. Although the Irish government would have been aware of minority grievances in Northern Ireland during the 1960s, it did not raise American awareness of the injustices taking place in Northern Ireland. This could be attributed, to some degree, not only to the indifference of the government in the Republic to the discriminatory nature of the Northern Ireland state, but also to the limited nature of the Republic's diplomatic presence in America.

In the late 1960s the Republic focused upon entry into the European Economic Community.[3] When civil unrest took hold in Northern Ireland in 1969 the Irish diplomatic service was virtually powerless to change the public tide of support for militant Republicanism. The profile of the Irish diplomatic service did not improve until well into the 1970s. Overlooking the importance of diplomacy in the Republic allowed Britain the main initiative in explaining events to the White House as they unfolded in Northern Ireland. Therefore, for the first six years of the Northern Ireland troubles the White House largely backed the official British position on the conflict.

Despite an acrimonious history between Britain and Irish-Americans, and in spite of the fact that there had been sixteen American presidents with Irish ancestry, American diplomats treated Northern Ireland as a domestic concern of the United Kingdom.[4] However, following the 'Bloody Sunday' atrocity of January 1972, New York Congressman Hugh Carey led a Congressional inquiry into the event, and witnesses from Ireland gave evidence.[5] Nonetheless, it was not until the Carter Presidency in 1977 that the US protocol of non-intervention in Northern Ireland was broken. That year was significant in that it saw embryonic US involvement in the contemporary Northern Ireland conflict. The later Clinton administration also committed itself to American involvement in the Northern Ireland peace process, as did, on a much reduced scale, the subsequent Bush administration.

John Hume in America

The role of John Hume in America was to dissuade Irish-American groups from supporting Republicans in Northern Ireland and from inadvertently financing violence. His focus was to promote the ethos of non-violence and the constitutional politics of the SDLP. During the short period of the five-month Power-Sharing Executive in 1974, Hume had been Minister of Commerce and had led high-profile economic missions to the United States. On these visits he regularly spoke against Irish-Americans who indirectly supported militant Republicanism.

Hume met Senator Edward Kennedy in 1972 and started the process of reversing what the SDLP leader regarded as over-simplified

Irish-American views of the Northern Ireland conflict. After the events of Bloody Sunday in January 1972 Kennedy took a very strong anti-British position, and indirectly aligned himself with the militant Republican position. He called for British army withdrawal, the ending of internment and the eventual reunification of Ireland.[6] As the complexity of the Northern Ireland conflict became more apparent, Kennedy contacted Hume in November 1972, and after an initial meeting at the Irish Embassy in West Germany, he changed his view of the issues of Northern Ireland and acted largely on advice given him by John Hume. Before this meeting, in 1971, Kennedy had suggested that Protestants 'who could not accept a united Ireland should be given a decent opportunity to go back to Britain'.[7] He gradually came to believe that Protestants should have an equal role with Catholics in whatever solution might come about.[8]

Kennedy understood the seriousness of the accusation that Irish-Americans were contributing money, ammunition and moral support to the Provisional IRA. Within a relatively short time he introduced Hume to senior American politicians in Washington: these included the Irish-American Democrats Tip O'Neill, Speaker of the House, Senator Daniel Moynihan and Governor Hugh Carey of New York—who, with Kennedy, became known as the 'Four Horsemen'. This group first came together on St Patrick's Day 1977 by issuing a statement to Irish Americans not to support or encourage violence.[9] The message was reinforced by President Jimmy Carter, although during his 1976 election campaign he had indicated support for Irish unity. The diplomatic efforts of Hume and Irish government officials with the Four Horsemen paid dividends. President Carter began to take an interest in Northern Ireland affairs, thanks largely to the lobbying of the Four Horsemen. Their influence was so great that, in August 1977, Carter issued a statement that held out the prospect of economic aid and heralded the importance of power-sharing and the Irish dimension in Northern Ireland. It marked a major coup for Hume, along with the Irish Embassy in America. The statement from Carter laid the foundations for subsequent White House strategy towards Northern Ireland.

Much as Hume wanted international pressure placed on the British government to concede the validity of power-sharing and an Irish dimension as an integral dimension of a political settlement in

Northern Ireland during the mid-1970s, he knew it was unrealistic for the 1977 Carter statement to attack Britain publicly. The section of the Presidential speech offering American economic assistance in the event of a political settlement in Northern Ireland was due directly to Hume. Carter, in his statement, included the suggestion from Hume that the US would join with others to encourage additional job creating investment in the event of an internal political settlement. This later became a key element in the 1985 Anglo-Irish Agreement.

It was a considerable achievement for Hume to steer the Four Horsemen into a cohesive force. Formerly they had each acted in a highly individual and outspoken manner in relation to Northern Ireland. Like Ted Kennedy, Tip O'Neill recalled his stridency concerning Northern Ireland matters. He admitted contributing to the Irish Northern Aid Committee (NORAID, a fundraising body established in 1970 for dependants of Irish Republican prisoners) until studying developments in Northern Ireland.[10] The real power of the Horsemen emanated from Tip O'Neill, for many years Speaker of Congress. O'Neill authorised Congressional hearings on Northern Ireland, whilst refusing permission to Congressman Mario Biaggi—a protagonist for militant Republicanism who had the support of 130 Congressmen, one third of the House of Representatives—permission to conduct a Congressional hearing on Northern Ireland. Hume's diplomatic efforts led to international pressure on the British government about Northern Ireland issues, although the pro-British State Department muted the impact of Hume's American initiatives.

The SDLP was under pressure from Sinn Féin's new electoralism in the early 1980s, epitomised by Gerry Adams' 1983 Westminster election victory in West Belfast. Hume contacted the Democratic Party in America, with the intention to obtain assistance through the National Democratic Institute for International Affairs (NDI) to broaden the political base of the SDLP. Hume gained the endorsement of the Friends of Ireland in Congress (a body created on St Patrick's Day, 1981) to support his case that the SDLP should receive assistance through the NDI. In June 1986 the NDI announced links with the SDLP through the formation of the Social Democratic Group (SDG). The SDLP institute was, to a large extent, autonomous. It had the authority to appoint its own personnel. It was established as a formal training and development organisation for the

SDLP with the overall objective of fortifying the SDLP infrastructure. In reality the institute was an American attempt to buttress the SDLP against the electoral challenge of Sinn Féin.

The NDI, which as a rule ran non-partisan programmes, made Northern Ireland the exception by working solely with the SDLP. The NDI involvement with the SDLP caused controversy across the political spectrum in Northern Ireland. Mark Durkan proved how effective the NDI training could be, putting electoral strategy into practice and being credited with the election successes of Seamus Mallon in Newry and Armagh in 1986 and Eddie McGrady in 1987. For most nationalist voters, the choice lay between advocacy of armed struggle or constitutional routes to Irish unity. However, some NDI mentors pinpointed Sinn Féin's seemingly 'pro-choice abortion stance as a potential weak spot in its armour' in the 1987 general election. This gave the SDLP significant advantage over Sinn Féin especially in traditional, Catholic rural areas of Northern Ireland.[11]

The survival of the SDLP-run institute, the SDG, depended on running non-partisan programmes under the remit of formal association with the NDI. From the start, the SDLP never fully understood the function of the SDG. Hume conceived it as an indirect funding mechanism for the SDLP. Along with senior SDLP figures, Hume was unhappy at the prospect that the SDG would develop into a service training body for other social democratic parties as well. Hume did not attempt to save the SDG. One of the sad ironies in the downfall of the institute was that it had the potential to become an international service training institute, especially for the SDLP on a European basis; and this would have been a triumph for Hume and his visions of international politics. However, international opportunities faded for the SDLP when the institute was overshadowed by criticism. The perception that senior SDLP figures in the institute were in a position to promote the domestic policies of the party caused its demise. In truth the SDLP hierarchy felt threatened by the NDI enthusiasm to include younger personnel, to expose the second tier of the party to leadership training. Senior SDLP personalities were unwilling to relinquish power at the cost of losing control of their fiefdoms.[12] The SDG closed down in 1989, although Tom Kelly, a former director of the institute, has argued that the SDG could have been saved if Hume had continued to support the body.

The main impact of Hume in America was his ability to moderate Irish-American ideas of romantic nationalism based on anti-Britishness, so that the politics of non-violent nationalism could be understood. Hume 'internationalised' the Northern Ireland problem, so that from 1985 the White House, insofar as it took a stance on Northern Ireland, adopted the principal arguments of the SDLP. The culmination of the efforts of Hume and the Irish government to advance the constitutional nationalist analysis of the Northern Ireland conflict had, by 1986, left the Provisional IRA isolated in a political *cul-de-sac*, with few political allies abroad, even though many countries had little sympathy with Britain's approach to Ireland. Hume spelt out clearly that supporting the armed struggle in Northern Ireland meant unnecessary deaths in Northern Ireland. Hume was effective in articulating the voice of the SDLP and its constitutional analysis of the Northern Ireland conflict over the competing voice of militant Republicanism, although his influence was perhaps greater in Congress than within the White House.

Hume was also effective in opposing the MacBride Principles, anti-discrimination measures strongly supported by Sinn Féin. The nine principles were based on similar lines to the Sullivan Principles that promoted equal opportunities for black workers in South Africa. Seán MacBride drafted similar principles to be applied to companies in Northern Ireland in order to increase numbers of the minority population in the workplace. Hume felt that the MacBride Principles were an obstacle to obtaining foreign investment in Northern Ireland. He believed republicans promoted the principles purely for propaganda purposes and exaggerated the plight of Catholics in Northern Ireland. In America, the Irish National Caucus ignored Hume's protestations and succeeded in having the principles adopted by sixteen states by 1994.[13]

In 1985 the American government endorsed the Anglo-Irish Agreement, offering substantial financial aid. The deal, registered as an international agreement at the United Nations, placed Northern Ireland's affairs within a bi-national context and appeared a vindication of the efforts of Hume and the Irish government. Together they had neutralised the militant Republican interpretation of the Northern Ireland conflict. In reality the Republican movement had little political leverage and less political force to fall back on in 1985, despite electoral gains. From the perspective of the State Department, the interests of the Northern Ireland nationalist community were identified with John Hume.

Hume and the Irish government

The Irish government initially took a 'Brits out' attitude after 'Bloody Sunday' in January 1972. The Taoiseach, Jack Lynch, withdrew Donal O'Sullivan as Irish Ambassador from London. The catastrophe marked a major turning point in the Irish government's attitudes to international lobbying in relation to the Northern Ireland conflict. The Irish government sent a cable to the US State Department stating it would 'use its limited leverage in attempt to make the milestone a turning point.'[14] Lynch sent the Minister for Foreign Affairs, Patrick Hillery, to brief the Secretary of State, William Rogers, but Seán Cronin has recalled that Lord Cromer, the British Ambassador, got to him first.[15] At Kennedy Airport in New York, Hillery stated he would 'seek help wherever I can get it' because Northern Ireland was 'a problem for the free world'.[16] However, in diplomatic terms Hillery's visit to America in 1972 was an embarrassment for the Irish government. The Irish government was unable to make its position on British Northern Ireland policy clear in America because there were excellent diplomatic relations between the United States and Britain. Nonetheless, by 1976 John Hume had taken up the role of building closer contacts between senior Irish-American politicians and the Irish government. On St Patrick's Day 1976 the Taoiseach, Liam Cosgrave, addressed Congress, and his speech was accompanied by a joint communiqué with President Ford.[17] This marked the first significant public demonstration that the Northern Ireland conflict was not simply a British problem. The statement called on Americans to renounce 'organisations engaged in violence'.[18] It was the first major gain for constitutional nationalism over militant Republicanism in Irish America.

Seán Donlon, who been a fellow seminarian with John Hume at Maynooth College, proved himself an invaluable colleague in promoting the constitutional analysis of the conflict in the United States. Donlon spent a period as Irish Ambassador when Michael Lillis was also appointed as Counsellor at the Irish Embassy in Washington. In the 1980s, both were crucial in persuading Garret FitzGerald that he could no longer wait for the unionists to be involved in a settlement.[19] This was against the background of the late 1970s, in which both Fianna Fáil under Jack Lynch and also Fine Gael took a conciliatory stance towards Northern Ireland. Garret FitzGerald, as Minister for Foreign Affairs and in his early period as Fine Gael leader, believed that responsibility for a settlement in the North lay with the British government, which should impose an internal solution, and significantly that the North-South relationship must be freely given by general consent.

The Irish National Caucus, an umbrella group representing the majority of Irish-American groups, was formed in 1974. This group largely lobbied the House of Representatives, and their activities led to the establishment of an Ad Hoc Committee on Irish Affairs in the House of Representatives, with Mario Biaggi as its Chairman. When Charles Haughey became Taoiseach in December 1979, the leader of the Irish National Caucus, Father Seán McManus, and Biaggi called for the dismissal of Donlon, even though he had only been Irish Ambassador in America for two years. Biaggi and McManus, along with NORAID, regarded Seán Donlon as hostile to Republicanism. Donlon, along with Hume, had developed the concept of 'consensus policy', involving the isolation of all IRA sympathisers in America. The Four Horsemen put pressure on the White House, and indirectly on the British government, to encourage peaceful political development. The intergovernmental initiative launched in 1980 by Humphrey Atkins, Secretary of State for Northern Ireland under the new Conservative government, came about partly because of the pressure on Mrs Thatcher from the United States.

In July 1980, Donlon was informed that he was being moved to the United Nations. The Four Horsemen, along with John Hume, rode to Donlon's rescue. When Charles Haughey, as Taoiseach by this point, decided to remove Donlon from his position as Irish Ambassador, on Capitol Hill the move was interpreted as a public capitulation by the Irish government to Republicans, reversing Irish government policy supporting John Hume. The Horsemen considered the Donlon issue an attack on them. They made it clear they would not cooperate with the Irish government if Donlon were transferred from his post as ambassador. Hume intervened in the matter, and condemned Haughey, demonstrating that the SDLP could oppose the Irish government. Combined pressures on Haughey meant he changed his mind about moving Donlon, although he felt he had surrendered 'his right to decide who should be Ireland's Ambassador in Washington'.[20]

On St Patrick's Day in 1981 the Friends of Ireland was formed, to offer an alternative to militant republicanism as represented by the Irish National Caucus and NORAID. It provided a forum in Congress for constitutional Irish nationalists in America to discuss the causes of the conflict and to explore solutions. In the 1980s the Friends of Ireland was an extension of the work carried out previously by the Four Horsemen. Ronald Reagan was elected US President in 1980 despite the high priority the Democratic Party placed on Northern Ireland in their Presidential electoral strategy, which included the idea of a peace envoy, a policy that was subsequently taken up by the Clinton administration. There was a natural concern among SDLP and Irish political sources that American foreign policy would revert to the former policy of taking the British position in line to Northern Ireland. The Reagan administration continued the policy of the previous administration by denying visas for entry to the USA to members of groups associated with terrorism. This was something of a reward for the efforts of Hume and Irish government diplomats, and prevented Sinn Féin gaining access to the USA to promote the interests of militant republicanism.

Despite limited American involvement in Northern Ireland after Reagan's election, the US administration endorsed the work of the New Ireland Forum published in May 1984. This White House intervention was vital in the aftermath of the statement 'Out, out, out' with which Margaret Thatcher condemned the New Ireland Forum Report. Both the traditionally Anglophile *New York Times* and the *Washington Post* combined with the Friends of Ireland in Congress in attacking the British Prime Minister. Seán Donlon was able to counsel Bill Clarke, a close confidant of Reagan, to persuade the President to express his concern about the deteriorating Anglo-Irish situation to Thatcher, who was visiting Washington just before Christmas 1984.[21] Reagan had received a letter from the Friends of Ireland urging him to give priority to Northern Ireland in his discussions with Mrs Thatcher.[22] At a further meeting between Reagan and Thatcher on 20 February 1985, Northern Ireland was on the agenda. It was a clear indication that the State Department were no longer passive observers of the conflict and did not consider the conflict as a purely British affair.

The support of the American administration for the Anglo-Irish Agreement in November 1985 was a blow to the American infrastructure of the Republican movement and strengthened the position of the SDLP as a representative of the nationalist community in Northern Ireland. The agreement also had the potential to address the strong sense of minority alienation in Northern Ireland; the agreement meant that the Republican movement's ideology in Irish America, based upon the irreformability of Northern Ireland, would become less convincing. The Anglo-Irish Agreement was the most practical manifestation of interventionist US policy initiated by President Carter in 1977. American economic commitment, which passed easily through both Houses of Congress, was the progression of a promise made by Carter eight years earlier, ensuring continuity for Irish policy in Washington. The Reagan administration was not interested in political intervention in Northern Ireland, but saw the Anglo-Irish Agreement as an opportunity to focus on economic support for the Province. The goal of the Anglo-Irish Agreement was to marginalise extremists and prevent violence.

From 1986 onwards the Republican leadership took lessons from Hume. If Hume was able to influence the British government by external pressure from the American administration aided by influential senior Irish Americans, then their strategy of achieving a united Ireland could more realistically be obtained through a similar alliance. This strategy became the backbone of Republican thinking, contributing to the development of the Hume-Adams talks in 1988.

The SDLP and Europe

Northern Ireland joined the European Community in 1973 with Britain and the Republic of Ireland. The Province was allocated three seats for the European Parliament. The system of proportional representation guaranteed the minority community in the province would have electoral representation, with John Hume elected to the European Parliament in 1979. John Hume obtained his induction into European politics working as a part-time special adviser to Dick Burke in the European Commission from 1977 to 1980. During this period of employment he made himself familiar with the mechanics of the European Parliament, and built up invaluable political contacts. When he took over the leadership of the SDLP after Gerry Fitt's resignation in November 1979, Hume benefited from his earlier famil- iarity with European politics and with American politics: European and American politics affected his style of leadership. His influence and standing in the European Parliament and America gave Hume a repu- tation as the statesman of Irish politics.

The SDLP perspective on the European dimension in Northern Ireland always implied cross-border regional development in social and economic matters. The issues were debated collectively, agreed and articulated in the earliest internal discussion papers in 1971. The concept of cross-border bodies was not originally an SDLP proposal, but could be traced to the Government of Ireland Act of 1920. Divided identities and loyalties have always been at the centre of the SDLP analysis of the Northern Ireland problem. The party believed that a traditional Irish unitary state was an unattainable goal because of unionist opposition. Therefore, when the party issued its first pol- icy document, *Towards a New Ireland*, policy was based on federal solutions. The concept of joint sovereignty of the British and Irish governments over Northern Ireland was also considered.

Hume remained a strong advocate of post-nationalism, believing that Irish unity could be developed in the context of a European na- tion state. The SDLP argues that Irish unity is not about territorial unity but is about unity of people. This post-nationalist, post-nation- state philosophy has not removed the SDLP's long-term objective for the political reunification of the island of Ireland, but the 'sover- eignty' of the governing body of such territory would be pooled. Yet the 'pooling' argument does not overcome the problem of a lack of unionist consent, or the 'Unionist veto'.

The European dimension for Hume was more than just the facili- tation of cross-border co-operation. He believed it diluted the Union- ist thesis that Northern Ireland was simply an integral part of the United Kingdom. European co-operation put into action his concept of unity, namely the unification of the Irish people on the whole island of Ireland. Hume also used the SDLP's European approach to attack the republican argument that Britain continued to have self-serving, economic reasons for remaining in Northern Ireland. British member- ship of the European Community, according to Hume, completely changes the idea that Britain has imperial and colonial interests in maintaining Northern Ireland as part of the United Kingdom.

The creation of the North-South Ministerial Council set out in the 1998 Good Friday Agreement was a direct manifestation of Hume's thinking in this context, although the top-down, institutional promotion of cross-border activity is perhaps at odds with the aspiration for a 'bottom up' unity of peoples held by the SDLP. The mechanism of the North-South Ministerial Council (NSMC) has some similarities to the European Council of Ministers. The level of North-South co-operation is at a level 'unprecedented since partition', although given its earlier absence, this might be seen as damning with faint praise.[23] The NSMC attempts to oversee cross-border co-operation via six North-South implementation bodies with executive powers, also presiding over the six pre-existing areas of North-South co-operation as agreed within the context of the Good Friday Agreement. Although the Agreement remains fragile, the formalisation of cross-border co-operation can be contrasted with Unionist resistance to such developments in the 1974 Sunningdale Agreement, and Republican opposition through violence at the time.

Hume played a major role among Social Democrats in matters pertaining to Northern Ireland. He successfully tabled a motion in the European Parliament about community regional policy and Northern Ireland.[24] The motion succeeded in leading to the Martin Report, prepared after Madame Simone Martin visited Northern Ireland in September 1980. Consequently, the European Parliament approved a financial package worth £63 million for Northern Ireland. In 1984 Hume obtained direct European involvement in the Northern Ireland problem. The Political Affairs Committee in the European Community chaired by the Danish Liberal, Neils Haagerup, examined the political crisis in Northern Ireland. The timing of the Haagerup Report in March 1984 was a coup for Hume because it came before the New Ireland Forum Report and the signing of the Anglo-Irish Agreement. The final version of the Haagerup Report took a strong SDLP slant on the need to find 'a legitimate and visible expression' of the Irish dimension to the Northern Ireland conflict. The report called on 'closer Anglo-Irish co-operation and a power-sharing form of Government in Northern Ireland'.

SDLP Anglo-Irish political ideas

At the beginning of the 1980s, the SDLP was still feeling the impact of the collapse of Sunningdale and the subsequent Constitutional Convention. The demise of political initiatives further convinced the party that an internal Northern Ireland settlement was not a viable option. The SDLP still regarded power sharing at executive level as a prerequisite for participation in any new system of government in Northern Ireland. The party also wanted some institutional acknowledgement of the Irish dimension that reflected the ethos and identity of the nationalist community in Northern Ireland. Despite Unionist opposition to these two key SDLP principles, in 1979 the party felt that to obtain these fundamental political structures in Northern Ireland, the British and Irish governments would have to take responsibility for ensuring their implementation as the basis for political negotiations among the local politicians.

If the British government maintained the *status quo* in Northern Ireland, the SDLP felt it would only reinforce an imbalance in the treatment of the two communities in Northern Ireland. Effectively this meant the SDLP believed that Northern Ireland policy gave Unionists unconditional guarantees to remain part of the United Kingdom without reciprocal guarantees to the aspirations of the nationalist community. Therefore, from the SDLP point of view an imbalance in concessions given to the Unionist tradition would work to the detriment of the nationalist community in Northern Ireland. Consequently any new political initiative by the British government in Northern Ireland would have to rectify this imbalance. The SDLP believed the government had to withdraw from its position of only conferring guarantees to the Unionist community, in order to coerce all local political parties towards a realistic solution for the Northern Ireland problem.

The SDLP wanted the British government to move forward from its position of leaving the responsibility of negotiating an acceptable political system in the Province with the local Northern Ireland politicians. The solution needed to be one of joint government, which could also be amenable to the Irish government. SDLP strategy was formed on the basis that Unionists might be unwilling to accept the principles of power-sharing and an Irish dimension. The party believed that unless the British government endorsed the necessity of these two principles as part of the overall political equation to a political settlement in Northern Ireland, no progress could be made. Any absence of an Irish dimension as part of further British initiatives in the Province would be bound to fail in the long term.

In a review of party strategy during 1979 the SDLP realised it was necessary to hold negotiations with local Northern Ireland politicians to obtain political progress in the Province. Consequently, the SDLP viewed Anglo-Irish co-operation as a means by which the British and Irish governments might surmount Unionist obstruction of SDLP solutions for Northern Ireland. The Anglo-Irish approach, from the SDLP standpoint, would debilitate Unionist control over political progress in Northern Ireland. By the end of 1979 the SDLP fully endorsed a joint Anglo-Irish strategy by both governments to set about the creation of a political framework that did not necessitate the support of the local parties in Northern Ireland. This change in strategy indicated the end of the SDLP search for a political settlement in an internal Northern Ireland context. The fundamental benefit of the shared Anglo-Irish advance by both governments was, for the SDLP, its ability to sustain Unionist opposition.

Within an Anglo-Irish framework, the SDLP believed unionists would still be involved, with the British government looking after their interests. To avoid the 1974 scenario, which allowed unionists and loyalists to overthrow a system of government in Northern Ireland containing power-sharing and an Irish dimension, the SDLP thought an Anglo-Irish scheme was an effective way for political progress to take place in Northern Ireland. This would prevent Paisleyism acting as a barrier to progress. In addition, the SDLP hoped that leaders of Provisional Sinn Féin might see the Anglo-Irish plans which included cross-border co-operation 'as a tacit declaration of eventual British disengagement'.[25]

In a policy reappraisal in 1979 the SDLP criticised the general inactivity of the Republic regarding Northern Ireland policy:

> The actions and attitudes of Southern people and Southern governments have a direct bearing upon Northern Ireland. It is inevitable that this should be so when over one-third of the people of the North look to Dublin as their real capital and the centre of their national identity. The Republic is involved in the problem. It must be involved in the solution.[26]

In relation to the Irish Republic, the SDLP called for an end to the authoritarian influence of the Catholic Church on social and moral issues pertaining to Southern society. The party wanted the Republic to move towards becoming a more pluralist state. This line of argument was further developed during the talks between the main constitutional parties in the South and the SDLP as the basis of the New Ireland Forum deliberations in 1984. The core of the 1979 SDLP review of party strategy focused on a discreet dilution of British control over political developments in Northern Ireland.

Moving away from the political inertia of the mid-1970s, in 1979 the SDLP promoted the idea that a Constitutional Commission could be formally established by the British and Irish governments. The function of the commission would be to support the two governments in accomplishing an acceptable constitutional agreement in Northern Ireland. It was envisaged that the commission would draw representatives from political parties in Northern Ireland, Britain and the Republic as well as constitutional experts led by an international figure from outside Northern Ireland. In the SDLP proposals, separate sectors of the commission would examine the social and economic domains of Northern Ireland and also of the Republic. Their objectives would be to streamline and harmonise services between the two states. The SDLP believed that economic and social organisations in particular would benefit from joint cross-border co-operation. Separate inquiries would analyse the needs of agriculture and fisheries, tourism, industry and commerce, health and social services, education, arts and sport. The SDLP recommended European funding should be administered on an all-Ireland basis for such projects.

By the end of 1979 the SDLP had formulated key policy positions for the Northern Ireland problem. Their policies provided the necessary infrastructure for British and Irish governments to make political progress during the 1980s. Advancing their proposals for an Anglo-Irish framework, the SDLP had conceived practical ways in which to negotiate a settlement to the long-term Northern Ireland conflict. These proposals encompassed the principles of power-sharing and an Irish dimension. To buttress this position the SDLP and its new leader, John Hume, procured external assistance from international political allies in Europe and in the United States.

Guns not government: Republicans and international 'solidarity'

For a movement awarded so many propaganda gifts by the British security forces during the early 1970s, Republicans were slow to internationalise their cause. Whilst the Republican aim of forcing British withdrawal troubled few internationally, the lack of a developed Republican political wing inhibited the spread of the Republican message. Republican concerns were in any case more practical; propaganda, though useful, was of less immediate value than the importing of weaponry. Internationalising the Irish Republican cause meant dealing with a variety of regime or client types, for whom the IRA and later Sinn Féin could tailor an individual message.

Most of the arms shipments to Republicans during the 1970s came from the United States. Socialist features of the movement were generally played down in favour of Fenian or Hibernian posturings in the appeal to Irish-American support for material and financial aid. Nonetheless, early arms procurers and fundraisers in the United States were themselves substantially left of centre, generally Irish-born Republicans still committed to the establishment of a fully independent Ireland.[27] The main fundraising body, established in 1970, was NORAID. Its supporters were caricatured and propagandised as partisan Irish Americans ignorant of the complexities of Northern Ireland. Its leadership, however, did not lack knowledge of Irish history. Diehards opposed Sinn Féin's ending of abstentionism in respect of the Dáil Éireann in 1986 and NORAID eventually split. Provisional Sinn Féin later enjoyed the considerable largesse of Friends of Sinn Féin, led by Chuck Feeney and supported by 'respectable' and wealthy Irish-American businessmen, willing to pay large sums for dinners with Gerry Adams. The party's chief fundraiser in the United States, whilst lamenting the loss of 'good people' in the split, acknowledged that fundraising, which had stalled in the 1980s under pressure from the United States administration, had been much easier during the 1990s.[28]

Sinn Féin found it difficult to gain influence on Capitol Hill or in the White House until after the election of Bill Clinton as US President in 1992. His election led to the award of an entry visa to Gerry Adams, to the somewhat synthetic chagrin of the British government.[29] Congressmen such as the Republican, Peter King, were regular visitors to Sinn Féin Ard Fheiseanna, but were voices in the wilderness in offering largely uncritical support to the Republican movement.

The other possible repository of sympathy for the republican movement, the European Union, was ignored by Sinn Féin until the 1990s, when the party's outright opposition to EU membership was replaced by a policy of 'critical engagement'.[30] Sinn Féin opened a European bureau to begin to articulate its case. The continued opposition to 'supra-nationalism' did not prevent the 2003 Ard Fheis endorsing the extension of the euro to Northern Ireland.

During the 1980s, as Sinn Féin developed as an electoral force, the IRA landed four large shipments of arms from Libya, whose leader Colonel Qaddafi had long offered succour to Republicans. The fifth and largest intended arms delivery was intercepted, however, probably because of betrayal from within the IRA. The interception rendered the IRA incapable of launching an all-out 'Tet' offensive, designed to render Northern Ireland ungovernable and prompt an oppressive response from the security forces, which would alienate the nationalist community and lead to enhanced support.[31] With the discovery of the arms, the IRA's final chance of winning the war evaporated, it is claimed, as the British security forces could from hereon contain the violence.[32]

Open political links remained underdeveloped by Republicans. The 1970s had seen endogenous political activity, whatever the internationalisation of secret arms gathering. The republican left turn post-1977 facilitated the forging of 'solidarity' links with a range of other organisations, although anarchist groups, such as the Red Brigades, remained beyond the pale. The closest links were developed with the Palestine Liberation Organisation (PLO), with resolutions expressing solidarity with the Palestinian people and condemning Israel a mainstay of Sinn Féin gatherings. As one example, the 2003 Ard Fheis agreed a boycott of all Israeli goods and services. Similar supportive links were developed and maintained with Herri Batasuna, the political representatives of the militant Basque armed group ETA, links which survived even the return to violence and collapse of the Basque peace process, which Herri Batasuna had modelled on developments in Northern Ireland. Lesser links were formed with Breton, Corsican and Kurdish 'political prisoners'. The 1970s and much of the 1980s were largely 'wilderness years' for Sinn Féin, however, prior to the moves towards the pan-nationalism and international approval of the peace process.

6

THE REPUBLICAN SECOND FRONT
HUNGER STRIKES AND BALLOT BOXES

The Republican movement of the 1970s had a greater political dimension than is sometimes acknowledged. As McIntyre notes, the two wings of the movement, military and political, had always existed.[1] By the 1980s, however, the Provisionals' disinterest in electoral campaigns had become a major burden. Republicanism had no political outlet and Republican supporters could not register their disaffection with the Northern state, other than through violent means By accident more than design, the hunger strikes of the early 1980s provided the opportunity for a transformation of republican politics, via the growth of Sinn Féin. By the end of the 1980s, Sinn Féin had established itself as the main voice of working-class Northern nationalism, welding community activism to more traditional Republicanism through a successful electoral strategy.

Legitimising a long war

Two distinct problems confronted Republicans by the late 1970s. Firstly it was evident that a military campaign would not in itself remove Britain from Ireland. The IRA stated the obvious in declaring that 'there is no question of us winning in the sense of driving the British Army into the sea'.[2] The military campaign was designed to sap the will of the British government to remain in Northern Ireland. The war was one of attrition, reliant upon psychology (triumph of wills) and economics (the cost of the British subvention). Secondly, there was a need to develop Republican political strength throughout Ireland. The Republican movement remained in what some of its leaders, suspicious of electoralism, appeared to regard as splendid isolation. The baldest acknowledgement of political reality came from Jimmy Drumm at the annual Wolfe Tone commemoration at Bodenstown in 1977:

'We find that a successful war of liberation cannot be fought exclusively on the backs of the oppressed in the six counties, nor around the physical presence of the British Army. Hatred and resentment of this army cannot sustain the war and the isolation of socialist Republicans around the armed struggle is dangerous and has produced, at least in some circles, the reformist notion that 'Ulster' is the issue, which can be somehow resolved without the mobilisation of the working-class in the twenty-six counties.'[3]

Optimistically, Drumm urged the forging of strong links between republicans, workers and trade unions to ensure 'mass support for the continuing armed struggle in the North'. The failure of the struggle thus far was noted:

'The British government is NOT withdrawing from the six counties and the substantial pull-out of businesses and closing down of factories in 1975 and 1976 were due to world economic recession though mistakenly attributed to symptoms of British withdrawal. Indeed the British government is committed to stabilising the six counties and is pouring in vast sums of money to improve the area and assure loyalists, and secure from loyalists, support for a long haul against the Irish Republican Army.'[4]

Drumm's assertions amounted to remarkable frankness when measured against the 'imminent victory' propaganda in evidence until only a few months earlier. They offered a realistic antidote to the idea that the failure of Sunningdale had led to such exasperation from the British government towards local politicians that withdrawal was now the favoured policy. Some academic accounts have asserted that slow withdrawal has been covert British policy ever since 1974.[5] Drumm offered a realistic appraisal of British policy. He outlined publicly thoughts that had been discussed in Republican circles since 1975, when Adams, then in jail, and Danny Morrison, later to become Sinn Féin director of publicity, concluded that the unrealistic promotion of the idea of imminent victory would induce cynicism among Republicans.[6] Far better, they mused, to condition Republican thinking to accept years of sacrifice rather than imminent gain. The promotion of such ideas carried implicit criticism that volunteers had been duped by the leadership, which Adams was keen to replace with his own circle of Republicans, led by him. The process of ideological conditioning was abetted by the establishment of a 'revolutionary council', designed to allow an influx of ideas into the IRA from outside the narrow confines of the Army Council.[7] The revolutionary council was a smaller body than the General Army Convention, which was unable to meet because of security concerns. Other Adams-inspired structural changes had more to do with the prosecution of a successful military campaign. Smaller IRA cells replaced large, but leaky, brigades; volunteers received 'proper' inductions, with anti-interrogation training introduced and a *Green Book* issued to IRA members, outlining the responsibilities of members. An internal security department, soon to be dubbed the 'nutting squad' and itself to be later penetrated by 'traitors', was established to 'take action' against informers. Meanwhile, the search for arms imports beyond the American sources of the early to mid-1970s was begun in earnest.

Initially, the new political strategy of the Provisionals was concerned with the adoption of tactical coalitions and the abandonment of exclusivity. Later, new methods of political organisation would be required, to facilitate electoralism. The restructuring of the IRA into cells in 1977 staunched the number of arrests of volunteers and prevented the collapse of the organisation. Nonetheless, its role could be overstated. The conversion of IRA brigades into cells was often more nominal than real.[8] The 'supergrass' system would later expose this, as arrested IRA members would readily name fellow members, some correctly, others indiscriminately. Furthermore, the IRA acknowledged that its ability to conduct bombing campaigns was impaired by a 'shortage of explosives'.[9] The political underdevelopment of the movement meant there was insufficient opportunity to develop struggles complementary to the armed effort. This inadequacy was only partly born of distaste for electoral politics, still a relatively minor issue within Sinn Féin until 1980. It also owed much to the elitism of the movement, which ignored conditional or limited offers of support from interested organisations. For the Provisionals the armed struggle required unequivocal support. Indeed, even when softening this stance the Provisionals criticised those on the left who claimed to support their aims for failing to back the 'war' unconditionally. For the Provisionals violence liberated the working class, as 'struggling

Irish people do get passionate satisfaction as well as results from the violent actions carried out'.[10] By 1979 Sinn Féin had made clear that support from other groups was welcome, provided such campaigners endorsed efforts to achieve British withdrawal from Ireland and the campaign for political status for Republican prisoners.

The Relatives Action Committee, campaigning for political status for republican prisoners, contained some individuals critical of aspects of PIRA activity. Until the late 1970s, republicans had been disdainful of those organisations expressing 'critical support' for the IRA, as adopting a contradictory stance. It was some time before the movement was prepared to accept that 'a position of critical support was better than one of no support at all'.[11] The frequency with which the armed campaign was accompanied by 'accidents', such as the death of twelve civilians in the La Mon restaurant bombing in 1978, reduced the numbers willing to express unqualified support for the Provisionals' campaign. Even supporters of political status attacked aspects of the PIRA's campaign at a conference at Coalisland in February 1978, in the immediate aftermath of La Mon.[12] Many of these partial supporters belonged to left-wing organisations, treated with disdain or even contempt by some Provisionals. This contempt was not merely because of quibbles over the use of force. Greener Provisionals also disliked the left because of their perceived Marxist, or 'Sticky' (Official IRA/Sinn Féin) politics, even though the Officials played little role in the prisoners campaign. From 1977 and the onset of the long war, it was nonetheless increasingly obvious that the Provisionals could no longer act in isolation. A strategy of economic resistance to British rule could unite the movement by broadening the base of armed struggle to include economic targets, whilst proving that the Provisionals had a socialist socio-economic agenda. At one level, this struggle was emphasised by the targeting of business leaders. Concurrently, the Provisionals moved leftwards, urging the development of socialist forms of republicanism.

Developing Republicanism as a political force

Initially, some Republicans held the optimistic view that public opinion within Britain might facilitate British disengagement. Indeed such opinion favoured British withdrawal from Northern Ireland throughout the Troubles.[13] Weariness or indifference did not, however, equate to mobilisation. The Troops Out Movement (TOM) attempted to raise consciousness in England, Scotland and Wales on the Irish question, but with minimal impact. By the 1980s TOM was already in decline. The TOM attempted to raise the Irish question within the trade union movement. Arguably, its campaigns impacted upon the Labour Party's policy shift towards support for Irish unity (albeit by consent within the Northern state) in 1981, a policy which survived until 1994. Generally however, TOM's dialogue was held with the already converted within Northern Ireland, on fraternal visits hosted by Sinn Féin.

The political advancement of the Republican agenda needed to come from within its own ranks. Different sections of the republican movement united in contempt for the SDLP and resented its near monopoly of the nationalist vote. This hostility was strong despite the apparent greening of the SDLP, as the party became more nationalistic in outlook. Urban, working class Republicans regarded the SDLP as the 'Stoop Down Low Party'. Nonetheless, the more nationalist tone of the SDLP and its 'increasing Irishness' were noted by republicans, as such 'sympathetic reformist appeals to revolutionaries' were 'real threats'.[14]

For a brief period in the late 1970s nationalism had an alternative political outlet to support for either armed struggle or the SDLP. Rural elements sympathetic to Republicanism were attracted to the Irish Independence Party. The Provisionals derided the way in which the IIP were 'prepared to ride on the back of the (IRA) volunteers', whilst acknowledging that they formed a 'welcome break from the pro-Brits of the SDLP'.[15] Formed in 1977, the IIP offered an electoral repository for those nationalists who desired a tougher line on partition than that usually offered by the SDLP. The IIP offered old-style anti-partitionism, which, whatever its limitations, held some attraction to those nationalists reluctant to support 'armed struggle' but unable to accept British rule in Northern Ireland. The initial electoral success of the IIP added weight to the arguments of those Republicans who believed that Sinn Féin could be developed as an electoral force. Following Sinn Féin's electoral participation in 1982, the IIP quickly withered.

A more vibrant role for Sinn Féin had been envisaged for some time, but under the strict direction of the IRA. The relationship between Sinn Féin and the IRA had, historically, fluctuated considerably since the two organisations were formed.[16]. At times Sinn Féin had been the dominant organ of the Republican movement; at other times Sinn Féin and the IRA had acted relatively independently. Alternatively, as in the early 1970s, Sinn Féin had been subordinate to the IRA's armed campaign. Although organisationally distinct, the overlap of personnel (one of the recurring features of the two organisations for most of the twentieth century) ensured that the movement's political and military wings continued to be intertwined. As late as 1997, as the party moved towards constitutionalism, the Sinn Féin President Gerry Adams referred to the possibility of the (Irish Republican) Army calling up activists.[17] During the 1970s, even the revitalised role of the party envisaged by the Republican leadership indicated a limited perception of Sinn Féin as a rallying movement of agitation rather than as a competitive political party. Ultimately, however, Sinn Féin's role was to expand beyond the limited perceptions of the Republican leadership.

The move towards electoralism followed an infertile period for the armed struggle. The Secretary of State for Northern Ireland from 1976 to 1979, Roy Mason, offered nothing to militant Republicanism. The loss of political status by Republican prisoners in 1976 was a major blow, undermining the IRA's insistence that it amounted to a legitimate army. The refusal of prisoners to wear prison uniform in the 'blanket protest' nonetheless attracted little interest from 1976 to 1979. Demonstrations attracted only limited support within Northern Ireland and virtually none in the Irish Republic. The situation changed dramatically when the 'blanket protest' was converted into the hunger strikes of 1980–1.

Shaping coalitions

The need to sustain a long war provided the impetus for the development of new forms of Republican politics. The 1977–80 period witnessed unimpressive attempts to develop coalitional politics with groups thought sympathetic to the overarching aims of Republicanism. Such coalitions, rather than electoralism, were seen as the way forward. They provided a relatively comfortable alternative for Republicans, as there remained a lack of any need to test the contemporary popularity of the politics of 1916–18. The continuing paramilitary campaign was also seen as having exposed the limits of the 'non-politics' of the Labour Secretary of State for Northern Ireland, Roy Mason. His attempt to diminish the IRA through a tough security response had some impact, but the limitations of the approach were exposed before Labour's election defeat in May 1979. The INLA's killing of the Shadow Secretary of State, Airey Neave, at the start of the election campaign was followed in August by the IRA's killing of eighteen soldiers at Warrenpoint and the murder of Lord Mountbatten on the same day.

Meanwhile, the 'blanket protest' had achieved no results, despite becoming a 'dirty' protest in 1978, after which prisoners smeared excrement on their cell walls. At the instigation of the prisoners themselves, the protest was transformed into a hunger strike in 1980. Although this initial fast was called off, the promised concessions from the British Government failed to materialise. The strike was thus reinstated in March 1981 by the prisoners, despite the reluctance of Sinn Féin, which feared defeat. For the first time the Republican movement attempted a more coalitional form of politics, having been encouraged by the condemnation of prison conditions by Cardinal Tomás Ó Fiaich, the somewhat strident leader of the Catholic Church in Ireland, broadcast on television in August 1978 and reiterated afterwards. After visiting the H-Blocks Ó Fiaich claimed that conditions were 'almost unbearable' and that he had been 'unable to speak for fear of vomiting'.[18]. This sympathy from the leader of Ireland's Catholics offered the first real encouragement to the Relatives Action Committees (RACs) outside the jails, whilst inside some IRA prisoners, irrespective of their personal faith or atheism, enjoyed good relationships with Ó Fiaich, even though the Cardinal denounced Republican violence.[19] The RACs were placed on a more organised footing with the establishment of the National H-Block/Armagh committee in 1979. Although the H-Block/Armagh Committees were dominated by the Provisionals, they contained a significant number of non-aligned individuals or representatives of other organisations outside Sinn Féin.

Although some on the far left disagreed with the broad front approach, Sinn Féin directed the H-Block Committee's attempts to arouse nationalist sentiment through appeals to the Church, Fianna Fáil and the SDLP. At a Special Conference of the National H-Block

Committee in January 1981, the prominent Republican Jim Gibney spoke of the necessity of 'getting the SDLP out of the "Six County" council chambers in order to emphasise to the British government the breakdown of the political system'.[20] Gibney argued that if local representatives were not urged to take action, how was it possible to pressurise the British government? The H-Block/Armagh Committee did not demand support for the wider ambitions of militant Republicanism. Instead, they appealed for support on the looser grounds of humanitarianism. The eclectic composition of the H-Block Committee, given its strategic domination by the Provisionals, was startling, containing a significant number of elements hostile to the armed struggle. A leader of the Peace People, Ciaran McKeown, was granted speaking rights at the Committee's inaugural conference in October 1979.[21] If, politically, it was still 'ourselves', there was a recognition by Sinn Féin and the PIRA that, in propaganda terms, reliance upon 'ourselves' offered a mere cul-de-sac.

Ó Fiaich's sympathy kept up the pressure on the British government and ensured that the Catholic Church refused to condemn as suicide—a mortal sin—the deaths of the hunger strikers. His episodic talks in 1980 with the British Secretary of State, Humphrey Atkins, nonetheless yielded little. The dead hunger strikers were given Catholic funerals and buried in consecrated ground. Indeed on Ó Fiaich's own death in 1990, *An Phoblacht/Republican News*, whilst insisting that the Cardinal was 'no political friend of the Republican movement', lamented the passing of a 'lone nationalist voice from the ranks of the Catholic hierarchy' who was 'a friend to the prisoners'.[22] Republicans had not always been so sympathetic. Angered by Ó Fiaich's assertion that participation in IRA activity was a 'mortal sin', *An Phoblacht/Republican News* condemned Ó Fiaich as someone who 'cynically used his position to break the relatives and so end the hunger strike' in November 1981, although this immediate post-strike period marked a low ebb in Church-Republican movement relations.[23] Whilst the Cardinal's pronouncements legitimised sympathy for the hunger strikes within greener elements of the SDLP, they antagonised others, notably Gerry Fitt, who believed they encouraged the strikes.[24] Two Catholic priests, Father Dennis Faul and Father Raymond Murray, produced a widely circulated pamphlet, detailing conditions in the H-Blocks.[25] Faul was later vilified by Republicans for his role in ending the strike, but in its early stages he found favour among the prisoners.

The five demands of the prisoners were the freedom to wear their own clothes; freedom of association; the lifting of the requirement for prison work; better educational facilities; and full remission of prison sentences. All sections of the anti-H-Block movement could unite in support of these core demands, although some, notably elements within the Church, shied away from the sum of the parts: the recognition that the IRA (and INLA) inmates were political prisoners who must be treated as such. Those who campaigned for more humane prison conditions were welcomed within the campaign, but for Republicans the hunger strike was a political action, designed to achieve recognition of the 'war', in addition to better treatment. Here there were clear differences between Sinn Féin/PIRA and their allies, glossed over for campaigning purposes. Aside from the novelty of having to work with other interested parties, the H-Block campaign also posed a test for those traditionalist elements who regarded intermediate demands, such as political status, as a distraction from the 'big prize' of fundamental constitutional change. Admitting that Sinn Féin had not welcomed the renewal of the hunger strike in 1981, Ruairí Ó Brádaigh argued that the 'total' diversion of the movement into the H-Block campaign was 'not welcome', declaring that over long periods it could be organisationally distracting for the movement.[26] Ó Brádaigh declined to invest the hunger strikes with special significance, arguing that they were 'just another front in the ongoing war of liberation in Ireland'.[27]

In 1979 Sinn Féin declined to test the electoral impact of the blanket campaign. Bernadette McAliskey decided to contest the European elections as an independent supporter of the protest. She was unmoved by the curious criticism from Sinn Féin, inspired more from fear of electoral rout than reality, that her participation was something desired by the British government. McAliskey polled respectably but hardly spectacularly, accumulating 33,969 votes, less than 6 per cent of the total cast. The result emphasised that much greater mobilisation was still needed. McAliskey's campaign on behalf of the prisoners was not helped by the condemnation of her electoral foray by the prisoners themselves. Nonetheless, by the time of the first hunger strike in 1980, there were further signs that electoral opportunities might be forthcoming. Demonstrations in Dublin in November and December 1980 attracted sizeable turnouts, although attendance at others remained modest. The stirring of nationalist sentiment had begun, but few in the movement could have foreseen the subsequent turn of events.

The election of Sands and Carron

The decision to enter the electoral arena in support of the prisoners was logical, given the need to develop a broader base in support of the Republican campaign. Nonetheless, it was a combination of fortuitous circumstance and the determination of the prisoners, rather than any strategic planning by Sinn Féin, that led to the decisive entry into electoral politics. The death of the independent Republican Frank Maguire created a Westminster by-election in Fermanagh and South Tyrone in 1981. Maguire, a supporter of the prisoners' campaign, had defeated the Ulster Unionist candidate by 5,000 votes and more than doubled the vote for the SDLP's Austin Currie to take the seat in 1979.

Started in March 1981 after an earlier strike in 1980 had failed to win sufficient concessions, the second hunger strike was staggered in order to maximise pressure on the British government. A steadily increasing number of prisoners participated in the fast, Bobby Sands being the first prisoner to decline food. The death of Frank Maguire then created an electoral contest, the by-election to be held as the prisoners proceeded with their strike. Sinn Féin saw the potential for the mobilisation of nationalist sentiment, but underestimated the extent to which this could develop. Despite the party's caution, the prisoners decided that Sands should stand for election on an 'Anti-H-Block/Armagh Political Prisoner' label. The main initial role of Sinn Féin was to dissuade other nationalist or Republican candidates, notably Bernadette McAliskey, from standing. This was achieved, at some cost to the SDLP's internal unity, and the contest was a straight fight between Sands and the Ulster Unionist Party candidate, Harry West. On a huge turnout of 86.9 per cent, Sands polled 30,492 votes, beating his Unionist rival by 1,446 votes.

The huge boost for Republican morale did little to alter the doomed course of the hunger strike itself, but the election victory demonstrated the extent of sympathy for the Republican cause, if not necessarily the armed struggle. Pan-nationalist political unity was nonetheless lacking, beyond a basic concern for prisoners' welfare. The humanitarian concerns of the Church were both a strength and weakness of the campaign. Interventions such as that from the (Church-based) Irish Commission for Justice and Peace, arguing that prisoners should be given their basic demands were undoubtedly useful in mobilising sentiment. The ICJP's timely intervention boosted the votes for hunger strikers standing as candidates in the Irish Republic's general election in June 1981. Yet humanitarianism was always likely to prompt Church interventions to ensure the ending of the strike. This risk, from what were termed the 'alien elements of the Church, SDLP and Haughey', was acknowledged by the prisoners' leader, Brendan 'Bik' McFarlane, in a communication smuggled out of the prison to Gerry Adams in late June. Humanitarian Church intervention led to increasing pressure being placed upon relatives to ask prisoners to end their fast. The removal of Paddy Quinn from the strike on 31 July signalled the beginning of the end.

The election results convinced most Republicans that electoralism need not be disastrous, but instead could offer sustenance for the Republican campaign. Bobby Sands died on 5 May and his funeral was attended by an enormous crowd, estimated at 100,000. The resulting by-election led to his election agent, Owen Carron, standing for the vacant seat, on an Anti-H-Block Proxy Political Prisoner label. The British government had introduced legislation prohibiting a convicted prisoner from contesting an election. Nationalist unity held, with the SDLP declining to field a candidate, aggravating internal friction. The Workers' Party Republican Clubs candidate made scant impact, as did the Alliance Party. In effect, therefore, the contest was another straight nationalist-Unionist fight, with the same outcome, Carron triumphing over the UUP's Ken Maginnis by 2,230 votes, on an even higher turnout. Perhaps even more remarkably, two Republican hunger strikers were also elected as TDs in the general election in the Irish Republic in June 1981. Nine prisoners stood, with Kieran Doherty (who died in August) and Paddy Agnew elected. However, the failure of all seven Sinn Féin candidates in the next general election, a mere nine months later, indicated that electoral politics required far deeper roots than those afforded by emotionalism. As the imprisoned Republican Gerry MacLochghlainn admitted publicly: 'There is no disguising the facts. This is a disappointing result for us… We can only conclude that we have failed to present ourselves to the people of the twenty-six counties as offering anything relevant to them.'[28]

Impacts North and South

After ten deaths, the hunger strike was finally called off on 3 October 1981. The electoral successes of the hunger strike were juxtaposed against the apparent failure of the campaign itself, although several of the prisoners' demands were met. Indeed, three days after the strike was abandoned, the Secretary of State announced that the prisoners would be allowed to wear their own clothes. The relative pan-nationalist unity of the previous months collapsed in rancour. Father Denis Faul was the subject of particular opprobrium, accusing of spreading 'demoralisation and defeatism' and opening up 'a gap for the cornered SDLP leadership to escape through'.[29] Father Faul had encouraged the families of the prisoners to intervene to call off the strike.

In the North, Sinn Féin hoped that the discomfiture endured by the SDLP would be turned to its electoral advantage. A well-sourced report of the SDLP's private conference in mid-September 1981 appeared in *An Phoblacht/Republican News* on 3 October, outlining the SDLP's fears of the new electoralism of the Republican movement. Sinn Féin believed it would capture much of the SDLP vote through social agitation. In particular, the party wished to expose what it saw as the SDLP's 'win some, lose some, easy relationship with public bodies in the North, such as the Housing Executive, DHSS and DOE'.[30] By acting as an agent for individuals encountering problems with these unpopular bureaucracies, Sinn Féin believed it could displace what was seen as an ageing, middle class nationalist party. The establishment of Sinn Féin advice centres facilitated such engagement with the community. Advice regarding benefits was particularly important in areas such as West Belfast, suffering enhanced deprivation in a period of acute economic depression in the early 1980s. This new political engagement meant considerable movement on the part of Sinn Féin from the abstract sloganising associated with *Éire Núa*. The architects of *Éire Núa* did not have disdain for campaigns on social and economic issues. Indeed Ruairí Ó Brádaigh highlighted the importance of unemployment and housing in his 1981 presidential speech to the Ard Fheis.[31] However Ó Brádaigh also highlighted land questions of minimal relevance to urban Northerners. Sinn Féin's increasingly influential Northern urban base recognised that welfare issues were of paramount importance to the daily lives of its core supporters. Assisting individuals in their contacts with officials brought Sinn Féin's elected representatives into much closer contact with the Northern state.

The IRA's military campaign did not reach the level many people expected after the end of the hunger strikes. During the strikes themselves, even after a number of deaths had occurred, there was an emphasis upon peaceful protest. In recognition of the fragility of alliances that had been built, it was argued that the 'most useless, most negative, most egotistical and most unthinking contribution…would be to exhort to violence from H-Block platforms.'[32] However, when the IRA did strike, its choice of targets became even more controversial. In November 1981 the organisation killed the UUP MP, the Reverend Roy Bradford. The Provisionals justified the first killing of a Northern Ireland Westminster MP on the grounds of Bradford's calls for the 'military suppression of resistance in the nationalist ghettos, his advocacy of summary executions of captured Republicans and his gloating and ghoulish comments after republican hunger-strikers died'.[33] Although the Provisionals stressed that the act should not be seen as sectarian, it was hugely provocative and could not be 'excused' as a 'shooting at the uniform'.

Sinn Féin hoped that election successes in the Irish Republic might undermine the Thatcher-Haughey Anglo-Irish intergovernmentalism favoured since the Conservative government's election victory in 1979. This Anglo-Irish axis had been seen as 'significant and dangerous'.[34] Disagreement over the Falklands conflict, rather than Republican successes, cooled those particular arrangements. Republicans had been fearful that the apparent rapport between the Fianna Fáil and Conservative administrations might shore up British rule. Thus the Republican commentator Peter Dowling argued that 'devolution, with a "unique relationship" with the Free State', condominium, and confederation were all possibilities for Northern Ireland under the new Anglo-Irish axis.[35] Dowling argued that 'pure militarism' was an inadequate response to intergovernmental activity. Instead, the movement needed to be educated that the development of political sophistry and electoral politics did not equate to becoming 'Sticks'. Many within the movement feared that the road to electoral politics would indeed follow the path of Sinn Féin the Workers' Party, renamed as simply the Workers' Party in 1982. It enjoyed some electoral success in the Irish Republic, holding three seats by the time of the name change. In the North, the Workers' Party fared poorly. The remnants of the old Official IRA had become 'bodyguards...extortionists and club bouncers' according to one critic.[36] More politically minded former Official IRA members in the North failed to tap into any leftist sentiment in republican circles. The increasingly virulent anti-Republicanism and condemnation of the IRA's 'mad-dog' campaign offered by the Workers' Party enjoyed a better reception in the South than in the urban constituencies of the North, sympathetic to the Provisional IRA. Provisional Sinn Féin welcomed the eventual disavowal of the title Sinn Féin by the Workers' Party, insisting that 'such a name (Sinn Féin) never belonged in Westminster, Stormont or Leinster House'.[37] Within two decades, Sinn Féin had entered two of those three parliaments. Wheels had yet to come full circle in 1982.

In 1982 the Conservative government temporarily moved from over-arching intergovernmentalism towards rolling devolution. The plan, introduced by a largely uninterested Secretary of State, James Prior, completely failed to engage republicans or nationalists. It was devoid of an Irish dimension, beyond an ill-defined Anglo-Irish Council. The proposals for a new assembly, gradually acquiring devolved powers, were boycotted by Sinn Féin and the SDLP. Republicans saw the proposals as a 'skilful scaling down of the ill-fated Sunningdale Agreement, giving a little more to loyalists and a little less to nationalists'.[38].

The new electoralism of Sinn Féin

The 1980 Ard Fheis took a decision not to contest the 1981 local elections. Given the emotions aroused by the hunger strike, this proved to be a missed opportunity, an error not to be repeated. With nationalist sentiment aroused, the Irish Independence Party offered an outlet, picking up 21 seats. The Irish Republican Socialist Party (IRSP) and Peoples Democracy (PD) also gained two seats each in Belfast. The 1981 Sinn Féin Ard Fheis voted to lift any blanket bans on contesting elections in Northern Ireland and the Irish Republic, in favour of allowing the Ard Chomhairle (executive) to decide. Motions from Sinn Féin *Cumainn* in Armagh, Cork, Belfast and Strabane, attempting to shore up anti-electoralism, were swept aside in favour of a more positive approach to electoral politics. The 'armalite and ballot box' strategy was confirmed, exemplified in the famous declaration of Danny Morrison, Sinn Féin's director of publicity, in an off-the-cuff address: 'Who here really believes that we can win the war through the ballot box? But will anyone here object if, with a ballot paper in this hand and an Armalite in this hand, we take power in Ireland?'[39] Later Morrision admitted that he knew there were 'contradictions' within the dual approach, although the negative impact of violence upon Sinn Féin's vote only later became an all-consuming issue for the movement.[40] The success of the hunger strike elections ensured that the steps towards electoralism were less controversial than might otherwise have been the case. Potential dissent was discouraged by the insistence that electoral politics were not to be conducted at the expense of armed struggle. Republicans were urged to vote Sinn Féin even though it was necessary to 'recognise the fruitless future of con-stitutional politics'.[41] The IRA emphasised that electoral intervention did not mean a dilution of the armed struggle.[42].

There was already a tension between those who saw the need for the diversion of Republican resources towards the establishment of Sinn Féin as a formidable electoral machine and those who saw the new electoralism as a diversion. An unsuccessful motion from the Molloy/Devlin *Cumann* in Strabane to the 1981 Ard Fheis urged that Sinn Féin 'do not enter any British election, Westminster or local, un-til British declaration of intent to withdraw immediately is given'. In his 'Revolutionary Rules', Gerry Adams, under the pseudonym Brownie, saw no contradiction between the simultaneous mainten-ance of a 'strong guerilla army' whose actions 'must be consistently and consciously aimed at increasing support and understanding of the republican position' and a 'strong party'.[43] Adams thus stressed the need for renewable mandates for the actions of Republicans. Although this was not explicitly stated, it was insufficient to regard the Rising of 1916 or the election result of 1918 as sufficient man-date. Such a proposition was elitist and failed to engage the popula-tion. Electoralism was seen as complementary, but not subordinate, to the military struggle. In otherwise divergent accounts, M. L. .R. Smith and Anthony McIntyre both argue that electoralism was not a new departure.[44]. McIntyre's point is that the two wings, political and military, of the Republican movement had always existed. Smith's account emphasises that the prosecution of the long war strategy post-1977 ensured that all military and political aspects of the campaign were tactics, rather than principles. Not everyone in the movement agreed, but the fundamentalists preaching abstentionism (and federalism) became marginalised by the need for a more subtle response to British pressure upon the Republican movement. Not unreasonably, fundamentalists began to ask of the modernisers, what were the principles of the Republican movement? Was everything tactical? The hunger strike elections gave new impetus, more sustainable than isolated military 'spectaculars'.

Sinn Féin was anxious to end the SDLP's dominance in electoral contests in the North. Although the IIP and the Irish Republican Socialist Party declined to contest the 1982 Northern Ireland Assembly elections, Sinn Féin fielded twelve candidates. Initially, Sinn Féin sought a unified nationalist boycott under a 'Stop Prior' banner.[45] Sinn Féin then announced that the party would contest the election only if the SDLP took part. On an abstentionist platform (in common with the SDLP) Sinn Féin polled an impressive 10.1 per cent of the vote, approximately one-third of Catholic voters. After another increase in violence immediately afterwards, the IRA again stressed that the military and electoral campaigns 'go together without contradiction'.[46] Furthermore, Sinn Féin's Ard Fheis in October unanimously passed a resolution demanding 'that all candidates in national and local elections and all campaign material be unambivalent in support of the armed struggle'.[47] Electoralism was nonetheless seen as crucial in its own right, offering a new facet to a military campaign more effective in terms of logistics than in the realisation of its political goals.

The hunger strikes opened for the Republican movement the strategic second front of electoral politics. Electoralism demonstrated that the IRA had significant support among a section of the nationalist population in Northern Ireland. Hence the propaganda value of election victories was considerable, even where such successes became less spectacular after the hunger strikes. The rapidity of the shift towards electoral politics in the early 1980s owed more to circumstance than to the strategic ideas of the emerging Northern leadership, but it was this group, led by Adams, which offered a vision of how electoral and agitational politics might complement the armed struggle. The existing leadership, gradually removed from influence, remained haunted by the politics of republicanism of the 1960s, fearing displacement of the armed struggle and absorption into the Northern state. By the late 1990s, this group claimed vindication, as politics displaced violence and participation in the Northern state replaced revolution. The newly emerging leadership of the 1980s, however, could point to the failure of violence to achieve Republican goals when used in isolation during the 1970s, necessitating the development of a twin-track approach if the entire struggle was to be maintained.

7

RESCUING THE SDLP
THE NEW IRELAND FORUM

The rolling devolution cul-de-sac

The election of Bobby Sands as MP for Fermanagh and South Tyrone damaged the efforts of the British government to portray an image of normality in Northern Ireland. Meanwhile fresh political initiatives were considered by the government, more in hope than expectation. When elected in 1979, the Conservatives' manifesto for Northern Ireland was designed to create a new context for 'a regional council, effectively a new, upper tier of local government'.[1] Like his predecessor Humphrey Atkins, James Prior, the Secretary of State for Northern Ireland from 1981 to 1984, realised that a regional council was not simply a proposal, but had to present some kind of solution for the province. The hunger strikes polarised the two communities in Northern Ireland and made any previous agreement on an interim political settlement virtually impossible.

Initial talks between Prior and the SDLP aimed to return some form of power to Northern Ireland. The party demonstrated interest in his suggestion of creating an Executive along the lines of the American Cabinet system.[2] In essence this meant that ministers could be members of the Executive without necessarily being part of the Assembly. Hume believed Prior was considering setting up a system of government in Northern Ireland whereby the Secretary of State could appoint ministers internally, in the Assembly, or on an external basis. The SDLP read the proposals to mean that if a political party refused to participate in the Assembly, the necessary mechanisms would be in place to safeguard government from collapse as happened in 1974.[3] According to SDLP internal documents from the mid-1970s, this strategy presented a political framework that could not be boycotted. Accordingly, the plan was discussed in depth by the SDLP leadership.

Prior dismissed the SDLP's own preliminary proposals, which in due course meant that the SDLP had to review the intentions of the Secretary of State as set out in the April 1982 White Paper. He was fully supportive of the Unionist position and in reality relegated the Irish dimension. Prior confirmed this line of argument in his autobiography; he noted that the British Prime Minister at that time, Margaret Thatcher, insisted he drop his chapter on Anglo-Irish relations and put forward 'a less positive version, incorporated at the end of the chapter on the "Two Identities" in Northern Ireland.'[4] Thatcher heightened SDLP concerns about the White Paper, and acknowledged later: 'Before publication I had the text of the White Paper substantially changed in order to cut a chapter dealing with relations with the Irish Republic and I hoped, minimise Unionist objections.'[5] The Taoiseach, Garret FitzGerald, warned Thatcher that the consequences of not helping the SDLP could mean that Sinn Féin might overtake it as the main nationalist party in Northern Ireland.[6]

In the House of Commons Prior remarked, 'I believe that our proposals are the most likely to tie Northern Ireland into the United Kingdom.'[7] The SDLP thought the subsequent proposals from Prior were an integrationist move to accommodate unionists. The party also believed that Prior's proposals contained two mutually exclusive concepts. On the one hand, the initiative conceded that the Northern Ireland conflict was based on differences in identity and aspiration. However, he insisted that any new forthcoming parliamentary body had to 'be seen within the context of Northern Ireland as part of the United Kingdom.'[8] The SDLP believed that the devolution scheme outlined by Prior presented a dilution of government commitment to the Anglo-Irish process. Seamus Mallon pointed out that nationalists were asked to give their 'consent to be governed in a constitutional framework, which by definition is exclusively British, and by yet another administrative system, which is based on Unionist majority rule'.[9]

Overall the SDLP opposed the 'rolling devolution' proposals set out by Prior, as the government failed to confront the political inequalities which remained and ignored the root causes of conflict. The SDLP position was that Britain was directly involved in the Northern

Ireland conflict, and not an innocent bystander. By supporting the constitutional guarantee of Northern Ireland as a sector of the United Kingdom—so the party spokesman, Seán Farren, argued—the government sanctioned 'undemocratic foundations' by which Northern Ireland was established. The British government was 'underscoring their own partisan involvement in the crisis… [and ignoring] … how this majority was contrived at in the first place'. They allowed unionists 'to reject with impunity all attempts to establish partnership'.[10]

Despite SDLP criticisms of Prior's overall project, the party welcomed Paragraph 17 of the White Paper stating, 'The difference in identity and aspiration lies at the heart of the "problem" of Northern Ireland; it cannot be ignored or wished away.'[11] However, from the SDLP standpoint, the White Paper acknowledged the Irish dimension of the conflict, but did not include any feasible guidelines as to how the Irish dimension was going to be an integral part of an overall solution. The government believed the Anglo-Irish process was still a mechanism for promoting co-operation in areas of mutual interest between Northern Ireland and the Republic. From the British government perspective, the constitutional question in Northern Ireland was an internal United Kingdom concern. On the other hand the SDLP viewed the Anglo-Irish process as a means for both governments to draw up a framework through which the local Northern Ireland political parties could reach agreement. It was only through the Anglo-Irish process that complex constitutional policy could be resolved.

Margaret Thatcher and Garret FitzGerald met for their first Anglo-Irish summit in November 1981. However, FitzGerald and his government fell because of the budget crisis of January 1982. Charles Haughey was re-elected as Taoiseach until FitzGerald was returned to office later in the same year. Anglo-Irish relations between the British and Irish governments were at a low ebb. During the tenure of Haughey as Irish Prime Minister in 1982 the Irish government opposed the British stance over the Falkland Islands. Haughey also opposed the devolution plans set out by Prior.[12]. The fall-out between Britain and the Republic over the Falklands strengthened links between Thatcher and the Unionists in Northern Ireland. Instead of Anglo-Irish progress during the Haughey era, there was concern in the SDLP that the plans of Prior for rolling devolution would lead to a return to majority rule in Northern Ireland. Figures such as Austin

Currie, Paddy O'Hanlon, Joe Hendron, Seán Farren, Eddie McGrady, Denis Haughey and Frank Feeley of the SDLP were initially in favour of participating in the Assembly as a means to show up the obdurate stance of the Unionists. The SDLP members' decision to refrain from taking their Assembly seats was partly due to frustration at what they perceived as partisan government support for the Unionist community. SDLP members also felt the government was unwilling to address the Irish dimension of the Northern Ireland conflict. Furthermore the SDLP wished to offset the publicity given to Sinn Féin following the hunger strikes.

Elections to the Assembly took place on 20 October 1982. The SDLP won 14 seats in the Assembly and gained 18.8 per cent of the valid poll, a somewhat disappointing performance. It demonstrated a decline of slightly over 40,000 votes for the SDLP from the polls for the 1973 Assembly election. Sinn Féin took part in the Northern Ireland electoral contest and gave the Provisional Republican movement 64,191 votes, 10.1 per cent of the poll. Sinn Féin only put up seven candidates, yielding the party a 2.5 per cent higher result than in the total H block vote in the 1981 local government elections. Prospects for political progress on the Anglo-Irish front looked extremely bleak and Margaret Thatcher privately expressed her doubts as to whether any solution was possible to resolve the Northern Ireland problem.[13]

Developing nationalist consensus

In an attempt to break the political deadlock, constitutional nationalist parties throughout Ireland convened the New Ireland Forum in 1983-4. The idea of an all-island discussion forum had emerged in SDLP thinking during the late 1970s, before the more emotional impact of the hunger strikes in 1981. At the 1978 SDLP annual conference the party called for the Northern Ireland problem to be reassessed in an Irish context with the main parties in the Republic. The objective of such a nationalist conference set out by the SDLP in 1978 was to attain a cohesive strategy for Northern Ireland that could be used in negotiations with Unionists for an overall political settlement. The futility of the devolution proposals from Prior prompted Hume to resurrect the All-Ireland forum concept. Hume concentrated his efforts on attaining a cohesive all-island nationalist body that could formulate an agreed analysis of the contemporary nature

of the Northern Ireland problem. He wanted an effective strategy
that would provide a framework for both governments to move the
political process forward. Hume envisaged using the elections to the
Prior Assembly as a mandate for his Forum initiative.

Charles Haughey's leadership of Fianna Fáil saw the party return
to its conventional Northern Ireland line, with rhetorical calls for a
British withdrawal in order to make Irish unity feasible. Haughey delivered a hardline speech on Northern Ireland at the Fianna Fáil 1983
Annual Conference. He called for a constitutional conference as 'a
prelude to a final withdrawal of Britain from Ireland within a stipu-
lated period of time, enabling the Irish people North and South to
come together and freely determine their future'. The objective of the
conference was to debate policies on which power could be transferred to new All-Ireland political structures.[14] However, at his party
conference, Haughey was nevertheless a proponent of the idea of
John Hume that a 'Council' for a new Ireland[15] should be put in place,
consisting of all the nationalist parties, but not including the unionists.

Garret FitzGerald took over as Taoiseach from Charles Haughey
following the general election in the Republic on 25 November 1982.
He had been briefed by his senior advisers on the possibility that Sinn
Féin might gain three or four seats in the forthcoming British general
election, while they suggested the SDLP might only gain one or two
seats. Consequently, FitzGerald made it his priority to prevent the
increasing apparent popularity of the IRA's armed struggle, if measured in terms of support for Sinn Féin. Reluctantly, he abandoned his
ambition to obtain a settlement in Northern Ireland through direct
negotiations with the British government which also involved the
unionists.[16] FitzGerald, like his predecessor Haughey, was concerned
at the potential threat the IRA posed to the stability of Ireland.
Assembly election results provided an impetus for Garret FitzGerald
to press ahead with the creation of a 'Council' of Ireland in his term
as Taoiseach.

In March 1983 the FitzGerald government disclosed its intention
of establishing an All-Ireland Forum on the basis set out by the
SDLP. FitzGerald viewed the New Ireland Forum as a 'mandate for
an Anglo-Irish agreement' that would address minority alienation in
Northern Ireland and consequently reverse the rising tide of support
for Provisional Sinn Féin.[17] The official announcement of a New

Ireland Forum by FitzGerald nevertheless made some amendments to the original SDLP proposals. Hume agreed to drop the term 'Council of Ireland' on the basis of FitzGerald's argument that such a phrase might rekindle Unionist fears of a mechanism towards Irish unity, similar to that of the 1974 power-sharing era. FitzGerald eventually gave in to pressure from Hume to opt for the SDLP concept of a nationalist Council for a New Ireland, which Hume was presenting to his party's Annual Conference in January 1983. The Taoiseach decided to invite all the constitutional parties on the island invited to participate in the Forum, with the intention that it was not just an exclusive nationalist exercise, as the SDLP had originally proposed.

Rather than face political alienation from the other mainstream nationalist parties in Ireland, Charles Haughey supported the aims of the Forum in public. The Fianna Fáil leader declared that the work of the Forum would result in an advance plan that could play a vital role in a constitutional conference, as a prerequisite to a final constitutional settlement. Seamus Mallon strongly backed this position.[18] The aim of the New Ireland Forum for the Irish government was to buttress the SDLP as the champions of Northern nationalism, against the rising tide of support for Sinn Féin. The British government was indifferent as to whether FitzGerald achieved his real intention of creating the Forum initiative to support the SDLP. Margaret Thatcher remained unsympathetic to the plight of the SDLP against the increasing popularity of Sinn Féin, telling FitzGerald, 'the SDLP are your problem' and complaining that the SDLP were 'anti-Unionist'.[19] However complacent the British government might have been as to the rise of Sinn Féin after the 1981 hunger strikes, the Westminster election results in June 1983 in reality must have given some credence to FitzGerald and his sense of urgency over the issue. The SDLP leader, John Hume, was elected to Westminster, but so was Sinn Féin's Gerry Adams, for West Belfast, at the expense of the former SDLP leader, Gerry Fitt, who stood as an Independent Socialist.

From the SDLP perspective, the Forum would enable the party to replace the disparate positions on Northern Ireland held by the main Irish constitutional parties with a cohesive nationalist strategy on which to negotiate with the Unionists. The Forum provided a framework which could also be described as an evaluation or revision of traditional nationalism in Ireland. The Forum could allow for this evaluated, revised nationalism to be applied in a contemporary setting in the North. Yet any attempt by the SDLP to show itself as a revisionist nationalist party by endorsing the New Ireland Forum was irrelevant as far as the Unionist tradition was concerned. From the Unionist viewpoint, since the SDLP did not attend the Assembly set up by Prior, it simply represented remnants of a traditional nationalist boycott strategy that the old Nationalist Party had used. Further, the fact that the SDLP held similar ultimate objectives to Sinn Féin meant that, for unionists, it might be a party of non-violence, but its nationalism was also strident, camouflaged by so-called democratic mechanisms.

SDLP policy positions: the New Ireland Forum

The SDLP desperately needed a focal point like the New Ireland Forum to assist its challenge to rising Sinn Féin support. By the beginning of 1983 Sinn Féin was increasingly confident after its electoral success following the hunger strikes. The armed struggle and entry into mainstream elections had mobilised a section of the nationalist party not merely against the British 'forces of occupation', but also against the 'Uncle Toms' of the SDLP. Prior's rolling devolution initiative did nothing to buttress the SDLP. Pádraig O'Malley has noted that the absence of the SDLP from the Assembly strengthened Sinn Féin arguments that the boycott undertaken by its nationalist rival affirmed 'that the SDLP had achieved nothing after twelve years of "collaboration"' with the British.[20] The challenges facing the SDLP at the beginning of 1983 were described at the time by the SDLP chairman, Seán Farren, at the 12th SDLP Annual Conference. He claimed that the SDLP faced 'a coalition of intransigent unionism, British conservatism and the fascism of the Provisional IRA and of its fellow-travellers in Provisional Sinn Féin'.[21]

The SDLP was totally opposed to Sinn Féin calls for an electoral pact in the 1983 Westminster elections. The SDLP fought the general election with the Forum as a key element of its election manifesto, arguing it was the 'most significant political development since 1920'.[22] The SDLP decided to fight all seventeen Westminster seats. The party thus reversed the 'step aside' approach evident in the Fermanagh and South Tyrone by-elections, despite the risk of letting Unionists win seats where the Catholic vote was split between the SDLP and Sinn Féin.

The objective of the negotiations in the Forum was, to the SDLP, to reach consensus in Northern Ireland as part of the broad-based constitutional nationalist family. The Forum would enable the Irish government to negotiate a new framework with the British government and political progress in Northern Ireland could be made. External pressure from the SDLP brought the main nationalist parties in Ireland together to agree on a common approach to the Northern Ireland conflict. From the SDLP point of view, a crucial element of the Forum talks was to get the main parties involved to agree on the 'basis for a new way forward in North-South and in Anglo-Irish relations... [and a] ...basis for future discussion with the British government and with the unionist parties'.[23]

The SDLP believed the Forum was an opportunity to examine Unionist fears of association with the South of Ireland. Unionist hostility to the Irish Republic was seen by the SDLP as the main problem thwarting efforts to obtain a political settlement on the island, preventing the obvious solution of power-sharing in Northern Ireland with an Irish dimension. Therefore the SDLP proposed that, rather than participating in the Assembly, the party should 'examine in detail the roots of division in Ireland, in particular the reasons for unionist opposition to co-operation with their fellow countrymen and women'.[24]

The Forum was placed by the SDLP in an Anglo-Irish framework because of the nature of partition. The emphasis on Anglo-Irish relations was paramount from the SDLP viewpoint, not only for moving the political process forward in Northern Ireland, but also for understanding the conflict in which Britain played a historic role. The in-depth examination of the causes of the current Northern Ireland divisions was, for the SDLP, not simply to point the finger of blame at Britain, but rather to get the British government to face up to its part as one of the causes of the conflict. The SDLP believed the Forum was to act as a basis for negotiation, which could give an accurate analysis of the causes of the Northern Ireland conflict. It provided the framework within which future discussions with the British government and Unionists could take place.

The Forum was about creating structures and principles for a political settlement in Northern Ireland.[25] There were four fundamental principles at the centre of the Forum talks: first, the need for the

British government to address 'its historical role in failing to come to terms with the widespread abuse of power in Northern Ireland since 1921 or to accommodate the nationalist position'; second, the need for Irish nationalists to assess their historic role and their inability to argue 'the merits of the nationalist aspiration' to the unionists and to the British government alike; third, the need to address the failure of Northern Ireland political structures, due to the denial of 'an adequate involvement in decision-making and an adequate symbolic and administrative expression of their Irish identity and aspiration' to the nationalist community; and lastly it was obligatory to comprehend fully the Unionist/loyalist position 'in any new structures'.[26] To demonstrate this last requirement major changes would have to be made to the Irish Constitution to accommodate Protestants and dilute the dominant role of Catholicism in cultural, social and moral matters.

The SDLP wanted its concept of a Council of Ireland to be an opportunity to redefine the meaning of Irishness in contemporary reality. John Hume solicited the support of the main parties in the Republic to examine the obstacles to building a new all-Ireland Irish society. In his address as leader of the party to the 12th SDLP annual conference, Hume outlined terms of reference for the negotiations between the main constitutional parties in the Republic. He wished to explore the 'economic implications of unity by consent', 'Church-State relations' and 'Anglo-Irish relations'.[27]

The SDLP discussed the main constitutional options internally during the talks leading up to the Forum. In relation to joint sovereignty, the SDLP debate focused on the 1972 document, *Towards a New Ireland.* The party review of joint sovereignty during the Forum debate led to change from the 1972 position. Instead of joint sovereignty being viewed as an interim arrangement, it was now seen as a permanent arrangement for as long as it could be accepted on both parts of the island. In further discussions the SDLP were swayed towards a secular schema leaving moral and ethical principles and guidance to specific churches in any new constitutional formulation.[28]

The main weakness in the SDLP conception of a unitary state was the unrealistic premise that Unionists would somehow accept the idea. It was a quixotic theorem to expect traditional Unionist cultural and religious concerns to be so easily overcome, or to believe that negotiations could ever take place between two sets of irreconcilable nationalisms. The SDLP proposed that in the unitary state the United Nations Charter would be the protector of all moral, ethical and social rights. In relation to specific domains between North and South, harmonisation was recommended to take place within a range of timetables. An Anglo-Irish Council was constructed as a mechanism to deal with the unionist desire to maintain institutional links with the UK. It was suggested that the Royal Ulster Constabulary and the Garda Síochána amalgamate as one police force.[29]

Of the three constitutional options the SDLP believed a federal/ confederal state would have most support among the Unionist tradition, largely because of the degree of autonomy that Unionists would have from the rest of Ireland. In this constitutional arrangement all-island political structures and powers 'would be restricted to external defence, foreign affairs, customs and excise, limited aspects of all-Ireland security and the provision of an all-Ireland court, again with limited jurisdiction'.[30] In essence the SDLP called for the four constitutional nationalist parties in the South to reassess the ideological, economic and social implications of Irish unity. The agreed Ireland the SDLP sought was one that had no 'pre-conceptions,' but rather had to encompass 'comprehensive agreement' to meet the 'criteria of justice, realism and durability'.[31]

Sinn Féin: rejecting federalism and the Forum

Sinn Féin denounced the New Ireland Forum as a 'show trial for Irish unity', which 'created the illusion of political movement when nothing at all was happening'.[32] The party argued that the Forum had been created by the SDLP to underline its nationalist credentials and undercut the growing Northern support base of Sinn Féin. The Irish government was aware that the Forum could consolidate the fortunes of the SDLP. As the Foreign Affairs Minister, Peter Barry, bluntly put it, 'The SDLP needs all the help it can get'.[33] The Forum placed the SDLP in a pivotal role in all-Ireland pan-nationalist alliances and highlighted the isolation of the Republican movement in its advocacy of political violence. Sinn Féin stressed that the main sections of the population not involved in the Forum were those that it spent much time addressing—Republicans and Loyalists. Sinn Féin attacked the Forum for devising safeguards for Loyalists without emphasising how the British government was going to be forced to withdraw, although

this was a criticism from which Sinn Féin was not immune. More realistically, Sinn Féin decried the cynical manner in which the Fianna
Fáil leader, Charles Haughey, saw the Forum as 'a platform to portray
himself as a "Brits out" republican leader', for party advantage.[34]
Indeed the mid-1980s formed the last period in which Fianna Fáil
openly expressed its Republican ideals, prior to the greater sophistry
of the peace process.

Sinn Féin had changed its own model of Irish unity. The merger of
An Phoblacht and *Republican News* in 1979 meant that there would be
only one main source of printed Republican propaganda, and this
source was lukewarm towards the federalism of the New Ireland or
Éire Núa. Both papers supported political programmes designed to
coerce loyalists 'into changing their sectarian ways and accepting that
being born and reared in Ireland makes one Irish and no better nor
worse than the next Irish person'.[35] The demands of motions at party
gatherings, the Ard Fheisanna, for full support from the papers for
Éire Núa were ignored by the editors. In military matters Northern
Command had operated semi-autonomously since 1976. In 1979 the
IRA had dropped the federalism of *Éire Núa* and it was inconceivable
that it could remain Sinn Féin policy for much longer. The Northern
leadership of the Republican movement, based around figures such
as Gerry Adams, Martin McGuinness and Danny Morrison, exerted
their authority. They resented the manner in which the federal principles of *Éire Núa* had been written into the constitution of Sinn Féin,
a move which Adams criticised as 'elevating federalism into a republican principle which it patently wasn't'.[36] Opponents of federalism
were particularly critical of the plans to establish a Dáil Uladh, a nine-
county parliament, presiding over Protestant and Catholic populations of broadly equal size. Adams played a sectarian card in moving
towards ending federalism, arguing that the preservation of an Ulster
parliament, with a possible Unionist majority, could leave Northern
nationalists vulnerable to discrimination.[37]

In 1980 Sinn Féin members at the Ard Fheis had attempted to
modernise the party's economic and social programmes. At the 1981
gathering the federal policy of *Éire Núa* was rejected, but a federal
Ireland remained an ambition in the Sinn Féin constitution. In 1982 a
two-thirds majority finally erased the concept of federalism from the
party constitution. Sinn Féin now proposed a unitary state model for

an independent, thirty-two-county Republic. The change in policy was accompanied by a commitment to decentralised socialism, which retained some of the earlier utopian ideals. Decentralisation would be implemented via the creation of regional councils, district councils and community, or 'People's Councils'.[38] There would even be a network of street committees, feeding into the Community Councils. The District Councils would be 'self-governing' areas, containing populations of 25,000–45,000, with responsibility for most public services, including policing, plus employment, agriculture and fishing. The fifteen Regional Councils, with variable populations, would be responsible for economic and educational planning. The National Parliament would comprise representatives from the Regional Councils who would be directly elected representatives (using a proportional representation system) and, vaguely, 'a limited number of people…from outside parliament'. Legislation could be initiated by the National Parliament, by the central Government via referenda, or via the Regional, District and Community Councils. The unanswered question was 'How much power would be ceded to Loyalist Regional or District Councils in the North?' given the concurrent determination of Sinn Féin to smash that 'neo-fascist' creed.

Federalism had been abandoned to demonstrate to Loyalists that 'There is no longer any "Stormont way"… To the Protestant people we offer no privileges, only the same rights as everyone else.'[39] An attempt to revive federalism, via a motion to the 1983 Ard Fheis from the Patrick Carty *Cumann* in Bundoran, Donegal, was defeated. The new approach amounted to a hardline, 'no sops to Loyalists' policy.[40] The Republican press had become increasingly critical of Loyalists, denouncing their 'reactionary, pro-imperialist philosophy'.[41] Loyalists had always been seen as a confused people, 'unable to liberate themselves'.[42] Republicans differed as to best way to deal with their 'fellow citizens': they understood that there would be 'psychological alienation of the Loyalist community' *en route* to Irish unity, yet knew that the loyalist tradition had to be accommodated somehow.[43] Republicans agreed that Loyalism was a reactionary product of colonialism, although it was sometimes labelled 'fascist'.[44] From 1970 to 1982, republicans could claim to offer institutional recognition of Loyalist identity, but from here on there would be none.

Moves towards the abandonment of federalism coincided with an internal reorganisation of Sinn Féin. Provincial Councils of the party, or structures that mirrored the federalism proposed externally, were seen as ineffective. The ending of the federalism of *Éire Núa* was particularly well received by those Northern Republicans who had endured years of sectarian discrimination and who had never been as wedded to abstract federal principles as the old Southern leadership. However, the decision to drop federalism did not come about merely simply because Northerners opposed the old Southern leadership. Proposers of the motion for abandonment at the 1981 Ard Fheis included Sinn Féin *Cumainn* from Waterford and Dublin. Urban-based Southern opponents of *Éire Núa*, like Seán Crowe, later to become a Dublin-based member of Dáil Éireann, were also more critical of 'pie-in-the-sky' federalism.[45] Nonetheless, the loss of a central plank of a republican agenda was too much for the old Southern-based leadership, with Ruairí Ó Brádaigh and Dáithí Ó Conaill resigning from their posts in 1983. There was a particular antipathy among many Northerners to 'concessions' to Loyalists under *Éire Núa*. All wings of the movement agreed that the exercise of Irish self-determination would end the Northern state. Northerners feared its reconstruction, albeit in larger form, via the Dáil Uladh. The Northern unitary state model of a united Ireland offered no such opt-out clauses. By the 1980s federal political structures offering institutional recognition of the diversity of tradition in the island were no longer in vogue. Although palpably unsympathetic, the Republican press had been relatively restrained in discussions of Orangeism during the 1970s, regarding members of the Order as misguided imperial dupes. Now the tone was harsher, the Order's Twelfth of July parades being criticised as demonstrations of the 'hatred of the coloniser for the colonised, the imperial domination upon which the institutions of the six county state have rested for over 60 years'.[46]

The unitary state model offered by the Northerners was also increasingly a socialist model, as Sinn Féin attempted to marry republicanism with leftist politics during the early 1980s. Revolutionary fervour was useful in the secret processes of procuring arms for the struggle. Although a shortage of arms obliged the movement to trade with a variety of groups and regimes, including, most profitably, the Qaddafi regime in Libya, such knowledge was kept from Sinn Féin, within which far-left anti-imperialism was never especially popular. The party passed motions at its 1982 Ard Fheis rejecting militant anti-imperialist organisations such as the Red Brigades.[47] The fusion of Republicanism with socialism replaced the Gaelic federalist romanticism of 1970–81, but it was a brief and unstable marriage. Aware of the moderate levels of interest in socialism in the party, Gerry Adams attempted to weld Republicanism and socialism by invoking the writings of earlier martyrs. During the 1970s he complained of how 'the "Irish" Labour Party and more recently the Sticks and the Communist Party were allowed for too long to monopolise the legacy that Connolly handed on'.[48] Sinn Féin socialism contained little of the aspirational cross-class unity aspirations of the old 'Sticks'. Meanwhile working-class Loyalists were derided as 'even more reactionary than the upper echelons' of society.[49] Republicans merged the language of revolutionary socialism with community activism, electoral change and militarism.

By 1988 Sinn Féin had settled for a more fruitful role as a greener (more nationalist) party than the SDLP, rather than a revolutionary organisation. Sinn Féin's moves to the left had been partly influenced by a similar drift in the British Labour Party during the same period. Sinn Féin hoped to shift Labour policy decisively in a pro-Republican direction. While the British Labour Party was busy making itself unelectable (though not through its policy on Ireland, as support for Irish unity chimed with the British electorate), sections of its left wing offered sympathy to the Republican cause. The leader of the Greater London Council, Ken Livingstone, rejected the criminalisation of Republicans and offered them a platform—which the leadership of Sinn Féin willingly accepted. Livingstone argued for 'fraternal links between Sinn Féin and the Labour Party as sister parties fighting for socialism in Europe'.[50] Sympathy for Sinn Féin was mainly confined to the far left in the Labour Party. Even figures such as Tony Benn were not immune from criticism by Republicans, as he stood accused of having a 'blind spot of calling for United Nations intervention, in spite of the record of such interventions demonstrating a clear advantage to the Western powers'.[51] Others willing to share platforms nonetheless included the future Labour Cabinet Minister Chris Smith, who defended the visit to London by Gerry Adams in July 1983 and indicated he 'would go a long way in agreeing the case for withdrawal'.[52] Links between Sinn Féin and sections of the British left assisted the political development of Sinn Féin. It is an exaggeration,

however, to assert that these links 'encouraged the evolution of republican policy away from national liberation towards the peace process'.[53] Such comments overstate the influence of the British left
during the period. Nonetheless, the dialogue was one element of the
encouragement to Sinn Féin to pressure the IRA into refining operations. The embryonic debate within the republican movement over
the viability of its bomb-and-ballot-box strategy was fostered by
dialogue with sections of the British left.

Margaret Thatcher's dismissal of the New Ireland Forum

Throughout the first half of the 1980s Margaret Thatcher maintained
her pro-Unionist stance in relation to Northern Ireland. The combination of the INLA killing of Airey Neave and the demands for political status by the Republican hunger-strikers in the early 1980s did
little to endear the British Prime Minister to a nationalist agenda. The
criticisms offered by Charles Haughey of Britain's Falklands campaign almost led to cessation of Anglo-Irish co-operation developed
at the 1980 summit in Dublin between Thatcher and the Taoiseach.
By the summer of 1982 Thatcher and her administration reverted to
traditional British policies in Northern Ireland, namely that the Province was the internal responsibility of the United Kingdom government. The Prime Minister pointed out that she would not look to the
Republic for co-operation in Northern Ireland, and noted at the time
'that no commitment exists for Her Majesty's Government to consult
the Irish Government on matters affecting Northern Ireland.... That
has always been our position.'[54]

The SDLP believed that the British government was going to rede-
velop the Anglo-Irish front on the basis of the Forum Report. Its
optimism was based on comments made by the Secretary of State,
James Prior, which referred to constructive aspects of the Report in
the House of Commons on July 1984. In particular Prior approved the
emphasis on 'consent....its unequivocal condemnation of violence....its
attempt to understand the Unionist identity and its openness to discuss other views' in the Forum Report.[55] The SDLP depended on the
success of the Forum proposals, measured by their impact on the
British government, in order to counteract the continuing political
rise in support for Sinn Féin.

Meanwhile the SDLP was bolstered by John Hume's European election success in 1984. In winning his European Parliament seat with 151,399 votes (22.1 per cent of the vote) Hume demonstrated that the SDLP's electoral crisis might not be as acute as predicted. The SDLP was gratified by the overall increase in votes for the party compared to the 1983 general election, when they obtained 137,012 or 17.5 per cent of votes cast. However, the reality for the SDLP was that Sinn Féin was still a significant electoral threat. Despite the fact that Sinn Féin did not come close to obtaining a European seat, they captured 91,476 votes, indicating that intra-nationalist electoral rivalry would remain intense.

After a scheduled Anglo-Irish summit at Chequers on the 19 November 1984 and at a summary press conference, the Prime Minister ruled out all three options of the New Ireland Forum with the three-pronged phrase, 'That is out, that is out, that is out'. She did not approve a unitary state, a federal system or joint sovereignty. The SDLP was astounded at the brevity and tone of her dismissal of months of effort and was disappointed that its hopes for the Forum as a means to urge the government to develop new structures and institutions for Northern Ireland might all have been in vain. The SDLP deputy leader, Seamus Mallon, described comments by the Prime Minister about the Forum as 'racist' and 'based on ignorance'.[56] On the basis of the words spoken by the Prime Minister, 'Out, out, out', the SDLP was convinced that parties to the Forum would find it difficult to change the attitude of Margaret Thatcher or the attitudes of her government to Irish nationalism. Political persuasion had little impact on Thatcher or her policy in relation to Northern Ireland. However, an IRA bomb at the Grand Hotel in Brighton on 12 October 1984, which killed five people attending the Conservative Party's annual conference, did cause a response.

For the SDLP the Brighton bomb was a deliberate attempt by the Republican movement to sidetrack progress on British-Irish relations and to spoil the Anglo-Irish summit to be held at Chequers in late November 1984. For the Provisionals the operation was a major coup, highlighting the vulnerability of the British government. Success arising out of the New Ireland Forum would be viewed by Sinn Féin as a political coup for the SDLP and would strengthen the constitutional nationalist analysis of the Northern Ireland conflict. Therefore, it was in the interests of the Republican movement to destabilise Anglo-Irish relations and to undermine the efforts of the SDLP to establish its own British-Irish framework for a political settlement pertaining to Northern Ireland. The SDLP's Seán Farren argued, not unreasonably: 'The IRA wanted to cause sufficient backlash that the British government would have imposed draconian measures against nationalists and republicans and measures like these in the past such as internment or torture or "shoot-to-kill" tactics usually rebound on the authorities and would further the Sinn Féin cause in terms of increased support.'[57] Farren might also have noted the particular desire of the IRA to take 'revenge' on Thatcher after the 1981 hunger strikes.

Despite the serious nature of the public attack from Thatcher on the Forum plans at the press conference at Chequers, Anglo-Irish negotiations resumed again early in 1985. These talks re-focused on areas of co-operation between both governments. Intergovernmental cooperation had begun to recover after the Falklands crisis, until the criticism of the Forum's deliberations from Thatcher. During 1983 Anglo-Irish Intergovernmental Conference Ministerial Meetings still took place on a regular basis despite the deterioration in Anglo-Irish relations in the Falklands crisis.[58] Monthly Ministerial Meetings took place in 1983 and dealt with issues such as language, regional development, youth matters and local government.

Against the background of the Forum talks in 1983, Garret Fitz-Gerald and Margaret Thatcher met at a European Council at Stuttgart in June 1983. At this meeting the Prime Minister for the first time expressed her dismay at the possibility that Sinn Féin might overtake the SDLP in the polls, despite disapproving of the SDLP reluctance to participate in the Assembly.[59] The Stuttgart meeting was also significant because Thatcher agreed with FitzGerald on talks between officials on impending co-operation on the Anglo-Irish front. Talks had been taking place between British and Irish officials on ways to improve security and co-operation between both parts of the island— particularly cross-border co-operation between the Gardaí and the RUC. During these negotiations the Dublin government had been pressing for joint Anglo-Irish courts and suggested the possibility of the Garda policing nationalist areas of Northern Ireland. Negotiators from the Republic pressed for some form of joint sovereignty in

Northern Ireland to address the sense of alienation experienced by Northern nationalists.

What was significant from the communiqué released after the Anglo-Irish summit on the 19 November 1984 was its proposal that 'the identities of both the majority and minority communities in Northern Ireland should be recognised and respected, and reflected in the structures and processes of Northern Ireland in ways acceptable to both communities'.[60] The communiqué stated that discussion and co-operation should take place between the two governments in relation to Northern Ireland. In particular the communiqué acknowledged the necessity 'to diminish the divisions between the two communities in Northern Ireland and to reconcile the two major traditions that exist in the two parts of Ireland.'[61]

Despite positive tones in the communiqué, from the SDLP point of view it appeared as though the Prime Minister continued to reject the alienation thesis of the Forum by resorting to a government *status quo* in Northern Ireland. At her press conference Margaret Thatcher explained, 'I have long taken the view that we cannot impose something from London.'[62] What was important by the end of 1984 was that Unionists believed the government had reacted to the Forum proposals in such a way as to commit the SDLP to negotiating with them in the political context of Northern Ireland. In this respect Unionists sorely underestimated the strength of the Anglo-Irish axis created for reasons of pragmatic security co-operation and lack of faith in the calibre of local politicians. This Anglo-Irish intergovernmentalism, a triumph for the SDLP, was to dominate Northern Ireland politics in future years, enshrined in the 1985 Anglo-Irish Agreement.

8

THE ANGLO-IRISH AGREEMENT

The Anglo-Irish Agreement, signed at Hillsborough by the British Prime Minister Margaret Thatcher and the Irish Taoiseach Garret FitzGerald in November 1985, owed its existence to a range of factors. It revived British-Irish intergovernmental contacts of the early 1980s. The Agreement reflected the concern of the British government that the Republic was a relatively safe haven for the IRA. Its worries were magnified many times by the bomb attack on the Conservative Party Conference delegates at Brighton in 1984, which might have killed most of the Cabinet. The Anglo-Irish Agreement also reflected a frustration among British politicians at the lack of progress towards power-sharing in Northern Ireland. As Bew, Gibbon and Patterson have indicated, power sharing was never an *essential* part of British strategy in Northern Ireland.[1] It was, however, a *desired* option.

The lukewarm and ultimately ineffective attempt to revive power-sharing under Prior was never more than a tentative attempt at the restoration of the idea. Its predictable failure provided an opportunity for the British and Irish governments to impose an agreement over the heads of politicians in Northern Ireland. After the embarrassment of the apparent rebuff to the unitary island ideas of the New Ireland Forum, here was the chance for the Irish government to exert some influence within Northern Ireland, without, as Aughey notes, the burden of accepting responsibility.[2] The Anglo-Irish Agreement offered the prospect of increased support for the constitutional nationalism of the SDLP against the electoral Republicanism and cheerleading for armed struggle of an increasingly vibrant Sinn Féin. The SDLP role in levering Dublin influence in the North was thought likely to improve its electoral fortunes and ward off the danger of the increasing popularity of Sinn Féin.

Impervious to boycott, the Agreement enraged Unionists who had, after all, cooperated in the rolling devolution initiative. Registered at the United Nations, the Anglo-Irish Agreement emphasised that the future of Northern Ireland would be determined on a bilateral basis, with hopes of a return to Unionist rule, or even unfettered British sovereignty, undermined. The Agreement was indeed 'a more crushing end to Unionist ascendancy than the suspension of Stormont in 1972', in emphasising that 'Unionism without the Unionists' would be operated, while power-sharing remained unattainable.[3] Unionists complained that they had become powerless, since decisions would be taken by an Anglo-Irish Conference of Ministers from London and Dublin, established under Articles 2 and 3 of the Agreement. This intergovernmental Conference had a permanent Secretariat. Articles 5 to 10 of the Agreement offered the government of the Irish Republic representation in the areas of discrimination and rights; employment; policing and security matters: economic and social issues. Unionists were also incensed that nationalists had not been persuaded by the British government of the merits of British rule. Instead, the Agreement heralded the onset of the politics of identity which were to dominate Northern Ireland in the future. Article 4 offered the opportunity to the Dublin government to make proposals relating to the interests of the minority in Northern Ireland. The government of the Irish Republic had a new role as guarantor of the rights and traditions of Northern nationalists.

Nonetheless, the extent of Unionist hostility might be seen as surprising, given that Article 1 of the Agreement was a clear restatement of the consent principle, namely, that there could be no change in the constitutional status of Northern Ireland without the consent of the majority of its citizens. The balance-sheet for Unionists was hardly frightening: consultation with the Irish Republic on political issues; co-operation on reducing the terrorist threat; and continuity in terms of the constitutional position of Northern Ireland. According to one of its architects, the civil servant Sir David Goodall, the Anglo-Irish Agreement moved the British government 'a shade further towards accepting a united Ireland as an attainable rather than simply a conceivable goal'.[4] Critics saw the Agreement as a substantial shift in the balance of political forces away from Unionists.[5] The introduction of what was described as 'direct rule with a green tinge' indicated the

new vulnerability of local Unionists in a British-Irish intergovernmental political framework.[6] Anthony Kenny was justified, however,
in calling the Agreement minimalist, at least in its actual operation.[7]
The areas in which the Irish government could be consulted were extensive; what mattered, however, was the depth to which the potential for bi-nationalism was realised. Since 1972 the British government
had indicated its desire that future policy in Northern Ireland should
be acceptable to the Irish Republic. The Anglo-Irish Agreement implemented this desire, but did not represent a substantial shift towards joint sovereignty. Both governments agreed that no derogation
of British sovereignty was involved. Instead, the Agreement represented a rearrangement of British rule in Northern Ireland, designed
to give such governance a greater all-island and world legitimacy than
it had previously enjoyed. The major advantage for the Irish government was that it increased its influence in the North, without any obli-
gation to change its constitutional claim to the territory. In that
respect Unionists were right to be concerned, as the Anglo-Irish
Agreement addressed aspects of fundamental political concern to the
Dublin government without reciprocation for Unionists in respect of
their biggest irritation.

The importance of the SDLP analysis

The 1984 Forum Report reflected a constitutional nationalist consensus. It was a document that focused on an agreed analysis of the complexities of the Northern Ireland conflict. Its analysis was based
largely on SDLP outlines. The Report focused on the concerns of the
nationalist community in the Province and urged the British government to reassess its role in the conflict. Despite the initial dismissal of
its findings by Margaret Thatcher after the Anglo-Irish Summit at
Chequers in November 1984, the government based its talks with the
Irish government on the alienation theory developed in the Forum
Report, which, along with the pressing need of the British government for security cooperation against the IRA, led to the signing of
the Anglo-Irish Agreement one year later. The Agreement was the
first step in the political process to address the issue of nationalist
alienation in Northern Ireland. Before this the Irish dimension had
usually been dismissed by the British government, or regarded as un-
enforceable, with the obvious exception of government legislation in

1973, which had established the 1974 power-sharing government. After the collapse of the 1974 experiment, the government had, until 1985, reverted to efforts to resolve the conflict predominantly in the context of Northern Ireland.

The Anglo-Irish Agreement gave institutional approbation to the legitimacy of the nationalist identity in Northern Ireland. It signified the beginning of a process in which British government broadly accepted the SDLP thesis for resolving the Northern Ireland conflict, ideas outlined in the New Ireland Forum Report. The Agreement was an attempt by the government to deal with the concerns of the nationalist community in Northern Ireland. The agreement or accord dealt with three key areas of the SDLP analysis of the Northern Ireland conflict. First, it recognised that the Northern Ireland problem could not be resolved purely in Northern Ireland, but involved the British and Irish governments. Secondly, it clarified the responsibility of the two governments to act as referees for the implementation of power-sharing in any new devolved system of government in Northern Ireland. For the first time since Sunningdale, a Dublin-London axis was responsible for acquiring cross-community support for an internal system of government in Northern Ireland. Thirdly, it marked the end of British claims that issues concerning Northern Ireland were purely internal domestic affairs. The Anglo-Irish Agreement started the process which the SDLP had outlined for joint government action in Northern Ireland. It initiated joint action by the two governments to concentrate on the genesis of the conflict and to address the issue of nationalist grievances on an equal footing with that of their Unionist counterparts.

From the SDLP's viewpoint Paragraphs 4.15 and 4.16 of the Forum Report underpinned Dublin-London negotiations that led to the signing of the Anglo-Irish Agreement. These two paragraphs represented the cornerstone of two aspects of SDLP ideology in resolving the Northern Ireland problem. For the first time since 1920 the British government addressed SDLP demands that Britain needed to confront the legacies of the partisan role it had played in establishing the Northern Ireland state. Central demands for equality outlined by the SDLP were not requests to the government to remove unionist consent in Northern Ireland for a constitutional political settlement. What was required was for the government to tackle the underlying malaise at the core of the Northern Ireland conflict. This could only be addressed by understanding the undemocratic and myopic nature of the 1920 partition. The SDLP argued consistently that structures and institutions in Northern Ireland were based only on the identity and ethos of the Unionist tradition. Therefore the framework for finding political consensus in Northern Ireland required the government to acknowledge the existence of another tradition in the Province, with a different identity and sense of allegiance from its Unionist counterpart. Hence the Anglo-Irish Agreement was basically the first step in acknowledging this actuality as set out in paragraph of 4.15 of the New Ireland Forum Report: 'The starting point of genuine reconciliation and dialogue is mutual recognition and acceptance of the legitimate rights of unionists and nationalists.'

Paragraph 4.16 of the Forum Report expressed the persistent SDLP argument that equality was impossible for nationalists in the Province because of Unionist intransigence. To obtain equality for nationalists in Northern Ireland, which was the main reason for the formation of the SDLP, negotiations could only take place beyond the remit of purely internal political dialogues. The wider framework for power-sharing or equality which the SDLP recurrently broached needed to be implemented in Northern Ireland by a London and Dublin alliance. Paragraph 4.16 of the Forum Report explained the SDLP position: 'A settlement which recognises the legitimate rights of nationalists and unionists must transcend the context of Northern Ireland. Both London and Dublin have a responsibility to respond to the continuing suffering of the people of Northern Ireland.' In the Anglo-Irish Agreement the British government set out the key SDLP principles of a wider framework than Northern Ireland. Joint British and Irish government became the basis for moving the political process forward to resolve retracted problems. The Anglo-Irish Agreement, founded on SDLP premises, articulated a coherent appraisal of the central issues at the core of the Northern Ireland conflict. The Agreement gave formal recognition from the two governments to the SDLP analysis for the creation of a viable scheme for resolving the conflict.

The impact of SDLP ideology on the two governments' involvement in Northern Ireland is evident through the creation of the 1985 accord. The threads of the SDLP political initiatives can be traced to the reappraisal of SDLP strategy in 1979 (as set out in Paragraph 5.5).

By 1979 the party believed that the two governments had to create the necessary mechanism for political progress to take place. This analysis was based on the evidence that Unionists remained intransigent after the collapse of Sunningdale in 1974. Such evidence was reflected in their continued opposition both to a power-sharing government with nationalists and to the formal recognition of an Irish dimension in Northern Ireland. In order for the two governments to obtain a framework that accommodated the intricacies of the Northern Ireland conflict, the SDLP argued in 1979 that, if necessary, negotiations between the two governments would have to take place over the heads of the Northern Ireland political parties. This was a fundamental concept behind SDLP advocacy of an Anglo-Irish dimension to resolve the conflict during 1979. Less than six years later the concept was adopted by the two governments in the negotiations leading to the Anglo-Irish Agreement in November 1985.[8]

SDLP gains

During negotiations between the two governments in 1985 that led to the signing of the Anglo-Irish Agreement, SDLP leader John Hume was notified of developments by the Taoiseach in Dublin at that time, Garret FitzGerald. Consequently, when the accord was signed at Hillsborough on 15 November 1985, SDLP politicians were not surprised by its contents, unlike members of the Unionist community. Set against Margaret Thatcher's initial 'Out, out, out' reaction to the New Ireland Forum Report in November 1984, the Anglo-Irish Agreement was a triumph for the SDLP. Unionists believed that the Prime Minister was sympathetic to their position, never conceiving she would negotiate a deal with Dublin over their heads. The former Northern Ireland Secretary of State, James Prior, recalled this position when he wrote: 'She more than any other British politician was trusted by the Unionists as being rock-solid on Northern Ireland's position within the United Kingdom.'[9]

For the SDLP the Anglo-Irish Agreement was a political framework devised by the British government that demonstrated a proper grasp of the complexities of the Northern Ireland conflict. The SDLP considered the accord arose from the alienation thesis, which it had illuminated in the New Ireland Forum Report. In particular the SDLP believed the accord showed a significant reassessment of strategy by the government. It removed the guarantee to the unionist tradition whereby traditionally progress did not take place without Unionist authorisation. The Agreement offered a suitable framework for conflict resolution for the first time since the partition of Ireland in 1920, and referred to the legitimate rights of two traditions in Northern Ireland.

The SDLP also felt the Anglo-Irish Agreement ended a Unionist 'veto' on political developments. With the Agreement in place the SDLP believed that unionist privilege in Northern Ireland enjoyed for over fifty years was finally over. Political progress could now take place in Northern Ireland on even terms under the supervision of both governments, which ensured equality, in principle, for the first time for both traditions in the Province. The Anglo-Irish Agreement was a public admission that the Northern Ireland conflict could not be resolved within the parameters of a British framework, or on unionist terms, as such attempts had failed in the past.

The new intergovernmental approach was simply the fruition of the earliest position set out by the SDLP that Irish unity in the traditional sense was an impractical reality. The original aim of the SDLP in 1970 was, like the former NDP, to attain primarily equality for the nationalist community in Northern Ireland, with the practical realism that agreement between the two traditions had to take place before the issue of Irish unity could be addressed. The SDLP thesis for the resolution of the Northern Ireland conflict was one that had repeatedly argued for a necessary political framework to end the division of the people on the whole island of Ireland, and the implementation of equality in Northern Ireland. The Anglo-Irish Agreement endorsed the earliest arguments of the SDLP that there was no immediate resolution of the Northern Ireland conflict. The SDLP believed the agreement moved towards its aim to establish unity and equality in a framework conferred by the British and Irish governments as appropriate means to resolve the Northern Ireland conflict. Article 4 (a) (1) of the Anglo-Irish Agreement presented the formulas for equality, which, according to the SDLP, aligned the nationalist tradition with the unionist. It stated that the 'United Kingdom Government and the Irish Government' would work through the Intergovernmental Conference 'for the accommodation of the rights and identities of the two traditions which exist in Northern Ireland'.

The SDLP view of a power-sharing principle was endorsed in Article 4 (c) of the agreement and stated: 'Both Governments recognise that devolution can be achieved only with the co-operation of constitutional representatives within Northern Ireland of both traditions there.' The SDLP did not see the Anglo-Irish Agreement as a final solution to the Northern Ireland conflict, but rather as the identification of necessary mechanisms for real reconciliation based on equality to take place. The party was stronger in outlining methods of addressing conflict issues than in providing an outline of the 'endgame'. The Agreement gave legitimacy to a sense of Irishness in the minority community and, from the SDLP perspective, denoted maturity in the British government perception of the minority community.

At an international level the Anglo-Irish Agreement was a coup for the SDLP largely because of the diplomatic efforts of John Hume. Hume, with the assistance of Irish officials since 1977, had taken the Northern Ireland problem beyond the domestic forum of UK politics to the international arena, and gained support from his close friendship with Seán Donlon. As former Irish Ambassador in the United States, Donlon used his political influence to persuade Ronald Reagan to place some external pressure on Margaret Thatcher to reconsider her position, following her infamous dismissal of the New Ireland Forum Report in November 1984. Once the Agreement was fully operational, the American administration became economically involved in the Northern Ireland conflict by contributing to the International Fund to support areas of deprivation in Northern Ireland. American economic aid in Northern Ireland can be traced to the successful efforts of John Hume in 1977 to request President Jimmy Carter to promise American financial assistance in the event of a major political settlement.

By the end of 1986 the SDLP saw a number of practical results from the Secretariat at Maryfield, outside Belfast, created under the auspices of the Anglo-Irish Agreement. The Anglo-Irish Secretariat gave the Irish government assistance in matters pertaining to British policy in Northern Ireland and in particular on issues that directly affected the nationalist community in Northern Ireland. The demolition of run-down housing schemes in nationalist areas such as the Divis Flats in Belfast and the Rossville Flats in Derry were practical examples of the impact of the Agreement in nationalist areas of

Northern Ireland. The Secretariat was also behind the repeal of the Flags and Emblems Acts, under which displays of the Irish tricolour had been prohibited. Permission was also given for Irish place names on public notices in nationalist areas of the Province. The Secretariat sought increased representation of Catholics in public bodies. Fair employment measures were also set in motion by the Anglo-Irish Secretariat.[10]

The Anglo-Irish Agreement was the first step in SDLP long-term strategies directed to evolving policies for an 'agreed' Ireland. The greatest net gain for the SDLP from the implementation of the Anglo-Irish Agreement was the removal of the Unionist veto, in terms of internal political arrangements, though not the constitutional position of Northern Ireland. Equality between the two traditions in Northern Ireland became feasible, as a result of the Anglo-Irish framework advocated by the SDLP to resolve the conflict since 1979. The SDLP also believed that the Agreement addressed the means for solving the conflict with reference to the three key dimensions of the dispute. These dimensions related, first, to the two communities in Northern Ireland, secondly to the relationship between North and South, and thirdly to connections between the Republic of Ireland and Britain. John Hume trusted that the Agreement would dismiss the justification for violence and believed that the basis of equality for both traditions in Northern Ireland had been established. Hume argued that the Anglo-Irish Agreement was 'not a solution' and noted, 'This Agreement is only an opportunity.'[11]

SDLP disappointments

Initially the Anglo-Irish Agreement was seen as a masterstroke for the SDLP because the Irish government had obtained a consultative role in Northern Ireland affairs. Constitutional nationalism was now 'joined up' North and South and thus seen as a stronger source of remedy to the sense of alienation felt by Northern nationalists. The Irish government took a role as guardians to look after the interests of the minority community in Northern Ireland. Also, in practical terms this meant the Irish government would scrutinise any new proposals for devolution in Northern Ireland and would make sure such proposals met the SDLP criteria for power-sharing. The SDLP believed that initial Unionist opposition to the accord would diminish once opponents realised that devolution was still a realistic option for Northern Ireland.

However, as Article 4, sections (b) and (c) of the accord set out, devolution in principle meant embracing the SDLP concept of 'partnership government' in Northern Ireland and these terms meant power sharing. The SDLP was genuinely disappointed at the level of opposition demonstrated by Unionists between 1986 and 1989 following the introduction of the accord. Attempts to make local government in Northern Ireland inoperable and the Unionist refusal to meet government ministers were lessons for the SDLP that little had changed since Loyalists brought down the 1974 power-sharing government.

It is useful to refer to Section 5.2 (7) of the New Ireland Forum Report to demonstrate the difference between SDLP proposals and the actual failure of the Intergovernmental Conference to achieve its agenda for equality in real terms. Section 5.2 (7) stated: 'New arrangements must provide structures and institutions including security structures with which both nationalists and Unionists can identify on the basis of political consensus; such arrangements must overcome alienation in Northern Ireland and strengthen stability and security for all the people of Ireland.' For the SDLP the accord failed to address 'security', 'legal matters' and 'the administration of justice'.[12] Because the proposals were not fully implemented, the continuing claim of Sinn Féin that Northern Ireland was 'irreformable' retained its salience.

Hume acknowledged at the 1986 SDLP Annual Conference that there was 'disappointment about lack of movement in the crucial area of the administration of justice and in particular the Diplock Courts'.[13] The British government rejected Irish government proposals for a three-judge court, suggesting that the Irish government's role in Northern Ireland was purely consultative. Another major disappointment for the SDLP was the lack of reform of the RUC. Peter Barry, then Irish Foreign Affairs Minister, had been involved in the negotiations leading to the signing of the Anglo-Irish Agreement. He called on Northern nationalists to join the RUC. However, Irish government proposals for the 'restructuring of the police, involving separate units, divisions or forces for such areas as Derry and Belfast' were not implemented.[14] In 1986 the former Deputy Chief Constable of Manchester, John Stalker, was inexplicably removed from the 'Shoot-to-kill' inquiry, concerning the deaths of six men shot by the RUC in 1982. The controversy led to calls from within the SDLP for the resignation of the head of the RUC, Sir John Hermon.[15] Partly owing to the Stalker affair and to the inability of the Irish government to bring about any visible signs of impartial policing in Northern Ireland, the SDLP felt that the Anglo-Irish Agreement did not fulfil its remit. The SDLP, in line with the broader nationalist family, believed that when Stalker was removed from the inquiry this was a deliberate move by the RUC to prevent him from making full exposure, as he neared the truth.

Additionally, by the end of the 1980s, the Anglo-Irish Agreement had not brought forward any proposals for reforming the Diplock Courts, courts that had no juries. Criminal law in Northern Ireland continued to operate in the framework of emergency legislation. This framework was totally opposed by the SDLP and by the broader nationalist community in Northern Ireland. The SDLP pressed the government to change the Diplock Court system and the Irish government in the Anglo-Irish Conference also pressed for the replacement of the one-judge Diplock Courts with three-man tribunals.[16] However it was clear that the government was not going to act. Overall, SDLP confidence in the administration of justice in Northern Ireland did not improve after the Anglo-Irish Agreement was signed.

The SDLP was also disappointed at the reaction of Charles Haughey and the Fianna Fáil party to the Anglo-Irish Agreement. As opposition leader, Haughey claimed the accord hindered rather than helped the nationalist cause. Fianna Fáil opposed the Anglo-Irish Agreement on the grounds that Article 1 recognised the state of Northern Ireland and enshrined partition. The party forced a close vote in the Dáil Éireann on whether to ratify the agreement. Indeed the vote in favour in the Dáil (88–75) was much narrower than in the United Kingdom Parliament (473–47). Haughey softened his opposition as it became apparent that the Anglo-Irish Agreement was popular with the Irish electorate. Nonetheless, it was claimed that the change to a Fianna Fáil government in 1987 led to 'under-utilisation of the agreement' and that its attitude contrasted with that of the previous Fine Gael/Labour administration.[17] This owed something to Haughey's resentment at having to support FitzGerald's crowning political glory.

On balance, SDLP disappointments were outweighed by the overall optimism in the party over the accord. As Hume explained at the

SDLP 1987 Annual Conference, the party appraised the Anglo-Irish Agreement on two separate counts. At one level the accord focused on the daily grievances of nationalists in Northern Ireland. Yet on a more important level, it addressed the core of the problem that caused 'the deep divisions' that existed in Northern Ireland society.[18] From the SDLP viewpoint the Anglo-Irish Agreement still provided a framework for equality.

By the end of the 1980s the provisions of the Agreement were far from establishing equality in Northern Ireland. Nevertheless, the Agreement remained a potentially feasible framework for desired reform. Whatever the practical shortcomings of the Agreement for delivering complete solutions to Northern Ireland, and the criticisms from unionists and Sinn Féin, the SDLP never viewed the accord as a 'final settlement' or an 'immediate solution'.[19] At the 1985 SDLP Annual Conference, held a week before the signing of the Anglo-Irish Agreement, Hume asked: 'Will the proposals which emerge from an Agreement if there is an Agreement, help us to make progress with the healing process?'[20] The eventual answer was 'yes'. Combined with a shoring of the SDLP's electoral support, the Anglo-Irish Agreement represented a good deal for the SDLP.

Sinn Féin's double-edged response

The basis of the Anglo-Irish Agreement did not surprise Sinn Féin. An internal party conference in early September 1985 discussed the measures likely to be included in such an Agreement.[21] The party feared it might be banned from contesting elections in the North, or would be obliged to sign anti-IRA election pledges. At this point, the British government had not clearly thought through the advantages of making Republicans go 'political' and preferred to defeat both wings of the movement. With prescience, Sinn Féin anticipated that the Irish government's (Section 31) broadcasting ban on their party would be imitated by the British government. The party did not, however, develop effective counter-measures. Sinn Féin also anticipated that the Anglo-Irish Agreement would be financed by US money and would bolster the fortunes of the SDLP.

A detailed response to the Anglo-Irish Agreement by Sinn Féin indicated the depth of concern in the party over the anti-Republican agenda in the accord. Sinn Féin needed to react carefully, given the popularity of the Agreement in Ireland. With the Irish press enthusiastically praising the terms and concessions of the Agreement, Sinn Féin was aware that it would be difficult to win any propaganda battle over its value. A further potential complication to the propaganda war was that the Agreement was roundly opposed by Loyalists, but Sinn Féin could afford to be dismissive of 'Loyalist hysteria at the most inconsequential change'.[22] More problematic was deciding the Sinn Féin line among its own potential electorate, on an Agreement that most nationalists accepted and which contained some changes in their favour. Sinn Féin directed its main criticism to the partitionist basis of the Agreement. The party also stressed its counter-insurgency measures and also pointed to the inadequacy of concessions to constitutional nationalists.

The basic acceptance of partition in the Agreement was clear, as the legitimacy of the Northern state was unquestioned in Article 1. Nonetheless the Irish courts concluded that if the Irish government accepted that Northern Ireland was part of the United Kingdom, this was a mere acknowledgement of the *de facto* reality of the balance of political forces in the North, rather than *de jure* concession of the position. As such, the constitutional imperative for unity, outlined in Articles 2 and 3 of the Constitution of the Republic, remained undiminished. As to consolidated security arrangements, Sinn Féin argued that the Conservative Party right wing had been influential in its October 1984 report, *Britain's Undefended Frontier: a Policy for Ulster*, which had been commissioned by the Institute for European Defence and Strategic Studies.[23] Much of the report had indeed been woven into British policy. It stressed the need for British-Irish unity in defeating terrorism and cited approvingly the common action taken against the 1956–62 Border Campaign. The report recognised that the main measure during that era, the internment of suspects, would encounter greater political difficulties. What was needed, therefore, was easier extradition of suspects from the Irish Republic. The British government was anxious to ensure that IRA personnel suspected of offences in England would face trial in British courts, where, if convicted, they would face long prison sentences. Political concessions to the SDLP and an institutional role for the Dublin government in Northern Ireland would be the selling points to nationalists.

Privately senior figures within Sinn Féin endorsed aspects of the Agreement. The implementation of the Agreement was a significant indicator of the willingness of the British government to confront Loyalists. This point was not lost on Mitchell McLaughlin, an increasingly influential figure in Sinn Féin and later Party chairman. He offered a much more sanguine view of the Agreement than that indicated by the public posture of his party, and noted, 'There is a negative counter-insurgency dimension to it, but in fact as a result of it the British Government position has changed and changed irrevocably. They have actually indicated, in terms of historical perspective that they can be moved along.'[24]

McLaughlin insisted that he wrote an internal paper outlining the benefits of the Anglo-Irish Agreement mainly to 'be provocative' and to prompt debate within Sinn Féin.[25] Furthermore, other prominent members of Sinn Féin saw scant merit in the Agreement, even with hindsight. Pat Doherty, later vice-chair of the Party, dismissed the accord as 'containing two elements; counter-insurgency and a rescue package for the SDLP'.[26] Micheál McDonnacha, editor of *An Phoblacht/Republican News* for part of this era, acknowledged that the Agreement was sometimes difficult to counter in propaganda terms, but insisted that 'increased repression against republicans was evident in the south' and maintained that 'material benefits to northern nationalists were negligible'.[27] Nonetheless, other members of Sinn Féin acknowledged that constitutional nationalists benefited from the Agreement. Danny Morrison was anxious that republicans be given credit, claiming that 'SDLP bartering power flows from IRA firepower'.[28] Gerry Adams adopted a slightly different argument, noting that the concessions to Northern nationalists were a consequence of the growing political strength of Republicans. Adams insisted that 'more support for Sinn Féin alarms the British Government and forces them to make concessions'.[29] Whatever its criticism of the SDLP role in brokering the Anglo-Irish Agreement, the Sinn Féin leadership offered the SDLP an 'anti-unionist unity' election pact in the by-elections prompted by the resignations of Unionist MPs at Westminster in protest against the Agreement.[30] The SDLP declined the offer and preferred to examine the extent of its new electoral benefits.

A primary motivation of the Agreement was the 'furtherance of an anti-Republican consensus'.[31] This was reflected in the creation of better cross-border security cooperation and alterations to constitutional politics. The Agreement could not be seen as a triumph for constitutional nationalism, if nationalism was defined as the pursuit of a united, independent national territory. The real meaning of the Anglo-Irish Agreement was made clear by the British Secretary of State, Tom King, in December 1985. King explained that it indicated the Irish government acceptance that 'for all practical purposes there will never be a united Ireland'.[32] His comment was criticised by an embarrassed Dublin government. The aim of the Agreement, according to King, was a 'united front against gunmen', Britain's favoured form of pan-nationalism.[33] The Agreement offered, via a carrot-and-stick approach, the prospect of power-sharing to Unionists, in what was labelled coercive consociationalism.[34] Without power-sharing the Agreement would remain in place for an indefinite period.

The balance-sheet for nationalists

The Anglo-Irish Agreement acted as a considerable influence upon the political thinking of republicans. Sinn Féin made a relatively careful, if somewhat cynical, assessment of the document, arguing that 'cosmetic internal reform and a powerless consultative role would be offered to Dublin and [to] the SDLP in return for their active assistance in creating political stability in the Six Counties'.[35] In these respects there was nothing new in the policies of the British government. Furthermore, Republicans made clear that the war would go on, despite the fears of increased repression, Martin McGuinness using the 1986 Bodenstown Wolfe Tone Commemoration Speech to warn republicans (erroneously) that internment might be revived.

Republicans faced an Agreement that was more difficult to confront than Sunningdale. Ultimately, the Agreement could bring neither peace nor a solution, given that it simply ignored the main actors in the conflict, Republicans and Loyalists. To treat such actors merely as security problems indicated the limited strategic visions on offer at the time among both governments. Highlighting the anti-Republican agenda of the Agreement was easy for Republicans. What was required, however, was a more sophisticated response to an Agreement which at least acknowledged, to various degrees, the dual British-Irish nature of the problem, the aspiration for Irish unity and the rights of Northern nationalists. The Thatcher government offered some hope to constitutional Northern nationalists in its willingness to confront Loyalist protests. However much Sinn Féin might urge Republicans to ignore Unionist claims of betrayal, the sheer size of the protests, including a 200,000 strong 'Ulster Says No' demonstration in November 1985, could not fail to impact upon the nationalist population. Republicans were also confronted by the popularity of the Agreement among many nationalists. According to one poll almost one third of Sinn Féin voters claimed to support the Agreement.[36] Gerry Adams, notwithstanding his numerous criticisms of the Agreement, agreed that it had some potential and argued, 'Of course concessions, even if made for the wrong reasons, are good. They show that the Establishment can be moved.'[37] Furthermore, Sinn Féin reluctantly conceded the point that the Agreement showed the Dublin government might be able to lever some influence in the North if it was able to engage in bilateral negotiations without 'interference' from Unionists.

It would be an exaggeration to claim that the Anglo-Irish Agreement created the prospect of a pan-nationalist alliance of the Dublin government, the SDLP and Sinn Féin. Changes were already taking place in Sinn Féin by the mid-1980s, alongside private peace initiatives, undertaken by Gerry Adams, which would inevitably bring the party into closer contact with other political parties and institutions, North and South. The practice of Sinn Féin abstention was already being criticised internally, in respect of the Dáil Éireann. The Agreement hastened the process by which Sinn Féin would abandon its political isolation. It engaged the party in a process in which it needed to seek common cause with the remainder of nationalist Ireland and ultimately made Sinn Féin tactically astute in the development of political allies. Many in the SDLP and, unsurprisingly, all of Sinn Féin opposed any return to Stormont now that the Anglo-Irish Agreement offered an alternative to unionist hegemony. Given the strength and unity of this proposition, Republicans could at least console themselves that any influence Dublin took in Northern affairs after 1985 would not immediately be aimed at a restoration of the Northern parliament. Instead, it might be channelled more fruitfully to achieve gains for nationalists on human rights or cultural issues.

Some Republicans still believed that influence was maximised through the maintenance of armed struggle, although Republican violence was conducted at a relatively low level around the time of the Anglo-Irish Agreement. The Sinn Féin leadership realised that without political shifts it would not be able to claim the credit for any move towards all-island political arrangements. This modernisation could only be achieved by offering a relevant programme to the public. The Anglo-Irish Agreement merely confirmed the need for Sinn Féin to bolster its political strength. The maintenance of appeals to the politics of 1916–18 was made even more irrelevant. In a speech at Bodenstown, Martin McGuinness criticised the 'element of romanticism within our ranks that, while not consciously defeatist, continues to look at the past for legitimacy'.[38]

The Republican leadership also wished to diminish the perceived threat to the South from the movement. This was partly tactical, given the fears of increased counter-insurgency, but also because of the dated feel to opposition to a twenty-six-county Republic which was clearly accepted by the overwhelming majority of its citizens. The IRA had increased its arms supply significantly via its Libyan supply line.[39] Its problem was finding sufficient volunteers on either side of the border. Sinn Féin had been contemptuous of British claims that Republicans wished to set up an 'offshore Cuba'. After 1985, republicans emphasised that there remained no threat to the South. This was achieved not merely by the reiteration of a Standing Order forbidding action against 'Free State' forces. Gradually, Sinn Féin jettisoned the left-wing agenda it had adopted without conviction in the late 1970s and early 1980s.[40] Gerry Adams had always rejected the idea that Sinn Féin was a Marxist organisation. In 1979, he declared; 'There is no Marxist influence within Sinn Féin. I know of no one in Sinn Féin who is a Marxist or who would be influenced by Marxism.'[41] Beyond 1985, as Sinn Féin quietly moved away from even verbal commitments to revolutionary socialism, the party's political agenda became greener, designed to appeal to mainstream nationalists more concerned over their rights in the North than any grander political project. This creeping moderation had the potential to gain votes from the SDLP. In the South the aim was, initially, to emphasise the unthreatening nature of the Republican agenda to the Irish government and, in the long term, to achieve more credible poll results. Developments in the party gathered pace as the Anglo-Irish Agreement encouraged greater political thinking concerning its internal problems; the diminishing enthusiasm for perpetual armed struggle; the perennial lack of support for socialism among the electorate, and the hamstrung nature of Sinn Féin's electoral tactics, still tied to abstention from constitutional roles.

9

REPUBLICAN REAPPRAISAL
THE INITIATIVES OF GERRY ADAMS

Electoral gains and plateaus

After the hunger strikes Sinn Féin developed political strength in the North, but failed abysmally in the South. The 1982 Northern Ireland Assembly elections saw Sinn Féin trailing the SDLP by nearly 9 per cent. The result was a reasonable one for Sinn Féin, although the party found itself fighting an SDLP increasingly green in political direction, following its criticisms of Prior's rolling devolution. Both parties fought the election on abstentionist platforms. This made the IRA's 1983 Easter Statement that 'Sinn Féin's victory stopped the SDLP from entering and propping up the assembly' curious, given that there was no such victory and the SDLP had been no keener than Sinn Féin to waste political energy on a futile Assembly.[1] Meanwhile in the South, Charles Haughey led Fianna Fáil into one of its periodic phases of more strident nationalism, criticising the failure of British rule in Northern Ireland.[2] These criticisms paved the way for the development of the New Ireland Forum, under which constitutional nationalist parties throughout the island attempted to develop a nationalist consensus.

In March 1983 a by-election victory gave Sinn Féin its first seat on a local council in the North since the 1920s. Later that year Alex Maskey became Sinn Féin's first Belfast councillor. Maskey, who became the city's mayor almost two decades later, described his tasks as exposing sectarianism, participating in committees and increasing the accessibility of local services.[3] The gap between the SDLP and Sinn Féin vote was halved in the Westminster general election of 1983. Sinn Féin polled over 100,000 votes, with Gerry Adams capturing the SDLP's West Belfast seat. Adams' victory represented a triumph for

153

the new politics of Sinn Féin. The party's community work, notably its emphasis upon local support for the unemployed, provided the basis for success more than any switch from federalism to 'decentralised socialism', or Sinn Féin's support for 'armed struggle'. Even controversial acts in the months before the election, such as the IRA's assassination of the Catholic judge William Doyle as he left Sunday mass in January 1983, appeared to have scant detrimental effect on Sinn Féin's core vote. Such actions were eventually to place a ceiling upon Sinn Féin's rise, but this could not be forecast with certainty in 1983. All Republicans could celebrate the fillip provided by electoral success. Even those supposedly suspicious of creeping politicisation devoted much attention to social and economic concerns. Such issues dominated Ruárí Ó Brádaigh's presidential address to the 1982 Ard Fheis.[4] Furthermore, Ó Brádaigh appeared keen to harness the potential of electoral politics. Flushed by the 1983 Westminster election success, he rashly predicted that 'in the 1985 local council elections in the six counties Sinn Féin will finally overtake the SDLP and nationalist politics will undergo their most radical and significant change since 1918'.[5] Apparently renewed mandates were of great significance.

By 1984 there were signs that the rapid rise in support for Sinn Féin in the North might be slowing, although too much extrapolation from the PR-STV single constituency European election appeared unwise. With each party fielding a single candidate, John Hume was always likely to deliver the bulk of the nationalist vote to the SDLP. Hume polled 60,000 votes more than Sinn Féin's Danny Morrison. Sinn Féin's vote, while respectable, was largely confined to its working-class core constituency. During the previous year, Martin McGuinness had claimed that the elections offered 'the best opportunity ever to beat the SDLP'.[6] Sinn Féin remained hostile to the EEC, although Republican delegations, when meeting the EEC Commissioner for Northern Ireland, demanded that more money should be allocated to North and West Belfast.[7] The contradictions of the Republican 'economic warfare' campaign were already exposed. From the outset of the electoral strategy, there were fears over the impact of IRA violence upon Sinn Féin's performance. Adams stressed that armed struggle was a 'necessary and morally correct form of resistance'.[8] Meanwhile, he urged the IRA to 'continue to refine its operations', to prevent 'any conflict between what we're doing and what they're doing'.[9]

After the local elections of May 1985, Sinn Féin had representatives on seventeen of Northern Ireland's twenty-six district councils, holding a total of fifty-nine seats, having achieved almost 12 per cent of the total vote and one-third of the votes of Northern Ireland's Catholics. Only thirty-nine seats were won in the Republic, where the national organiser, Caoimhghín Ó Caoláin, told an internal party conference in September 1985 that in many areas Sinn Féin did not function or exist.[10] A combination of factors explained the deficiency: the link to political violence; poor organisation; the impact of the Section 31 broadcasting ban on Sinn Féin, and the perception of the party as an organisation concerned exclusively with the North. Redress was more difficult than analysis and Sinn Féin did not become a registered political party in the Republic until January 1987. Adams' early insistence upon use of the term 'socialist republican' to distinguish Sinn Féin's creed from Fianna Fáil's Republicanism was hardly likely to inspire the conservative electorate.[11] In the general election in the Republic early in 1987, Sinn Féin achieved a dismal 2 per cent of the vote. Even the cautious director of elections had predicted the party might achieve between 3 and 5 per cent of the vote.[12]

In the North, however, Sinn Féin performed well, beyond even the leadership's expectations. By the mid-1980s, the Party held more seats than the SDLP (seven to six) on Belfast City Council. Sinn Féin offered a different type of councillor from the middle-aged and, often, middle-class individuals normally serving as elected representatives. A large number had been active within the IRA (a few remained so). One quarter of Sinn Féin's election candidates were aged under thirty.[13] The proof that militant Republicanism had support was more important than what could be achieved on largely powerless local councils, the weakest in Western Europe. The dismal sectarianism which passed for political life, most especially but by no means exclusively on Belfast City Council, achieved little. The suspension of business by many Unionist-controlled councils after the Anglo-Irish Agreement served only to emphasise the insignificance of these bodies. More worrying than the Unionists' self-inflicted wounds was the prospect of the Agreement damaging Sinn Féin's vote by bolstering the electoral fortunes of the SDLP. In the Westminster by-elections of January 1986, prompted by the resignations of Unionist MPs, the SDLP decided to contest four constituencies. Its offer of an electoral pact rebuffed, Sinn Féin decided to fight the SDLP in each of these seats. Sinn Féin's vote fell by over 18,000 across the constituencies, whilst the SDLP vote rose by over 11,000, compared to the 1983 Westminster general election.[14] The impression of an SDLP resurgence was heightened by the party's capture of Newry and Armagh from the Ulster Unionist Party. The rise of Sinn Féin's vote, seen as inevitable only two years earlier, appeared to have been halted. This stalling preceded the Anglo-Irish Agreement. Nonetheless, the firming of the SDLP vote following the Agreement indicated that Sinn Féin still needed to change its political approach if it was to move out from its solid core of voters. For party strategists, the best hope of doing that was to engage in meaningful dialogue with its nationalist rival.

Goodbye fundamentalism, hello pragmatism: the end of abstentionism

Although the peace process did not fully emerge until the 1990s, an early important element in its development was Sinn Féin's decision to end abstentionism in respect of the Dáil Éireann in November 1986. The party had been engaged in vociferous internal debate throughout the year. Supporters of change criticised opponents for their use of labels such as 'Stickyism', 'De Valeraism' and 'creeping reformism', and attacked the 'self-righteous' and 'holier than thou' attitude of those for whom abstentionism remained a core principle.[15] There were two core themes to the anti-abstention argument. One emphasised the pragmatic electoral value of the lifting of the prohibition. The other concerned the historical role of abstentionism, with supporters of participation insistent that abstention had never been more than a tactic, erroneously elevated to a principle. Opponents of change failed to counter the electoral value argument. They preferred to argue on historical points, relying upon the old adage that the system changes revolutionary parties far more than vice versa. The example of the Officials, or 'Sticks', was freely cited. The historical turning point in their development, the end of abstentionism, offered an uncomfortable precedent, given that, as the most eloquent correspondent of *An Phoblacht/Republican News* noted, 'Their organisation contained men and women, who in their day risked everything for the republican cause.'[16] At their most extreme, opponents of change called for the expulsion of advocates of any dilution of abstentionism.[17]

The decision to end abstentionism signified the end of republican purism, based upon loyalty to the Second Dáil. Although the move produced few defectors, it removed some dissidents from the organisation, casting them into the political wilderness. The end of abstentionism acted as recognition of a reality already apparent to all outside Sinn Féin, that the people of the twenty-six counties had accepted their nation state. Above all, it indicated that Sinn Féin was a party with which other nationalists could do business. Mark Ryan argues that Republicanism from this point onwards lost its distinctiveness.[18] However, the IRA's ongoing military campaign meant that Sinn Féin could still not be regarded as just another anti-system party.

The 1986 decision did mark a decisive step on the road to conventional parliamentary politics. The movement towards change had been in the offing for some time. Gerry Adams dropped a broad hint in his Bodenstown oration of 1983, arguing that the people of the twenty-six counties accepted state institutions as legitimate. Failure to accept this was to 'blinker republican politics'.[19] This attitude was toned down marginally at the time of Adams' election as Sinn Féin president later that year. In respect of abstentionism, Adams declared—falsely—in his inaugural presidential address that 'it is not my intention to advocate a change in this situation', although he also stressed that 'emphasis needs to be upon the 26 counties'.[20] It was certainly Adams' intention to allow others to raise the questions of abstentionism, but he recognised the balance of forces within Sinn Féin was not yet in his favour. As late as 1985 Adams studiously ignored the abstentionism issue in his presidential address to the Ard Fheis. Yet in 1987, after change had occurred, Adams insisted that he was 'sorry that abstentionism wasn't dropped years ago'.[21] Despite Adams' initial caution, the 1983 Ard Fheis indicated that the tide was turning. A motion from the Galway Comhairle Ceantair seeking to reaffirm the ban on discussion of abstentionism was defeated by 180 votes to 140. A motion that 'no aspect of the constitution and rules be closed to discussion' was passed by 208 votes to 98. The Ard Fheis also decided that the 1984 European election would not be fought on an abstentionist basis. To propose abstentionism in respect of that election would be 'madness', declared Martin McGuinness.[22] The prohibition extended only to Westminster, Stormont and Leinster House elections.

Adams and McGuinness were obliged to move cautiously, as there remained some elements within the movement suspicious of the entire election strategy. A letter to the republican press accused Sinn Féin of 'being struck down with election fever'.[23] Seán Crowe, one of the 'new breed' of Sinn Féin members with no previous connections to the PIRA, a type which Sinn Féin still found difficult to recruit, offered a sharp riposte:

> The electoral strategy, if used correctly, can break our self-imposed isolation, expand our base of support, give people a real alternative to the corrupt establishment parties, encourage our supporters, help assess our membership's commitment, recruit new members and so on.... We've had enough whinging.[24]

Crowe's comments were also important in belying the idea that the ending of abstention was driven solely by 'Northerners'. The Dublin-based member believed that it was possible to achieve electoral support through social agitation in urban areas and that abstention denied supporters in these areas the prospect of representation. The 1985 Ard Fheis rejected a motion that abstentionism was to be regarded as a principle rather than a tactic. However, the removal of abstentionism as a principle (asserted in rules 1 and 5 of the party's constitution) required a two-thirds majority. At the 1985 Ard Fheis, the leadership declined to show its hand on the crucial motion 187. The end of the policy was widely trailed in the Republican press prior to the 1986 Ard Fheis. The decision to end abstention, taken by a very substantial majority at that gathering in November, was inevitable after the IRA, having held a rare General Army Convention, declared itself in favour of ending abstention during the previous month. The Convention removed the ban on IRA members discussing or advocating the taking of parliamentary seats and lifted the prohibition on supporting successful Republican candidates taking seats in Leinster House.[25] The IRA's decision effectively clinched the debate in favour of Sinn Féin's modernisers, whatever the assertions in the Republican press that the following month's Ard Fheis vote was 'not a foregone conclusion'.[26]

The policy of abstentionism was seen as outdated and devoid of contemporary relevance. The senior Republican Jim Gibney was forceful in his dismissal:[27] 'The idea that in 1986 you could put on the mantle of Republicanism and say that we do not recognise Leinster House because it emerged from the Treaty is not a credible position. Not only is it not credible, you cannot build a political party without recognising and accepting the institutions of that state.' Gibney's arguments had implications for the development of Sinn Féin in the North. Modernisers could also argue that so-called 'principles' had never been more than tactics in the struggle. During the Dáil Éireann abstention debate, it was pointed out in the vigorous correspondence on the abstentionism debate in *An Phoblacht/Republican News* that 'at one time, Republicans wouldn't even send their children to Free State schools or recognise Free State courts', but that a more realistic perspective was now required.[28] Opposition to recognition of the courts had indeed featured in Sinn Féin debates. At the 1982 Ard Fheis, two motions from Dublin *Cumainn*, both heavily defeated, had urged the leadership to reject the use of partitionist courts throughout Ireland. The criticism followed the unsuccessful challenge by Sinn Féin to the Section 31 broadcasting ban on the party in the Irish Republic. The use of the Irish High and Supreme Courts had outraged one Dublin delegate, who argued that the entire morality of the movement was brought into question.[29] By the 1980s, however, Republican 'purism' was waning in favour of a new realism.

The 1986 Republican split

There were genuine fears of a major republican split over the abstentionism decision. *An Phoblacht/Republican News* was dominated by calls for unity. The paper was solidly in favour of a change in policy. It published the statement from Tom Maguire, the last surviving member of the Second Dáil, refusing to recognise the legitimacy of any IRA Army Council supportive of Sinn Féin's entry to the 'partition parliament of Leinster House', but issued a sharp rebuttal of Maguire's arguments.[30] *An Phoblacht/Republican News* declared that the IRA's mandate predated the Second Dáil and was derived from the 'legitimate right of the Irish people to resist the British presence... The abstentionist issue does not affect that legitimacy one whit'.[31] Modernisers thus used ultra-traditionalist interpretations of the IRA's mandate to defeat opponents of change. Supporters of change were also anxious that the party did not divide on right (pro-abstention) versus left (anti-abstention) lines. The 1986 Bodenstown oration offered by Martin McGuinness emphasised that 'not every person who argues new positions is a trendy leftie and not everyone who advocates orthodox Republicanism is a right-wing traditionalist'.

Sinn Féin was anxious to convey the message that, by entering Dáil Éireann, it was not laying the foundations for tactical pan-nationalist alliances. Ritual denunciations of the Leinster House parties accompanied Sinn Féin's crucial change. Understandably, given the previous history of splits, the party was anxious to preserve unity. The end of abstentionism had provoked some disquiet within the IRA Army Council. Indeed, the IRA 'came extremely close to splitting', with even some of its senior Northern elements opposing the policy change.[32] According to Brendan Hughes, the end of abstentionism 'meant the end of the domination of the Republican Movement by people from the South', although the Adams-McGuinness Northern axis had been increasingly in control for some time.[33] The appeal to traditional republicans to remain within the movement was based upon three things. First, there was a need for Republican unity. Secondly, the IRA's campaign would remain unaffected. Thirdly, although this was not an issue at the time, it was assumed that abstentionism would remain policy in respect of any reconstituted Northern parliament. Supporters of change argued that the movement was failing its own supporters by not offering to represent them in Leinster House. The view of modernisers was that acceptance of a partitionist state in the South was simply acknowledgement of popular opinion in the twenty-six counties. It was not tantamount to abandonment of the campaign for Reunification. In a letter from an Amsterdam jail, Gerry Kelly urged Republicans to accept that the majority of people 'accept the twenty-six-county state as their own—however flawed and partitionist it may be'.[34] Kelly's subsequent assertion that the end of abstentionism 'does not mean that we legitimise the twenty-six-county state' was thus superfluous, in that the citizens of the Irish Republic had already determined the issue. The decision of Sinn Féin to play belated catch-up was of huge significance in respect of the party's political development, but barely registered with the Republic's electorate.

'Purist' republicans remained unimpressed by the proposals for change, but could offer little as an alternative other than the continuation of meaningless electoralism (given their unwillingness to accept any dividend) and armed struggle. It was this absence of a viable alternative, allied to an image problem of 'tired Southerners', that placed the Ó Brádaigh-led traditionalists in difficulty. This was most bluntly expressed in the comments from Seamus Ryan that 'sitting back and citing principles may appease their egos, but it will not beat the British'.[35] The scepticism of some in the movement concerning the increasingly political direction of Republicanism was dismissed as the 'groundless fears and suspicions generated by some elements of a former leadership', a phrase which neatly linked political direction to personalities.[36] Whilst the 'sacrifices' of this former leadership were acknowledged, such figures were denounced for endangering the 'Irish Republican revolution' through instigating the 1975 ceasefire and maintaining support for federalism.[37] The Northern leadership was probably correct on the first point; the latter, however, was irrelevant, in that support for federalism had not endangered anything. It was the failure to engage in complementary electoral and community politics that had been the problem.

The strongest argument of the purists concerned the implications for future republican politics. As Ruairí Ó Brádaigh commented, it was 'impossible to ride a horse that wishes to travel in two opposite directions'.[38] For Ó Brádaigh participatory electoralism and armed struggle to overthrow the state amounted to a zero-sum game. Ó Brádaigh lost the argument less because of the merits of his case (although abstention from the Dáil Éireann was futile) but because his mode of politics had achieved only limited results in the 1970s, with very little in terms of tangible gain since 1972. The arguments of modernisers that the ballot box and armed struggle could co-exist and that republicans could increasingly participate within the state were delusions, as the co-existence of ballot and bomb could only be advanced for a limited period. Nonetheless, the movement towards more participatory politics should not be seen in conspiratorial terms. There was no plot to dupe Republicans into full acceptance of constitutional politics just over a decade later. Instead, there was a belief that Sinn Féin could make electoral gains in the South and shape the political system. Within fourteen years the party had become sufficiently 'constitutional' to discuss whether to enter into coalition with the former 'untouchables' of Fianna Fáil and Fine Gael.

A split was inevitable in 1986, despite the plea from McGuinness in his conference speech to traditionalists to 'stay and we will lead you to the Republic'. The decision to end abstentionism was taken by 429 votes to 161, just (by 11 votes) over the two-thirds majority needed. The victory for the modernisers was achieved through quality of argument, an influx of IRA personnel into Sinn Féin and the creation of largely fictitious Sinn Féin branches, swelling Ard Fheis delegate numbers way beyond the usual level.[39] Defeated, Ó Brádaigh led a number of colleagues from the conference hall and, in a re-enactment of the 1970 split, announced the formation of a new party, Republican Sinn Féin (RSF), with the same set of allegiances as declared by the Provisionals at their formation. Lacking political strength and a military wing, RSF made scant impact. Early in 1996 a military wing, the Continuity IRA, emerged. It claimed that the IRA Executive had voted against an end to abstentionism in 1986, but had been over-ruled unconstitutionally at a General Army Convention.[40] But with no in weaponry and with its political 'representatives' comprising mainly older figures, the Continuity IRA was derided as by Provisionals as a 'Dad's Army'.

The road to Hume-Adams

The Irish peace process has no easily defined starting point, but it clear that the revisionist account of Ed Moloney alters conventional wisdom that dialogue between Gerry Adams and John Hume marked the opening of the peace process.[41] Criticism of the IRA's armed struggle from the Catholic Church had always been a sensitive issue and had stung Adams into demanding alternatives for political change. Father Alec Reid, a Redemptorist priest in West Belfast, approached Adams to discuss devising such alternatives. The initiative was backed by Cardinal Tomás Ó Fiaich, Primate of Ireland, but opposed by some other senior Church figures.[42] It remained secret from other leaders of the republican movement, many of whom, after the hunger strikes, were more hostile to the Catholic Church than at any other juncture in Irish history.[43] By 1987 the Reid-Adams initiative became more formalised, privately culting a set of questions to the British government.

As has been acknowledged, the British government has always kept open indirect lines of communication with the IRA, whatever its rhetoric of 'not talking to terrorists'.[44] Hence the indirect dealings between the government and Gerry Adams should not come as a huge surprise, its masking being part of the necessary public duplicity and off-stage choreography of the peace process.[45] However, the unilateral basis of the Adams initiative would have startled Republican colleagues had they been aware of it and, so soon after the Brighton bomb and the Anglo-Irish Agreement, exposure of such dealings might have precipitated a political crisis at Westminster.

The core of the Reid-Adams initiative was to establish the extent to which the British government was prepared to concede the right of the Irish people (not defined in the indirect dialogue) to self-determination. In a secret reply to Adams' equally secret six questions, the Secretary of State for Northern Ireland, Tom King, insisted that the 'problem is not that the British government will not agree to Irish self-determination but that the people of the two divided traditions do not at present agree among themselves on how to exercise it'.[46] The British government insisted its presence in Ireland was not colonial and acknowledged that Republicans, if acting peacefully, should be represented in constitutional negotiations.[47] These positions were eventually to be broadly accepted by the much-changed Sinn Féin of the late 1990s, but had Adams publicly revealed the dialogue, or expressed any satisfaction with its contents, in 1987, his position as leader of the Republican movement would surely have been untenable. For orthodox Republicans, any shift towards the British position would have been heretical. The British denied colonial involvement, yet King's statement determined the conditions upon which Irish people could enter negotiations to shape the future of their country. There was no acknowledgement of how the 'Unionist tradition' had been awarded a statelet under the threat of violence, nor was there acceptance of Britain's historical responsibility for the problem. Furthermore, there was scant recognition that a British claim to sovereignty over part of the island, conditional or otherwise, might impinge upon 'Irish political self determination'. The significance of the 1987 initiative is that it was evident that any 'peace process' would involve shifts in the republican political position from that of the demand for British withdrawal; any changes in the British position would be much more nuanced and amount to far less in terms of *Realpolitik*. This is how the process unfolded.

The ending of abstention in respect of the Dáil Éireann offered the first significant visible signs of change within Sinn Féin. Nonetheless, the party's positions on Northern Ireland and in relation to the utility of political violence, the role of Unionists and the 'colonialism' of the British government remained unchanged. The 1985 Anglo-

Irish Agreement contributed to the internal debate taking place within Sinn Féin over the party's long term strategy, and the IRA's use of armed struggle to attain its objective of a united Ireland. However, the party needed greater encouragement to shift its position. John Hume believed that there might be sufficient movement within Sinn Féin to make a nationalist party dialogue worthwhile. Some form of dialogue between the SDLP and Sinn Féin had long been advocated by certain members of both parties. Such urging prompted more disquiet within the SDLP than within Sinn Féin, which by the late 1980s was in greater need of political allies. Some discussions had taken place between the two parties in the autumn of 1980. Subsequently the discussions within either party centred upon the desirability of electoral alliances with its nationalist rival. In 1983 Danny Morrison urged discussions on how to 'secure maximum nationalist successes'.[48] Morrison argued that a clear distinction was to be drawn between the 'betrayal' of the SDLP leadership and the aspirations of the party's supporters. Morrison was correct in hinting at a green element within the SDLP's support. The evidence that this wing was at variance with the leadership was less forthcoming, Instead, the party itself had gone greener than the cluster of original 'red' Socialists had envisaged.[49].

In a BBC radio interview with John Hume and Gerry Adams in 1985, the Sinn Féin President called for discussion between the nationalist rivals on 'pan nationalist interests'.[50] Hume expressed interest in talking to the IRA. In February 1985 Sinn Féin's Ard Chomhairle invited the SDLP for talks, but Hume dismissed Sinn Féin as 'mere surrogates'.[51] Republicans argued that the 'average SDLP voter has no qualms about talks with the IRA—nor for that matter with Sinn Féin'.[52] Retrospectively, this is confirmed, in that 94 per cent of SDLP supporters believed that John Hume was right to engage in dialogue with Gerry Adams.[53] However, this figure is based upon a 'hindsight' survey question, after Hume had achieved his aims in respect of Sinn Féin and more, widely, the peace process.

With some justification Adams claimed that Sinn Féin's electoral intervention had led to the 'greening' of the SDLP. He argued that this was 'especially true West of the Bann where it is recognised that Sinn Féin is right in opposing loyalism. In such areas the SDLP cannot afford not to side with Sinn Féin.'[54] Yet the backdrop to the Hume-Adams dialogue which finally commenced in 1988 was, publicly at least, unpromising. Sinn Féin had issued a largely unreconstructed document in 1987, *Scenario for Peace*. The title was based upon the contention that Sinn Féin wanted to 'create conditions' that would 'lead to a permanent cessation of hostilities' and the end of their 'long war' of military tactics. Despite its title, *Scenario for Peace* amounted to a traditional set of republican demands. The suggestion of repatriation for Unionists unable to accept a united Ireland was omitted from the final version, but the exclusion of that idea was the closest that the document came to compromise. Although designed as a discussion paper and not the definitive Republican position, *Scenario for Peace* had a familiar litany of ideas and was perhaps the last statement of unreconstructed republicanism ever to emerge from Provisional Sinn Féin. It insisted that the conflict was colonial; British withdrawal within the lifetime of a British government was required; the British security forces of the RUC and Ulster Defence Regiment must be disbanded and all Republican prisoners must be released without conditions. Britain's only role was to provide a subvention during the establishment of the new state. Loyalists would accept the decolonisation of the North.[55]

Disastrous military operations, such as the bombing of a Remembrance Day parade at Enniskillen in 1987, added to the increasing sense of futility over the military campaign. The IRA apologised for the action in a particularly contrite tone, but this did little to improve its standing.[56] The IRA action even angered an otherwise apathetic British public to the extent that the withdrawal of British forces from Northern Ireland was opposed, for the first time during the Troubles.[57] With its electoral strategy still yielding successes, but not at the rate envisaged in the heady days of 1981–3, Sinn Féin believed it had little to lose from serious dialogue with the SDLP. It was evident that the dialogue begun in January 1988 would pose serious questions about Sinn Féin's colonial analysis of the conflict. For Sinn Féin, colonialism and imperialism provided easy historical explanations of Britain's role in Northern Ireland, but little serious thinking had been done on the modern basis of Westminster involvement. Although Adams was working privately towards cleverly worded declarations of the right to Irish self-determination from the British government, Sinn Féin's solutions remained rooted in straightforward ethno-geographical determinism—the island of Ireland and therefore the people of Ireland were one. As such, there should be a unitary government. A substantial shift in mindset was required for Sinn Féin to move towards the arguments of Hume concerning the need for unity of peoples. Whilst Sinn Féin conceded the existence of two traditions, the party still saw Loyalism as illegitimate, or even quasi-fascist. Northern Protestants would have their civil and religious liberties guaranteed, but there were to be few concessions to Unionist identity and none to Unionist political aspirations. Irish self-determination, as espoused by Sinn Féin, precluded any prospect of co-determination, in which Unionists would decide their future as a separate unit.

SDLP-Sinn Féin dialogue

The first meeting between Hume and Adams as part of the new dialogue took place in January 1988, followed by three meetings of party delegations. Sinn Féin's team of four, Gerry Adams, Tom Hartley, Mitchell McLaughlin and Danny Morrison, were favourably disposed to the concept of pan-nationalism. The talks took place at the instigation of Father Alec Reid, priest, who was based at the Clonard monastery in West Belfast and a close confidant of Gerry Adams. The purpose of the talks between the two parties was an attempt to identify a common strategy on bringing about Irish unity, and also on issues affecting nationalists in Northern Ireland.

Sinn Féin produced a further document, *Towards a Strategy for Peace*, urging cooperation between the SDLP and Sinn Féin. It acknowledged the possibility of co-operation between the parties on a range of micro-issues connected with nationalist rights. Sinn Féin was keen to see nationalist grievances addressed via an equality agenda. The SDLP could hardly be seen to reject much of this agenda, but argued that pan-nationalism could only develop if there was a reassessment of Sinn Féin's position on constitutional questions and if IRA violence ceased. Sinn Féin urged the SDLP to join in an effort to persuade the Dublin government to pursue Irish self-determination.

John Hume's arguments to Sinn Féin in 1988 can be traced to relevant sections of the New Ireland Forum Report.[58] Section 3.20 of the Report points to 'the negative effect of IRA violence on British and unionist attitudes'. This section of the Report blamed IRA violence for intensifying Unionist opposition 'to any form of dialogue and accommodation with nationalists'. This theme was reiterated by Hume in written correspondence with Adams during the 1988 talks.[59] Here Hume argued that IRA violence only contributed to rigid security measures whose effect in turn was only to 'further alienate the nationalist section of the community' in Northern Ireland.[60] Also Hume maintained that IRA violence played a major contribution to the lack of economic investment in Northern Ireland, and consequently to high unemployment within the very community the IRA was proclaiming to represent.

The debates between Hume and Adams covered the same questions to the Republican movement aired by Hume at the SDLP's annual conference in 1986. As part of the formal exchange of dialogue between the two parties in 1988, John Hume also set out the SDLP's view of the Northern Ireland problem in written correspondence with Gerry Adams. Hume's assessment was the antithesis of the public Republican analysis of the situation. Hume believed the ending of IRA violence could remove 'the stated justification for security force activity'. He also disagreed 'that the British presence was the primary source' of the Northern Ireland problem.[61] He argued that Sinn Féin's call for a British withdrawal from Ireland or a declaration of intent would only precipitate a potentially dangerous vacuum. He claimed it could create Cyprus- or Lebanon-type scenarios with the prospect of 'permanent division and bloodshed'. He argued that the 12,000 'armed members of the RUC and UDR' were likely to become the 'defenders' of their own community, leaving the Catholic community very 'vulnerable'. Hume inferred that there could be no 'military solution'.[62] Hume also argued that Britain had 'no selfish or economic interest in Northern Ireland'.[63] The SDLP leader maintained that the Anglo-Irish Agreement was an international agreement demonstrating the British government's neutrality in relation to Irish unity. He contended at the 1986 conference: 'The British Government has declared that Irish unity is a matter for those Irish people who want it persuading those Irish people who don't'.[64] His challenge to the Republican movement was to join with the SDLP in taking up the peaceful challenge by the British government in its commitment on Irish unity through article 1 (c) of the Anglo-Irish Agreement.

Each party produced four documents during the talks. Sinn Féin's opening document was confined to constitutional issues and amounted to a restatement of the views of *Scenario for Peace*. Britain was not neutral and unionism was the 'child of imperialism'.[65] Perhaps the most interesting paragraph, in view of Sinn Féin's U-turn a decade later, was the unambiguous rejection of transitional routes to Irish unity:

> The SDLP—with the conditions of power-sharing and a variable 'Irish dimension'—have continually given the British succour and allowed them to believe that an internal arrangement may be possible, a belief that would be reinforced by an SDLP involvement in a devolved assembly.
>
> Sinn Féin is totally opposed to a power-sharing Stormont assembly and states that there cannot be a partitionist solution. Stormont is not a stepping stone to Irish unity. We believe that the SDLP's gradualist theory is therefore invalid and seriously flawed.[66]

The SDLP's reply posed a series of questions to Sinn Féin, mainly concerning definitions of Irish self-determination. The SDLP emphasised that what was needed was agreement on the most appropriate means of national self-determination, without indicating how this might be achieved. The SDLP's arguments were answered in Sinn Féin's presentation to the second meeting of the delegations in May. Sinn Féin's reply argued that the exercise of national self-determination could not permit Unionists a veto over the reunification of Ireland. Furthermore, implicit in the exercise of national self-determination was a renunciation of British claims to the Six Counties. Crucially, Sinn Féin insisted than any all-Ireland conference to determine the most appropriate future constitutional arrangements needed to be preceded by a declaration from the British government of its intent to withdraw from Northern Ireland. The issue of the Unionist veto remained vexed. The SDLP agreed with Sinn Féin that Unionists had 'no right whatsoever' to a veto over British policy, but qualified this by referring to a 'natural veto since they live on this island', as if residence provided a sufficient qualification for any group of people to override the wishes of others. The SDLP's final document argued that the Unionist veto was a matter of fact, based upon 'numbers, geography and history'.[67] Loyalist weaponry and the post-withdrawal 'bloodbath' scenario, arguably determinants of British policy, were unmentioned.

The two delegations met in June, with private Hume-Adams discussions taking place in July. At the June meeting, Sinn Féin's outlined with greater clarity its new view of Britain's role. The party argued that the British government should act as 'persuaders' to Unionists for Irish unity. Whilst admitting that such a scenario was 'improbable at present', Sinn Féin argued that such a development was possible if the SDLP analysis (of British open-mindedness on the future of Northern Ireland) was correct. There was little to justify such optimism. Sinn Féin did hold the upper hand, however, in its definition of the Irish people. Strangely, for a party insistent upon the need to reconcile two traditions, the SDLP accepted (in its fourth document) that the Irish people should be defined as those people domiciled on the island of Ireland.[68] This endorsed Sinn Féin's view that Unionism was reducible to a religious and cultural tradition held by a certain number of Irish people, rather than the legitimate political identity or allegiance of non-Irish citizens based on an island.

Throughout all of Sinn Féin's dialogue with the SDLP in 1988, republicans disregarded the legitimacy of the Unionist community in Northern Ireland and the right of that tradition's claim to its own self-determination and long-term destiny. Hume believed republicans confused two vetoes in their analysis of the Northern Ireland conflict. First, he argued that historically the veto Unionists had over British policy in Ireland was an abuse of power to the detriment of Irish unity. Hume maintained that this veto which was at the core of the Northern Ireland conflict had been eradicated by the implementation of the Anglo-Irish Agreement. However, on the other side of the equation, Hume stressed that Unionists had a natural veto on any exercise of self-determination since they lived on the island of Ireland. Hence the challenge for the Republican movement from Hume's viewpoint was to abandon its military campaign, and enter democratic politics to persuade the Unionist constituency of the benefits of Irish unity. Hume challenged Adams on the question of self-determination, focusing on determining whether Sinn Féin accepted the Unionist tradition's right to exercise self-determination. If Sinn Féin accepted this principle, Hume wanted clarification that they would attend a conference 'convened by an Irish government, at which all parties with an electoral mandate would attend'.[69] The clear message from Hume to Sinn Féin was that the process of Irish unity could only be started by uniting the people on the island of Ireland. The central dilemma according to the SDLP thesis was attaining agreement with the Unionists over the exercise of self-determination. Therefore, the real challenge for the republican movement in tangent with the SDLP was how to search for analogy within the two traditions comprising the Irish people on how to exercise 'the right to self-determination'. Hume's 1988 approach followed the Secretary of State's private line to Adams a year earlier. Ultimately, Sinn Féin would be faced with the decision whether to stick to its formula that self-determination meant that all on the island of Ireland must determine their future, *without opt-outs for any section of that population*. Shorn of nuanced language, that meant eradicating the unionist veto, in favour of an aggregate outcome.

The discussions on British policy centred upon whether the Anglo-Irish Agreement indicated British neutrality. Unsurprisingly, Sinn Féin thought it did not, but the significance of this opening phase of the Hume-Adams dialogue was that both parties held an optimistic view that Britain might act as persuader for Irish unity. This eased the way forward, as both parties could concur that the most likely method of persuading Britain in this direction was by bringing the Dublin government into a nationalist coalition. Although the parties predictably remained divided over the Unionist veto, the extent of tacit agreement on the best way to end the veto (British persuasion) meant that a pan-nationalist alliance was under construction.

The talks ended in disagreement in September 1988. Aside from the obvious disagreement over the role of armed struggle, the continuing dissent between the parties centred upon interpretations of British policy and the Unionist veto. There were obvious disparities between the SDLP and Sinn Féin in relation to the British government's motives and position on Northern Ireland. However, the principal logic behind the termination of the talks was simply that the SDLP could not agree a strategy with a Sinn Féin party still supportive of IRA violence.

The SDLP and Unionists

The Hume-Adams dialogue had concentrated upon the role of Unionists. During this period, however, Unionists were uninterested in political dialogue without the scrapping of the Anglo-Irish Agreement. In addition to bringing Sinn Féin into a political process, the SDLP was also interested in moving Unionists from this position. As with Sinn Féin, the SDLP leadership detected signs of movement among Unionist parties. During 1987 the loyalist Ulster Defence Association (UDA) published a policy document, *Common Sense*. Significantly, the document rejected the return of former majority rule in Northern Ireland and acknowledged the SDLP analysis that Northern Ireland was 'a divided society'. However, the document insisted that unionists would not accept the SDLP's Irish dimension and rejected 'formal Irish government involvement in Northern Ireland'.

The prospects for new political dialogue in relation to devolution in Northern Ireland were bleak because of unionist election pledges in the 1986 by-elections in Northern Ireland. Unionists promised their electorate that they would work towards the replacement of the Anglo-Irish Agreement. Nonetheless, as the 1980s came to a close it became apparent that Unionists were moving to the reality of the existence of an Irish dimension in resolving the Northern Ireland conflict. Yet Unionists had the dilemma of how to move into party negotiations on devolution with the Anglo-Irish Agreement still in place. Since the signing of the Anglo-Irish Agreement in November 1985, no formal discussions had taken place between Unionists and government ministers owing to protest against the accord.

In October 1988 talks took place in Duisburg, West Germany, between the four main Northern Ireland constitutional political parties: the Alliance Party, SDLP, UUP and DUP. Eberhard Spiecker, a German lawyer, brought together representatives of the four parties. Father Alec Reid, having already played vital roles in bringing Sinn Féin towards the political mainstream, was present at Duisburg. Father Reid was able to transmit the Sinn Féin analysis at the talks to the other four main Northern Ireland political parties. The Duisburg talks took place after two years of an absence of formal dialogue between the main Unionist parties and the SDLP. The SDLP had been approached four months earlier to see if it was possible to hold formal discussions in relation to political progress in Northern Ireland. However, in testing the possibility of holding the talks with the SDLP, unionists first wanted reassurances on getting a suspension of the Anglo-Irish Agreement.[70] At the time the success of the talks depended on the SDLP's willingness to 'agree on a formula for the suspension of the Hillsborough agreement', according to other party participants in the talks.[71]

What was apparent from Duisburg was the change in the Unionist mindset towards a desire for negotiations on devolution. The Duisburg talks were aimed 'at a formula to secure full blown negotiations'.[72] Unionists wanted the suspension of the Anglo-Irish Agreement, and the closure of the Maryfield secretariat, otherwise Unionists would refuse to attend formal negotiations. They had an election pledge that they would work towards 'an alternative to the Anglo-Irish Agreement' in the 1986 Westminster by-elections.[73] The Duisburg talks amounted to exploratory movement in that direction. Unionists wanted sufficient time to elapse before the next meeting of the Anglo-Irish Intergovernmental Conference in order to hold formal party negotiations on the future of Northern Ireland. Therefore they requested that the British and Irish governments should announce a fixed date for the Anglo-Irish Conference to take place, allowing sufficient time to elapse for dialogue to take place with the four main Northern Ireland constitutional parties. The SDLP rejected the Unionist proposals, believing they were designed by Unionists to give the impression that the Anglo-Irish Agreement was suspended.[74]

Some members of the SDLP, including Austin Currie and Eddie McGrady, felt the party should accommodate the desire of Unionists to hold formal dialogue. This wing of the SDLP felt there was an obvious softening by Unionists in relation to the Anglo-Irish Agreement. Unionists had evolved from a position of demanding a total scrapping of the Anglo-Irish Agreement to now only calling for a suspension of the accord. The leaders of Fine Gael and the Irish Labour Party were in favour of the Duisburg idea of a limited suspension of the Anglo-Irish Conference.[75] However, the Fianna Fáil government led by Charles Haughey was opposed to a suspension of the Agreement, ironically given Fianna Fáil's initial opposition to the deal. John Hume also backed this line, claiming there would 'serious political consequences' if the Agreement was suspended.[76]

Austin Currie advocated a formula of words which partly accommodated Unionist demands. He agreed in principle that meetings of the Anglo-Irish Conference would not be held for a specified period to enable talks to take place. This formula of words would have paved the way to formal discussions. However, this was not explored further by John Hume.[77] Currie did not receive the necessary mandate from his party leader—dominant, if aloof from other leadership figures—to follow up what had been agreed at Duisburg.

The Duisburg talks clearly demonstrated the tensions within the SDLP. There were members of the SDLP reflecting the Eddie McGrady position that the party should operate devolution within the terms of the Anglo-Irish Agreement, and viewing the proposals arising out of Duisburg as an opportunity not to be missed. The SDLP was an ageing party with party activists unable to hold any anti-cipation of office. Therefore members of the party, such as Austin Currie and Seán Farren, felt the need to do a deal with Unionists which might result in jobs within a power-sharing administration for senior members of the party and younger members of the party such as Mark Durkan and Alex Attwood, presently denied office. Hume's quandary was how to get the practical benefits for his party colleagues that a devolved administration in Northern Ireland would provide. He wanted to preserve the main gains of the Anglo Irish Agree-ment—an all-Ireland component and the Republic's role in resolving the Northern Ireland conflict. Hume was now focused on an all-Ireland settlement which included Sinn Féin. The differences that clearly existed between Austin Currie and John Hume arising from Duisburg were soon forgotten, as Currie left Northern Ireland and was elected as a Fine Gael TD for Dublin West in 1989.

The Hume project, fostering pan-nationalism in the wider interest of a peace process rather than a 'quick fix' for devolution, won the day. Hume's dialogue with Adams had not started the peace process, having been preceded by unilateral, private actions by the Sinn Féin leader. However, Hume-Adams made the process public and pro-vided political impetus. By the end of the 1980s, there had been sig-nificant shifts in Republicanism. A new constitutionalism had yet to fully emerge, but traditional Republicanism was being displaced, to be replaced during the 1990s with a new pragmatism. Grounded partly in the circumstances of 1969, Provisional Republicanism had never been fully wedded to the politics of 1916–18, but nonetheless the 1970s leadership of the movement had attempted to preserve the connection. In ending abstentionism and recognising the Irish Re-public, the ideological baggage of 1916–18 had been jettisoned. Meanwhile Sinn Féin had developed as an electoral force in Northern Ireland. This growth could only be checked by political exclusion or hostility to armed Republicanism. Sinn Féin thus embarked on a new phase in the 1990s, shaped by developments in the 1980s, in which political allies were sought, as was a way out of continued 'armed struggle'. In moving in this direction, the party would be obliged to accept considerable sections of the political agenda of the SDLP, a party it had long derided for selling nationalists short.

10

TOWARDS PEACE, PAN-NATIONALISM AND CO-DETERMINATION

The Brooke talks: creating a basis for change

Towards the end of 1989, unionists were clearly predisposed to activating political discussions with the British government, the Irish government and the SDLP. This change in attitude was attributable to a realisation that their strategy of non co-operation with government ministers in opposition to the Anglo-Irish Agreement was counterproductive. It was clear that, despite Unionist hostility, Irish government involvement was set to become a permanent feature of the Northern Ireland political landscape. Consequently the Northern Ireland Secretary of State, Peter Brooke, announced to the House of Commons on 21 March 1991 that talks involving the Alliance Party, SDLP, UUP and DUP would proceed. Brooke confirmed that the talks would take place within a three-stranded approach involving each of the fundamental sets of relationships: those within Northern Ireland, those within the island of Ireland, and those between the British and Irish governments. All three strands were interlinked, in that no final agreement in relation to any particular strand could take place until everything in the talks process was agreed.

The Anglo-Irish Intergovernmental Conference was suspended on 26 April 1991 for ten weeks to enable the talks to proceed. Instead of the talks dealing with substantive issues, they centred on debates over where the Strand Two talks should take place and who should chair the Strand One talks. With little progress in the initial stages, Peter Brooke formally announced to the House of Commons that the current round of talks had ended. As the ten-week gap in meetings of the Anglo-Irish Intergovernmental Conference had elapsed, Unionists were not willing to continue in the talks process beyond 9 July

175

1991. Throughout the first series of talks the SDLP was accused by Unionists of not taking the process seriously in their reluctance to submit formal proposals to the negotiations. Sir Patrick Mayhew replaced Peter Brooke as Northern Ireland Secretary of State after the 1992 Westminster election, Brooke having blotted his copybook in January when, under pressure from an eager television chat show host, he burst into song on the night of the IRA's killing of eight workers at a British Army base at Teebane.

As Northern Ireland Secretary from July 1989 to April 1992 Brooke demonstrated an assiduous commitment to establishing a political process for Northern Ireland. He set in place a framework for dialogue between the Northern Ireland political parties. Although Brooke's sympathies lay with the 'pro-Union camp', his frankness in outlining British security and economic thinking for the Republican movement and addressing their analysis of the British presence in Ireland helped lay the foundations for the 1994 IRA ceasefire.[1] Although his predecessor, Tom King, had indicated privately and indirectly to Gerry Adams the thinking of the British government, Brooke sent important public signals to the Republican movement that played an enormous part in bringing Sinn Féin into eventual all-party talks. In speeches in 1989 and 1990 he indicated with a surprising frankness that the IRA could not militarily be defeated. He also declared that Britain had no 'selfish strategic or economic interest' in Northern Ireland and would accept unification of Ireland if desired by the people of Northern Ireland.[2] The sub-text of Brooke's message was that continued violence was futile, as it was not part of a war against a colonial aggressor.

The former Brooke talks were resuscitated by Mayhew, with Strand Two discussions resuming in Lancaster House in London in July 1992. Strand Three of the negotiations between the British and Irish governments also commenced during this month. As part of the Strand Two negotiations, James Molyneaux headed a UUP delegation to Dublin. Although Ian Paisley's DUP did not attend the Dublin talks, this phase broke sterile Unionist attitudes in relation to North-South co-operation. The talks broke the deadlock over constitutional negotiations between Unionists and nationalists evident since the mid-1970s. Nonetheless, Unionists pulled out of the talks in November 1992, as the Maryfield secretariat started preparations for an

Anglo-Irish intergovernmental meeting in Dublin the following week. The secretariat had ceased operations for three months as part of unionist preconditions for engaging in the Brooke-Mayhew talks. Unionist hostility was as strong as ever, but might no longer preclude political negotiations.

During Strand One negotiations the SDLP was demanding direct Irish and European involvement in the internal government of Northern Ireland. The SDLP proposed a system of government by six commissioners and an elected assembly to question and make proposals. The SDLP's Strand One proposals involved the election of three commissioners, who would appoint a cabinet to run the various Northern Ireland departments. Such a strategy might overcome the problem of nationalist representation and articulation of interests.[3] John Hume described his proposals as no different to the American system of government.[4] However, the European Commission President, Jacques Delors, indicated he did not feel it appropriate for the European Commission to meddle in the internal matters of any country.[5] The SDLP's European proposals were a reiteration of earlier policy proposals designed to achieve joint sovereignty pending Irish unification. The concept of commissioners holding power over Northern Ireland was first set out in the SDLP's 1972 document *Towards a New Ireland*. It can also be argued that these proposals by the SDLP were nothing more than a ploy by John Hume to camouflage his focus on bringing the Republican movement into the democratic arena.

The SDLP's 'three commissioners' idea was regarded as unworkable by the Unionists and the British government and the party appeared isolated. Nonetheless, the Brooke initiative did demonstrate the influence of John Hume and the SDLP's philosophy as the basis for healing division in Northern Ireland. The three-stranded analysis for resolving the conflict, and the famous term 'nothing is agreed, until everything is agreed', originated from Hume and key SDLP personnel. Brooke used this reasoning as the bedrock for starting his talks. These conditions were accepted by the British and Irish governments, but also by the Unionists and, later, Sinn Féin. The Brooke-Mayhew talks were important because they enabled the four main Northern Ireland constitutional parties to exchange analyses of the Northern Ireland problem. It set in place a mechanism for dialogue between the divergent sides on an equal footing, something absent since the collapse of the Sunningdale experiment in 1974. The Brooke talks also indicated to Unionists that an 'Irish dimension' was non-negotiable, although its terms were to be the subject of considerable later bartering.

Self-determination, co-determination and persuasion

Although in most respects a failure, the Brooke talks had sketched the three-stranded nature of any future agreement. For a worthwhile deal to be reached, however, Republicans needed to be on board. By the 1990s the IRA was moving towards a ceasefire, Gerry Adams having formulated a sufficiently ambiguous formula to achieve Irish self-determination. In parallel with secret, indirect contacts with the British government, Adams finessed the concept through similar approaches to the Taoiseach, Charles Haughey.[6] Moloney suggests that Haughey fashioned the suitably ambiguous definition, which allowed Unionists to self-determine their own future within the broader framework of all the people on the island of Ireland determining their own future, uninhibited by interference from the British government. This formula would allow Adams to claim a triumph, in that a deal amounted to Irish self-determination and it would require repeal of the 1920 Government of Ireland Act, under which the British laid unconditional claim to Northern Ireland.[7] Self-determination, so defined, replaced the demand for an independent Ireland.

Adams had no desire to reveal the indirect dialogue, partly to protect Haughey, but also because revelations of its contents would have enraged those Republicans fighting and dying for independence.[8] 'Self-determination' permitting Unionists to determine their own future was the unionist veto rewritten. It allowed a geographically concentrated section of the population to preference its constitutional outlook against the wishes of the majority of the Irish people. Searching for a formula to end armed struggle, Adams could argue that this 'opt-out' did not matter, provided that such a solution was agreed by the Irish people as a whole. Of course, the working out of the formula in the subsequent peace process indicated the flaw in Adams' approach. The final formula for self-determination, for which the door was left ajar by Adams, meant that it did not matter how those in the twenty-six counties voted in a subsequent referendum.

British sovereignty would remain over the North, even if the entire population of the South preferred the British to leave the six counties (not that the population of the Republic was allowed to vote on such an option). British sovereignty over Northern Ireland did become more conditional upon the will of its people, as the 1920 Act was replaced by the 1998 version, but the net effect of this, in the short term at least, was to strengthen and legitimise the existing territorial border so opposed by republicans and to uphold the 'unionist veto' for so long as unionists remained in a majority. Adams had accepted co-determination for the peoples of the island, a concept far removed from an independent state or even self-determination. It was to be the beginning of the end for the Provisionals' articulation of traditional republican goals.

After the secret Adams-Reid-King and Adams-Reid-Haughey initiatives, the field was broadened. The public SDLP-Sinn Féin dialogue of 1988 was run in parallel with an equally significant set of meetings between representatives of the Irish government and Sinn Féin, which broadened the Adams-Reid-Haughey axis. The secret dialogue in the Irish Republic, encouraged and facilitated by the Catholic Church, involved three Fianna Fáil representatives, including the party's main political strategist Nicholas Mansergh and the Dundalk TD Dermot Ahern, with Gerry Adams, Mitchell McLaughlin and Pat Doherty representing Sinn Féin.[9] The main purpose of the Irish government's approach was to establish prospects for an IRA ceasefire. In common with the SDLP-Sinn Féin discussions, the talks centred upon questions of self-determination and the role of Unionists. Fianna Fáil's discussants revived the notion that the party remained Sinn Féin's 'first cousin', by sympathising with the arguments of Adams that Britain was not a neutral actor. The Fianna Fáil team believed that a combination of Adams' search for an exit strategy, war-weariness and generational factors would impact upon changes in republican strategy as much as a more nuanced British approach to Northern Ireland. The Sinn Féin team gave the impression that it was genuine in seeking an end to the conflict without conceding defeat.[10]

For a dynamic to be created, three things were required. Firstly, republicans needed to accept at least some of the arguments of the SDLP and soften their demand for British withdrawal, accepting the possibility of an interim role for Britain. Given that Adams and his team were moving away from the idea of physical British withdrawal, this was not an insurmountable difficulty, although the issue would pose problems internally for the Republican movement. Secondly, a cessation of the armed struggle was required to allow politics to flourish. Finally, the British government began to offer some original thinking on Northern Ireland, even though the essence of its policy, upholding the 'consent principle' and therefore the Union, remained unchanged. The British government was anxious to entice Republicans into a political process. By the late 1980s the aim was no longer to inflict outright military defeat on the IRA and the organisation's violence had been largely contained.[11] It was evident that Sinn Féin was some years away from replacing the SDLP as the major repository of nationalist votes. Whilst IRA violence continued, the growing Catholic middle class remained 'impervious to Republicanism'.[12] Instead, the aim of the British government was to enmesh the Republican movement within constitutional politics, with Sinn Féin shifting the IRA away from violence. Within the IRA, there were those who feared the move towards politics. As one example, the (temporary) informer, Eamon Collins, recalled being asked to take over the Sinn Féin *Cumainn* in Newry on behalf of the IRA, whose South Armagh members feared that militarism was being usurped in favour of 'soft' politics.[13] The end of Southern abstentionism, the realisation of the possibilities of Hume-Adams and the arrival of a more enlightened Secretary of State for Northern Ireland, Peter Brooke, facilitated the shift in British policy towards inclusion of Republicans within a political process.

As Secretary of State, Brooke's main role was to insist that Britain had no 'selfish, strategic or economic interest' in Northern Ireland.[14] This was not an assertion of British neutrality, for the word 'political' was excluded from the catalogue of non-interests. Brooke was aware that he could not impress even increasingly moderate republicans with claims of neutrality, given his government's support for the constitutional status quo, albeit support which was conditional upon a particular demographic situation. Nonetheless, the Secretary of State made some important points, which offered the prospect of political development. First, he insisted that partition was not an expression of British self-interest, but an acceptance of reality. Secondly, he insisted that the British presence was not that of a colonial aggressor. Brooke accepted that national self-determination for the Irish people was a legitimate pursuit for Sinn Féin and the SDLP, but that a border was likely to remain. His promise to respond imaginatively in the event of a cessation of violence was a thinly coded message to republicans that inclusion in talks could soon follow and that an amnesty, or prisoner releases, might be forthcoming if the conflict were to be drawn to a permanent conclusion.

For Sinn Féin there were four political tasks at the beginning of the 1990s. First, how could it respond positively to the Brooke agenda, in terms of constructing a new British role in Ireland? Secondly, the leadership needed to sell to the Republican grassroots a mode of national self-determination which did not guarantee British withdrawal. Thirdly, Sinn Féin needed to develop tactical alliances with other nationalist forces throughout Ireland and elicit external support, notably from the US administration. Finally, the task of ending IRA violence had to be undertaken.

By now the British government was in secret contact with the broader Republican leadership. It was later claimed by the British government that a message was sent by Sinn Féin at the beginning of the decade, stating that the conflict was effectively over, but that a means of properly ending it was required. Embarrassed, Sinn Féin vehemently denied the assertion and claimed that the British government had indicated the inevitability of a united Ireland.[15] Yet the validity of armed struggle was being openly questioned within the movement by the early 1990s. In an important speech soon afterwards at Bodenstown a senior Republican, Jim Gibney, a 'kite-flyer' for Adams within the movement, urged Republicans not to be 'deafened by the deadly sound of their own gunfire'.[16] A necessary replacement was the construction of a pan-nationalist alliance, which might impact upon British policy and the outlook of Unionists. Even after the end of abstentionism in the Irish Republic in 1986, there remained residual hostility to the 'Free State', with some Republicans continuing to use the term to describe the Republic.[17] By the early 1990s this was evaporating fast, in favour of the Irish government playing a crucial role in the North.

Sinn Féin's new approach to the role of the British state was heralded by the arrival of the party's discussion document, *Towards a Lasting Peace in Ireland*, in 1992. *Towards a Lasting Peace in Ireland* was a far subtler document than anything offered by Sinn Féin during the previous two decades. It reassured the Irish government and the SDLP that Sinn Féin's commitment to a pan-nationalist alliance was secure and indicated to a wider audience outside Ireland that Sinn Féin was a fully developed political party. *Towards a Lasting Peace in Ireland* replaced the old mantra of 'Brits out' with a call for Britain to 'join the ranks of the persuaders' to Unionists that their better interest lay in a united Ireland. Although the document amounted to utopianism, given that such a task of persuasion lay beyond the smoothest salesperson, *Towards a Lasting Peace in Ireland* represented a crucial shift in Sinn Féin policy. For the first time since the formation of the Provisionals, there was no specific timetable for British withdrawal from Ireland. Previously, negotiations would merely concern issues of detail regarding Britain's departure. Now, mere acknowledgement of the failure of partition, rather than a promise of withdrawal, would be sufficient for dialogue. Interim arrangements, prior to withdrawal at an unspecified time, could be negotiated. Most important of all, Sinn Féin recognised that Loyalists, their Irish brethren, would not come quietly, but instead would need persuading of the advantages of Irish unity.

It remains unclear whether Sinn Féin's leadership ever really believed that Britain would act a persuader for Irish unity. There had been false expectations of a Labour Party victory in the British general election in 1992, which, had it occurred, may have led to a more viable basis for the development of the persuader strategy. One of the architects of the policy, Mitchell McLaughlin, acknowledged that the strategy might be not be realisable.[18] Nonetheless, Sinn Féin's new approach created space for a more public formulation of appropriate mechanisms of Irish self-determination first developed by Adams in the 1980s. As Hume-Adams discussions revived, the two party leaders issued an essentially bland statement in April 1993. This agreed that the Irish people as a whole had a right to national self-determination and that the exercise of self-determination was a matter for agreement between the people of Ireland. Such agreement was 'only viable if it can earn and enjoy the allegiance of the different traditions' on the island.[19] Hume and Adams pledged to continue to search for agreement on the most appropriate means of self-determination. The principles of self-determination were converted by Hume into the draft British-Irish declaration which became, in heavily modified form, the Downing Street Declaration. The final Irish draft, handed by the Taoiseach Albert Reynolds to John Major, declared that the 'democratic right of self-determination as a whole must be achieved and exercised with the agreement and consent of the people of Northern Ireland'.[20] In effect Republicans had conceded the idea of co-determination.

The 1993 Downing Street Declaration

The Downing Street Declaration (DSD) was a Joint Declaration for Peace made by the British and Irish governments in December 1993. The final version watered down even the limited form of self-determination favoured by Adams and Hume. The DSD made explicit the 'consent principle' in declaring that the British government would 'uphold the democratic wish of a greater number of the people of Northern Ireland on the issue of whether they wish to support the Union or establish a sovereign united Ireland'. The green language of self-determination was matched by the practical language of co-determination. The declaration insisted that it is 'for the people of the island of Ireland alone, by agreement between the two parts respectively, to exercise their right of self-determination on the basis of consent, freely and concurrently given, North and South, to bring about a united Ireland.' Shorn of the green language, British policy was largely unchanged since Sunningdale in 1974. The Declaration did provide further acknowledgment that Northern Ireland was 'a place apart', ending any flickering integrationist hopes within the Conservative Party and the Ulster Unionist Party. Nonetheless, as a broad set of principles, it offered the prospect of a political settlement way short of traditional Republican objectives, an aspect evident despite Sinn Féin's request for 'clarification'. Sinn Féin's input into the draft declarations devised by Hume, Adams and the Irish government moved towards acceptance of the consent principle, provided that the British government accepted the need for Irish self-determination and moved to persuade Unionists to accept the outcome of such an exercise.

In offering the self-determination formula, the Republican leadership could at least argue, however unconvincingly, that Republican principles were not abandoned as national self-determination and possible British withdrawal remained on the agenda. Furthermore,

Sinn Féin publicly acknowledged the contradictions between the British government's acceptance of Irish self-determination and its constitutional guarantee for the Union. The British government was to be charged with the role of persuading Unionists of the advantages of a united Ireland. The difficulty for Sinn Féin was that insufficient thought had been given to policy formulation if the British government declined to adopt the task, or if Unionists were unwilling to listen.

Given that Sinn Féin's leadership had considerable indirect input into the Downing Street Declaration, the party's subsequent call for 'clarification' appeared an attempt to further muddy the waters of compromise into which the party had inexorably headed. Republicans had already begun what one critic of the new direction caustically described as 'the burdensome task of selling the internal settlement as an interim arrangement which will weaken the institution of partition and hence act as a dynamic towards eventual unity'.[21] Pretending to ignore the real meaning of the DSD was the opening sales pitch. Amid the ambiguity, the British government had been frank with Sinn Féin in exchanges earlier in 1993, declaring that it 'does not have, and will not adopt, any prior objective of ending partition'.[22] A united Ireland could only be achieved on the basis of the consent of the people of Northern Ireland. These pronouncements reappeared in the DSD, wrapped in cotton wool. The DSD may have been green-flavoured Unionism, but Unionism it remained. For McIntyre the 'Irish Peace Initiative' and the subsequent Anglo-Irish pronouncements formed merely the endgame of a process in which Republicans had been forced to respond to British state strategies.[23] Such an account nonetheless needs to explain the timing of Sinn Féin's new approach, given that temptation to move towards a settlement with a mere Irish dimension, rather than the utopian independent republic, had lain in wait for two decades. McIntyre's account also overlooks the increasing concern of the British government over IRA actions in the 1990s, easily the most effective of the Troubles, as the IRA's South Armagh unit became increasingly influential in the British mainland campaign.[24]

Republican reaction to the Downing Street Declaration

It had been a Republican mantra that there were not 'two parts' of the island to exercise self-determination respectively. The DSD maintained the territorial integrity of Northern Ireland for as long as the people there wished it to continue, even though 60 per cent of its land mass, Sinn Féin argued, contained populations opposed to partition.[25] Yet the DSD made clear that the Northern 'consent principle' remained and the British government confirmed that it would not act as a persuader to unionists for Irish unity. Sinn Féin held a special conference at Letterkenny in July 1994 to discuss the DSD. The successful motions at the conference confirmed the direction of policy signalled by *Towards a Lasting Peace in Ireland*. The Irish Peace Initiative was designed to establish a progress of agreement on an exercise in national self-determination, the format of which was a 'matter for agreement between the people of Ireland'. The consent and allegiance of Unionists were 'essential ingredients for a durable peace', although Sinn Féin continued to fudge whether such consent and allegiance were pre-requisites or inevitable consequences of fundamental constitutional change. The issue could not be avoided in perpetuity. As the Ulster Unionist Party councillor Chris McGimpsey remarked in 1995, the 'entire process…boils down to acceptance of the consent principle'.[26] The Letterkenny Conference also again urged Britain to join the 'ranks of the persuaders' for Irish unity, although it was evident that there would be no movement in this direction from the Conservative government under John Major.

The Downing Street Declaration 'outed' the informal, largely secret, earlier moves of the peace process. The vitality of IRA operations in the 1990s both obscured and facilitated Sinn Féin's increasingly rapid moves towards historic compromise. Some, such as the Warrington bomb which killed two children in 1993, were catastrophic blunders devoid of strategic rationale. Others, such as mortar attacks on Downing Street and the Bishopsgate bomb, were effective reminders of the continuing potency of armed Republicanism. The Bishopsgate bomb was hugely expensive for the British government, forcing it into a position of 're-insurer of last resort' for the finance houses of the City of London.[27] The rationale of continuing armed struggle had been removed by Sinn Féin's peace strategy, according to critical accounts of change within the movement.[28] For such analysts, Republican violence was now mainly concerned with preserving the unity of the movement, or disguising its political failure. Whatever the merits of such explanations, they fail to explain the willingness of the overwhelming majority of republicans to forgo violence so readily by the mid-1990s. One of the more startling aspects of the peace process of the 1990s, given the historical propensity for division and recrimination, was the unity of republicans.

Sinn Féin found itself on difficult political terrain during the early 1990s. The party performed only moderately well in elections, forced to defend armed struggle whilst attempting to convince the electorate of the prospective gains of its social and economic policies. Whatever the disdain held towards the ageing, middle-class SDLP among some Catholics, there was also the feeling that economic progress meant that they 'didn't need the Provos to pursue their civil rights'.[29] The nadir of the electoral fortunes of this period was the loss of Gerry Adams' West Belfast seat in the 1992 Westminster general election to Joe Hendron of the SDLP.[30] Sinn Féin performed effectively as ward representatives on councils, despite attempts by Unionist parties to marginalise the party. Sinn Féin councillors suffered considerably outside the council chambers, with a number being assassinated, among thirteen Sinn Féin members killed between 1989 and 1992.[31]. There were also a number of less dramatic attacks upon the homes of SDLP councillors as part of the Loyalist targeting of the 'pan-nationalist front'.

Although the DSD was an obvious disappointment in terms of the advancement of Republican objectives, Sinn Féin was anxious not to simply reject its ideas, not least because they originated in part, albeit in greener form, from its leader. To pull out at this stage would have collapsed the party's growing influence with the Fianna Fáil dominated government of the Republic, led by the sympathetic Albert Reynolds. The Irish government's recognition of the changes within Sinn Féin meant that it was prepared to exert international pressure to further end the political isolation of Republicans. A successful example was Reynolds' backing for the application for a US visa for Gerry Adams in 1994. Sinn Féin knew that it could continue to win propaganda contests, given the global unpopularity of Britain's position in Ireland. Furthermore, there was no need for outright rejection or support of the DSD. Its set of core principles did not rule out a 'transitory' route to Irish unity, via demographic change. At this stage, Sinn Féin did not have to sign to the SDLP's ideas of Sunningdale-type three-stranded forms of governance, and as such the leadership could hold out public hopes of substantial constitutional change. In 1994, the Irish government and Gerry Adams both mused about the possibility of joint sovereignty as a possible way forward.[32] In an attempt to reassure supporters alarmed by this prospect (although they were to gain less eventually), Martin McGuinness insisted that a five- to seven-year British disengagement programme was acceptable, but withdrawal must be complete at the end of the programme.[33] For Sinn Féin there was in any case no need to sign up to the principles of the DSD, because the British government made explicit in May 1994 that its full acceptance would not be a prerequisite for any entry by Sinn Féin into talks. The ending of PIRA violence remained the condition for further political developments.

Ceasefire

On 31 August 1994 the IRA called a 'complete cessation of military operations'. The word 'ceasefire' was not used, as a full Army Convention would have been required in advance before such a step could be taken. A cessation did not necessarily mean a permanent silencing of the guns, a point not lost on the Conservative government. Instead, the republican movement had moved into what was described a Tactical Use of Armed Struggle phase. Any such phraseology was unintentionally ironic. Republican use of armed struggle had always been tactical, having been designed as the blunt instrument to effect British withdrawal and, since the late 1970s, deployed as a necessary but insufficient device for British withdrawal. Mallie and McKittrick argue that TUAS stood for Totally Unarmed Strategy.[34] Patterson cautions against a 'teleology of the peace process', which 'inexorably brought the doubters and traditionalists towards acceptance of the need for a Totally Unarmed Strategy.'[35] Indeed the role of armed struggle was not mentioned in the document.

The title of the TUAS document was less important than its contents. Whether strategies are 'totally unarmed' depends upon subjective viewpoint. For critics, the refusal of the IRA to surrender its weapons indicated that a 'totally unarmed strategy' did not exist. The new republican reliance upon pan-nationalism and international forces nonetheless indicated that PIRA might soon stand for Peaceful IRA. The cessation of violence was hugely significant, coming despite a lack of any substantial evidence that republicans had advanced their historical goals. TUAS argued that 'for the first time in twenty-five years all the major nationalist parties are rowing in roughly the same direction', which was true; only one of those parties, Sinn Féin, had altered course.[36] 'Humespeak' also appeared in the document, with the assertion that an 'agreed Ireland needs the allegiance of varied traditions to be viable'. Britain's unpopularity within the EU and the influence of the Irish-American lobby on the Clinton administration were highlighted as helpful factors in movement towards Republican goals, although the conservative moderation of influential sections of Irish America diluted its strength. TUAS remained faithful to traditional Republican objectives in its assertion that the DSD was 'not a solution' and its insistence upon national self-determination.

Few within Sinn Féin dissented from the TUAS. The IRA cessation was reciprocated seven weeks later by loyalists, allowing Sinn Féin respite. The suspension of violence allowed the lifting of the broadcasting bans on Sinn Féin. The cessation also allowed Sinn Féin a public forum for the articulation of its increasingly sophisticated political outlook. The Irish Forum for Peace and Reconciliation was established in October 1994 and invited submissions on the future of Ireland from various interested parties, although the two main Unionist parties boycotted the event. The Forum allowed Sinn Féin to illustrate its flexible peace strategy, bereft of the demands characteristic of party policy prior to 1992. Equally, the Forum offered the party a chance to prove that its traditional Republican analysis of the problem remained largely unaltered. The British presence was still seen as the root of all evils.[37] The contemporary problem of Unionism was, as ever, addressed in two fundamentally different ways. There was an insistence that nationalists had 'no wish to coerce' Unionists, whilst concurrently Sinn Féin's submission rejected the Unionist veto. A belief in voluntary action by unionists was juxtaposed with the need to remove their autonomy. As expected, Sinn Féin remained dismissive of the two nations analysis of Ireland's historical development.[38] Sinn Féin highlighted the ambiguity of the DSD in this respect. Part of the DSD appeared to respect the territorial integrity of the island of Ireland by speaking of the right of self-determination for the people of the island and Ireland alone (one nation theory) whilst qualifying this by referring to the North and South (two nations).

Yet for Sinn Féin the legitimacy of Unionism as a political creed remained the most problematic aspect of the British presence. The three other aspects of the British presence outlined earlier by Peter Brooke could all be dealt with or replaced, namely the Army, the subvention and the Northern Ireland Office.[39] For Sinn Féin, acceptance that Unionists were a distinct national community, rather than a separate Irish tradition, would go some way towards conceding the legitimacy of partition. Sinn Féin offered guarantees of religious freedoms in a 'new Ireland'. At the 1995 Ard Fheis, the notion of covenantship with Protestants was articulated.[40] This built upon the pledge outlined one year earlier of 'full recognition of the Protestant identity in the new Ireland. The right of those in Ireland who wish to retain a British passport must be guaranteed.'[41] This represented a shift in Sinn Féin thinking from the repatriation ideas of the 1980s, whilst remaining abhorrent to Unionists.

Sinn Féin offered a measured response to the Framework Documents published by the British and Irish governments in 1995. The documents offered practical proposals based upon the principles of the DSD. The British government's proposals for devolved government in Northern Ireland were contained in Part 1, *A Framework for Accountable Government in Northern Ireland*. The second part of the document, *A New Framework for Agreement*, was the British-Irish plan for North-South cross-border bodies and East (London)-West (Dublin) intergovernmental cooperation. The Framework Document, or Part 2 at least, amounted to the high-water mark for the green pan-nationalism of 1992–5. Gerry Adams claimed:[42] 'The ethos of the document and the political framework envisaged is clearly an all-island one. It deals with the general concept of one-island social, economic and political structures, and moves the situation closer to an all-island settlement'. This was not an outlandish claim, given the promises of a strong North-South council and the transfer of rafts of legislation to be dealt with on an all-Ireland basis. The British government conceded that it had 'no limits of its own' to the amount of legislation that could be produced on an all-Ireland basis. Despite being partitionist, being based upon Northern consent and incorporating a revival of a Northern Ireland Assembly, the Framework Documents offered the most potent all-island approach to politics since partition. Sinn Féin clung to the view that Britain should act formally as persuader to unionists for a united Ireland, even though the all-Ireland economic arrangements were a clear signal from the British government that unionists needed to look south as well as east in future.[43] The problem with the Framework Document for Republicans seeking compromise was not the document itself. Instead, the difficulty lay with the non-implementation of the Document by the Major government, dependent on Unionist votes at Westminster. The Framework Document ought to have been the baseline for a Republican settlement. Instead, Sinn Féin lost ground over the next three years.

The US conundrum

The developing peace process was aided by US activism. Access to Irish America for Sinn Féin from 1994 onwards provided a much needed boost to its capacity to raise funds and, in making the party 'respectable', helped revive political support. The Irish diaspora dominated sections of American business and politics, with one in five chief executives of top US companies being of Irish descent. This diaspora proved important in providing success for the Democrats in the 1992 US Presidential election campaign.

During Clinton's campaign a new Irish-American pro-Clinton group, coordinated by Niall O'Dowd, publisher of the *Irish Voice* in New York, lobbied the prospective President. The aim was for Clinton to promise to give the Northern Ireland problem top priority if elected to the White Office. The new group, 'Irish Americans for Clinton', obtained an election promise that he would send a 'special envoy' to Northern Ireland if elected as President of the United States.[44] Clinton promised an American-Irish Forum in Manhattan that he would grant Gerry Adams a visa to enter the United States.[45] Once Clinton was elected, O'Dowd and his colleagues wasted no time holding the new President to his election promises in relation to Northern Ireland. Meanwhile, this group encouraged an IRA ceasefire. The SDLP felt the group was too identified with the Sinn Féin agenda. However, the real antipathy by the SDLP towards this new group perhaps had more to do with the dilution of John Hume's influence within the White House.

Niall O'Dowd played the key role of informing the Clinton administration of the Republican movement's sincerity in abandoning violence. O'Dowd did this mainly through the deputy head of the

National Security Council, Nancy Soderberg. The other key player influencing Clinton was Edward Kennedy. In the early stages of the peace process, O'Dowd relayed his messages in relation to Sinn Féin through Trina Vargo, senior foreign policy adviser to Kennedy from 1987 to 1998. These contacts were vital in bringing about a successful conclusion to Gerry Adams' visa application in 1994. Between 1994 and 1997 Tony Lake, the head of the National Security Council, and his deputy effectively steered American policy for the White House in relation to Northern Ireland. The US State and Justice Departments were against the visa. The Adams visa episode demonstrated the willingness of Lake and Soderberg to taking a position at variance from the State Department.[46] During this period, the leverage of the State Department was considerably reduced.

The Presidential invitation to Gerry Adams for the St Patrick's Day celebrations in 1995 was accompanied by the lifting of the ban on fund-raising for Sinn Féin. The British government felt its position in relation to decommissioning had been weakened by Clinton over the successful Adams visa outcome. John Hume, in association with the Irish government, supported Adams' visa application, arguing 'for the use of the carrot rather than the stick' approach.[47] Clinton's authorisation for Adams' visa was not a solitary decision, but one that was largely attributable to Edward Kennedy's approval, a response that would not have been forthcoming without the agreement of John Hume.[48]

The appointment of Jean Kennedy Smith as US Ambassador to Ireland in June 1993 indicated the influence of the Kennedy clan on President Clinton. Ray Seitz, the US Ambassador in London, described Jean Kennedy Smith as 'an ardent IRA apologist'.[49] Yet the Kennedys traditionally echoed John Hume's stance towards the Northern Ireland conflict. Sinn Féin's promise to turn aside from violence and embrace constitutional politics was beginning to impact upon Irish America, blurring distinctions with the constitutional nationalism which had been supported by the majority. In early 1995 Sinn Féin opened a Friends of Sinn Féin office in Washington, backed by wealthy and influential supporters. Sinn Féin's move was in marked contrast to the SDLP's lack of organisational presence in the United States, dependent upon the representations of John Hume. Sinn Féin now had the upper hand over the SDLP in making its voice heard in the United States.

Temporary fracture

Adams had performed a remarkable job in holding Sinn Féin and the IRA together, confounding historical determinists who believed in the inevitably of a serious split in the movement. Unity had been achieved through a constructive ambiguity in the political process, based upon vagueness over what self-determination meant or where it could lead. This ambiguity was replicated in the peace process, in which the possibility of a return to violence was dangled as a possibility to hardliners, whilst governments were informed of a lasting Republican commitment to peace.[50] The dual approaches could not be maintained forever.

Sinn Féin expected publication of the Framework Document in 1995 to be followed by the entry of the party into negotiations. A weak Conservative government did not facilitate this, preferring an unrealistic insistence upon prior IRA decommissioning of weapons. In October 1995 the IRA's Army Council took the decision in principle to return to violence, although a final decision was delayed until after President Clinton's visit in late November. In January 1996, the Independent International Commission on Decommissioning (IICD) under the chairmanship of George Mitchell, recommended that the decommissioning of paramilitary weapons should take place in parallel to multi-party constitutional talks. In Washington, in May 1995, the British Secretary of State for Northern Ireland, Patrick Mayhew, had demanded that some decommissioning of weapons take place prior to Sinn Féin taking part in full political discussions on a equal basis with the other Northern Ireland parties. The British government adopted a tentative suggestion, found later in the Mitchell Report, of an elected forum to produce negotiating teams from the political parties for future talks. For the PIRA this amounted to further prevarication, and the ceasefire was ended with a huge bomb at Canary Wharf in London in February 1996, killing two. This action and the even bigger Manchester bombing which followed in June were designed to achieve a place at the negotiating table for Sinn Féin. In his speech at the 1996 Ard Fheis in March, at the Ambassador Cinema in Dublin, Gerry Adams dropped unsubtle hints that the peace process would be restored, although it might need the imminent removal of the floundering Major government for a restoration.[51] Adams was also critical of the damage done to pan-nationalist unity by the election of a Fine Gael-Labour-Democratic Left coalition in the Republic in December 1994. Whilst the Taoiseach, John Bruton, was indeed less favourably disposed to Sinn Féin than Albert Reynolds, it was the impact of his virulently anti-Republican coalition partners that was more damaging to the fragile nationalist alliance.

Adams emphasised the need for continuing commitment to a peace strategy to Sinn Féin members at an internal conference at Athboy in Meath in 1996, declaring, 'This party is not going back to the days when we were cheer-leaders for the Army [IRA]…whatever the Army does is the Army's business…let us not use the Army in whatever it does as an excuse for us not to make peace'.[52] Adams needed to maintain the peace strategy pending the arrival of more favourably-disposed governments in Britain and Ireland during the following year.

Within the IRA, however, there was considerable discontent. The Army Council's decision to call the cessation in 1994 had not been unanimous.[53] After the resumption of violence in 1996, Adams was heavily criticised at an IRA convention in October, particularly for the indefinite nature of the 1994 ceasefire without any guarantee of entry to talks for Sinn Féin. Sinn Féin's willingness to endorse Senator Mitchell's six principles of non-violence in May 1996 had disturbed some IRA members. Although the IRA later insisted that, unlike Sinn Féin, it did not endorse such principles, there was an undercurrent of unrest within the movement, even though many leading IRA personnel accepted that compromise well short of a united Ireland was inevitable. Delegates to the Convention insisted that any future ceasefire be time specific and the Convention even passed a motion, later ignored by the Army Council, forbidding decommissioning of weapons until a united Ireland had been achieved.[54] Ceasefire sceptics, opposed to the Adams' peace strategy, achieved a majority on the twelve-person IRA executive, but, owing to absence and late defections, could not translate this into a majority on the all-important ruling Army Council.[55]

A split in the movement duly arrived in 1997, when a second ceasefire was called by the IRA leadership, contradicting its pledges of 1996.[56] The ceasefire followed Labour's landslide British election victory in 1997. With a huge majority Prime Minister Blair was less hidebound than his Conservative predecessor over Unionist sensitivities.

Accordingly, the Prime Minister moved swiftly to postpone the requirement of the IRA to decommission its weapons to facilitate the entry of Sinn Féin into talks. Unfortunately for Republicans, Blair wasted equally little time in ruling out a united Ireland.[57] Given that the British Prime Minister, if his words were taken at face value, was ruling out what Republicans had fought for, the question begged was why renew the ceasefire? Those who had long seen the Adams strategy as a *cul-de-sac* saw no case for a ceasefire, given that Republican objectives had been specifically ruled out as an outcome to any talks process. The 'Real IRA' (RIRA) was formed as a breakaway from the Provisionals, led by the former PIRA quartermaster general, Mickey McKevitt. The RIRA drew its limited support mainly from border counties in the Irish Republic. By the autumn of 1997, Provisional 'dissidents' had been marginalised, or been given preferment, requiring unequivocal support of the Adams' strategy, or, in a few cases, left, to form the 'Real IRA'.[58] The Adams' peace strategy was now secure.

Adams had also enjoyed a political triumph in the 1997 Westminster elections, recapturing West Belfast. Sinn Féin's capture of Mid-Ulster from the DUP at the same election and a strong performance in the local elections later that month, boosted party morale. The Republican leadership maintained a large number of supporters in Sinn Féin, partly through its advanced system of party consultation and the propensity to deploy Adams supporters on visits to 'educate'.[59] Within Sinn Féin, the *Cumainn* were actively consulted throughout the peace process. In part, this reflected a commitment to debate, including public discussion at the Ard Fheis beyond that of other parties, which encouraged the private voicing of grassroots sentiment, provided that the leadership was eventually supported. The consultation also had a pragmatic basis, in addition to any commitment to democracy. It reflected the fear of a split, which still haunted the movement. Sinn Féin's Ard Chomhairle remained a fluid body, with an elected membership fluctuating sufficiently to frustrate charges of oligarchy. The party thus travelled in the same direction as a united body. Party members were nonetheless obliged to embark on campaigns ending in extraordinary U-turns, the nadir of which was the 'No return to Stormont' sloganising as multi-party talks began, leading to the Good Friday Agreement—and a Northern Ireland Assembly at Stormont. Later, the party faithful were asked to campaign for a return to

Stormont when the Assembly was suspended, a scenario which embarrassed even party stalwarts.[60] By now, however the party was locked into an Agreement which kept Northern Ireland in the United Kingdom, provided an Assembly of Northern Ireland and offered, to revisit the republican phrase of the 1975, the 'sickening term' of an Irish dimension. Republicans had indeed travelled a long way, but the question begged was whether Republicanism had been left behind.

11

THE GOOD FRIDAY AGREEMENT
SDLP TRIUMPH?

The contents of the Agreement

The climax of the Northern Ireland peace process finally arrived on 10 April 1998. After prolonged multi-party negotiations, the Good Friday Agreement was reached. Although nationalists lost some ground during negotiations, the Agreement was not markedly different from the Heads of Agreement document presented by the British and Irish governments in January 1998. The Agreement contained few surprises, given that the principles of a settlement had been outlined in the 1993 Downing Street Declaration and the basic institutional framework had been drafted in Framework Documents in 1995. The Good Friday Agreement nonetheless changed some of the mechanics of the 1995 proposals. The all-Ireland dimension was reduced slightly from the 1995 plan; the idea of a 'panel of three' senior politicians to adjudicate on controversial issues was rightly dropped as unworkable, and a confederal element was added to the 1998 deals. With the IRA having renewed its ceasefire in July 1997, Sinn Féin was admitted to negotiations. Give that the party had mobilised supporters on a 'No return to Stormont' platform, Sinn Féin could hardly be an enthusiastic participant in Strand One talks on the form of a new Northern Ireland Assembly. Accordingly, the party attempted to maintain its 'purity' by ignoring most of the constitutional aspects of the deal and instead concentrating upon human rights, policing and prisoners.[1]

The Good Friday Agreement contained separate, but interrelated Strands. Strand One outlined the Northern dimension, creating a legislative Assembly of 108 Members, eighteen more seats than had been proposed three years earlier. Equivalent representation at Westminster, according to population figures, would produce a House of

Commons containing over 4,000 members. Strand Two established a North-South Ministerial Council (NSMC), weaker than the cross-border element proposed in the Framework Document, in which the British government indicated it 'had no limits of its own' on the number of policy areas to be dealt with on an all-island basis. The Good Friday Agreement was more prescriptive. The NSMC was required to consult or reach agreement on common policies, North and South. To implement policies, a minimum of six new all-island bodies, with executive powers, would be established, whilst the NSMC would also oversee cross-border cooperation in six further policy areas in which existing implementation bodies would remain. The dynamic of these all-island arrangements was restricted by the requirement that approval for more cross-border bodies was conditional upon approval from the Northern Ireland Assembly, requiring an unlikely change of attitude among unionists. Strand Three replaced intergovernmental arrangements made in the Anglo-Irish Agreement, substituting new administration under the control of a British-Irish Intergovernmental Conference. A new, fairly weak confederal aspect was created, in which devolved institutions throughout Britain and Ireland were linked via the British-Irish Council to facilitate bilateral or multilateral agreements.

If this confederal aspect of Strand Three offered some novelty, many of the themes and constitutional arrangements amounted to a reheating of old provisions.[2] In constitutional terms this was, as the SDLP Deputy Leader Seamus Mallon put it, 'Sunningdale for slow learners', although other aspects of the package contained limited conflict amelioration measures absent in 1973–4. Overriding all else in 1998, as in 1973–4, was the principle of consent for constitutional change in the position of Northern Ireland within the United Kingdom. Only with the consent of the majority of its citizens could Northern Ireland leave the United Kingdom. This effectively neutralised the language of Irish self-determination, as there was a Northern Ireland veto over the desires of the remainder of the Irish population, if that population desired Irish unity. Consent would be based on the will of members of the Northern state, the exact territorial boundaries of which (in addition to the principle of partition) had never been agreed by the Irish people. The Agreement did offer co-determination, in which the people of Ireland, North and South would (separately) determine their future. The historic role of British nationalism in shaping that future was overlooked.[3] Another long-standing theme was consociation. Although the mechanics of cross-community institutional co-operation were different from Sunningdale, the principle remained the same: power sharing in a multi-party executive, but one designed to include Republicans, rather than exclude as in the earlier consociational experiment.

In the short term at least, Unionist and nationalist ethnic blocs were entrenched through the requirement that all members of the Assembly were required to designate as either Unionist, nationalist, or other. Parallel consent was required on key issues, requiring Unionist *and* nationalist support. Provided that the Assembly could embed, Strand One would be the dominant element of the Agreement, given that the range of devolved powers awarded to the Assembly and the governing Executive was considerable, even allowing that responsibilities for security and taxation remained at Westminster. Strand Two, the all-island dimension, attempted greater precision than Sunningdale in defining cross-border arrangements. Strand Three's confederal arrangement, a British-Irish Council devoid of legislative powers but linking parliaments and assemblies in Britain and Ireland, was a Unionist idea. Arguably more important within Strand Three was continued intergovernmental administration via the Intergovernmental Conference, which replaced the machinery of the Anglo-Irish Agreement.

Given that institutional arrangements maintained partition, how could such a deal be sold to Republicans? Despite campaigning for 'no return to Stormont', the Republican leadership privately accepted the inevitability of a revival of the institution. Of course, there was the considerable consolation for senior Sinn Féin members that they would find themselves in government for the first time, within the Power-Sharing Executive, albeit presiding over a statelet they had originally intended to smash. Other than the limited cross-border dimension, the only constitutional aspect in which Sinn Féin could possibly find a positive element was the British government's commitment to repeal its claim to Northern Ireland under Section 75 of the 1920 Government of Ireland Act. Gerry Adams could thus claim at the 1998 Sinn Féin Ard-Fheis that there was 'no longer any raft of legislation' to maintain Northern Ireland as part of the United Kingdom.[4] Yet this overlooked the post-Good Friday Agreement implementation of precisely such legislation.[5] Nonetheless, the repeal of Section 75 did signify that Northern Ireland was at the edge of the union. The provisions of the Agreement amounted to the creation of a 'state within a state' whose long-term constitutional future was yet to be determined.[6] As a necessary part of the deal, the Irish Republic downgraded its territorial claim to Northern Ireland to that of a mere aspiration. The symbolic legitimation of the Republican struggle, contained in the Constitution of the Irish Republic, was now removed. Republicans could, however, see the potential of improvements in the more novel aspects of the Agreement, which were based on the politics of inclusion and identity.

Whereas Sunningdale was an attempt to marginalise republicans, the Good Friday Agreement was an attempt to co-opt them into a permanent political settlement. Sinn Féin studiously avoided use of the term 'settlement', preferring to highlight the deal's dynamic aspects and 'transitional' potential. Beyond largely unsubstantiated claims of transition, there was a big selling point for Republicans, the release of prisoners. This was a key element of the package, non-negotiable, other than on timescale, for Sinn Féin. Adams made this clear at the 1998 *Ard Fheis*, insisting that he had informed Prime Minister Tony Blair at the outset of negotiations that without full prisoner releases there would be 'no deal'.[7] The tough line, necessary to preserve party unity and deliver Republican 'ultras', was successful. It raised the question as to whether a better deal could have been achieved on cross-border co-operation had Sinn Féin been similarly strident on that point in negotiations. Lamely, the possibility that better terms could have been reached on cross-borderism was put down to 'insufficient political strength', as if the number of cross-border bodies was directly connected to the electoral performance of Sinn Féin in Northern Ireland.[8]

The politics of identity, which underpinned the Good Friday Agreement, suited Sinn Féin. The British government made no attempt to persuade nationalists that they were British and nationalists were no longer 'disloyal' citizens in an increasingly bi-national state. Sinn Féin could campaign with success on issues such as Orange parades, which were deemed to impinge upon the rights or identities of the nationalist population, and the Parades Commission, formed in 1997, prevented most parades from entering nationalist areas. Despite the genuine holistic vision of Republicanism for the long-term, sectarian issues continued to occupy many nationalists.

An SDLP analysis of the Agreement

The nationalist elements built into the Good Friday Agreement echoed elements of SDLP political strategy contained in unpublished internal documents dated September 1971. The documentation sets out the long-term thinking of the SDLP on the constitutional issue. It had a strong 'green' tinge and one could be forgiven for associating it with contemporary Sinn Féin political strategy. The SDLP noted 'that it is essential to create a system, which has the capacity to move forward at a later stage to a United Ireland'.[9] As an interim measure, the SDLP clearly desired a Northern Ireland administration 'in which the process of persuasion could take place'. John Hume directed 'persuasion' to the Republican leadership during the formal Hume-Adams dialogue in 1988, and again when talks resumed in 1993. The logic of the use of persuasion on Sinn Féin by Hume was to convince the republican movement that Irish unity could be best achieved if the armed struggle was abandoned.

The broad shape of the Good Friday Agreement reflected SDLP thinking, causing one republican to lament that the 'fingerprints of the SDLP are all over the Good Friday deal'.[10] The mechanics of the 1998 Agreement varied from those envisaged in SDLP policy documents of the 1970s. The same limits of devolution were in existence in 1998 as earlier, as the SDLP throughout this period did not support the idea of Northern Ireland institutions being able to control policing or judicial matters. Party views reflected the lack of confidence among nationalists in the RUC, the judiciary and security policy in the Province. These security issues remained reserved powers, resting with the Secretary of State for Northern Ireland, under the Good Friday Agreement, although the British government envisaged the eventual devolution of policing matters. The SDLP of the early 1970s envisaged the formation of a Commission with cross-party representation, to elect a fifteen-member executive, which in turn would appoint its own Directors of Northern Ireland Departments. The Good Friday Agreement allowed for the allocation of ministerial posts via party choice, according to the D'Hondt mechanism, based upon party strength in the Assembly. Further early proposals by the

SDLP in 1971 suggested that, following consultation with the Northern Ireland devolved administration, the British and Irish governments should legislate for a Bill of Rights in the Province. The purpose of the Bill of Rights was to guarantee equality before the law for all Northern Ireland citizens. The Good Friday Agreement makes provision for upholding human rights according to the European Convention of Human Rights and the Agreement created a Human Rights Commission for Northern Ireland.

The framework for Strand Two of the Good Friday Agreement stems from the earliest articulation of North-South relations by the SDLP in internal policy documents of late 1971. At that time, the party called for the British and Irish governments to create a Supreme Council of Ireland with representation from Northern Ireland and the Republic. Their proposed remit for the Council envisaged that it would have far greater powers than those ultimately set out in the final Agreement. Nevertheless, key ingredients of former SDLP policies are an integral part of Strand Two. In particular, they mirror early proposals for the initiation of schemes for cross-border co-operation, and 'educational, cultural and social development and the interchange of ideas' relate to principal ingredients of the Strand Two section of the Good Friday Agreement.[11]

Another dimension of early SDLP documentation is the proposition that Britain should show 'she actively desires re-unification whenever this can be achieved on such terms as will win the consent of the majority of people in Northern Ireland.'[12] The British government did not go this far in the Agreement, although some unionists feared this was the logic of its policy. In its early years, the SDLP had called on Britain to adopt this strategy of developing structures of unity in consultation with the Irish government and through the equivalent of the current Northern Ireland Assembly. The SDLP saw the potential benefits of harmonisation between co-operative bodies in the North and South and believed this would facilitate institutional persuasion of unionists of the benefits of Irish unity.

A synopsis of the early SDLP documents reveals that 'a 32-county Socialist Republic … cannot be realised immediately'. Therefore what was required were interim measures before the long-term objective of Irish unity could be attained. Other early SDLP proposals noted that the Republic might amend its Constitution to allow the citizens of Northern Ireland the opportunity to vote in presidential elections. Interestingly, the party also called for an amnesty for anyone 'convicted of or charged with "political" offences since 13 August 1969'.[13] Also, the idea of joint referendums in both North and South as the basis for expressing self-determination between both parts of Ireland was articulated by the SDLP from 1975 onwards. In short, the Good Friday Agreement put into action the ideas of the SDLP as articulated 27 years earlier. The SDLP argued that such structures could be transitional towards Irish unity, a contention now publicly held by Sinn Féin, although, privately, at least one senior party figure stated baldly that he 'never believed that the Good Friday Agreement would lead to a united Ireland in 20–30 years time'.[14] The first step for both communities, the shared governance of Northern Ireland, was described by John Hume as the 'healing process', which could lead to an agreed Ireland.[15]

Early SDLP documentation makes clear that Irish unity in the traditional sense was the ultimate goal of the party. The moderate front presented by the first leader, Gerry Fitt, camouflaged the real 'green' intentions of others, shared by the majority of rank and file SDLP members, particularly those joining after the collapse of Sunningdale.[16] It becomes apparent that the initial analysis of the Northern Ireland conflict by the SDLP has survived the passage of time and formed the basis of the current agreement. The modern Sinn Féin has become the major nationalist ambassador, even custodian, of similar policies.

There remained tensions within the SDLP's approach. Whilst Sinn Féin's 'end of history' was apparent, via ultimate British withdrawal, the SDLP was ambiguous over the extent to which the Good Friday Agreement ought to represent a final settlement, or a staging post to Irish unity. As indicated above, the SDLP believed in Irish unity. Hence, the Agreement, unionists could conclude, was a mere staging post even for its constitutional architects. This gave the Agreement, positively spun, a dynamic, or, negatively, an impermanence as its nationalist architects did not see the deal as the endgame, but merely the means to the endgame. There were also questions over what constituted the SDLP's 'Plan B' should the Agreement fail, although the same questions applied to Sinn Féin. The SDLP reverted to support for intergovernmental approaches after the collapse of Sunningdale in 1974, and there remained elements in the party as comfortable with bi-national movement towards joint British-Irish authority as with risky devolved power sharing with unionists. The electoral problems of the SDLP made intergovernmentalism an attractive prospect, compared to the risk of electoral defeats by Sinn Féin in polls for the Northern Ireland Assembly.

The SDLP membership

The peace process in Northern Ireland had been driven by a number of factors, most notably the changes within Republicanism and the development of 'pan-nationalist' commonalities. SDLP members were incidental to John Hume's largely unilateral initiatives in helping draw Gerry Adams' route map away from violence. As Feeney notes, Hume tended to go on a 'solo run', continuing to meet Adams after the formal SDLP-Sinn Féin dialogue ended in 1988, with only Mark Durkan being aware within the SDLP.[17] Nonetheless, SDLP policy was formulated more broadly, by the party executive. Although the first decade of the party's existence saw considerable tension between socialist and nationalist factions of the party, these debates petered out by the late 1970s, with the nationalist element dominant. The nationalism of the SDLP is apparent when the views of the party membership are examined. The SDLP never achieved its initial aim of attracting cross community support and it is overwhelmingly (95.1 per cent) Catholic. It developed as a nationalist party with left leanings. Most members see the party as nationalist and a majority also think the party is, as its title suggests, social democratic, but the membership is divided over whether the party is socialist (Table 11.1).[18]

Table 11.1. IDENTIFICATION OF THE SDLP BY PARTY MEMBERS (%)

| | The SDLP is a ...... party | | | | |
	Strongly agree	*Agree*	*Neither agree/disagree*	*Disagree*	*Strongly disagree*
Nationalist	31.6	24.3	7.4	2.3	2.1
Social Democratic	32.4	56.3	9.5	0.6	0.4
Socialist	9.7	40.7	24.6	16.7	3.2
Catholic	7.2	31.1	24.2	29.5	7.0
European	39.4	49.2	7.6	1.7	0.0
N = 528					

Table 11.2. CONSTITUTIONAL PREFERENCES OF SDLP MEMBERS (%)

The best solution for Northern Ireland is......					
	Strongly agree	*Agree*	*Neither agree/disagree*	*Disagree*	*Strongly disagree*
United Ireland	20.5	29.5	25.8	16.9	2.8
Joint sovereignty	6.8	27.7	21.6	26.9	8.9
Good Friday Agreement and power-sharing	41.1	39.4	11.2	4.0	1.3
Remain in UK	1.5	6.4	18.4	34.8	36.7
N = 528					

As indicated earlier, the SDLP's early policy and strategy documents indicate that the party's origins were much more nationalist than is sometimes believed. Nonetheless, the location of the party within the Civil Rights movement meant there was also a reddish, left of centre hue. Those members identifying the party as socialist were most likely to have joined between 1970 and 1974.[19] There was a greening of the party membership after this period, in that post-1975 joiners are more likely to see the party as nationalist. A section— almost exclusively post-1975 joiners—is clearly Catholic nationalist to the exclusion of competing identities. This green wing of the party is most supportive of Irish unity, or joint British-Irish sovereignty, and is the section of the party most in favour of electoral pacts with Sinn Féin. It was also the section most strongly favouring the early release of republican prisoners. Most importantly, its views are closer to those of the mainstream than those held by people seeing the party as socialist but rejecting the 'Catholic' party label.[20] A section of the party, located mainly within this green wing, believes some IRA actions may have been justifiable.

Overall, although most SDLP members see their party as nationalist, this does not necessarily lead to unanimity over constitutional solutions. Over two-thirds of members (67.6 per cent) believe that power sharing is more important than Irish unity to the SDLP and the belief that a united Ireland is the best solution is far from overwhelming, as Table 11.2 indicates.[21]

The overall figures from the author's survey are explicit: 80.5 per cent of members support the Good Friday Agreement plus power sharing; in contrast only 50 per cent support a united Ireland. The figures confirm support for partnership government in Northern Ireland with an Irish dimension, namely cross-border bodies, as outlined by the party. The findings also bolster the current SDLP policy on Irish unity as set out in the amended constitution of the party. The constitution states that the object of the SDLP is 'to promote the cause of Irish unity freely negotiated and agreed to by the people of the North and the people of the South'.[22] This philosophy is an integral dimension of the Good Friday Agreement and represents the nationalist view. Yet the views of the SDLP membership are contradictory. A substantial majority of members reject the idea that Northern Ireland should remain in the United Kingdom—the inevitable outcome, for the foreseeable future, of the Good Friday Agreement, given that the Accord enshrines the Northern consent principle. An overwhelming majority (82.4 per cent) of party members believe that the SDLP has 'achieved the bulk of its objectives through the Good Friday Agreement'. If so, a united Ireland cannot have been a primary objective of the party, or, as is confirmed by the survey, a substantial number of members believed that for the party power-sharing was of greater importance than Irish unity, irrespective of their personal nationalist tendencies. Seventy per cent of SDLP members did, however, believe that the Good Friday Agreement brought a united Ireland nearer. Four-fifths of the SDLP members identified themselves as Irish, with only 15 per cent preferring the hybrid label of Northern Irish.

Nationalists and policing

One fundamental, non-constitutional change demanded by nationalists of the Good Friday Agreement was in the policing of Northern Ireland. 'Pan-nationalism' was evident in a shared critique of the Royal Ulster Constabulary. There was less unity over proposals for change. Sinn Féin desired abolition; the SDLP wanted, and got, reform, but the shared criticism was important in achieving change. Both parties regarded the RUC as a partisan police force, unacceptable to the nationalist community. They argued that the force developed as the armed wing of Unionism when it was established in 1921. Under unionist control from 1921 to 1972 and backed by emergency security legislation, the RUC used repressive measures to suppress Republicans in Northern Ireland. Despite the introduction of direct rule from London after the end of the Stormont regime in 1972, the RUC remained largely unchanged and was rejected by the broader nationalist community. Although less vocal than Sinn Féin in condemnation of the security forces, the SDLP nevertheless acknowledged the authenticated findings of international agencies, of abuse and inhumane treatment of terrorist suspects. However, the SDLP also acknowledged the tragedies inflicted on the RUC. As onetime policing spokesman, Seán Farren publicly extended his sympathy and the sympathies of the SDLP to the families of bereaved and injured RUC members. Farren also publicly acknowledged that the RUC defended sections of the nationalist community against attack during the Troubles.[23]

The 1998 *Northern Ireland Life and Times Survey* noted a significant difference between SDLP and Sinn Féin supporters on the issue of police reform. While 63.4 per cent of SDLP supporters polled maintained the RUC should be reformed, only 26.5 per cent of Sinn Féin supporters held the same view, preferring abolition.[24] In the author's sruvey, SDLP members overwhelmingly (94.1 per cent) backed 'radical reform' of the police. Unlike Sinn Féin, the SDLP never called for the RUC to disband, but rather requested 'fundamental changes' to policing in the context of 'new wider arrangements'.[25] The SDLP always maintained that support for policing in Northern Ireland could only occur 'when both traditions agreed on how the province was to be governed'.[26] The SDLP and Sinn Féin demanded judicial inquiries into the killings of Pat Finucane, Rosemary Nelson and Robert Hamill. All three of these killings, nationalists believed, were tarnished by RUC collusion with Loyalist paramilitaries and inadequate police 'investigations'.

The establishment of an Independent Commission on Policing, chaired by Chris Patten, heralded change.[27] When the Patten Report was published in 1999, the SDLP took the position that if the government fully implemented the recommendations of the report there would be a police force acceptable to the whole community in Northern Ireland.[28] Sinn Féin was in a tricky position, having demanded the disbandment of the RUC, preceded by its disarmament and withdrawal from nationalist areas.[29] The Patten proposals promised substantial changes to the composition and ethos of the police force, renamed the Police Service of Northern Ireland. As such it was difficult to oppose the report in the name of a purist abolition stance and rejection of a 'neo-colonial' police force. Sinn Féin compromised, by viewing the report as a reasonable baseline for change. Gerry Adams argued that 'Patten, implemented in full, could provide a minimum threshold from which to achieve acceptable policing'.[30] Owing to the attempted watering down of the implementation of the Patten proposals under the Police Act of Peter Mandelson, Secretary of State for Northern Ireland from 1999 until 2001, Sinn Féin refused to take seats on the newly constituted Policing Board.[31] The longer-term expectation was that Sinn Féin would eventually take seats. This would of course mean presiding over a six-counties police service dedicated to arresting diehard Republicans keen to maintain 'armed struggle'. In addition to Sinn Féin representation on the Province-wide, 19-strong Board, District Policing Partnerships would have Sinn Féin majorities in areas such as West Belfast.

By 2003 most of the Patten proposals had been implemented, new impetus having been provided through negotiations at Weston Park in England in 2001 and the replacement of Mandelson by John Reid. The new Police Service was less associated with 'Unionist' symbols of the state, such as the Crown or the Union flag. New recruits were no longer required to swear an oath of allegiance to the Crown and recruitment was undertaken on a 50–50 Protestant-Catholic ratio. In February 2001 John Hume hinted that he was encouraged by the negotiations relating to policing because ultimately the changes could lead the SDLP to accept and propose members for the new Policing Board.[32] Prior to the 2001 general and local government elections in Northern Ireland the SDLP indicated that the party wished to endorse the new police service, and became the first political party to nominate members to the new Policing Board and District Policing Partnerships. The party declared itself satisfied with the estimated 94 changes to the original Mandelson Police Act of May 2000.

Key SDLP concerns were addressed in the new implementation plan. These included full powers to be given to the Oversight Commissioner to manage the necessary changes recommended in the Patten Report; the phasing-out of the full time reserve over three years; the designs for a flag and badge of the new police force, to be ideologically neutral; a 50 per cent reduction in employees of the former RUC Special Branch; the introduction of a part-time reserve whose members will be enlisted primarily from nationalist areas of Northern Ireland; new legislation to enable members of the Gardaí join the new Northern Ireland police service; and the promise that the British and Irish governments will appoint an international judge to look at the Nelson, Hamill and Finucane cases.[33] The SDLP involvement in the first cross-community supported policing in Northern Ireland marks realignment in nationalist communities. Rather than taking credit for their input to the changes to the RUC, Sinn Féin indicated hostility to the revised policing arrangements, stressing that they remained a considerable dilution of the Patten proposals.

The SDLP was partly responsible for the idea of an Independent Commission on Criminal Justice matters.[34] The concept was set out in Annex B of the Good Friday Agreement Review of the Criminal Justice System. It obliged the British government to charge the Commission to pursue a full review of the criminal justice system in Northern Ireland. The Report of the Criminal Justice Review Group was published in March 2000. Generally the SDLP welcomed the broad principles in the review. In particular the party welcomed the establishment of a 'Judicial Appointments Commission and Independent Prosecution Service, proposals for the treatment of juvenile offenders, restorative justice, justice co-operation on the island and training in human rights for criminal justice practitioners'.[35] SDLP submissions to the Criminal Justice Review recommended the 'appointment of Judges at all levels' and the establishment of an Independent Prosecution Service to cover criminal prosecutions at every level of the Criminal Justice system. The SDLP also welcomed other aspects of the Rights, Safeguards and Equality section of the Good Friday Agreement. These have included provisions that British law is incorporated into the European Convention of Human Rights and that equality of opportunity is enacted with reference to the 1998 Northern Ireland Act. Other measures welcomed by the SDLP and Sinn Féin included the creation of the Human Rights Commission in March 1999 and the establishment of the Equality Commission in October 1999.

The impact of the Agreement: electoral problems?

The claim of the SDLP that it was the architect of the Good Friday Agreement may have much validity. However, a triumph for its political thinking has not been translated into electoral success relative to Sinn Féin. Having effectively produced the 'big idea' of the Good Friday Agreement, a legitimate question to ask of the SDLP leadership was 'What next?' The SDLP was respected as the producer of the constitutional architecture, but it was Sinn Féin that was increasingly trusted with the furnishing.

Helped by larger turnouts in nationalist-held constituencies than unionist areas, the nationalist vote has risen across the two parties, but most of the increase can be attributed to the rise in Sinn Féin support from 78,000 in 1992 to 176,000 in 2001.[36] The percentage transfer votes from the SDLP to Sinn Féin jumped to nearly 75 per cent in 2001 and 2003, from 53 per cent in 1993 and only 32 per cent in 1989.[37] Table 11.3 indicates the closeness of the electoral contests between the two parties and demonstrates the electoral rise of Sinn Féin.

Table 11.3. SDLP-SINN FÉIN ELECTORAL COMPETITION, 1982–2003

Election		Vote share (%)	
		SDLP	Sinn Féin
1982	Assembly	18.8	10.1
1983	General	17.9	13.4
1984	European	22.1	13.3
1985	Local	21.1	11.4
1987	General	21.1	11.4
1989	Local	21.0	11.2
1992	General	23.5	10.0
1993	Local	22.0	12.4
1994	European	28.9	9.0
1996	Forum	21.4	15.5
1997	General	24.1	16.1
1997	Local	20.7	16.9
1998	Assembly	22.0	17.6
1999	European	28.2	17.4
2001	General	21.0	21.7
2001	Local	19.4	20.7
2003	Assembly	17.0	23.5

Although the 1998 Assembly elections confirmed the continuing rise of Sinn Féin, they were reasonably pleasing for the SDLP, leading to false optimism concerning the electoral benefits accruing to the party from the Good Friday Agreement. The SDLP gained more votes than any other party for the first time in its history. With 177,963 votes, 22 per cent of the total poll, the SDLP won twenty-four seats in the Assembly. Sinn Féin won 142,848 votes, 17.7 per cent of the electorate, yielding eighteen seats. Sinn Féin picked up two-thirds of the vote transfers of SDLP supporters. By 2001 any SDLP hopes that the Good Friday Agreement, like the 1985 Anglo-Irish Agreement, would strengthen the party's vote relative to Sinn Féin had evaporated. For the first time Sinn Féin outpolled the SDLP, in the Westminster and local elections. Sinn Féin now had four Westminster MPs, compared to the SDLP's three. In the local elections the SDLP obtained 117 seats in Northern Ireland, a higher figure than Sinn Féin's 108, but this did not disguise the significance of the electoral switch. In eight years, Sinn Féin had more than doubled its number of councillors, from 51 in 1993 to 108 in 2001.

By 2001 the only safe SDLP Westminster seats appeared to be Foyle and South Down, held by John Hume and Eddie McGrady respectively, but Hume's retirement in 2001 left Foyle vulnerable to Sinn Féin's advance. In the 2003 assembly elections, the SDLP's vote there declined by almost 12 per cent, compared to a 5 per cent overall drop. The SDLP had relied heavily upon Hume's personal vote, which delivered the highest first preference vote ever for the SDLP, 190,731 (28.1 per cent) in the 1999 European election. Hume polled 24,538 votes in the 2001 Westminster election, a 2.3 per cent drop from the previous general election, but sufficient for a comfortable 11,550 lead over his Sinn Féin rival Mitchell McLaughlin. A problematic development for the SDLP in the 1998 Assembly election was the low level of support for Mark Durkan, the new leader of the party. In the 1998 election Mitchell McLaughlin of Sinn Féin polled 5,341 votes, 918 more than Mark Durkan.

Despite the high profile of Seamus Mallon in his role as Deputy First Minister in the Belfast Assembly, his majority over Sinn Féin dropped to only 3,575 in Newry and Armagh. In South Down the SDLP obtained three Assembly seats to only one for Sinn Féin at the 1998 Assembly elections. The SDLP member Eddie McGrady has held the Westminster seat since he defeated Enoch Powell (UUP) in 1987. McGrady held the seat at the 2001 general election, obtaining 24,136 votes (46.3 per cent) to Sinn Féin's 10,278 (19.7 per cent). However, the vote for McGrady decreased by 2,045 from the 1997 general election, while Sinn Féin doubled its vote from 5,127 votes. The SDLP was particularly disappointed by the result in West Tyrone at the 2001 General Election. In the 1998 Assembly Elections, the SDLP and Sinn Féin held two seats each. The party candidate in the 2001 Westminster election, Bríd Rogers, was popular in her role combating the foot-and-mouth epidemic as Agriculture Minister in the Northern Ireland Assembly. Despite the large amount of effort the party assigned to her campaign, she was not only beaten, but came third with 13,942 votes (28.7 per cent). Sinn Féin's Pat Doherty polled 19,814 voted (40.8 per cent) to win the seat.

In West Belfast the SDLP was crushed. In 1992 Joe Hendron won back the seat for the SDLP from Gerry Adams with 17,415 votes, a majority of 589. However, Adams regained the seat for Sinn Féin in the 1997 General Election with 25,662 votes (56 per cent) to the 17,753 (39 per cent) votes cast for Joe Hendron. In the 2001 contest the SDLP's representative, Alex Attwood, achieved only 7,754 votes (18.9 per cent) to 27,096 votes (66.1 per cent) cast for Gerry Adams and Sinn Féin. In the 1998 Assembly Elections for West Belfast, the SDLP won two seats (24.93 per cent) while Sinn Féin won four (58.98 per cent). Adams' counterpart, Martin McGuinness, also won an overall majority of votes cast (50.1 per cent) in retaining his mid-Ulster seat. Meanwhile, Michelle Gildernew won a fourth Westminster seat for Sinn Féin, elected MP for Fermanagh and South Tyrone with 17,739 votes (34.1 per cent), a majority of 53 votes over the UUP. The SDLP candidate, Tommy Gallagher, obtained only 9,706 votes (18.7 per cent of the overall vote). At the 1997 General Election Gallagher polled 11,060 votes (23 per cent) for the SDLP, only marginally behind Gerry McHugh of Sinn Féin.

For the SDLP the new 'respectability' of Sinn Féin was bad electoral news. Hume's altruism in helping Sinn Féin from the political wilderness was aimed at resolving the 'big picture', but it ensured that the SDLP lost much of the supposed 'moral' edge over its rival, crucial among middle-class Catholics. Recruitment to the SDLP was static and the average age of a party member was fifty-seven. Two-thirds of members declared themselves inactive within the party.[38] For the SDLP there was no vote to farm. Whilst Sinn Féin could pick off the SDLP by adopting its agenda and promising vigorous delivery of the Good Friday Agreement, the SDLP had only the rising nationalist population and its position as a repository of Sinn Féin lower preference transfers as sources of electoral solace. There was a small Catholic Alliance vote to be picked up, given the centre party's demise, but this was insufficient compensation. The other hope, of cross-community vote transfers from pro-Agreement Unionists, could not be entirely discounted, but the evidence from the 2001 local elections and 2003 assembly contest was not encouraging, as the early hopes of electoral thawing produced by the Agreement began to subside. In 2003, less than one per cent of surplus votes for the first elected candidate were transferred across the community divide at the next count. Although lower preferences across the divide were more evident, they were still very much minority choices.

The electoral implications of the new politics of Northern Ireland were clear. Although the Good Friday Agreement could be viewed as predominantly an SDLP accord, the nationalist electorate did not see the party as the most appropriate defender of its interests in the new political dispensation. Sinn Féin was seen as the party more likely to ensure full implementation of the Agreement. The SDLP membership remained divided over how to cope with the rise of Sinn Féin; almost half (47.3 per cent) favoured electoral pacts, but Sinn Féin's interest in these was diminishing as it overtook the SDLP. Republicans promoted the Good Friday Agreement even more strongly than it theoretical architects in the SDLP. Meanwhile, the SDLP looked increasingly old and middle-class, lacking radical zeal. Such shortcomings were acknowledged in a leaked internal party review in April 2000. Under a consociational, ethnic bloc settlement, it was likely that the centrifugal forces of Sinn Féin and the Democratic Unionist Party would gain, as the best defenders of their respective ethnic pillars.

12

TRIUMPH OR SELL-OUT?
SINN FÉIN AND CONSTITUTIONAL REPUBLICANISM

Republican politics and the Good Friday Agreement

Sinn Féin played little part in the construction of the constitutional aspects of the Good Friday Agreement, preferring instead to concentrate upon the Agreement's micro-agenda, seen as more likely to deliver tangible rewards. Insofar as Republicans offered a position on the constitutional agenda, it was to ensure that Strand Two of the Agreement contained an all-Ireland dimension approaching that of the 1995 Framework Documents. Only on 24 March 1998, less than three weeks before the final Agreement, did Sinn Féin submit its proposals for the three strands of the Agreement.[1]

Predictably, the party insisted that any agreement needed to be part of a transitional process towards Irish unity and independence, and that therefore powerful, all-Ireland bodies were required. Whether the six new bodies created could be viewed as powerful was a moot point, dependent upon whether the range of competences of each body could be expanded. Sinn Féin also insisted that North-South bodies needed to be 'immune from the veto of any proposed six-county institutions, with no limit on the nature and extent of their functions, with the dynamic and ability to grow'.[2] In this respect, the Republican project was a failure, as expansion of the number of North-South bodies was conditional upon the approval of the Northern Ireland Assembly (and Dáil Éireann). Even greater political strength for Sinn Féin would not finesse this difficulty, given the need for cross-community support within the Northern Assembly for expansion of cross-border arrangements. A change of political approach from Unionists, embracing acceptance of the logic of cross-border co-

213

operation, was needed. On cross-border cooperation the Sinn Féin leader declared:[3]

> The All-Ireland Ministerial Council will plot a course to harmonise and strengthen the political, economic, cultural and social relationships among all sections of our people. Taken together, we can see that these institutions provide a dynamic that will transform Ireland and its people, and provide a meaningful process of national reconciliation.

Allowing that Adams appeared to ask a great deal of Food Safety and Inland Waterways Boards, the symbolic value of the North-South Ministerial Council was nonetheless considerable. The first meeting of ministers from the Northern Assembly and Dáil Éireann in 1999 saw historic 'enemies', David Trimble and Martin McGuinness, sitting around the same table and offered hope that the two parts of the island might be reconciled via an institutional and economic logic, whatever the restrictions upon such progress contained within the Good Friday Agreement. Diehard Republicans attempted to dampen the effect of Sinn Féin's parade. Bobby Sands' sister, Bernadette Sands-McKevitt, offered the most wounding comment in her assertion that 'Bobby did not die for cross-border bodies with executive powers. He did not die for nationalists to be equal to British citizens within the Northern Ireland state.'[4]

On the plus side, executive cross-border bodies represented the first withering of the border since partition. A limited exercise in co-determination took place in the vote on the Good Friday Agreement. Against this, the British government retained sovereignty over Northern Ireland and the 'consent principle' was embedded. Leading Republicans could insist to their followers that there was no longer a raft of legislation maintaining Britain's claim to sovereignty. However, as Hadfield points out, the replacement of the 1920 Government of Ireland Act after the Good Friday Agreement was legally 'of no significance'.[5] Furthermore, even if Britain's claim *had* been reduced, this was nothing compared to the reversal in the Republic's position on Northern Ireland, the reintegration of the 'national territory' now reduced to mere aspiration. In an assessment of surprising frankness, Sinn Féin's solitary member of Dáil Éireann at the time the Good Friday Agreement was reached, Caoimhghín Ó Caoláin, acknowledged that the 'incorporation of consent into Article 3 presents a major difficulty. Consent here, once again, is unarguably the Unionist veto in disguise.'[6] The perceptions that had long dominated republicanism, North and South, that partition and British rule in Northern Ireland were illegitimate and that the Northern state was a 'failed' political entity, were downgraded, although the end of British rule remained an objective. Instead the emphasis was upon ending the formal British claim to sovereignty.[7] The real meaning of this was that Sinn Féin supported a deal that reconstituted British sovereignty by making it even more dependent explicitly upon the will of the people of Northern Ireland, irrespective of the view of the people of Ireland as a whole. Despite Sinn Féin's unwillingness to formally accept the 'consent principle', this amounted to recognition of Northern Ireland, as its population unit would continue to determine which government acted as the sovereign power. Meanwhile the limits to the all-Ireland basis of the agreement were evident in the refusal of the Irish government to support Sinn Féin's demand for voting rights for Northern nationalists in Irish presidential elections and referenda.

Selling the deal as transformative was an understandable necessity. It allowed the grassroots to believe progress was being made. The leadership's message was reinforced at the crucial 1998 Ard Fheis by a helpful speech from Thenjiwe Mtintso, Deputy Secretary General of the African National Congress, which used the discourse of transformation, transition and evolution favoured by the Sinn Féin leadership.[8] The ANC model was indeed used by the Sinn Féin leadership, although the difference, put simply, was stark—the ANC had achieved its primary objectives. Sinn Féin's Ard Chomhairle, encouraging support for the Good Friday Agreement, offered the following: the deal was not a permanent settlement; it is 'clearly transitional'; it 'weakens the union'; 'it promotes conditions for advancing the equality, rights and justice'; it 'can be a basis for pushing forward national and democratic objectives'; and 'it allows us to move our struggle into a new and potentially more productive phase'.[9] The biggest difficulty lay in the 'transition' claim, when a literal reading of the Agreement (on which Sinn Féin often proved keen) neutered this assertion, whilst the 'weakening' of the union insistence was more aspirational than actual.

Conflict resolution measures

Away from constitutional issues, Republicans fared rather better. The non-negotiability of the demand for prisoner releases led to Republicans gaining virtually all they desired in this area. The only concession made by Sinn Féin's leadership was to extend the period for the completion of prisoner releases from one year to two. Sinn Féin also had a broader 'justice and equality agenda'. The party saw itself as the chief exponent of the demand for nationalist 'rights'. With Commissions on Policing, Human Rights and Equality established under the Good Friday Agreement, Sinn Féin was able to articulate plans for change across broad areas. The Northern Ireland Human Rights Commission issued a consultative document paving the way for the introduction of a comprehensive Bill of Rights in Northern Ireland.[10] For Sinn Féin the development of 'parity of esteem' for the nationalist community would be located within a legalistic, rights-based framework. The party's demand that movement from 'equity' to 'equality' of treatment must be through statutory provision appeared likely to be realised. Nonetheless, the party line softened from 1998, when it demanded that policing, human rights, the legal system and the administration of justice should come within the remit of North-South institutions.[11] None of these areas came under the remit of cross-border bodies established under the Good Friday Agreement.

Whatever the wideness of the equality agenda, the Ard Chomhairle's (executive's) 2000 political report on Justice and Equality concentrated exclusively upon the need for policing changes and demilitarisation.[12] During the 1990s Sinn Féin's demand for disbandment of the RUC, dismissed as a slogan by the SDLP, had remained. Yet the party reduced its demands in 2000 to full implementation of the Patten Commission report on policing, a swift policy change generally overlooked amid Unionist hostility to Patten's recommendations. Some members noticed the shift in attitude from RUC disbandment to support for Patten, with the North Belfast *Comhairle Ceantair* tabling a critical motion to the 2000 Ard Fheis arguing that 'our party leadership should be promoting a more clearly defined policy on our attitude to the Patten Report on policing'. At the 2003 Ard Fheis, the Newry *Cumann* put forward a motion resolving that 'no Sinn Féin representative can sit on any Policing Board or similar body while Britain has jurisdiction over the Six Counties', a motion defeated by the conference. Instead the Sinn Féin president promised that any decision to enter the Policing Board would be determined by a special Ard Fheis.[13] Although radical in parts and offering substantial change, including that of the name of the force, the Patten Report fell short of traditional Republican ideas and reconstituted a 'Six Counties' police force. Nonetheless, in 2001, Sinn Féin's spokesman on policing, Gerry Kelly, declared that 'if the Patten Report was implemented in full there may be a basis for a new policing service'.[14]

Sinn Féin shared much of the critique of the RUC offered in the Patten Report, particularly that the force was seen by many nationalists as a Unionist defender of the state rather than as a policing service. Sinn Féin representatives were also offered the prospect of input into aspects of the operations of the force, at national level, via a nineteen-member Policing Board and locally through the creation of District Policing Partnership Boards. A diluted version of Patten offered sufficient gains to nationalists in respect of the composition and accountability of the force to entice the SDLP on to the new policing boards, but Sinn Féin declined its seats, claiming that only eleven of the original Patten proposals remained undiluted in the British government's implementation plan offered in 2000. Sinn Féin remained aggrieved over the changes to Patten in a number of key areas. These included the new oath (to be sworn only by new officers); the ban on former prisoners serving on District Policing Partnership Boards (DPPBs); the changes to DPPBs; the retention of plastic bullets; the retention of Special Branch (the 'political police') and the Police Reserve; and the retention of the title RUC within the name of the 'new' police force.[15] Many of Sinn Féin's concerns were addressed in the 2001 Police Act.[16]

Although support for Patten was indicative of a further reversal of Sinn Féin policy, the refusal by the party to take seats on the new Policing Board indicated the strength of feeling on the issue. Several of the party's councillors indicated their hostility, suggesting that the 'RUC had to go';[17] 'that there will be no compromise on this one';[18] and that 'only disbandment and a new police force could attract Catholics into policing'.[19]

Selling the Agreement: the maintenance of Republican unity

Despite the inevitability of a return to Stormont, given Sinn Féin's acceptance of Strand 1 of the Good Friday Agreement, there was some nervousness within the Sinn Féin leadership in the selling of the GFA to the membership. For this reason, the Ard Chomhairle recommended that the April 1998 Ard Fheis be reconvened in May for a decision on the Agreement. In the event, support for the GFA was overwhelming. At the reconvened conference, meeting under the optimistic slogan 'Our Future—a United Ireland', 97 per cent of delegates voted in favour of allowing Sinn Féin's elected representatives to enter Stormont. It is possible to speculate that the margin of victory for the leadership might have been lower had a secret ballot taken place. The debates at the April and May conferences contained a sizeable number of speakers hostile to the Agreement, mainly representatives from the Irish Republic. Nonetheless it is inconceivable that the Ard Chomhairle would have failed to secure the two-thirds majority required for change. Whilst there was acceptance that the GFA was far from ideal, all supporters saw it as a dynamic agreement rather than a final settlement.

Doubters were reassured by the presence of an unusually large number of IRA figures, supportive of the leadership's new political approach. This was signalled most dramatically by the arrival of the 'Balcombe Street Gang' on the platform, released temporarily from their life sentences for the Ard Fheis. Support from this section of the movement signalled that the Good Friday Agreement represented an honourable compromise to those that had endured most and that the IRA was fully supportive of historic change. Nonetheless one former Belfast IRA commander, although present in Ballsbridge in Dublin, declined to enter the RDS conference hall when the decision to enter Stormont was being debated. Brendan Hughes was later to publicly criticise the Republican leadership, claiming that dwindling enthusiasm amongst Republicans was 'not because people are war weary— they are politics weary…The political process has created a class of professional liars and unfortunately it contains many Republicans.'[20]

The totally unarmed phase of Republican struggle had begun with the 1997 revived ceasefire and was now embedded, with the need to preserve unity weighing heavily. The 'Brighton bomber', Patrick Magee, argued that the IRA had been defeated in the past because of the 'lack of unity, especially between the soldiers and the politicians'.[21] For some time the Sinn Féin leadership had been fairly open in trying to end the IRA's campaign of violence. After the 1994 ceasefire former IRA personnel moved seamlessly into positions within Sinn Féin, acting as election candidates, joining negotiating teams and participating within public forums, such as the Irish Forum for Peace and

Reconciliation. Publicly the separation of the two wings of the movement was emphasised to an unprecedented extent. As one example, Sinn Féin's 1997 Westminster general election manifesto insisted that 'Sinn Féin can only speak for itself and on behalf of its electorate. Sinn Féin is not the IRA.'[22] This of course was true, but increasingly, the IRA was becoming Sinn Féin. The IRA's Convention in October 1996 had marginalised potential dissidents by allowing them to remain a majority on the IRA's Executive, but a minority on the Army Council.[23] Following the re-election of a Labour government at Westminster in June 2001, the Army Council unilaterally announced the reinstatement of the IRA's cessation. Technically, it could still do this, as the restoration of a cessation was not tantamount to a permanent ceasefire, whatever the private ambitions of the leading figures on the Council. Such figures sold the revival of the cessation to doubters on the grounds that violence remained a tactical option.[24] Having sold peace to the IRA, Adams now had to sell a deal way short of Irish independence to the politicians within the movement. At an internal Sinn Féin conference in County Meath later in November, Adams urged the membership to endorse greater pragmatism. Whilst insisting that Republican goals remained unaltered, Adams prepared the movement for a negotiated settlement short of desired objectives. In a theme to become familiar, Adams insisted that pan-nationalist alliances were a necessary evil arising from Sinn Féin's lack of political strength.

The decision to revive the cessation indicated the decisive triumph of the political approach. The Labour government, enjoying a huge parliamentary majority, offered a more pragmatic approach in inviting Sinn Féin to talks. The decommissioning of IRA weapons was downgraded as a requirement, although Unionists maintained pressure on the issue. Furthermore, Sinn Féin was given assurances that the government would make headway on prisoners and the 'equality agenda'. Nonetheless, changes in Labour Party policy since 1994 indicated that the constitutional deal would differ little from that offered by any Conservative government. Labour's approach would be based loosely upon the Framework Document, which heralded a return to Stormont.

Keeping the flame burning? Republican ultras

As the ceasefire was revived and Stormont loomed, there were significant defections from the PIRA, although less than might have been expected given the extent of change. Most 'purist' Republicans had left in 1986, although there remained hardcore militarists, satisfied at the time by the leadership's continuing commitment to the use of force. The formation of the 32-County Sovereignty Committee during the 1990s, initially as a 'pressure group' within Sinn Féin, offered a challenge to the Sinn Féin leadership, as it contained prominent figures within the movement, including the Republican hunger strike pioneer, Bobby Sands' sister Bernadette Sands-McKevitt. By the beginning of 1998, the Committee had developed a military wing, the Real IRA (RIRA) comprising defectors from the PIRA. The renewal of the Provisionals' ceasefire, despite the British Prime Minister's insistence that there would be not be a united Ireland, left senior IRA figures, such as the quartermaster general, Mickey McKevitt, so unimpressed that they left to form the Real IRA.

The 32-County Sovereignty Committee and the RIRA had little interest in the republican purity of the earlier 'dissidents' of Republican Sinn Féin. The Committee tried to press Ireland's right to indivisible sovereignty via the United Nations. Members of the new grouping had supported the end of abstentionism in the Republic in 1986. However, the RIRA/32-County Sovereignty Committee had tired of the U-turns of the Republican leadership. The end of abstention regarding Dáil Éireann in 1986 had been accepted because a continuation of armed struggle was promised. Now, that struggle was being ended. Republicans had been mobilised on a 'No Return to Stormont' platform, yet the Sinn Féin leadership was heading inexorably in that direction. According to the same leadership, no decommissioning of Republican arms would occur, yet an International Commission on Decommissioning was about to be established. Sinn Féin had signed up to the Mitchell Principles of non-violence. Despite the PIRA's later statement pointing out that it had not taken Sinn Féin's course, adherence to the Mitchell Principles meant that Sinn Féin could not support armed struggle, even whilst the British government claimed sovereignty over Northern Ireland for the foreseeable future. Critics of the Adams-McGuinness line argued that the Mitchell Principles meant that the second IRA cessation had far greater implications than did the first, as it now needed to be permanent. The 32-County Sovereignty Committee and Republican Sinn Féin scorned the idea that the Stormont route offered any form of transition to a united Ireland. Sinn Féin was derided as a 'typically reformist' party'.[25]

The numbers supporting the RIRA/32 County Sovereignty Committee and Republican Sinn Féin/Continuity IRA were small. Nonetheless, two commentators have argued that their growth was considerable in the first half of 1998, as Republicans disillusioned with Sinn Féin's entry to Stormont at last found an alternative.[26] However, the RIRA's disastrous bombing of Omagh in August 1998, killing 29 civilians, confirmed the danger and futility of continued armed struggle to wavering Republicans. As Adams condemned the bombing, highlighting Sinn Féin's swift moves away from support for Republican violence, the RIRA was forced to call a cessation. With PIRA prisoners to be freed by the summer of 2000, and thus in debt to the leadership for the negotiated deal, the challenge to the authority of the Sinn Féin and Provisional IRA leaderships of 1996–7 had evaporated. Overall, it appeared that the Adams project had been hugely successful in its ability to 'reconcile subtly all but the most intransigent idealist to a settlement which contains nothing that can be realistically be seen as even "transitional" to a united Ireland'.[27]

Although the RIRA revived with a London bombing campaign in 2000, its support remained negligible, confined mainly to border areas, despite attempts to develop in Ballymurphy in Belfast. The organisation suffered internal disputes among prisoners and appeared to be heavily penetrated by the security services, with a large number of operations intercepted. The continuing presence of 'prisoners of war' and their demands for political status, reminiscent of the Provisionals' campaigns of the late 1970s and early 1980s but without the levels of support, was an embarrassment for Sinn Féin, which preferred to ignore the plight of incarcerated ultras.

The difficulty for dissidents was articulating a coherent alternative to Sinn Féin's strategy. The Provisionals' leadership was regularly denounced in the pages of *Saoirse* (Republican Sinn Féin) and the *Sovereign Nation* (32 County Sovereignty Committee), the latter disappearing from view in 2002. A more eclectic set of criticisms could be found in the pages of *Fourthwrite*, the journal of the Irish Republican Writers Group, most of its contributors rejecting armed struggle whilst criticising the Sinn Féin leadership. Republican Sinn Féin offered the standard 1919 Republicanism of abstentionism, allied to demands for a federal Ireland. Its criticisms extended even to the 32 County Sovereignty Committee, seen as 'impure' owing to its lack of interest in

Southern abstentionism. Disinterested in engaging with opponents, Republican Sinn Féin claimed its mandate from British occupation and the need to fight partition. The party offered no particular vision of how the British government was to be removed from Ireland, nor was there any consideration of the British identity of Northern Protestants, who would nonetheless be given autonomy via the federalism of *Éire Núa*. Armed struggle was the answer to British occupation, although this was rarely discussed in detail the pages of *Saoirse*. Occasional items praising the Continuity IRA appeared, citing the CIRA's denunciations as 'nauseating hypocrites' of those, such as 'British Crown minister' Martin McGuinness, calling for the organisation's disbandment.[28] The *Sovereign Nation* offered left-leaning critiques of the pan-nationalism of the 1990s.[29] It offered a number of criticisms of how, through the 'gains' of the 'equality agenda' of the GFA, working-class Republicanism had been translated into middle-class nationalism during the peace process. *Sovereign Nation* and its apparent successor, *forum*, did not elaborate a clear form of oppositional politics.

The logic of the Republican ultra position could be summarised thus: armed struggle is a necessary and morally correct form of resistance to British colonial occupation. Even if armed struggle could not be guaranteed success in forcing British withdrawal, it performed the function of destabilising the Northern state, whereas constitutional approaches conferred legitimacy and allowed the Six-County state to became embedded. Armed struggle did not require a formal mandate from the people any more than the rebels of the 1916 Rising required a mandate. A vanguard role was necessary for the IRA, justified on the basis of the infringement by Britain of Irish national sovereignty. Partition had been imposed against the will of the majority of Irish people. The strongest case amid these shibboleths was the scepticism over whether the 'Stormont deal' was transitory. In this respect Republican Sinn Féin quoted approvingly one of the architects of the Irish government's involvement in the pan-nationalist alliance, Dr Martin Mansergh, who stated that 'there is no evidence, let alone inevitability, from international experience, that cross-border cooperation necessarily leads to Irish reunification.'[30]

Dissent against the Provisionals could be forcefully discouraged. A prominent Republican Sinn Féin supporter in Derry, Michael Donnelly, was attacked in June 1998.[31] One of the few Real IRA supporters in Belfast, Joseph O'Connor, was killed, apparently by PIRA, in 2000. After blaming the Provisionals, Anthony McIntyre, a former PIRA prisoner and frequent contributor to *Fourthwrite*, was temporarily forced to leave his Ballymurphy home. Critics remained isolated and Sinn Féin's electoral successes, combined with divisions in Unionism, the 'records' of those staying with Sinn Féin and the legacy of Omagh, all combined to preserve unity. This was abetted by divisions among dissidents and the lack of a clear alternative to Sinn Féin's strategy.

Decommissioning physical force Republicanism

Those within the Republican movement nervous over the changes demanded by the Good Friday Agreement were partly reassured by the refusal of the IRA to surrender its weaponry for three years after the Agreement. For critics of the new Republican direction, the main-tenance of the Provisional IRA as merely a 'self regenerating military machine' was useless without a 'political dynamic'.[32] For supporters of Sinn Féin, the politics of change offered via electoral growth and internal change within Northern Ireland provided that political dynamic. Although the Good Friday Agreement was ambiguous on decommissioning, a combination of the necessities of the political growth of Sinn Féin and Unionist outrage at the lack of movement on the issue led the Republican leadership to move towards the placing of weapons beyond use. Meanwhile, guns were used merely for 'inter-nal housekeeping', in maintaining 'order' within a section of the na-tionalist community. Sinn Féin's chair, Mitchell McLaughlin, insisted in June 2001 that 'only a fool would say that the IRA are completely silent'.[33] Nonetheless, two days later McLaughlin invited an audience in London to 'compare the IRA's position in Easter 1998 where it was "not a bullet, not an ounce" to where it is now'.[34] By June 2001 Gerry Adams spoke at the Weston Park summit, involving the two govern-ments and all parties except the DUP, about working to end physical force Republicanism. This was a new form of words to bolster his earlier assertion that 'the violence we have seen must be for all of us now a thing of the past, over, done with and gone.'[35]

'Not a bullet, not an ounce' was little more than a slogan, useful during the uncertainties of the forging of the Good Friday Agree-ment. It did reflect a determination among Republicans that weap-onry would not be publicly handed over to historic enemies. Also irritated by unionist demands for such a humiliation, the IRA's historic opponent, the British government, had no desire for the public surrender of the IRA, with its inherent risk of Republican disunity. The British government ensured that the Good Friday Agreement fudged the issue of decommissioning, and at no stage did the Ulster Unionist Party leadership ever receive an indication from the British government that an arms handover (as distinct from decommissioning as defined and initiated by republicans) would be pressed.

The decommissioning issue became a debate over essentialism versus voluntarism in respect of the process. As early as June 1998, the Provisionals' OC in the Maze, Pádraig Wilson, indicated that 'voluntary decommissioning' would be a 'natural development of the peace process'.[36] The implication was that Republicans, like Unionists, accepted that resolution of the weapons issue was part of the process, but that differences remained on control over decommissioning. Republicans stuck to several points. First, the organisational separation of the IRA and Sinn Féin was emphasised. According to the Good Friday Agreement, Sinn Féin's ascribed role was no more than that of persuader to the IRA on decommissioning. This formal separation was useful, given the second point that, on any reading of the Agreement, there were no sanctions to be taken against Sinn Féin should the IRA fail to decommission. The Good Friday Agreement did indicate that weapons should be decommissioned by 22 May 2000, which turned the Unionist case from, arguably, mere moralising to something of more substance. Finally, the IRA linked decommissioning to the 'removal of the causes of conflict', an ambiguous assertion which, on a reading of 'true' Republicanism, could only mean removal of British sovereignty.

In July 1999 Sinn Féin declared that 'all of us, acting in good faith, could succeed in persuading those with arms to decommission them in accordance with the agreement…in the manner set down by the International Commission on Decommissioning within the terms of the Good Friday Agreement'.[37] Decommissioning was now seen as an achievable outcome in the statement, produced as a response to the *The Way Forward* initiative by the British and Irish Governments. Nonetheless, the Ulster Unionist Party rejected *The Way Forward*, leading to the brief formation of an all-nationalist Executive at Stormont, in the absence of Unionism's largest party. Without cross-community consensus, this 'Executive' lasted ten minutes before being declared invalid under the terms of the Good Friday Agreement.

In October 1999 the former Northern editor of *Republican News*, Mickey McMullan, argued for 'tactical decommissioning'.[38] In November, the UUP 'jumped first', voting to enter into government with Sinn Féin, but with the failsafe that movement on decommissioning needed to occur by February 2000. Such a default mechanism impinged upon Republican control of the decommissioning process, but it did produce increased verbal commitment to decommissioning from the IRA, now promising to 'initiate a comprehensive process to put arms beyond use'. The Independent International Commission on Decommissioning was sufficiently impressed to declare that the IRA's statement 'holds out the real prospect of an agreement which would enable it (the Commission) to fulfil the substance of its mandate'. Less impressed, the UUP was about to withdraw from the Northern Ireland Executive when the Secretary of State announced its suspension. The IRA promptly announced its decision to end its engagement with the IICD, but few thought this a permanent development and the 'break-offs' formed part of a regular pattern. Reinstatement of political institutions in May 2000 led to the IRA's announcement of its willingness to 'completely and verifiably put arms beyond use'. The plan involved the inspection of arms dumps by the former Finnish President, Martti Ahtisaari and the former Secretary-General of the African National Congress of South Africa, Cyril Ramaphosa. As had been clear from the outset, placing weapons beyond use was a development on the IRA's terms, avoiding the handover of 'product'.

By June 2001 three inspections of arms dumps had taken place, with the arms inspectors insisting that the IRA had 'fully honoured their commitments and complied with the terms of our engagement'.[39] The IRA also met the IICD four times in the first half of 2001. The alleged lack of movement on decommissioning led to David Trimble's resignation as First Minister in July 2001, creating yet another 'crisis' in the peace process. As Unionists remained unimpressed, they threatened to withdraw other ministers from the Northern Ireland Assembly in the autumn of 2001, as global events enhanced the unacceptability of terrorism. An alternative view was that the placing of any weapons beyond use by the IRA was remarkable, given the non-realisation of the organisation's political goal. Given the lack of interest within the

PIRA in returning to violence, combined with the irrelevance, other than in symbolic terms, of decommissioning, it was unsurprising to hear Gerry Adams complain how the 'issue of IRA weapons had been made a pre-condition for progress on all other issues'.[40]

Envisioning a 'future free of IRA weapons', Adams' central point was that decommissioning, the 'virus' within the Agreement, was a *political* imperative, not something which could or should be driven by *military* or security agendas.[41] In October 2001 the IRA announced that it had decommissioned some of its weapons. Gerry Adams admitted that the move had provoked 'considerable emotion among many Republican activists'.[42] The Sinn Féin President also admitted he had been called a 'traitor' in his own West Belfast constituency, albeit by 'only one constituent'.[43] The muted response in Republican constituencies came as little surprise; this was merely the completion of the Republican U-turn. 'No return to Stormont' and 'Not one ounce; not one bullet' had long been decommissioned as slogans. The IRA's statement that it had decommissioned to save the political process from collapse was true; the unstated sub-text was that the decommissioning move was to maintain Sinn Féin's political advances. Adams had insisted that 'the UUP can no more pressurise the IRA than the IRA can pressurise the UUP'.[44] In direct terms this was true. However, the UUP could collapse the Agreement, arguing that the IRA had not moved, thereby threatening Sinn Féin's strategy. Thus the UUP was pressurising an IRA now dominated by Sinn Féin. Decommissioning represented the final 'triumph' of electoralism within the movement.

Whilst desiring IRA decommissioning, the SDLP did not regard its instigation as central to political progress. Bríd Rogers, Minister of Agriculture in the Belfast Assembly, acknowledged the symbolic importance which a refusal to decommission represented for Unionists, referring to the issue 'as a question of trust, a confidence-building issue for ordinary Unionists'. With reference to Republican misgivings, she asked: 'Surely the Republican movement, which during the whole peace process has so vociferously articulated the need for confidence-building measures for themselves, cannot fail to recognise this reality?'[45] In sympathy with 'Trimbleite' Unionists she claimed, 'Sinn Féin's repeated commitment to initiate a process of decommissioning and their repeated failure to do so has clearly sapped the confidence of pro-agreement Unionists.'[46]

Another leading SDLP figure Seán Farren, Minister of Higher Education in the Belfast Assembly, also equated decommissioning with the necessity to build trust and confidence between the two communities. He argued that lack of decommissioning was an ominous warning to Unionists that Republicans could resort to violence if political developments did not go their way. Decommissioning thus created an unnecessary distrust, which was entirely contrary to the spirit of the Good Friday Agreement.[47] Before the resignation of David Trimble as First Minister on 1 July 2001, his Deputy Seamus Mallon suggested that the two governments might ascertain if Sinn Féin was in breach of its obligations under the terms of the Good Friday Agreement. He indicated that Section 30 of the Northern Ireland Act 1998, which referred to non co-operation with the International Commission as the basis for possible dismissal of individual ministers or a political party, provided possible grounds for expulsion from the devolved institutions under the Good Friday Agreement. Mallon claimed the two governments could take sanctions against Sinn Féin if it failed to honour their obligations undertaken in the Good Friday Agreement. Mallon also pointed out that the Northern Ireland Secretary of State had the power to submit a motion of exclusion, which could be put to the vote, to the Belfast Assembly.[48] Sensitive to the difficulties within the Republican constituency, John Hume appeared less concerned with decommissioning, but nonetheless declared 'that decommissioning must happen within the context of the implementation of the overall settlement...[and]...cannot be made conditional upon the full implementation of all other aspects.'[49]

Sinn Féin overtakes the SDLP

The vibrancy of Sinn Féin's electoral strategy had long threatened the primacy of the SDLP as nationalism's primary force. In June 2001 the decisive moment arrived as Sinn Féin overtook John Hume's party in the Westminster and local elections. Intra-nationalist rivalry concerned which party could best promote the interests of the ethnic bloc it sought to represent. Although the Good Friday Agreement reflected much SDLP thinking, a sizeable portion of the nationalist electorate was unconvinced that it had the political clout to implement a 'green' agenda. Adams claimed that the SDLP 'isn't a nationalist party...it is a "Northern Ireland" party, a social democratic party.

There are nationalists in it—good nationalists in it'.[50] Adams was correct in highlighting distinctions within the SDLP membership. Yet as the SDLP attempted to conduct its 2001 election campaign on a post-nationalist, pro-European agenda, Sinn Féin campaigned on core issues of housing, schools, jobs and policing, emphasised as part of the creation of parity of esteem for nationalists under the Good Friday Agreement, itself linked to the party's peace strategy. As a former member of Sinn Féin's leadership, Danny Morrison put it, the nationalist electorate were looking to 'embrace a party which will robustly defend their interests on policing, equality, justice and freedom'.[51]

Sinn Féin's support for the peace process and the Good Friday Agreement narrowed the SDLP's campaigning ground. Moreover, Sinn Féin could also claim an electoral 'success' in the South, with a victory for the 'No' campaign in the first referendum on the Nice Treaty, designed to enlarge the EU, which took place in the Irish Republic on the same day as the elections in Northern Ireland. In Dublin particularly, sizeable 'no' votes were recorded in constituencies subject to considerable Sinn Féin campaigning, based upon arguments that a diminution of sovereignty and compromise of Irish neutrality would result from the Treaty.

Sinn Féin maintained its policy of abstention from Westminster, although the party chair, Mitchell McLaughlin, claimed that this was not because abstentionism was a fundamental Republican principle, but because 'there was no strategic value in going to Westminster'.[52] The party vice-president, Pat Doherty, offered a more traditional view in insisting that members of Sinn Féin 'will not take an oath to the British monarch'.[53] However, Doherty also offered a model of representation within the British state, insisting that Sinn Féin's MPs 'want to represent our constituents and we want the facilities to help us do that'.[54]

Sinn Féin benefited from the presence of two ministers in prominent positions within the Northern Ireland Executive. The Executive, at best an uneasy alliance of the UUP, DUP, SDLP and Sinn Féin, developed little sense of collective responsibility during its existence, ironically because of continued wrangling over non-devolved matters such as policing and decommissioning. Within his Education Ministry Martin McGuinness initiated a review likely to end the 11-plus examination. He abolished league tables for secondary schools and took measures likely to further integrate education (although McGuinness remained supportive of denominational schools) and Irish-language schooling. At Health, Bairbre de Brún presided over reviews of health services and was involved in controversial location decisions in respect of hospitals and health services. Both had been accused by opponents of 'playing the green card', although the accusers were hardly devoid of partisanship.

The promotion of green politics was logical for Sinn Féin, in its attempt to promote itself as a 'catch-all' party among the nationalist electorate. Northern Ireland's consociational political system, legitimising ethnic bloc politics, encouraged, at least in the short term, the furtherance of 'pillar politics'. Thus the intra-bloc contests within nationalism and, even more importantly, among Unionists overshadowed longstanding inter-communal rivalries. Consociational arrangements, based upon enforced power-sharing, were designed to prevent majority dominance and allow segmental autonomy. The long-term aspiration underpinning such agreements was permanent co-operation between elites and movement towards a depoliticised democracy and an increasingly homogeneous polity.[55] Within Assembly committees, cross-communal bloc consensus was often possible. Nonetheless, the accommodation of political elites found in the Good Friday Agreement often looked fragile, with the Executive and the North-South Council both failing to function properly for part of their existence. In addition to the temporary suspensions of the Executive in 2000 (for three months), 2001 (twice, on technicalities) and 2002 (indefinitely from October), the reluctance of the IRA to decommission its weapons also led to sanctions initiated by the First Minister. David Trimble barred Sinn Féin's representatives from the North-South Ministerial Council, a move leading to a successful legal challenge from Sinn Féin.

The internal divisions within Unionism continued to plague the Good Friday Agreement. Allegations of continued IRA activity raised the siren voices of 'no' Unionists, who proved difficult to silence within the Ulster Unionist Party, which lacked a 'top-down' management structure. As the political institutions created by the Good Friday Agreement collapsed in October 2002, the long-term future of the deal remained uncertain. The British and Irish governments, via a joint declaration in April 2003, promised continued implementation of aspects of the Agreement. In this respect, the problems accruing to the deal were of no major concern to Sinn Féin in respect of its political (as distinct from electoral) objectives, whatever the party's protestations, using the language of British Secretaries of State, that the Good Friday Agreement was the 'only show in town'. A Unionist failure to accept the Agreement was likely to be followed by a period of growing bi-nationalism, with the British and Irish governments engaged in intergovernmental policy cooperation on Northern Ireland matters. This threatened Unionists with a sharper shift towards joint authority than the ringfenced cross-borderism of the Good Friday Agreement.

The electoral squeezing of the SDLP: irreversible gains for Sinn Féin?

Sinn Féin consolidated its electoral successes. The party increased its percentage vote by 4 per cent, to 6.5 per cent, in the Irish general election in 2002, acquiring five seats in Dáil Éireann. The party's rise was rapid; ten years earlier, 40 of its 41 candidates had forfeited their deposits.[56] In June 2002 Alex Maskey was elected Sinn Féin mayor of Belfast, despite the opposition of Unionist councillors. Maskey won the respect of some opponents, although not Unionist diehards, in articulating the pluralist tone of modern Sinn Féin politics, launching an anti-sectarian campaign under the broad slogan of a 'city of equals'. Sinn Féin expected to comfortably defeat, but not crush, the SDLP in the 2003 Northern Ireland Assembly election.[57] The election was postponed until November, on revisionist democratic grounds. Prime Minister Blair indicated that a reason for cancellation was that the DUP and Sinn Féin might emerge as the largest parties, further reducing prospects for a viable governing Executive. Sinn Féin's aspirations for Irish self-determination looked overly optimistic, set against a classic piece of neo-colonial governance, which set aside elections for fear of the 'wrong' result. The decision to postpone the election went against the public advice of the Irish government and the private counsels of the Northern Ireland Office.[58]

With the UUP leader, David Trimble, unimpressed by a further act of decommissioning by the Provisional IRA in October 2003, amid much grandstanding by the British government, the 'Save the UUP leader' approach of the Prime Minister was abandoned in favour of allowing elections. The election delay did not affect the widely predicted result. The DUP emerged as comfortably the largest Unionist party, whilst Sinn Féin reversed its number of Assembly seats with the SDLP, emerging with 24, compared to a modest 18 for its more moderate rival. Sinn Féin opened a large lead over its nationalist rival, of 6.5 percentage points and, following post-election UUP defections to the DUP, Adams' party was now the joint second largest in Northern Ireland.

Of course, there was a rather substantial problem confronting Sinn Féin; there was no Assembly and, under a DUP led by Ian Paisley, there was little immediate prospect of Sinn Féin returning to government. Even in a changed Northern Ireland, a Paisley-Adams First and Deputy First Minister duopoly stretched the imagination. With 70 per cent of elected Assembly members being pro-Agreement, Sinn Féin remained sanguine over prospects for an eventual deal, Adams calling on Paisley to engage in the 'Christian philosophy...of conversation and healing'.[59] Yet, a substantial majority of Unionists had voted for anti-Agreement candidates. The DUP's ascendancy, fighting a war that is over, represented an 'impasse of unprecedented magnitude'.[60] It meant that optimists relied upon a touching belief in a new pragmatism within Paisley's party, based upon a view that the DUP was at the stage the UUP reached in 1998, reluctantly accepting compromise.[61] Given that the DUP had entered an Executive with Sinn Féin in 1999, a deal remained possible, but the terms of any renegotiation of the Agreement would not favour Sinn Féin.

Sinn Féin's political balance sheet thus read: substantial electoral gains with every likelihood of further triumphs and equality for Catholics in Northern Ireland, versus removal from limited power, with any renegotiation of the Agreement being on unfavourable terms; a neutered, increasingly irrelevant IRA, which, whatever the debates over its legitimacy, had provided a 'cutting edge' to the movement; and the non-realisation of Sinn Féin's supposedly overarching political goal, of a united Ireland. As such, electoral victories were somewhat pyrrhic. Elections to a non-existent assembly would not trouble a British government whose primary motivation in the peace process was to end the IRA's campaign, not introduce devolution to Northern Ireland. Sinn Féin's restoration to power would now be conditional upon the completion of a process of surrender by instalments by the IRA. Sinn Féin was reduced to urging an Irish government which had explicitly renounced its claim to the North (if not all of its citizens, who could form part of an 'Irish nation) to produce a green paper indicating how it intended to progress towards a united Ireland. Even joint British-Irish authority appeared a distant prospect and Sinn Féin did not engage in calls for such, despite the near-collapse of the Agreement. Nationalists remained supportive of the Agreement and turnout in nationalist-majority constituencies in 2003, at 68 per cent, was 8 per cent higher than in Unionist areas. Nonetheless, the fall in turnout in nationalist areas, at 9 per cent, was almost double that in Unionist areas, providing some evidence of growing disenchantment among nationalists.

Despite the political vacuum, the Provisionals had long moved from a position where a return to violence remained a tactical option. The language now was of 'complete and final closure of the conflict', despite the non-realisation of traditional Republican objectives and the failure to achieve durable power-sharing.[62] The IRA indicated its willingness to embark on a process which put 'all arms' beyond use.[63] Adams publicly envisaged a future without the IRA.[64]

The short- to medium-term Republican objectives were apparent. The movement had gone from abstention and revolution towards a determination to hold office North and South, with the Assembly in the North and Dáil Éireann in the South the new 'sites of struggle'.[65] Speakers at Sinn Féin Ard Fheisanna had objected to the party being a possible coalition partner for Fianna Fáil in the Irish Republic, but resolutions at conferences did not tie the leadership's hands on the matter of entry in to government in the Irish Republic as a junior coalition partner. Sinn Féin still required more seats to force the issue. No institutions will be off limits. Sinn Féin will join the Police Service of Northern Ireland Board.[66] As early as October 2002 Adams stated publicly that he could 'conceive of a world in which it would be appropriate for Sinn Féin to join the Policing Board'.[67] Sinn Féin ministers in the North will demand more money from a British government to run departments should an Executive eventually be reconstituted. Participation in six-county institutions will be justified on the grounds that such institutions are mere 'staging posts' to Irish unity, or an 'Ireland of equals' in a 'lengthy transitional phase'.[68] The short-term aspiration for Sinn Féin is to provide linkages between the Irish parliament and others, creating an all-island institutional ethos. This includes giving citizens in Northern Ireland the right to vote in elections to the Seana and in Presidential elections, with rights of attendance in Dáil Éireann for Northern Ireland's Westminster MPs.

Progress or sell-out? Theorising Republican change

The way forward for Republicanism had been indicated by Jim Gibney at Bodenstown in 1992. Whilst Gibney's reference to the need for republicans to be no longer 'deafened by the sound of their own gunfire' attracted most attention, the strategic alliances for Republicans in future years were also apparent:

> 'We know and accept that the British Government's departure must be preceded by a sustained period of peace and will arise out of negotiations. We know and accept that such negotiations will involve the different shades of Irish nationalism and Irish Unionism engaging the British Government together or separately to secure an all-embracing and durable peace process.
>
> We know and accept that this is not 1921 and that at this stage we don't represent a government in waiting. We're not waiting in the airport lounge to be flown to Chequers or Lancaster House....'

Gibney's reference to 'Irish' Unionism indicated that revisionist Republicanism still required much more serious thinking on the identity and role of Unionists. Nonetheless, the speech prepared Republicans for new forms of coalitional politics, which would not deliver traditional Republican objectives in the short term. By the mid 1990s such coalitions were accepted as the norm. Sinn Féin made clear distinctions between the Republican-leaning Fianna Fáil governments of Albert Reynolds and, later, Bertie Ahern and the 'partitionist' analysis of Fine Gael under John Bruton. In 1996 and 1997, as the IRA ceasefire fractured, Bruton's hostility threatened the pan-nationalist alliance painstakingly constructed during the 1990s. After the ceasefires there was a steady downgrading by the Republican leadership of what could realistically be expected from political negotiations. By 1996 it was possible for Gerry Adams to no longer mention British withdrawal as an outcome.[69] Critics pointed to the shift from the 'agreed policy of the movement', expressed in the 1992 *Towards a Lasting Peace* document, that nationalist opinion needed to persuade the British government to withdraw from Northern Ireland.[70] The idea of the British government acting as a persuader to Unionists, so important in the revisionist Republican thinking of the early 1990s, withered when the approach of the Blair government, with its emphasis upon 'consent', became apparent soon after election in May 1997. From Easter 1998 the Republican baseline became full implementation of the Good Friday Agreement, which palpably, given the consent principle, would not achieve British withdrawal in the immediate future, whatever its other attractions to Republicans. The Good Friday Agreement, rather than any commitment to Irish unity, became the 'benchmark against which Sinn Féin will judge the two governments'.[71] Republicans sceptical about revisionist forms of the creed had difficulty expounding a credible alternative. As Alex Maskey put it: 'My reply to those in our movement who are critical of our strategy is to say: "Well find another one…give me a better one".'[72]

The literature on the extent of change in Republicanism is divided over its significance. Even those Republicans broadly supportive of the peace process acknowledge that there have been 'bitter pills to swallow'.[73] In the Republican debit account Danny Morrison cited the end of abstentionism; the abandonment of the territorial claim to the north; the acceptance of a Northern Assembly; the acceptance of British-appointed commissions on human rights, equality and policing; and the 'implicit recognition of the principle of unionist consent'. Yet Morrison declined to draw from this catalogue of disasters the conclusion that the peace process was an abject defeat for republicans. Participation in consociational arrangements need not *automatically* be the death-knell for Republican ambitions. Instead, by linking consociational arrangements with intergovernmental associations, the northern 'minority' are linked with 'their' nation in a way never previously achieved. The minority position of Unionists becomes more readily apparent. The previous problem was the relative isolation of Northern nationalists, abandoned by the Irish government and unloved by the British and Unionists.[74] Jennifer Todd has suggested that Sinn Féin remains wedded to the core ideology of Republicanism, centred upon the idea of an indivisible island.[75] M. L. R. Smith sees republican ideology as teleological, in that it sees an end to history.[76] Whatever the level of delusion, the Good Friday Agreement offered a step on that road. Republicans could claim that, despite the acknowledged flaws in the Agreement, it represented a new phase of struggle by redefining Northern Ireland's place within the United Kingdom. Political and economic decisions in relation to that part of Ireland were now to be determined initially by the population of the entire island and henceforth by bi-governmental or devolved institutions.

Other observers agree that the changes in Republican politics have been seismic without necessarily agreeing upon the reasons. The main dynamic of change has been located in one account in external factors, in particular the end of the Cold War.[77] Cox suggests that the end of the Cold War reduced the significance of Northern Ireland to the British government and allowed the possibility of accommodation.[78] Clearly the collapse of the left also hastened the rightward shift of Sinn Féin after its revolutionary posturing of the late 1970s and early 1980s. but it remains doubtful whether there has been a significant shift in British *constitutional* policy on Northern Ireland. Among Republicans, significant changes preceded momentous events in the Soviet Union and Eastern Europe, with the decisive shift away from fundamentalism coming in 1986, with the end of abstention from Dáil Éireann, followed by the development of pan-nationalism via the Hume-Adams dialogue, Furthermore, in the context of a 700-year conflict, the end of the Cold War might yet be seen as a mere 'blip'.[79] Guelke highlights the impact of peace processes elsewhere in encouraging accommodation.[80] The external referents offered by Cox and Guelke are useful in avoiding entirely insular, internal explanations of change. Nonetheless, the commencement of Republicanism's shift from violence to electoralism predated the end of the Cold War, even if the decline of revolutionary leftism (never central within republican thinking and rejected by some) hastened the process. The influence of peace processes elsewhere was important, notably the South African model. Nonetheless, the return to violence by the IRA's long-standing allies in ETA after the collapse of the Basque peace process indicated the fragility of such processes.

The crucial question of whether the Republican movement compromised its principles in accepting the Good Friday Agreement requires an identification of what constitutes Republican fundamentalism. If Republicanism was defined by the desire for a particular end product, an independent, united thirty-two-county republic, surely Sinn Féin had not abandoned Republicanism, but had adopted new strategies to accomplish this goal? As Joe Cahill declared in the closing speech at the 2000 Ard Fheis, tactics had regularly changed. Cahill highlighted instances, such as recognition of the courts and electoral campaigning, as instances in which Republicans had been obliged to adapt, but this did not make them any less republican. Using Cahill's model and accepting that the pursuit of Irish unity remained the key party goal, Sinn Féin could still be defined as an actively republican party, as opposed to a latently Republican party such as Fianna Fáil, an organisation which declined the pursuit of a united Ireland even when such a role was a constitutional imperative.

Not all are convinced by the above arguments. Mark Ryan argues that Sinn Féin has moved towards becoming another system party.[81] Ryan's death of Republicanism thesis highlights how historical objectives have been 'quietly abandoned'. A return to programmes of civil rights and largely meaningless notions of 'transitory' routes to unity cannot disguise the basic political failure of the Republican project. According to Ryan, Sinn Féin has been reduced to the status of a minority party within the Northern state, representing a core constituency. Ryan's analysis may be correct in the assessment of the departure from Republican principles, but he underestimates Sinn Féin's ability to break from its core constituency and develop vibrant politics throughout the island. Already Sinn Féin is no longer, as Ryan put it, the representative of a minority of a minority in Northern Ireland. Furthermore, the final impact of Sinn Féin's attempted 'greening of the North' cannot be accurately assessed at this stage, as it is a novel project. With their acute awareness of history, it is hardly as if Republicans were unaware of the dangers of adopting 'transitory' routes to unity.

The 'sell-out' thesis is also expounded by the journalist Suzanne Breen in her contention that most of the Good Friday Agreement was on offer in 1974. In constitutional terms this is broadly true, although executive cross-border bodies were not present in Northern Ireland's previous experiment in consociational power-sharing (nor, or course, were prisoner releases). In expanding her 'defeat' thesis, Breen argues: 'If it wasn't for the appalling loss of life, it would be side-splittingly funny realising that it was SF recently demanding "Bring Back Stormont".'[82]

These analyses are modified by McIntyre, who suggests that the extent of fundamental Republican principles within the Provisionals has been persistently overstated.[83] Any commitment to the Republican ideals of 1798 or 1916 was tagged on to Northern Catholic defender-ism. The division between tactics and principles was always arbitrary. Hence changes in strategy do not constitute a 'sell-out'. The nature of Provisional Republicanism has allowed historic compromise. A prod-uct of perceived necessity, or sense of outrage, following Loyalist attacks in 1969, Provisional Republicanism lacked the ideological com-pass of traditional Republican forms, based upon the blood sacrifice of 1916.[84] Northern urban Republicanism took a fundamentally dif-ferent form from the lingering traditional version, confined since the 1956–62 campaign to isolated rural areas. The Provisionals' urban base was a strength in terms of numbers, recruitment and sustained support, but a weakness, for the military campaign, if material im-provements could be made in the lives of its core working-class sup-port. The explanation has the advantage of outlining the historical origins and ideological location of the Provisionals, indicating the vul-nerability to compromise, given that the politics of 1916 were, partly at least, a 'bolt-on' to the immediacies of the crisis of 1969. It is less clear why compromise should only be accepted after a prolonged struggle from 1970 until 1994, fuelled for the vast part by a 'Brits Out' agenda. Given the indifference to core Republicanism, compromise might have been expected far earlier. The thesis also drifts towards economic reductionism in highlighting the importance of improve-ments in the economic circumstances of the Provisionals' base in di-minishing support for the 'long haul'.

Ryan and McIntyre concur, however, that acceptance of the 'con-sent principle' does signify Republican defeat. Acceptance that one million Protestants could not be coerced into a united Ireland was ac-knowledgement of what the Taoiseach, Albert Reynolds, had de-clared in 1994: that the physical force tradition had come to an end because it could go no further.[85] The question begged was its purpose during the previous twenty-eight years. As Brendan O'Brien puts it, the issue of Northern consent is 'where the story of the IRA's long war began'.[86] McIntyre concurs with Gerry Adams' assertion that the Good Friday Agreement was a 'historic compromise between nation-alism and Unionism'.[87] The problem was that it was nationalism that had done all the compromising. Application of the consent princi-ple and the maintenance of British sovereignty; the collapse of the constitutional claim to the North under Articles 2 and 3 of the Irish Republic's Constitution; the retention of an (armed) Northern police force and the resurrection of Stormont had all been conceded, in return for six cross-border bodies and an internal 'equality agenda'.[88]

Bean develops the idea of the importance of the Provisionals' urban base in shaping its version of Republicanism in two ways. The main role of Sinn Féin in the early days of electoralism was to act as a vanguard party (although a mere equal of its armed wing) in educating the population whilst being receptive to their social and economic concerns. This process of articulation at institutional level drew the party into closer contact with the Northern state. In order to demonstrate continuing progress, Sinn Féin needed to co-operate with these institutions and quangos rather than seek their destruction. Simultaneously, the party needed to expand its electoral horizons beyond the core base it vigorously and ably represented. Movement from local hegemony towards widespread support resulted in Sinn Féin moving from revolutionary organisation towards a mass bureaucratic party.[89]

Gilligan also offers a critical view of the effect of the peace process upon Republican politics. He notes how republicans became enmeshed in the process, making it difficult to withdraw. The Irish government was keen to suck Republicans into a process from which there was no retreat, an analysis with supportive evidence from the Irish government.[90] Peter Taylor's account of the Provisionals quotes an anonymous British civil servant as indicating that the process from ceasefire in 1994 to Sinn Féin signing up for an agreement would take about five years.[91] Sinn Féin was locked so tightly into the process that the party became anxious not to be excluded, despite its lack of tangible gains. The fracturing of the IRA ceasefire in 1996 was, ironically, an attempt to resurrect a process giving little hope to Republican constitutional ambitions. Gilligan's argument is that the abandonment of long-held cherished principles was part of a wider process of disengagement from politics by citizens, allowing their political representatives to take decisions more easily on 'their behalf'. There is much substance in this, but it overlooks the relatively high level of political activism in Northern Ireland. A further caveat to such arguments is, however, the extent to which the Good Friday Agreement was discussed at length within Sinn Féin *Cumainn*. The party leadership trod cautiously in 'selling' the deal to the party membership, although consultation, as distinct from policy formulation, does not negate the view that the party is 'top-down' in terms of decision-making.

Sinn Féin's electoral gains were juxtaposed with a retreat from its demands for British withdrawal from Northern Ireland. Electoralism had displaced armed struggle by 1997, although some unionists remained sceptical. Nationalist politics at the beginning of the twenty-first century contained two great ironies. The party that had achieved most of its political objectives, the SDLP, was in electoral crisis. Meanwhile, the party that had achieved few of its political goals was now the more popular among the nationalist electorate.

13

NEW AGENDAS?
NATIONALIST SOCIAL AND ECONOMIC POLICIES

Developing other political agendas

The economic and social policies of the SDLP and Sinn Féin were largely ignored outside the nationalist parties themselves (and at times even within) from 1970 until 1998. Such neglect was perhaps understandable. The SDLP oscillated between participatory and abstentionist approaches to politics until 1972, after which, apart from the brief period of power sharing in 1974, powers to implement policies were removed from Northern Ireland's politicians. Whilst the party developed a detailed socio-economic agenda, it was powerless to implement any policies. Sinn Féin's rejection of the Northern state precluded the party from developing detailed policies for the area, which would in any case remain the prerogative of the regional parliament for Ulster to be created under the federal structures of *Éire Núa*.

During the 1980s and 1990s, Sinn Féin's policy agenda became more comprehensive. This highlighted the contradictions inherent in an approach seeking the destruction of the state through armed struggle and, simultaneously, attempting its reconstruction through policies designed to attract inward investment and improve social conditions. Sinn Féin's participation in the Northern Ireland Executive put the party on a rapid learning curve in terms of policy formulation and delivery. Under the D'Hondt system, Sinn Féin claimed the key posts of Education, under Martin McGuinness, and Health, under Bairbre de Brún. Meanwhile, the SDLP held the posts of Finance, Higher and Further Education and Agriculture and Rural Development. Both parties were also enthusiastic participants in the North-South ministerial council, designed to facilitate the work of the six new cross-border bodies established under the Good Friday Agreement.

Sinn Féin placed its emphasis upon increased health spending within a broader political framework of a 'Republican labour' agenda, unveiled at the 2000 Ard Fheis. The party argued that the creation of appropriate economic and social conditions had been a core theme of Irish Republicanism, whatever the difficulties created by the fusion of nationalism and socialism.[1] The Republican labour agenda dwelt upon the need for a sharing of wealth throughout the island and was critical of the inequalities of the 'Celtic tiger' economy, but lacked details as how equality was to be attained. Plans for redistributive taxation were noticeably absent from Sinn Féin's agenda. Yet by 2000, party policy was more meaningful, North and South. Installed in the Northern Ireland Executive, the party used its 2000 Ard Fheis to begin the debate over whether it could enter into coalition in the Irish Republic after the next election. In other policy areas, all-Ireland provision could be expanded via cross-border bodies. The initial workings of the North-South Ministerial Council were impeded by the refusal of the Northern Ireland First Minister, David Trimble, to nominate Sinn Féin ministers to the Council, as the IRA decommissioning argument rumbled onwards. Sinn Féin's use of judicial review eventually led to the restoration of the party's ministers to the Council in 2001.

A radical approach to education policy

The nationalist parties had much scope to determine education policy, with ministers controlling all sectors. Martin McGuinness was fortunate in inheriting a primary and secondary educational system arguably superior to other countries within the United Kingdom, if measured in terms of educational attainment. In developing his own strategy, he was impressed by the manner in which the 'Unionist' civil servants at the Department of Education worked 'diligently, professionally and cordially'.[2] As Further and Higher Education Minister, the SDLP's Seán Farren could point to the egalitarianism of Northern Ireland's university system, in which 97 per cent of entrants to the Province's two universities came from state schools. Nonetheless, the educational system also contained divisive elements at all levels, at odds with the left-of-centre, egalitarian approach of either party. Sinn Féin opposed the 11-plus examination, a position endorsed at the 2000 Ard Fheis.[3] Prior to the suspension of the Executive and the

Assembly, McGuinness pledged the abolition of the 11-plus by 2004 and the introduction of all-ability 11–18 year-old schooling provision. Only one in ten children of manual worker, working-class parents entered grammar school.[4] Here there was a common nationalist position, the SDLP also opposing selection at 11.

McGuinness established a ten-member review body, the Burns Commission, assisted by academic advisers from Britain and Ireland, to explore the question of selection in post-primary education. Accused (erroneously) by opponents of favouring Catholic schools and generally unwelcome in non-Catholic ones, the Sinn Féin minister made clear his support for a continuation of denominational schools on the basis of parental choice, whilst increasing funding for the growing number of religiously integrated schools. McGuinness attempted to introduce a wider clarity to the funding of schools in Northern Ireland through a largely consensual consultative process. Previously, the Department of Education and local education and library boards had used seven different formulae to fund the state's 1,200 schools.[5] In addition to expanding pre-school provision towards a stated target of 75 per cent, the Education Minister also abolished school performance league tables, a move supported by the SDLP.[6] McGuinness also attempted to develop a consensual approach to change by establishing Education Working Groups in the areas of special needs, child protection, exchange programmes and North-South teacher mobility. Sinn Féin was committed to an all-Ireland literacy campaign with the objective of reducing adult functional illiteracy to under 10 per cent in 2003–7, from an average of 22.6 per cent in the Irish Republic and 24 per cent in Northern Ireland.[7] Amid clear targets, policy documents sometimes offered vacuity and mirrored the language of British New Labour; one of Sinn Féin's educational priorities was to establish 'Schools as Learning Organisations in a Learning Neighbourhood'.[8] Nonetheless, the strategic objectives of access and measurement of achievement through quality of delivery rather than via narrow performance indicators, were clear enough. At primary level Sinn Féin offers a target of reduced (to 15:1) pupil-teacher ratios. At primary and secondary levels, the party supports the development of Irish language schools.

As Higher Education Minister, the SDLP's Seán Farren was confronted by the problem of university tuition fees, imposed by the

Labour government after its 1997 election victory. SDLP policy was to end the student loans system introduced by the Conservatives in 1990 and to reinstate the former grants system. The sizeable number of Northern Ireland students living at home during their studies did not reduce the salience of the issue of financial burdens, although 50 per cent of students in Northern Ireland are exempt from tuition fees, 20 per cent pay partial fees and only 30 per cent pay full fees.[9] The SDLP minister acknowledged the difficulty in trying to deliver free education to all given the constraints of the devolved assembly in Northern Ireland, devoid of tax-raising powers. In these circumstances the SDLP faced a dilemma over the issue of abolishing tuition fees. The proposals that emerged mirrored those of the Scottish Executive in Scotland, with student tuition fees to be deferred, and later charged to the student once they are employed over a specified earnings threshold. The party moved away from advocacy of the restoration of the former grant maintenance scheme and proposed that students should have access to 'low-cost loans'. The Higher Education Minister did not recommend the outright abolition of fees, although the Assembly Education Committee investigating the issue was more hostile.

Sinn Féin unanimously endorsed opposition to the abolition of student grants at its 1998 Ard Fheis.[10] The party supported the restoration of student grants indexed according to family income. Sinn Féin also supported a broader post-16 curriculum, 'inspired by the models of the (Irish) Leaving Certificate and Baccalaureate'.[11] Sinn Féin opposed performance-related pay for teachers, on the grounds of its supposed divisiveness. Both nationalist parties offer life-long learning strategies through community education in particular, to offer the educationally marginalised such as parents, the unemployed and those lacking basic qualifications the opportunity to obtain further certification. Sinn Féin's control of the Education Department also saw an expansion of pre-school provision. Sanguine over primary school provision in the North, the party is critical of the extent to which such schools are dependent upon voluntary aid in the Irish Republic.

Local government

Local government in Northern Ireland still reflects the divisions prevalent in the Province: it has sustained rather than deconstructed sectarian divisions. In constituencies where the SDLP held a majority such as Derry, Down, and Newry and Mourne, the SDLP was the first to rotate the positions of mayor and deputy mayor. Despite reconstituted local government, following the McCrory Review in 1973 and the subsequent creation of twenty-six local government councils that remain in Northern Ireland, Unionists continued to resist partnership with Catholics at local government level. In protest the SDLP boycotted the Association for Local Authorities in Northern Ireland. However, the SDLP has moved towards full representation at local government level. The party assumed membership of the Local Government Association established on 2 October 2001, which replaced the former Association for Local Authorities in Northern Ireland. The legacy of mistrust of local government remained. SDLP members saw the most appropriate vehicle for devolved power sharing as the Northern Ireland Assembly. Nearly four-fifths of party members believed that the Assembly would create more jobs and investment and a majority (although only a slight one) thought that the new devolved administration would improve services.[12]

Sinn Féin shared the contempt of the previous operation of local government in Northern Ireland. As the party's control of councils, and representation increased dramatically, the party saw a more advanced role for local councils, hitherto the weakest in Western Europe. The party supports the concept of a 'social economy' developed through 'community regeneration initiatives', involving public-private partnerships.[13] Local regeneration and service provision are to be based upon three priorities: environmental and ecological concerns; reskilling of the workforce; and improvements in childcare provision.[14]

Health and housing

Until 1999, many of Sinn Féin's health policies concentrated upon provision in the Irish Republic. In particular, the party linked environmental policies to health issues, often concentrating on landfill sites, waste management, or the alleged impact of alleged nuclear processing discharges into the Irish Sea from the Sellafield nuclear plant in England. Sinn Féin advocates the release of funds to local authorities through green taxes to tackle environmental problems. The arrival of Bairbre de Brún as Health Minister in Northern Ireland ensured something of a shift in focus, facilitated by the 1998 Ard Fheis decision to agree a review of party health policy by the Policy Review and Development Department.

De Brún was accused by critics of pursuing sectarian politics in hospital locational decisions, favouring nationalist areas. In particular, her early decision to move maternity services to West Belfast caused acrimony, coming against the advice of the Assembly Health Committee.[15] Sinn Féin argued that provision in nationalist areas, particularly west of the Bann, was worse than elsewhere, owing to a concentration of resources in the Greater Belfast area.[16] In addition to the establishment of a review of acute service provision, the conclusions of which were rejected as inadequate at the party's 2001 Ard Fheis, and the development of a public health strategy, De Brún's immediate avowed priorities were reductions in hospital waiting times, increased provision for the elderly and the creation of extra training places for nurses. The party's *Health for All* document, adopted at the 2001 Ard Fheis, indicated a slight shift towards a preventive care approach, whilst also concentrating on healthcare inequalities.[17]

The SDLP offered a similar critique of government funding of the health service compared to levels of funding in other European countries, also lamenting the wastage of financial and labour resources linked to the administration of the National Health Service. In urging a more preventive approach to healthcare, the SDLP emphasises that health policy should be related to policies for education, housing, the economy and the environment.[18] Acute housing problems in the Irish Republic, with 100,000 people on housing waiting lists (10,000 in Dublin alone) in 2000, meant that Sinn Féin's focus on this issue remained south of the border and the party made electoral headway in poorer parts of the capital. Indeed a senior Dublin party representative argued that campaigns on housing and drugs had been responsible for reviving the party in the South, after Sinn Féin's vote had collapsed following the temporary post-hunger-strike fillip.[19] Within the Northern Ireland Assembly, Sinn Féin found the going tougher. Although much consensual work was undertaken within Assembly committees, housing disputes were sometimes linked to the defence of territory, inhibiting cross-community co-operation. Thus Michelle Gildernew MLA complained that cooperation with Billy Hutchinson of the Progressive Unionist Party was sometimes impeded, not because of a differing analysis of social conditions, but by the need of elected representatives to be seen to be defending their community.[20] More generally, Sinn Féin's MLAs found the greatest common ground with representatives of working-class Loyalism a product of similarity of class background, with Gildernew arguing that pan-nationalism 'simply does not exist within the Assembly'.[21]

Housing was central to basic demands for equality for all the citizens of Northern Ireland in the Civil Rights Movement of the late 1960s, and the SDLP emphasises its status as an essential component of a 'just and inclusive society'.[22] The party believes the Housing Executive should remain the agency of central housing administration in Northern Ireland. The remit of the Housing Executive, according to SDLP policy, should be to regulate control of housing associations in relation to 'rent levels, standards and quality of dwellings and the allocation of houses'.[23] Also they believe the allocation of public sector housing, including housing associations, need to be controlled by the Housing Executive through one specific waiting list and selection scheme.[24] The SDLP opposes the increasing role of the private sector in supplying 'social housing'.[25]

Employment and the economy

Employment differentials remain a source of nationalist grievance. The unemployment rate among Catholics is twice as high as that found in the Protestant community in Northern Ireland. There remain pockets of considerable deprivation, exacerbated by seemingly sectarian employment practices and not greatly alleviated by a raft of fair employment legislation since the collapse of the 'Orange state'. In overwhelmingly (80 per cent) Catholic West Belfast, fewer than half of government-sponsored industrial jobs were given to Catholics.[26] Such inequities offered fertile campaigning ground for Sinn Féin in the area, although the party's approach, favouring a tightening of fair employment legislation and more inward investment programmes (particularly in the neglected west of the Province), was little different from that offered by the SDLP.

There is a considerable reliance on employment from the public sector in Northern Ireland. Thirty per cent of the overall workforce in the Province is employed in the public sector, compared to an average of 15 per cent in the rest of the United Kingdom and 18 per cent in the Republic. The SDLP argues that the 60 per cent of GDP consumed by public expenditure ought to be reduced to a more acceptable level of 40–45 per cent of GDP. One possible way to cut public sector finance might be to effect a reduction in the costs of the security services on the basis that peace prevails.[27] The economic challenge in Northern Ireland is to move away from a dependence culture to one of self-sustaining growth. Although both parties stress the dependent nature of the Northern Ireland economy, there are different emphases. The SDLP stresses local structural factors, notably the excessive dependence on a number of declining industries in Northern Ireland such as ship-building and textile production, whilst the manufacturing base in the Province is limited in scope. The party has criticised lack of government spending on research and development and the absence of an entrepreneurial culture in the business sector. Economic reviews from the SDLP have pointed to the small number of indigenous enterprises in Northern Ireland that had 'world class status' and the consequent inability of such industries to expand and develop. The thrust of any new economic strategy for Northern Ireland, the SDLP has pointed out, should be to obtain world-class status for local enterprises in the Province.[28] The SDLP believes that to develop the Northern Ireland economy, a long-term regional strategy over a period of twenty-five years is necessary. At the core of this approach is the need to develop North-South institutional bonds to promote areas of growth in sectors such as agriculture, industry and tourism. There is a need to create a cohesive liaison between the public and private sectors to co-operate rather than to compete with each other. There is the additional necessity to develop educational provision for a flexible and skilled workforce to meet the requirements of the market.

Sinn Féin continues to stress the negative impact of partition upon the Northern Ireland economy. Much of the party's thinking is centred upon the need to create all-island bodies in each economic sector. The party claims that even under direct rule 'the aim of economic policy…has been one of discrimination and distorted economic planning aimed at maintenance of the inequitable status quo'.[29] Uneven levels of employment were historically associated with the promotion of discrimination by the British government and the failure to apply the MacBride anti-discrimination principles. Subsequently the party has emphasised the rights-based agenda of the Good Friday

Agreement as a vehicle for the creation of social justice. Despite its left-wing approach, Sinn Féin is anxious to deny it is a 'tax-and-spend' old-style labourist party. The party states that it 'supports the principle of cutting income tax'.[30] At other times, Sinn Féin was less clear on the issue, stating that 'extra taxes must be progressive'.[31]

Sinn Féin offers a detailed critique of the Private Finance Initiative (PFI), on ideological and practical grounds. Sinn Féin deploys similar arguments against Public-Private Partnerships (PPPs) in the Irish Republic. The ideological antipathy rests upon a hostility to privately financed projects as a form of privatisation, with the party arguing that in terms of shared ownership and public accountability, capital projects require state funding. The practical case rests upon the contention that private finance is more expensive.[32] The PFI is less extensive in Northern Ireland than elsewhere in the United Kingdom, owing to a shortage of suitable private sector investors, but its deployment is growing, particularly in the education, and culture sectors. Sinn Féin's chairing of the Assembly Finance and Personnel Committee within the Assembly led to a public inquiry into the PFI.

In the North, Sinn Féin argues that financial constraints created by the Barnett formula, a population based funding mechanism based upon population rather than social need, encourages use of the PFI rather than public money. Yet with national fiscal self-determination still distant, there is acceptance of the inevitability of retention of the PFI, with Sinn Féin arguing for a regulatory approach, including the establishment of an all-island PFI/PPP watchdog. The party condemns PPPs outright, as entirely unnecessary given the existence of economic sovereignty for the Irish Republic. Despite these criticisms, Sinn Féin ministers launched PFI initiatives in Northern Ireland.

The European agenda

Recent years have seen a considerable narrowing of the differences between the two nationalist parties on attitudes to the European Union, a convergence created by reversals in Sinn Féin policy. From outright opposition to the EU, Sinn Féin now advocates 'critical engagement'.[33] EU policies are assessed on their merits, according to whether they have been arrived at democratically, whether they are subject to accountability, whether they benefit the less well off, whether they have the potential to promote Irish unity and whether local sovereignty is protected.[34] In 1999 the party concluded that 'advocacy of withdrawal from the EU is no longer a feasible option'.[35] It nonetheless opposed European Monetary Union, asserting in 1999 that EMU was a 'project that stands in stark opposition to our socialist Republican objectives of national sovereignty in political and economic terms'.[36] Four years later Sinn Féin advocated the extension of the euro from the Irish Republic to Northern Ireland.[37]

The change in Sinn Féin policy was based upon arguments that wherever possible Irish Republicans should use the institutions of the EU.[38] By 1997, the party urged that funding from the EU's Special Support Programme for Peace and Reconciliation should be used to develop local communities. Sinn Féin nonetheless insisted that its agenda was not post-nationalist, arguing that reports of the death of the nation-state had been grossly exaggerated. According to the Sinn Féin President, 'post-nationalism is both factually and politically wrong'.[39] The party attempted to redefine notions of sovereignty in markedly changed circumstances, encouraged by successful opposition to EU expansionism in the first Nice Treaty referendum in 2001, a victory overturned in the second such contest.

The SDLP points to the European Community as the model institution for resolving conflict at home and abroad. Drawing particularly on the post-nationalist philosophy of John Hume as party leader until 2001, the party supports European co-operation and integration. It endorses the direction of the European Union set out in the Single European Act 1986 and the 1992 Maastricht Treaty. In short the party engages with Europe politically and economically. It welcomed the plans for enlargement of the European Union to incorporate the Central and East European states such as the Czech Republic, Hungary and Poland.[40] Also it is in favour of Britain joining the single European currency.

The SDLP views European Union legislation and administration as effective mechanisms to tackle social exclusion. In particular the party points to the European Social Chapter as a framework for the rights of employees, including part-time workers. Economically the SDLP further endorses the European Pact for Employment as a positive commitment to employment and training: in particular it welcomes the focus of this scheme on research as well as its provisions for the expanding service industry. The party acknowledge the role of

European Structural Funds in upgrading the transport system and infrastructure throughout the North and South of Ireland.

Early in the 1990s the SDLP called for the establishment of an 'Irish Peace and Reconciliation Fund'. The Fund would be designed to bring maximum economic and social impact to bear on identified areas of deprivation in the Province and in the border regions of Northern Ireland and the Republic. The Special Support Programme for Peace and Reconciliation in Northern Ireland and the Border Counties of Ireland was officially launched in July 1995 by the EU Commission. In the first five years of the scheme £300 million sterling was spent in Northern Ireland. Unsurprisingly, both nationalist parties are highly supportive of cross-border EU initiatives, Sinn Féin continuing to stress how partition acts as a structural impediment to the functioning of an effective all-island economy. The Special European Union Programmes Body was the most important cross-border body created as a result of the Good Friday Agreement, enjoying the widest remit and most extensive funding.

Moral agendas

The SDLP takes a traditional Catholic stance on the issue of abortion, perhaps unsurprising given that 95.1 per cent of its members are Catholics. It opposes all forms of abortion even when the life of a mother is in danger. It supports full legal protection for the rights of unborn children and legislation to lessen the number of abortions in Northern Ireland. Also, closely allied to Catholic doctrine, the SDLP opposes all forms of experimentation on embryos: the party advocates legislation 'to ban the sale or purchase of human embryos, their use as sources of human transplant tissue or as objects of research or experimentation'.[41]

Abortion continued to be a sensitive issue within Sinn Féin. Indeed the issue produced a more heated debate at the 1998 Ard Fheis than the decision to enter Stormont. At the end of the party policy remained unchanged. Many speakers sought change, but an important intervention from Gerry Adams at the end of the debate helped maintain the status quo. The convoluted policy recognised that some women need abortions without necessarily supporting liberalisation of the law. Adams insisted that Sinn Féin already had the 'most progressive policy on the issue in Ireland' and that the party was 'not a

Catholic party'. Clearly, however, there was a sizeable section of the membership for whom Catholic teaching remained influential, with this grouping opposing any extension of abortion provision. Sinn Féin did not support extension of the 1967 Abortion Act to Northern Ireland in the Assembly debate in 2000, Mitchell McLaughlin declaring that the 'overwhelming majority in our community do not support abortion on demand'.[42] The party did support an amendment from the Women's Coalition to refer the issue to the Health and Public Safety Committee. Party policy documents criticised the lack of clarity regarding the law in Northern Ireland, but made no proposals for change.[43] Sinn Féin opposed the 'attitudes and forces in society which compel women to have abortions and criminalise those who do make this decision'.[44] The party accepted the need for abortion on grounds of rape or sexual abuse and where life or mental health was at risk. Although the issue remained problematic within the party, senior women within the party believed an acceptable formula had been reached, one describing the ambiguity of the policy as amounting to a 'necessary compromise, given the type of party membership we have'.[45]

For Sinn Féin, the development of progressive social policies offered evidence that the party was not reduced to playing 'green cards', but was instead prepared to offer a newly progressive politics, centred upon universal rights and entirely separate from conservative, green, Catholic nationalism.[46] The party's endorsement of gay, lesbian and bisexual rights at the 1995 Ard Fheis provoked little comment. Both parties demonstrate liberal policies in relation to homosexuality. At the 1977 SDLP Annual Conference the party endorsed the legalisation of homosexuality in accordance with British law in the Sexual Offences Act (1967). At its 1999 Annual Conference the party supported the motion calling for the government to lower the age of consent for gay people in line with the age of consent for heterosexual people. Also, at the same conference the party attacked the Northern Ireland Secretary of State for failing to elect a member of the 'sexual minorities community' to the newly created Equality Commission and Human Rights Commission.[47]

Sinn Féin argued for the civic forum established under the Good Friday Agreement to be representative of all sections of the community and expressed disappointment at the apparent middle-class bias in selection.[48] The Forum's lack of powers meant that any republican enthusiasm for its potential had been replaced by fears that it would be 'no more than a talking shop'.[49]

For Republicans the articulation of equality and individual emancipation has always been an essential accompaniment to the wider question of the assertion of national self-determination. The ethos of equality in the SDLP stems from founding members of the party who were associated with the Civil Rights movement and its stated aims to establish equality of opportunity and social justice for all. However, the use of the term 'equality' by the SDLP has been largely obscured. Dominant media coverage over the last thirty years in Northern Ireland has concentrated on the constitutional nature of the conflict rather than on political, social and economic party policies. According to the SDLP 'inequality' is defined by marginalisation in society, not only in political terms but also in a social and economic framework. Consequently inequality in society is determined by biases based on gender, race, sexual orientation, age and disability. To tackle injustice the SDLP argues that the issue of inequality must be addressed across a broad range of public policies to meet a range of criteria that include more effective legislation, target-setting, monitoring and public education programmes.

Both parties have criticised the government for the absence of initiatives to encourage women into the workplace. They support the universal availability of childcare for women in the workplace to allow equality of opportunity. The SDLP wants the government to address the under-representation of women at decision-making levels in the top echelons of public institutions in Northern Ireland. In terms of gender equality the parties argue that married women should receive independent legal status. In terms of its own organisation the SDLP was proud to acknowledge that 47 per cent of its members were women.[50] Sinn Féin's election of an all-male Ard Chomhairle at the 2000 Ard Fheis was openly acknowledged as an embarrassment.[51] Although it was widely regarded as a freakish result, the party leadership was anxious to ensure that there was to be no repeat. However, after a lively debate at the 2001 Ard Fheis, a proposal for a quota system, dismissed by critics as tokenistic, but supported by many as a necessary measure to boost the representation of women, failed to obtain the two-thirds majority required to change the party's constitution. Instead of endorsing positive discrimination, the party attempted changes in internal structures to boost the representation of women, and a Gender Equality Section was established. Sinn Féin also set targets of 30 per cent women candidates in local and European elections.

Both parties support ethical and social values that are representative of a secular society, with the exception of abortion and experiments on embryos. Bríd Rogers, Minister of Agriculture in the Belfast Assembly, gave a synopsis of SDLP policy and the all-inclusive interpretation of equality by the party at a public address on 'Women in Public Life'. She spoke of a society in Ireland 'where women and men, regardless of class, creed, political belief, national identity, race, sexual orientation or possible disability can enjoy equality of treatment and equality of opportunity, a society which accepts difference for what it is, the essence of humanity.'[52]

Overall, it is not unrealistic to speak of 'pan-nationalism' in the social and economic agenda of the two nationalist parties. Sinn Féin played a rapid game of catch-up with the SDLP in advancing a social and economic agenda. The SDLP had emerged from the Civil Rights movement and, whatever its middle-class composition, was skilled at articulating an equality agenda for nationalists. Furthermore, Sinn Féin suffered reverses in its plans for the shaping of the equality agenda. The party was obliged to downgrade its demands for its location within all-island institutions and was defeated by Unionists and the SDLP on proposals to establish a dedicated Department of Equality.[53]

Sinn Féin was aware of the need to develop a coherent rights agenda in a post-conflict Northern Ireland to maintain electoral progress. It was assisted in this not merely by the somewhat staid and middle-class image problem of the SDLP, but also by Sinn Féin's status as an all-Ireland party. This allowed the party to develop all-island strategies designed to transcend partition, which, in a new context of cross-borderism, had greater appeal than the inward-looking, 'North only' SDLP policy agenda. In an attempt to forge an all-island, mildly left-of-centre alternative, Ruairí Quinn, as leader of the Labour Party in the Irish Republic, proposed a merger between his party and the SDLP, at the SDLP's 1998 annual conference. The proposal elicited little interest within the SDLP; in the authors' survey only 22 per cent of members supported the idea. Yet the vibrancy of Sinn Féin's all-island strategy would be difficult to counter in an exclusively Northern context.

The Good Friday Agreement offered the institutional mechanisms for the articulation of a rights-based agenda. In taking advantage, Sinn Féin played green card politics, in that policing and legal changes were at the heart of its equality agenda. Meanwhile, the acquisition of the two Executive ministries through which a progressive leftist agenda could most prominently be articulated was a huge boost for the party. The prominence of their two ministers helped Sinn Féin in its intra-bloc rivalry with the SDLP, whilst any criticisms from unionists over 'sectarian' ministerial decisions, largely exaggerated for political ends, did the party little harm among its electorate.

CONCLUSION

By the early part of the twenty-first century, nationalist politics in Northern Ireland had been transformed. Abstention and insurrection had been displaced by participation and constitutional politics within a reformed six-county Province. At the margins there persisted tiny groups determined to pursue the destruction of Northern Ireland by armed struggle. Most nationalists, however, believed that the Provisional IRA's war was over.[1]

Despite the collapse of the Good Friday Agreement's political institutions in 2002, the election triumph of the DUP in 2003 and the insistence of that party that Sinn Féin would not be allowed into government in 2004 and beyond, the PIRA did not return to war. Instead Sinn Féin placed faith in a hitherto undetected aspect of Ian Paisley's and the DUP's political approach compromise and negotiation with historic enemies. The Good Friday Agreement, which had produced Sinn Féin's political participation and ended the PIRA's armed struggle, appeared in mortal danger, although it lingered (as of course had its predecessor, the Sunningdale Agreement) as a framework for a possible future negotiated pact.

Traditional Republican demands for an end to partition and the ending of British sovereignty over Northern Ireland had been downgraded to long-term aspirations, to be preceded by participation in political institutions linking Northern Ireland, the Irish Republic and the British and Irish governments. The constitutional architecture of the Good Friday Agreement reflected the political thinking of the SDLP, described by one opponent, a former editor of *An Phoblacht/Republican News*, as 'the most consistent party' in the political process (although of course the party said less about final constitutional outcomes than its rivals).[2] However, it is Sinn Féin's new constitutionalism which has reaped the electoral reward of the support of a majority of the nationalist electorate, even if there has been only marginal movement towards its overall political objective of Irish reunification. Sinn Féin hegemony among nationalists appears irreversible, as the party is seen as the stronger defender of the interests of the nationalist bloc.

Even after the Good Friday Agreement seemingly collapsed in 2002, Sinn Féin continued to support a deal with only a modest all-Ireland dimension. Although 30 of the 32 counties on the island of Ireland have nationalist majorities, joint British-Irish authority has yet to appear as a republican minimum demand. Sinn Féin's support for the Good Friday Agreement is based upon electoral calculation, rather than the fulfillment of historical objectives. Notwithstanding continued electoral advance, new constitutionalism risks heading for a political *cul-de-sac* if the institutions established under the Good Friday Agreement are not revived. The other republican 'tool', the Provisional IRA, itself isolated and marginalized, has been run down, whatever the claims to the contrary of anti-Agreement Unionists.

Whither the SDLP?

In the first academic study of the SDLP Ian McAllister noted the total absence of an indigenous tradition of Catholic parliamentary politics in Northern Ireland.[3] The Good Friday Agreement offered the first serious prospect of nationalist parliamentary politics within Northern Ireland, conducted on an equal footing with Unionism. However, the Agreement and its associated institutions remained fragile. Three short suspensions of the Assembly and Executive were followed by prolonged suspension in October 2002, amid allegations that an IRA spying ring existed at Stormont. Northern Ireland remains a dysfunctional polity, devoid of a standard democratic system of government and opposition. Post-1998, however, nationalist parties participated in the governance of a statelet they ultimately wished to see disappear.

The SDLP set in place an alternative to the sterile policies of abstentionism that characterised the former Nationalist Party in Northern Ireland. After nearly three decades of struggling to overthrow the Northern state, the Republican movement also moved decisively towards constitutional, participatory politics. Despite the omission of the term 'nationalist' from its constitution, the SDLP became in effect the official opposition to the Unionist parties in Northern Ireland. It was the first Northern Ireland political party, and for that matter the first constitutional party in the whole of Ireland to set out in policy documents a three-stranded set of proposals to address the Northern Ireland conflict. Drawing ideas and personnel from the civil rights movement, the SDLP initiated the process for equality for Northern nationalists, to end the sense of alienation felt by that community.

The Provisional IRA also drew its strength from the civil rights campaigns, but formed different conclusions. Whereas the response of the SDLP was to demand integration for nationalists in decision-making structures within the state, the PIRA believed that Northern Ireland was irreformable and needed to be smashed. This belief that the North was a failed political entity attracted sympathy (but not much else) from Fianna Fáil in the Irish Republic. In this way the origins of the Provisionals were concerned with dealing with 'unfinished business' from the time of partition and are not reducible merely to Catholic defenderism, although this was an important element. Arguments concerning the primacy of the politics of 1969 and the impact of Loyalist attacks upon urban nationalist areas are important in explaining why Provisional Republicanism became, in sharp contrast to the militant Republicanism of 1956–62, a mass campaign. However, the Provisionals were not formed until 1970. The first few months of that year were relatively quiet in Northern Ireland. Misguided operations by the British army between 1970 and 1972 fuelled resentment and led to the growth of the Provisionals, to a greater extent than the Loyalist attacks of 1969.

Having attempted for nearly three decades to bring down the Northern state and end British sovereignty, the Provisionals headed, at a quickening pace, towards a civil rights and equality-oriented agenda. The Good Friday Agreement was based primarily on SDLP analysis and that party's framework for resolving the Northern Ireland conflict. Not only did the SDLP help convince the British government by enlisting the help of the US government; the party also had to educate the main constitutional parties of the Republic of Ireland in the necessity to include these two core principles as part of an overall political settlement. Through the New Ireland Forum Report, the SDLP outlined the stark realities for the political elite in the Republic and brought it to broadly accept the SDLP analysis of the conflict. Consequently, arising from the New Ireland Forum, a broad consensus emerged among constitutional nationalists on how to engage with the British to resolve the conflict.

The subsequent Anglo-Irish Agreement, signed by Margaret Thatcher and Garret FitzGerald in November 1985, meant that the British government acknowledged the SDLP thesis concerning the alienation of Northern nationalists. The direct involvement of the Irish government in Northern Ireland arising from the 1985 accord was central to SDLP views on resolving the conflict. From the SDLP point of view, the Irish government had to play a parallel role with the British government in order to ensure that true equality for nationalists would emerge in every facet of public life in the Province. Despite the instant formal dismissal by the Sinn Féin leadership of the Anglo-Irish Agreement as consolidating partition, informally they understood that the Agreement added to the need for serious scrutiny of the viability of the armed struggle.

John Hume, SDLP leader for over twenty years, presented the Northern Ireland conflict to an international forum. He promoted a post-nationalist philosophy in the SDLP, by arguing that Irish unity could be engineered in the context of the European nation-state. Espousing a European dimension to the conflict, he argued that the irreconcilable differences in the area of tradition and culture in Northern Ireland could be overcome. The SDLP's approach was that traditional concepts of exclusive national sovereignty were redundant. Instead, nations pooled sovereignty within supranational institutions. This, the SDLP believed, was the best way forward for Northern Ireland, ensuring that control over the territory was not exclusively British, but instead shared within a complex, interlocked set of political institutions between Britain, Northern Ireland and the Irish Republic, aided and abetted where appropriate by the European Union.

Post-nationalism formed a dimension of the Good Friday Agreement, although the Agreement was essentially bi-national, rather than post-nationalist. These two themes, resting uneasily alongside each other, are expressed through the foundation of North-South bodies and to a lesser degree through the British-Irish Council. Cross-border co-operation, which helps remove economic and social barriers between the North and South, has eased some tensions between Northern Ireland and the Irish Republic. While these mechanisms have not been a final solution to the conflict, they have formed a basis for a range of improvements in social and economic spheres. The core of SDLP analysis of the Northern Ireland conflict, that the root of the problem is the division of the people in the island of Ireland, was the conviction and constant claim of John Hume. He firmly opposed the traditional Republican viewpoint that the British occupation of Northern Ireland was the modern cause of the problem, whatever Britain's historical responsibilities.

Until the development of Sinn Féin as a mass party, the international community generally accepted John Hume as the main representative for Northern nationalists and Republicans. Hume's courage and political altruism in taking part in the Hume-Adams process, for the sake of peace and at the expense of his party, has to be acknowledged. However, the Hume-Adams process enabled Gerry Adams to overtake John Hume as the new 'Man of Peace'. The roots of Sinn Féin policy to overtake the SDLP as the chief political representatives for the Northern minority community can be traced back to the early 1980s, being epitomised in the comment of Danny Morrison that Sinn Féin's priority should be to 'devastate and demoralise the SDLP'.[4] Sinn Féin proposals 'to make the final thrust against the SDLP in the North, replacing it as the majority party there' began in 1983, but its effects were not fully felt until after the IRA ceasefires and the emergence of Sinn Féin as the larger party in the 2001 general election.[5]

If John Hume had retired as leader of the SDLP after the Good Friday Agreement had been signed, or during the subsequent Assembly elections, his successor, Mark Durkan, would have come into the political arena with the SDLP vote at its highest since the formation of the party. The departure of Hume at this stage might have given Unionists more incentive to endorse the Good Friday Agreement. It appeared that the Hume-Adams model of pan-nationalism, emphasising green politics and placing less stress upon contentious aspects such as IRA decommissioning, formed a focus for Unionist opposition to aspects of the peace process. The criticism was harsh, given that the SDLP has consistently argued for partnership arrangements with Unionists. However, Hume was seen as complacent over decommissioning. Furthermore, the SDLP lost an opportunity to distinguish itself from Sinn Féin, both before unionists and before the nationalist constituency, by presenting an equivocal viewpoint in the debate over the sensitive issue of decommissioning.

Selling a 'partitionist' settlement

In selling the Good Friday Agreement to its own base, the Republican leadership showed remarkable skill. The Agreement fell well short of Republican objectives; led Republicans into a parliament they had earlier buried; upheld the principle of Northern (unionist) consent for constitutional change rejected for so many years by Republicans; offered cross-border bodies, the numerical expansion of which could occur only with the approval of a Northern Assembly; and abandoned the Irish Republic's constitutional claim to the North, which provided the Republican movement with historical legitimacy. As late as February 1998 *An Phoblacht/Republican News* stated: 'The six-county assembly idea is an attempt to produce an internal settlement. It would move nothing forward.'[6] The early release of prisoners and the effectiveness of the PIRA in England during the 1990s could not disguise the failure to realise historic demands. As Hennessey puts it: 'It was true that the PIRA were not defeated militarily; but the British only need a draw to win.'[7]

Yet the leadership of Sinn Féin avoided the sizeable split in the movement that might have been expected, given the extent of compromise. Although the 32-County Sovereignty Committee had existed in embryonic form since 1994, it did not take many members. The formation of the Real IRA did not lead to widespread defections, nor did the emergence of the Continuity IRA. The existence of dissident 'micro-groups' could occasionally irritate or embarrass Sinn Féin, but continued armed struggle appeared futile and unpopular. Sinn Féin could use the Omagh bombing as a clear indication of the senselessness of continued military struggle, even if it had represented the type, if not the outcome, of IRA operation that had been commonplace for almost three previous decades and condoned by Sinn Féin. Thus a senior Sinn Féin figure argued that a 3,000 lb bomb in Manchester in 1996 (adequate warning; no dead; 200 injuries) was planted by 'heroes' (i.e. the PIRA), but a smaller bomb in Omagh in 1998 (incorrect warning; 29 dead; 300 injuries) was planted by people who must be condemned (the RIRA).[8] 'Good bomb, bad bomb' distinctions were indicative of the internal loyalty within the Provisional Republican movement. There is no single explanation for the solidity of Sinn Féin's members, but instead a combination of theoretical and practical factors allowed the leadership to sell the deal to the grassroots.

At the theoretical level, the nature of Provisional Republicanism permitted tactical flexibility. A product of a particular set of circumstances and a creature largely of disaffected but pragmatic working-class Republicans, Provisional Republicanism has been 'whatever the leadership said it was'.[9] Thus Republicanism that declared 'No return to Stormont' in 1997 was still Republicanism when it meant Executive ministries at Stormont in 1999.

The importance of interpersonal skills and personal histories should not be overlooked amid theorising. Articulate and forthright, the Sinn Féin leadership did not oversell the deal to the membership. Although overblown claims regarding its potential for transition were evident, there was enough acknowledgement that the GFA was not a republican document to pre-empt most critics. Sections of the leadership also had enough military 'stripes' to influence the grassroots that the GFA was a worthwhile advance for republicans. The support of large numbers of former and current prisoners for the Sinn Féin leadership had a huge effect in marginalising sceptics. Thus a Derry republican could dismissively ask of republican dissidents, 'Where were they when the bullets were flying?'[10] The conspiratorial nature of the IRA was, at a lesser level, reflected in Sinn Féin's structure. Linked to a genuine pride and internal loyalty over what had been achieved by Republican struggle, notably the downing of a sectarian Orange regime, Adams' task of steering the movement in a new direction proved manageable.

The promotion of tactical flexibility was greatly assisted by the successes of electoral politics. In its limited aim of making Sinn Féin the largest nationalist party in Northern Ireland, electoralism had achieved its goal by 2001. After the IRA ceasefire, the spectacular electoral gains for Sinn Féin could maintain an image of political advance. That electoral victories would not bring about the declared overarching aim of the party, a united Ireland, was of no great concern to electors or elected. In the shorter term, the nationalist electorate placed its faith in Sinn Féin as the party most likely to articulate its demands in a consociational system which attempts to accommodate rival ethnic blocs, but, in the short term, may heighten inter- and intra-bloc rivalries. The danger for Sinn Féin was that electoralism could become a mirror image of the military campaign: self-sustaining, undefeated and containing spectaculars, but not achieving its stated ends. Sinn Féin's leaders do not concur on when electoral politics will achieve a united Ireland. On any reading of the GFA, it remains only the remotest possibility, a point conceded by Mitchell McLaughlin, although Michelle Gildernew, elected Westminister MP for Fermanagh and South Tyrone, argues that a united Ireland will be created 'in 15 to 20 years'.[11]

For Sinn Féin, the essential problem was the articulation of any coherent strategy had the party remained outside the multi-party negotiations leading to the Good Friday Agreement. The party entered talks fully aware that they would lead to a three-stranded framework, which would be based upon Northern consent for change, hitherto derided as a unionist veto. In this respect, Sinn Féin was indeed a prisoner of its own electoralism. Three options confronted the Republican movement: a return to full 'armed struggle', with potentially disastrous electoral consequences for Sinn Féin and little prospect of military victory, notwithstanding the impact of IRA actions in England during the 1990s; a retreat to sullen abstentionism and a boycott of the Northern Assembly, a move with considerable electoral risks; or full participation and support for a political agreement, a measure almost certain to generate extra nationalist electoral support. The Agreement could then (justly) be sold to the majority of nationalist electors as a genuine advance towards full nationalist parity of esteem within the state, allied to a modest strengthening of an Irish dimension. For many Northern nationalists, this will suffice, as Irish unity is seen as an ultimate aspiration, rather than an immediate imperative. Sinn Féin have camped on the SDLP's political territory in Northern Ireland and used structural advantages and political acumen to make important advances in the Irish Republic.

Sinn Féin's increased contacts with institutions in Northern Ireland have developed rapidly over previous decades. Dealings with the local state began through community activism in the 1980s. The prospect of Sinn Féin ministers actually *controlling* parts of the local state was appealing to many nationalists. To core Republicans, the deal could be sold as transitory to Irish unity, although not all republicans bought this argument.[12] The symbolism of the first all-Ireland vote since partition in the GFA referendum of May 1998 helped the selling of the deal as one offering qualified national self-determination, even if the outcome was one of Sinn Féin being a co-manager of British rule in

Northern Ireland, until even that responsibility was halted by unionists and the British government in 2002.

Post-Republicanism?

To answer the question of whether Sinn Féin remains a 'true' Republican or 'post'-Republican party, one needs to examine whether a core
set of Republican principles has ever been identifiable. Insofar as they
exist, they have operated as goals, rather than as dictates of strategies
of achievement. The twin goals of Republicanism have been the creation of a sovereign, independent, united 32-county Irish Republic
and the emancipation of all citizens within that Republic. It is perhaps
the existence of the latter goal which has led to Todd's claim that republicanism has not been abandoned by Sinn Féin, but instead di-
verted into the pursuit of radical transformist egalitarianism.[13] Even
leaving aside the question of whether Sinn Féin's policies are either
'radical' or 'egalitarian', in what sense are the party's principles transformist? The party's rigid insistence upon full implementation of the
Good Friday Agreement is transformist in respect of the internal politics of Northern Ireland, but is a tacit recognition of the legitimacy
of the Northern state and as such, non-transformist in terms of constitutional politics. Sequentially, at least, there has been a reordering
of Republican principles. Whereas in the past the severing of the British connection was the precondition to the promotion of equality and
the development of citizenship, now it appears to be merely a useful
accompaniment.

Sinn Féin has moved towards a civic Republicanism, which acknow-
ledges the plurality of identities in Northern Ireland and recognises
an independent existence for Unionists beyond their British 'colonial
masters'.[14] The revised thinking dates back to the prison experience
of many Republicans, prepared to play 'Devil's advocate' and argue
the unionist case to imprisoned colleagues. The result was discomfiture with the traditional republican position.[15] This movement away
from an ethnic Republicanism which assumed homogeneity of identity on the island of Ireland has been recognised, in institutional
terms, through tacit acceptance of the consent principle in respect of
the constitutional position of Northern Ireland.

The debate over what constitutes core Republican principles has
been clouded by a failure to distinguish between what ought to be

recognised as principle and what is merely strategic or tactical. For Sinn Féin, principle is defined by intention. It is the intention of the Republican leadership to produce a united Ireland through entry to Stormont and by offering participatory politics to the nationalist electorate. Therefore there has been no departure from Republican principles, as the core objectives of all Republicans—self-determination and equality—are still dearly held. Tactical adjustments, the leadership point out, have always been made, hence the variation between politics and armed struggle, recognition and non-recognition of the courts, or electoralism and abstentionism, at different times. On the basis of this argument, there are no fundamental Republican principles beyond a commitment to core goals; abstention, even from Westminster, need not be seen as a core principle, although the oath of allegiance to a British monarch might be too much for Republicans to bear. How, then, can modern Sinn Féin be distinguished from Fianna Fáil, 'the Republican party' or the SDLP, as a nationalist party? After all, Sinn Féin's movement into parliamentary politics is reminiscent of Fianna Fáil's in 1926, a switch accompanied by continuing protestations of the party's Republicanism, yet followed decades later by renunciation of the claim to the North. Here, the difference rests upon the basis of organisation. As the only significant all-Ireland party, Sinn Féin, as an organisation, transcends partition. It is this key difference, becoming ever more important as Sinn Féin develops in the Irish Republic, which inhibits attempts to portray Sinn Féin as merely a communal party, representing a nationalist segment in the North.[16] Although Sinn Féin has moved away from its earlier avowed Republican principles, all-island organisation may eventually be matched by an all-island governmental presence, dependent upon the balance of political forces in the Irish Republic. Such a presence would not, of course, deliver the Holy Grail of the independent Republic, but would have implications for the all-island organisation of some key policy areas.

All-Ireland organisation does not of course, in itself, refute the 'sellout' or 'verbalised Republicans' charges aimed at Sinn Féin's leadership by diehard Republicans, who argue that Sinn Féin's 'sellout' is even worse than Fianna Fáil's decades earlier, in that De Valera *et al.* at least never became Crown ministers![17] The importance of Sinn Féin's all-island structure has yet to be determined and can only be assessed ultimately if and when the party is in government North and South.

Undoubtedly the Republicanism of Sinn Féin is a fundamentally different entity from older versions. Obliged to update the assumption that the mandate of 1918 gave automatic legitimacy to a modern cause, Sinn Féin altered its *modus operandi*, but was forced to engage in duplicity towards its own supporters, reassuring doubters that armed struggle remained a tactical option. Meanwhile, electoralism displaced militarism and constitutionalism and participation ousted insurrection. The result has been that, as Bean puts it, Republicanism has 'ceased to be a universalizing and transformative ideological framework and, in true pluralist and post-modern fashion, become one voice amongst many shouting for attention in the political market place'.[18] Respect for Sinn Féin's mandate has displaced the universality associated with traditional Republicanism. A section of Republicanism would naturally consider this a betrayal, as it dilutes a conflict against a colonial aggressor to a struggle for influence amid a diverse set of political forces and recognises that 'aggressor' as a referee within the Northern political market place. The journey from 'ourselves alone' to 'equal treatment for our mandate' has been the most striking transformation in republican politics.[19]

Endogenous and exogenous explanations of change are apparent. The 'external events thesis' suggests that the end of the Cold War contributed substantially to the shifts in republicanism and helped shape the Good Friday Agreement.[20] Undoubtedly the demise of discredited Eastern European regimes speeded the movement of Sinn Féin and the IRA away from leftist politics, but their commitment to such was only ever partial. Irish Republicanism was already changing prior to the collapse of Communism, as was illustrated publicly in 1986 through the end of abstentionism in respect of Dáil Éireann and in 1988 through the commencement of a pan-nationalist exit strategy through Hume-Adams. British government tactics shifted, in talking to historic enemies, but British policy, centred upon an unemotional maintenance of the consent principle, is unaltered. The basic architecture of the Good Friday Agreement was in evidence twenty-five years earlier at Sunningdale. Hence the main role of external players has been to act as honest brokers, or as facilitators of the peace process. They have accelerated change and influenced end-of-conflict negotiating positions (the African National Congress influenced Sinn Féin), but they are not causal agents of the peace process.

Endogenous structural explanations are perhaps the most convincing in explaining changes within Sinn Féin.[21] The rise of a Catholic middle class, seeking representation through political institutions, has accelerated in recent years in Northern Ireland. Sinn Féin's traditional agenda risked ghettoisation, confined mainly to an urban proletariat in the North and a small working class, chiefly in Dublin, in the South, allied to traditional pockets of rural support. The communal basis of voting in Northern Ireland and the diminishing working class ensured that Sinn Féin had to broaden its appeal and attempt to become a 'catch-all' nationalist party, capturing the votes of the SDLP, if it was to expand. Within this context, Republican baggage was expendable and the IRA was 'a political liability'.[22] By 2001 it was claimed that 94 per cent of SDLP supporters and 72 per cent of Sinn Féin supporters backed IRA decommissioning of weapons.[23] For Sinn Féin the demands of electoralism did not require renunciation of longer-term objectives, but rather the adoption of different means. In 2001 Catholic support for Irish reunification was reasonably high, at 59 per cent.[24]

For republican ultras, the dominance of electoralism ignores the opportunities created by vanguardism. Sinn Féin's election victory of 1918 was preceded by armed rebellion, which came to be supported by large sections of the population. The removal of the 'cutting edge' of the IRA would leave Republicans powerless, irrespective of the votes accrued by Sinn Féin.

For the Republican mainstream, however, the IRA had served its purpose in removing the sectarian essence of the Northern state, helping nationalists to become part of an 'Ireland of Equals', even if that Ireland remained partitioned. The emergence of Sinn Féin and the DUP as the largest parties at the 2003 Assembly election meant that a permanent deal could now be struck with Unionism, which would guarantee Sinn Féin a major place in government and transform Northern Ireland into a bloc duopoly, with Unionism and nationalism represented largely by single parties acting as 'catch-alls' within their ethic bloc. As the barriers to a Sinn Féin-DUP settlement were whittled down to the mere modalities and transparency of decommissioning, it was evident that the transformation of Republican politics was almost complete. A DUP led by Ian Paisley indicated its willingness to have Sinn Féin as a coalition partner in the government of Northern Ireland, a scenario unthinkable only a few years earlier. There remained questions concerning the viability of coalition arrangements in Northern Ireland amid continuing communal politics. Nonetheless, a coalition presence for Sinn Féin was a prospect sufficient to entice all but diehard Republicans.

Post-nationalism?

The new SDLP leader Mark Durkan needs to be cautious in continuing to deploy the post-nationalist philosophy of Hume to the detriment of nationalism. Election trends indicate growing confidence in the dynamism of Sinn Féin, particularly among the young nationalist constituency in Northern Ireland, which needs to be matched by creative regeneration of SDLP policies. Durkan needs to consider the views of Seamus Mallon, former SDLP deputy leader, that nationalism 'will always be a vibrant and legitimate political philosophy on the island of Ireland'.[25] Durkan must put the Hume legacy behind him and change the flagging organisational basis of the party. The difficulty for the SDLP is in avoiding the charge that the arrival of its own 'outstanding achievement' in 1998 means that the party's best days are now left behind. From a different perspective, hardline Republicans agree, arguing that the SDLP has fulfilled its role as 'a brake on the revolutionary forces within the nationalist population until such time as the British and Irish governments could persuade a majority of Republicans to abandon insurrection and participate in the Northern Ireland system.'[26]

Mark Durkan has a seemingly impossible task to place the party at the forefront of the nationalist constituency again in Northern Ireland. He stressed at his party's conference in 2002 that he was '100 per cent for a united Ireland' in a reinforcement of his nationalist credentials, whilst claiming as a 'strength' of the Agreement the fact that others who supported the Agreement were 100 per cent Unionist.[27] The SDLP leader pinned his hopes on continuing implementation of aspects of the Good Friday Agreement, even in the absence of devolved institutions. Durkan's main assets are the organisational and strategic skills he obtained through professional training at the National Democratic Institute in the United States during the 1980s. He played an important role in implementing an effective electoral strategy in 1986 and 1987 for Seamus Mallon and Eddie McGrady.

However, his ability to reverse the diminishing electoral support for the SDLP will prove a challenge. The SDLP failed to capitalise on its positive performance in the elections of the early 1990s and allowed Sinn Féin to use the peace process as a vehicle to reverse its dwindling support. Although continuing to poll respectably, the measurement of SDLP performance is invariably against Sinn Féin. The SDLP has faced difficult elections since the IRA ceasefires, a problem exacerbated by the ethnic bloc politics legitimised under the Good Friday Agreement. The party wishes to be seen as stoutly nationalist, but also needs to offer something to the moderate centre, in the hope of cross-community vote transfers from Alliance (a dwindling band) and moderate UUP supporters. The appeal to moderate Unionism has embraced nominations to the new policing boards, but this has had little electoral impact. Meanwhile, the beneficiaries of greater intra-nationalist voting will be Sinn Féin, as ever increasing SDLP members transfer within the bloc and allow Sinn Féin to continue to make gains.[28]

Presenting viable alternative policies to the supporters of Sinn Féin throughout the island of Ireland would require immediate and radical steps by the SDLP. An unlikely merger with Fianna Fáil would give the party a new 'green' nationalist image. The SDLP needs such an alliance to give it new impetus against the electoral drift in favour of Sinn Féin. Merger with the Irish Labour Party would still only give the SDLP minority political status and would not enthuse the SDLP membership. A post-nationalist, post-Unionist realignment of politics in Northern Ireland may yet emerge, in which the SDLP makes common cause with the UUP and Alliance, but this is at least one generation away and might be impossible to build under the current terms of the Good Friday Agreement.

The SDLP's capacity to rebuild itself as the main nationalist party in Northern Ireland is seriously hampered by the ageing profile of its members. The departure of Mallon and Hume saw the end of the party's Civil Rights era and the modern exponents of a civil rights agenda are more prominent within Sinn Féin. The SDLP may follow in the footsteps of the former Nationalist Party and become obsolete. In the absence of Hume and Mallon, the defects in party organisation will be fully exposed. The party, hitherto strongly identified with John Hume, Seamus Mallon, Eddie McGrady, Seán Farren and Bríd Rogers, may lose representatives with whom a younger electorate can engage. For a party that fermented pan-nationalism by helping persuade republicans that armed struggle was counter-productive, electoral demise may seem unfair. Furthermore, for a party that wrote a considerable section of the most important political agreement since partition, the verdict of nationalist voters may seem exceptionally harsh, not least amid allegations of continuing IRA activity, including the largest bank robbery ever committed in Britain and Ireland, in 2004, actions which threatened enduring political paralysis. However, the community activism, new constitutionalism and, above all, the near rabid insistence of Sinn Féin upon full implementation of the Good Friday Agreement chime with a nationalist electorate for which militant Republicanism was always a minority taste.

NOTES

Preface

1. E. Moloney, *A Secret History of the IRA*, Harmondsworth: Penguin, 2002.
2. I. McAllister, *The Northern Ireland Social Democratic and Labour Party*, Basingstoke: Macmillan, 1977
3. G. Murray, *John Hume's SDLP*, Dublin: Irish Academic Press, 1998.

Chapter 1 The Development of Nationalist Politics in Northern Ireland

1. Participants in the rising included Irish Volunteers, Cumann na mBan (the women's ancillary force) and the socialist Citizen Army. See M. Laffan, *The Resurrection of Ireland: The Sinn Féin Party 1916–1923*, Cambridge University Press, 1999.
2. E. Staunton, *The Nationalists of Northern Ireland, 1918–1973*, Dublin: Columba, 2001, pp. 101–3.
3. B. O'Leary, T. Lyne, J. Marshall and B. Rowthorn, *Northern Ireland Sharing Authority*, London: Institute for Public Research, 1993, p. 53.
4. P. Arthur, *The People's Democracy 1968–1973*, Belfast: Blackstaff, 1974, p. 12.
5. E. Phoenix, *Northern Nationalism: Nationalist Politics, Partition and the Catholic Minority*, Belfast: Ulster Historical Foundation, 1994, p. 359.
6. Ibid.
7. Ibid.
8. Ibid. p. 160.
9. Ibid. p. 362.
10. T. Hennessey, *A History of Northern Ireland 1920–1996*, Dublin: Gill & Macmillan, 1997.
11. The Free State became known as Éire following the 1937 constitution.
12. P. Arthur, *Government and Politics of Northern Ireland*, London: Longman, 1974, p. 57.
13. P. Arthur, *The People's Democracy*, Belfast: Blackstaff, 1974, p. 18.
14. B. Lynn, *Holding the Ground: The Nationalist Party in Northern Ireland, 1945–72*, p. 242.
15. P. Buckland, *A History of Northern Ireland*, Dublin: Gill & Macmillan, 1981, p. 125.
16. Ibid.
17. Interview with Michael McKeown, 13 July, 1995.
18. I. McAllister, 'Political Opposition in Northern Ireland: The National Democratic Party, 1965–70', *Economic and Social Review* V1/3, 1975, p. 357.
19. Ibid. p. 358.

271

20. Ibid. p. 360.
21. NDP Aims, NDP File, NIPC, LHL.
22. McAllister (note 17), p. 363.
23. NDP Attitude to Southern Ireland, NDP File, NIPC, LHL.
24. Statement by P. Ritchie, Secretary of the Lisburn Branch of the South Antrim Divisional Association of the National Democratic Democratic Party. NDP File, NIPC, LHL.
25. Ibid.
26. NDP General Election Manifesto, 18 June 1970, NDP File, NIPC, LHL.
27. McAllister (note 17), p. 363.
28. Interview with John Duffy, 23 January 1995.
29. Ibid.
30. Interview with Paddy Devlin, 2 November 1994.
31. *Irish News*, 20 August 1990.
32. *Irish News*, 18 August 1995.
33. Interview with Austin Currie, 2 August 1995.
34. Interview with Ben Caraher, 28 September 1994.
35. Ibid.
36. *Irish News*, 20 August 1990.
37. *Irish Times*, 15 September 1970.
38. Interview with John Duffy, 23 August 1995.
39. J. Bowyer Bell, *The Secret Army: The IRA*, Dublin: Poolbeg, 1998.
40. T. P. Coogan, *The IRA*, London: Fontana, 1989.
41. Bowyer Bell (note 38), p. 281.
42. See H. Patterson, *The Politics of Illusion: a Political History of the IRA*, London: Serif, 1997, pp. 91–4.
43. Bowyer Bell (note 38), p. 332.
44. M. Farrell, *Northern Ireland: the Orange State*, London: Pluto, p. 221.
45. P. Bishop and E. Mallie, *The Provisional IRA*, London: Corgi, 1988.
46. Coogan (note 39), p. 421.
47. Patterson (note 41), p. 99.
48. M. L. R. Smith, *Fighting for Ireland: the Military Strategy of the Republican Movement*, London: Routledge, 1995.
49. P. Walsh, *Irish Republicanism and Socialism: the Politics of the Republican Movement 1905 to 1994*, Belfast: Athol, 1994.
50. B. Feeney, *Sinn Féin: A Hundred Turbulent Years*, Dublin: O'Brien, 2001.
51. *This Week*, 31 July 1970.
52. Irish Police Intelligence reports suggest that the movement was not as dormant as widely claimed. Patterson (note 42), also notes a steady increase in IRA personnel in Belfast, although he suggests that this occurred largely independently of any activity undertaken by the Dublin leadership.
53. Bowyer-Bell (note 38).
54. See appendix to the Inquiry of Lord Scarman: 'Violence and Civil Disturbance in Northern Ireland in 1969', Report of a Tribunal of Inquiry, Belfast: HMSO, Cmnd 556, vol. 2, p. 45, 1972.

55. Sinn Féin (1967), *The Lessons of History*, Dublin: Sinn Féin, cited in Patterson (note 41), p. 105.

56. Walsh (note 48), p. 72.

57. *United Irishman*, December 1967.

58. T. P. Coogan, *The Troubles: Ireland's Ordeal 1966–1995 and the Search for Peace*, London: Hutchinson, 1995, p. 56.

59. For a detailed assessment of the composition of the civil rights movement, see B. Purdie, *Politics in the Streets*, Belfast: Blackstaff, 1990.

60. Coogan, 1995 (note 57), p. 63.

61. Republican Education Department quoted in Patterson (note 41), p. 117.

62. P. Taylor, *Provos: The IRA and Sinn Féin*, London: Bloomsbury, 1997, p. 24.

63. Smith (note 47), p. 76.

64. *United Irishman*, May 1966.

65. Walsh, op. cit.

66. S. Mac Stiofáin, *Memoirs of a Revolutionary*, Edinburgh: Cremones, 1975.

67. *United Irishman*, May 1969.

68. Patterson (note 48), p. 108.

69. D. O'Hagan, 'The Concept of Republicanism' in N. Porter (ed.), *The Republican Ideal*, Belfast: Blackstaff, 1998, p. 87.

70. G. Boyce, *Nationalism in Ireland*, London: Routledge, 1995, p. 363.

71. D. Keogh, *Twentieth Century Ireland: Nation and State*, Dublin: Gill and Macmillan, p. 289.

72. Seán Garland, Speech at Wolfe Tone Commemoration, Bodenstown, June 1968.

73. Mac Stiofáin (note 65).

74. *An Phoblacht/Republican News*, 19 August 1999.

75. P. Bishop and E. Mallie, *The Provisional IRA*, London: Corgi, 1998.

76. Ibid.

Chapter 2 Collapsing Stormont: Politics and Rebellion in the Early 1970s

1. *Irish Times*, 17 July 1971.

2. *Irish Times*, 6 November 1971.

3. *Irish News*, 12 January 1972.

4. Chapter 4, S. Greer, 'Powers of the Army' in B. Dickson (ed.), *Civil Liberties in Northern Ireland: the CAJ Handbook*, Belfast: CAJ, 1997.

5. Information supplied by Kris Brown, Northern Ireland Political Collection, Linen Hall Library.

6. PRONI D. 3072/1A/22A

7. PRONI D. 3072/1A/22A

8. The term 'Stickie' or 'Stick' was common parlance in Republican areas in describing the Officials. It derived from their habit of gumming, rather than pinning, an Easter lily to their lapel during Easter Rising commemorations. The National Liberation Front was the formal term by which the 'Officials' were often referred to in the newspapers of the Provisionals.

9. *Republican News*, 8 December 1972.

10. *Irish Press*, 5 January 1970.
11. *Republican News*, January–February 1971.
12. *United Irishman*, January 1970.
13. *United Irishman*, January 1975.
14. Ibid.
15. P. Bishop and E. Mallie, *The Provisional IRA*, London: Corgi, 1998.
16. Ibid.
17. For several such examples, see the contributions to K. Bean and M. Hayes (ed.), *Republican Voices*, Monaghan: Seesyu, 2001.
18. Interview with Alex Maskey, 17 April 2000.
19. *United Irishman*, August 1976.
20. *Voice of the North*, 12 October 1969.
21. *Voice of the North*, 31 January 1970.
22. Ibid.
23. *Voice of the North*, 12 September 1970.
24. Bishop and Mallie (note 15); J. Bowyer-Bell, *The Secret Army: the IRA*, Dublin: Poolbeg, 1998; T. P. Coogan, *The IRA*, London: Fontana, 1980; H. Patterson, *The Politics of Illusion: a Political History of the IRA*, London: Serif, 1997;
25. R. English, *Armed Struggle: A History of the IRA*, London: Macmillan, 2003.
26. G. Adams, *Free Ireland: Towards a Lasting Peace*, Dingle: Brandon, 1995.
27. From the IRA's *Green Book* (IRA Training Manual).
28. *Republican News*, January–February 1971.
29. *Republican News*, 2 October 1971.
30. Ibid.
31. *Republican News*, 25 August 1972.
32. *An Phoblacht*, 30 June 1972.
33. *Republican News*, June 1970, repeated frequently thereafter.
34. Sinn Féin, *Éire Núa* (New Ireland) Dublin: Sinn Féin, 1972.
35. 'What is Irish Republicanism?' *Irish Independent*, 9 December 1970.
36. P. Walsh, *Irish Republicanism and Socialism: The Politics of the Republican Movement, 1905–1994*, Belfast: Athol, 1995, p. 104.
37. Ibid. p. 105.
38. *Republican News*, July 1970.
39. *An Phoblacht*, July 1972.
40. Sinn Féin, op. cit., 1972.
41. See M. Ryan, *War and Peace in Ireland: Britain and the IRA in the New World Order*, London: Pluto, 1994; S. Cronin, *Irish Nationalism: a History of its Roots and Ideology*, Dublin: Academic Press, 1980.
42. Ruairí Ó Brádaigh, Presidential address to Sinn Féin Ard Fheis, 29 October 1972, in R. Ó Brádaigh, *Our People, Our Future: What Éire Núa Means*, Dublin: Sinn Féin, 1973.
43. *United Irishman*, September 1970.
44. Ruairí Ó Brádaigh, 'Green Paper Solves Nothing' in Ó Brádaigh (note 40).
45. See *Republican News*, 24 Nov. 72.
46. *Republican News*, 17 Nov. 72.

47. Ruairí Ó Brádaigh, Presidential Speech to Ard Fheis, 29 October 1972, (note 40), 12,000 copies of the economic and social programme had been sold.
48. Cited in J. Bowyer-Bell, (note 24) p. 379.
49. Ibid. p. 374.
50. Ibid. p. 382.
51. *Sunday Times*, 3 July 1977.
52. For a detailed account of the rivalry between McKee and Adams, see E. Moloney, *A Secret History of the IRA*, London: Penguin. 2002.
53. Patterson (note 24).
54. Ibid. p. 152.
55. J. Holland and H. McDonald, *INLA: Deadly Divisions*, Dublin: Torc, 1994.

Chapter 3   The Sunningdale Experiment

1. For a detailed outline of consociational ideas, see A. Lijphart, *Democracy in Plural Societies: a Comparative Exploration*, New Haven: Yale University Press, 1977. See also J. McGarry (ed.), *Northern Ireland and the Divided World*, Oxford University Press, 2001, pp. 15–16.
2. H.M. Government, *Northern Ireland Constitutional Proposals*, London: HMSO, Cmnd. 5259, 1973.
3. W. Flackes, *Northern Ireland: a Political Directory*, London: BBC, 1983.
4. J. Bowman, *De Valera and the Ulster Question, 1917–1973*, Oxford University Press, 1982, p. 101.
5. See P. Bew, P. Gibbon, and H. Patterson, *Northern Ireland: Political Forces and Social Classes, 1921–1996*, London: Serif, 1996.
6. G. Gillespie, 'The Sunningdale Agreement: Lost Opportunity or An Agreement Too Far?' *Irish Political Studies*, 1998, vol. 13, pp. 100–14.
7. SDLP Draft Proposals Relating to Negotiations on the Present Situation in Northern Ireland, Dublin, 17 September 1971, PRONI, D. 3072/1088.
8. Ibid.
9. Social Democratic and Labour Party Towards a New Ireland, PRONI, D. 3072/1088.
10. Ibid.
11. Ibid.
12. Ibid.
13. Ibid.
14. Ibid.
15. Interview with John Hume, 16 August 1995.
16. Interview with Eddie McGrady, 26 July 1995.
17. Interview with Paddy Devlin, 2 November 1994.
18. Interview with Austin Currie, 2 August 1995.
19. Interview with Eddie McGrady, 26 July 1995.
20. Interview with John Duffy, 23 January 1995.
21. Joint statement by the SDLP Executive Committee and Assembly Party, 3 Sept. 1974, PRONI, D. 3072/4/74/34.
22. Ibid.
23. Ibid.

24. Ibid.

25. Review of SDLP Strategy on the Convention election, 18 November 1974 (PRONI, D. 3072/1B/63).

26. Ibid.

27. Ibid.

28. Part 7. The Next Steps: Paragraph 50, Cmnd. 5675, The Northern Ireland Constitution, July 1974.

29. Ibid. Paragraph 45 (c).

30. Ibid. Paragraph 54.

31. Also known as the Ulster Coalition. It was established in January 1974 to fight the Sunningdale Agreement which it viewed as an embryonic move towards a united Ireland. It followed the split in the Ulster Unionist Party, which elected Harry West as leader in succession to Brian Faulkner, who had become Chief Executive in the Power-Sharing Executive.

32. Northern Ireland Convention, *Northern Ireland Convention Report*, Part IV, Belfast: NIC, 1975.

33. Ibid. Paragraph 28.

34. Ibid., Appendix I.

35. Ibid., Appendix 3 IV, The British Dimension.

36. H.M. Government, *Northern Ireland Constitutional Proposals*, London: HMSO, 1972, para. 78.

37. *Northern Ireland Convention Report* op. cit., Ibid., XI: *Authority, Legitimacy and Consent.*

38. Ibid., VIII. Police Service.

39. Ibid., Paragraph 94.

40. P. Devlin, *Straight Left*, Belfast: Blackstaff, 1993, p. 261.

41. *News Letter*, 4 February 1976.

42. D. Hamill, *Pig in the Middle: the Army in Northern Ireland, 1969–84*, London: Methuen, 1985, pp. 176–7.

43. I. Fallon and J. Strodes, *De Lorean: the Rise and Fall of a Dream Maker*, London: Hamish Hamilton, 1983, p. 228.

44. *Irish Times*, 17 March 1979.

45. See for example S. Bruce, *At the Edge of the Union*, Oxford University Press, 1994.

46. *News Letter*, 4 December 1976.

47. *Guardian*, 20 February 1976.

48. *News Letter*, 4 May 1978.

49. R. Mason, *Paying the Price*, London: Robert Hale, 1999, p. 178.

50. See comments of Sean Hollywood, in G. Murray, *John Hume and the SDLP*, Dublin: Irish Academic Press, 1998, p. 68.

51. Speech to SDLP Annual Conference, 1978.

52. *Irish Times*, 13 February 1978.

53. *Irish Times*, 24 May 1978.

54. Gerry Fitt had been a constant supporter of the Labour Party at Westminster. In particular, his vote was vital to the Wilson and Callaghan governments. His abstention in the important 1979 confidence vote which led to the downfall of the Labour administration demonstrated his antipathy towards Roy Mason as Northern Ireland Secretary of State.

55. *Irish Times*, 21 November 1979.
56. M. Rees, *Northern Ireland: a Personal Perspective*, London: Methuen, 1985, p. 305.
57. Interview with John Hume, 16 August 1995.
58. *Irish Times*, 23 November 1979.
59. Ibid.
60. *Irish Times*, 6 November 1978.
61. See Murray (note 50), pp. 78 and 79.
62. *Irish Times*, 2 November 1979.
63. *Irish News*, 6 December 1976.

Chapter 4 Marginalisation, Exclusion and Rebirth: Republicanism, 1972–9

1. *United Irishman*, August 1971.
2. M. McGuire, *To Take Arms: My Year with the Provisionals*, New York: Viking, 1973.
3. M. L. R. Smith, *Fighting for Ireland? The Military Strategy of the Irish Republican Movement*, London: Routledge, 1995, p. 105.
4. Ibid. p. 105.
5. *Republican News*, 2 January 1972.
6. *An Phoblacht*, 19 April 1974.
7. See P. Dixon, *Northern Ireland: the Politics of War and Peace*, London: Palgrave, 2001, for a discussion of British contemplations of withdrawal.
8. See P. Bew, P. Gibbon and H. Patterson, *Northern Ireland, 1921–1996: Political Forces and Social Classes*, London: Serif, 1996.
9. B. Hayes and I. McAllister, 'British and Irish Public Opinion towards the Northern Ireland Problem', *Irish Political Studies*, vol. 11, pp. 61–82, 1996.
10. T. P. Coogan, *The Troubles: Ireland's Ordeal and the Search for Peace*, London: Hutchinson, 1995, p. 147.
11. W. Whitelaw, *The Whitelaw Memoirs*, London: Aurum, 1989, p. 100.
12. See E. Moloney, *A Secret History of the IRA*, London: Penguin, 2002, for the most detailed account of the betrayal of IRA operations.
13. See Sinn Féin, *The Quality of Life in the New Ireland*, Dublin: Sinn Féin, 1973; Sinn Féin, *Mining and Energy: the Sinn Féin Policy*, Dublin: Sinn Féin, 1974.
14. *Hibernia*, 16 January 1976.
15. See *An Phoblacht*, 31 October 1975.
16. *An Phoblacht*, 26 July 1974.
17. 'Freeman', *An Phoblacht*, 12 June 1974.
18. Sinn Féin, *A Broader Base: the Need for Local Involvement*, Dublin: Sinn Féin, 1974, p. 3.
19. Ibid. p. 8.
20. *An Phoblacht*, 21 March 1975.
21. *An Phoblacht*, 19 December 1975.
22. *An Phoblacht*, 20 September 1974.
23. P. Bishop and E. Mallie, *The Provisional IRA*, London: Corgi, 1988.

24. E. Moloney (note 12), p. 141.
25. Ibid. p. 271. N.B. During the 1970s, the *Sunday Times* claimed that Dáithí Ó Conaill was the only member of the Army Council to oppose the ceasefire.
26. P. Taylor, *Provos*, London: Bloomsbury, 1997, p. 177.
27. P. Bew, P. and H. Patterson, *The British State and the Ulster Crisis*, London: Verso, 1985, p. 87.
28. *An Phoblacht*, 4 April 1975.
29. M. Ryan, *War and Peace in Ireland: Britain and the IRA in the New World Order*, London: Pluto, 1994.
30. *An Phoblacht*, 21 March 1975.
31. *An Phoblacht*, 21 November 1975.
32. *An Phoblacht*, 12 December 1975.
33. Quoted in K. Bean and M. Hayes (ed.), *Republican Voices*, Monaghan: Seesyu, p. 71.
34. *Republican News*, 14 August 1976.
35. *Republican News*, 22 May 1976.
36. J. Holland and H. McDonald, *INLA. Deadly Divisions*, Dublin: Torc, 1995.
37. P. Walsh, *Irish Republicanism and Socialism: The Politics of the Republican Movement 1905 to 1994*, Belfast: Athol, 1994, p. 153.
38. Gerry Adams in *An Phoblacht/Republican News*, 21 July 1983.
39. Gerry Adams, Bobby Sands Memorial Lecture, 5 May 1985, *Iris*, July 1985.
40. *An Phoblacht*, 7 November 1975.
41. Ibid.
42. Ibid.
43. *An Phoblacht*, 4 April 1975.
44. Walsh, op. cit.
45. Smith, op. cit., p. 98.
46. McGuire, op. cit., p. 128.
47. R. White, 'The Irish Republican Army and Sectarianism: Moving Beyond the Anecdote', *Terrorism and Political Violence*, vol. 9, no. 2, 1997, p. 130.
48. See J. Stevenson, *'We Wrecked the Place': Contemplating an End to the Northern Irish Troubles*, New York: Free Press, 1996.
49. Ibid.
50. Coogan (note 10), p. 149.
51. See, for example, *An Phoblacht*, 29 August 1975.
52. Bishop and Mallie (note 23), p. 275.
53. Interview with Rita O'Hare, 27 April 2000.
54. Éamonn McCann, *Hibernia*, 16 January 1976.
55. Peter Caraher, in T. Harnden (ed.), *Bandit Country: the IRA and South Armagh*, London: Hodder and Stoughton, 1999, p. 190.
56. Harnden (note 55), p. 181.
57. *An Phoblacht*, 28 March 1975.
58. S. Elliott and W. Flackes, *Northern Ireland: a Political Directory 1968–1999*, Belfast: Blackstaff, 1999, p. 451.
59. T. P. Coogan (note 10), p. 247.
60. T. P. Coogan, *The IRA*, London, Fontana, 1989, pp. 578–81.

Chapter 5   Ending Political Inertia: the Internationalisation of the Northern Ireland Conflict

1. D. N. Doyle and O. Dudley Edwards (eds), *America and Ireland, 1776–1976: The American Identity and the Irish Connection*; the proceedings of the United States Bicentennial conference of Cumann Merriman, Ennis, August 1976, Westport, CT: Greenwood Press, 1980, p. 81.
2. Ibid.
3. See comments by Seán Donlon (former Irish Ambassador in the USA) in chapter 10: 'Mobilising Europe and America', in G. Murray (ed.) *John Hume and the SDLP*, Dublin: Irish Academic Press, 1998.
4. S. J. Leonard, 'How "Green" is the White House?', unpublished MA Thesis, University College Dublin, October 1994.
5. Ibid.
6. B. White, *John Hume: Statesman of the Troubles*, Belfast: Blackstaff, 1984, p. 125.
7. *Irish Times*, 6 September 1979.
8. Ibid.
9. Ibid.
10. B. White (note 6), p. 188.
11. *Sunday Tribune*, 6 Nov. 1994.
12. Interview with Tom Kelly, former second director of the SDG, 9 July 1996.
13. S. Elliott and W. Flackes, *Northern Ireland: a Political Directory 1968–1999*, Belfast: Blackstaff, 1999, pp. 324–5.
14. S. Cronin, *Washington's Irish Policy, 1916–1986*, Dublin: Anvil, 1987, p. 303.
15. Ibid. p. 304.
16. Ibid.
17. B. White (note 6), p. 191.
18. Ibid. p. 193.
19. *Sunday Tribune*, 5 February 1995.
20. S. Cronin (note 14), p. 319.
21. G. FitzGerald, *All In a Life*, Dublin: Gill & Macmillan, 1991, p. 527.
22. *Irish Times*, 22 Dec. 1984 quoted in S. Cronin (note 14), p. 322.
23. *Irish Times*, 30 Aug. 2000.
24. Committee on Regional Policy and Regional Planning, Doc. 1–517/79.
25. G. Murray, *John Hume and the SDLP*, Dublin: Irish Academic Press, (note 3) p. 79.
26. G. Murray (note 3) p. 77.
27. R. English, *Armed Struggle*, London: Macmillan, 2003, pp. 115–17.
28. Interview with Rita O'Hare, 9 April 2000.
29. P. Dixon, *Northern Ireland: the Politics of War and Peace*, London: Palgrave, 2001, suggests that the 'anger' of the British government was largely staged as part of the choreography of the peace process.
30. Sinn Féin, *Sinn Féin and the European Union*, Dublin: Sinn Féin, 2003.
31. E. Moloney, *A Secret History of the IRA*, London: Penguin, 2002.
32. Ibid.

Chapter 6 The Republican Second Front: Hunger Strikes
and Ballot Boxes

1. A. McIntyre, 'Modern Irish Republicanism: the Product of British State Strategies', *Irish Political Studies*, vol. 10, 1995.
2. T. P. Coogan, *The IRA*, London: Fontana, 1980.
3. *Republican News*, 18 June 1977.
4. Ibid.
5. R. Fisk, *The Point of No Return: the Strike Which Broke the British in Ulster*, London: André Deutsch, 1975; C. Kennedy Pipe, *The Origins of the Troubles in Northern Ireland*, London: Longman, 1997.
6. E. Moloney, *A Secret History of the IRA*, pp. 150–1.
7. Ibid. p. 153.
8. P. Bishop and E. Mallie, *The Provisional IRA*, London: Corgi, 1988.
9. *Republican News*, 7 Jan. 1978.
10. *Republican News*, 6 Jan. 1979.
11. G. Adams, *Free Ireland: Towards a Lasting Peace*, Brandon: Dingle, 1995, p. 75.
12. *Hibernia*, 23 February 1978.
13. B. Hayes and I. McAllister, 'British and Irish Public Opinion towards the Northern Ireland Problem', *Irish Political Studies*, 11, 1996, pp. 61–82.
14. *Republican News*, 6 January 1979.
15. *Republican News*, 11 March 1975.
16. M. Laffan, *The Resurrection of Ireland: the Making of the Sinn Féin Party 1916–1923*, Cambridge University Press, 1999.
17. B. O'Brien, *The Long War: the IRA and Sinn Féin*, Dublin: O'Brien, 2000.
18. Quoted in Bishop and Mallie (note 8), p. 353
19. See, for example, comments by Tommy McKearney in K. Bean and M. Hayes, *Republican Voices*, Monaghan: Seesyu, 2001.
20. *An Phoblacht*, 31 January 1981.
21. P. Walsh, *Irish Republicanism and Socialism: the Politics of the Republican Movement 1905 to 1994*, Belfast: Athol, 1994.
22. *An Phoblacht/Republican News*, 10 May 1990.
23. *An Phoblacht/Republican News*, 26 November 1981.
24. Walsh (note 21), p. 186.
25. Ibid.
26. *Iris*, no. 1, 1981.
27. Ibid.
28. *An Phoblacht/Republican News*, 4 March 1982.
29. *An Phoblacht/Republican News*, 26 September 1981.
30. *Iris*, no. 5, March 1983.
31. *An Phoblacht/Republican News*, 5 November 1981.
32. *An Phoblacht/Republican News*, 6 June 1981.
33. *An Phoblacht/Republican News*, 19 November 1981.
34. *An Phoblacht/Republican News*, 12 November 1981.
35. *An Phoblacht/Republican News*, 17 January 1981.
36. J. Bowyer Bell, *The Secret Army. The IRA*, Dublin: Poolbeg, p. 521.

37. *An Phoblacht/Republican News*, 29 April 1982.

38. *Iris*, No. 3, July–August 1982.

39. Speech to Sinn Féin Ard Fheis 1981.

40. Quoted in R. English, *Armed Struggle*, London: Macmillan, 2003, p. 225.

41. Letter to *An Phoblacht/Republican News*, 7 October 1982.

42. *Iris*, no. 2, 1981.

43. *An Phoblacht/Republican News*, 17 June 1982.

44. M.L.R. Smith, *Fighting for Ireland: the Military Strategy of the Republican Movement*, London: Routledge, 1995; A. McIntyre (note 1).

45. *Iris*, No. 4, Nov. 1982.

46. *An Phoblacht/Republican News*, 28 October 1982.

47. A. Guelke, 'The "Ballot Bomb": the Northern Ireland Assembly Election and the Provisional IRA', paper presented to at the ECPR Joint Sessions, Freiburg, West Germany, 20–25 March 1983.

Chapter 7   Rescuing the SDLP: The New Ireland Forum

1. J. Prior, *A Balance of Power*, London: Hamish Hamilton, 1986, p. 193.

2. Ibid. pp. 195–6.

3. *Belfast Telegraph*, 18 January 1982.

4. Prior (note 1) p. 197.

5. M. Thatcher, *The Downing Street Years*, London: HarperCollins, 1993, p. 385.

6. Interview with Dr Garret FitzGerald, 23 January 1995.

7. Parliamentary Debates (Commons), 21 (1982), Col. 699.

8. Ibid.

9. Seamus Mallon, Speech to INC, 3 May 1984, PRONI, D. 3072/46 (1993).

10. Seán Farren, Speech, 22 March, PRONI, D. 3072/B/1097 (1982).

11. *A Framework for Devolution*, 5 April 1982, Cmnd. 8541.

12. The crisis in the Falkland Islands began on the 1 April 1982 with the Argentine invasion of the British-held Falkland Islands. The UK government sent a task force to remove the Argentine forces. The sinking of the Argentine cruiser *Belgrano* by a British vessel during the conflict, with the loss of 368 lives, led to Haughey's government withdrawing co-operation from EC states which were implementing economic sanctions against Argentina.

13. G. FitzGerald, *All in a Life*, Dublin: Gill and Macmillan, 1991, p. 462.

14. B. Arnold, *Haughey: His Life and Unlucky Deeds*, London: HarperCollins, 1993, p. 217.

15. Ibid. p. 218.

16. FitzGerald (note 13), p. 463.

17. Ibid. p. 464.

18. Ibid. p. 466.

19. Ibid. p. 471.

20. P. O'Malley, *The Uncivil Wars: Ireland Today*, Belfast: Blackstaff, 1983, p. 402.

21. *Irish News*, 29 January 1983.

22. *Irish News*, 26 May 1983.

23. Farren, 'The New Ireland Forum—a Hope for the Future', PRONI, D. 3072/30 (July 1983).
24. Ibid.
25. *The Fundamental Problems*, PRONI, D. 3072/10 (10 August 1983).
26. Ibid.
27. *Irish News*, 31 January 1983.
28. S. Farren, *Forum for a New Ireland Constitutional Issues*, PRONI, D. 3072/30 (10 April 1983).
29. H. Logue, *The New Ireland as a Unitary State*, PRONI, D. 3072/30 (27 August 1983).
30. G. Murray, *John Hume and the SDLP*, Dublin: Irish Academic Press, 1998, p. 132.
31. *The Fundamental Problems*, PRONI, D. 3072/10 (10 August 1983).
32. *An Phoblacht/Republican News*, 10 November 1983.
33. Ibid. 17 March 1983.
34. Ibid. 7 July 1983; *Iris*, 6 July 1983.
35. *An Phoblacht/Republican News*, 14 February 1981.
36. P. Bishop and E. Mallie, *The Provisional IRA*, London: Corgi, 1988, p. 330.
37. E. Moloney, *A Secret History of the IRA*, London: Penguin, 2003.
38. Sinn Féin, *Government Details*, Dublin: Sinn Féin, 1983.
39. *An Phoblacht/Republican News*, 11 November 1982.
40. T. P. Coogan, *The IRA*, London: Fontana, 1987, p. 633.
41. *An Phoblacht/Republican News*, 17 October 1981.
42. Ruairí Ó Brádaigh, quoted in *Iris*, 1 April 1981.
43. *An Phoblacht/Republican News*, 8 July 1982.
44. Ibid. 10 December 1981.
45. Interview with Sean Crowe, 27 April 2000.
46. *An Phoblacht/Republican News*, 21 July 1983.
47. *An Phoblacht/Republican News*, 4 November 1982.
48. *Republican News*, 11 December 1976.
49. *An Phoblacht/Republican News*, 10 October 1981.
50. *An Phoblacht/Republican News*, 28 July 1983.
51. *An Phoblacht/Republican News*, 16 December 1982.
52. *An Phoblacht/Republican News*, 28 July 1983.
53. M. Ryan, *War and Peace in Ireland: Britain and the IRA in the New World Order*, London: Pluto, 1994, p. 42.
54. *Irish Times*, 30 July 1982.
55. *Irish News*, 4 July 1984.
56. *Belfast Telegraph*, 22 November 1984.
57. Interview with Seán Farren, 30 May 1984 in John T. Greene, 'The Comparative Development of the SDLP and Sinn Féin 1972–1985', MSc thesis, Queens University, Belfast, 1986.
58. AIIC Ministerial Meetings were set in motion following the Haughey-Thatcher Summit in Dublin on 8 December 1980. See G. Murray, *John Hume and the SDLP*, Dublin: Irish Academic Press, p. 101.
59. Thatcher (note 5) p. 395.

60. *Belfast Telegraph*, 20 November 1984.
61. Ibid.
62. Margaret Thatcher quoted in *Fortnight*, 10 December 1984.

Chapter 8   The Anglo-Irish Agreement

 1. P. Bew, P. Gibbon and H. Patterson, *Northern Ireland, 1921–1996: Political Forces and Social Classes*, London: Serif, 1996.
 2. A. Aughey, *Under Siege: Ulster Unionism and the Anglo-Irish Agreement*, London: Hurst, 1989.
 3. B. O'Leary and J. McGarry, *The Politics of Antagonism: Understanding Northern Ireland*, London: Athlone, 1996, p. 227.
 4. *The Tablet*, 25 December 1993, cited in M. Ryan, *War and Peace in Ireland: Britain and the IRA in the New World Order*, London: Pluto, 1994, p. 158.
 5. Aughey (note 2).
 6. Bew *et al.* (note 1), p. 217.
 7. A. Kenny, *The Road to Hillsborough: the Shaping of the Anglo-Irish Agreement*, Oxford: Pergamon, 1986.
 8. G. Murray, *John Hume and the SDLP*, Dublin: Irish Academic Press, pp. 77–8.
 9. J. Prior, *A Balance of Power*, London: Hamish Hamilton, 1986, p. 243.
10. G. Murray, op. cit., pp. 154–5.
11. BBC Northern Ireland, *Behind the Headlines*, 28 November 1985.
12. Article 2 (ii–iv), *Anglo-Irish Agreement*.
13. *Irish Times*, 24 November 1986.
14. G. FitzGerald, *All in a Life*, p. 529.
15. *Irish Times*, 24 November 1986.
16. *Irish News*, 30 October 1986.
17. *Irish Times*, 15 November 1995.
18. *Irish Times*, 9 November 1987.
19. *Irish Times*, 24 November 1986.
20. *Irish Times*, 24 November 1986.
21. *An Phoblacht/Republican News*, 12 September 1985.
22. Ibid. 21 November 1985.
23. Ibid.
24. E. Mallie and D. McKittrick, *The Fight for Peace: the Secret Story behind the Irish Peace Process*, London: Heinemann, 1996, p. 36.
25. Interview with Mitchell McLaughlin, 28 June 2000.
26. Interview with Pat Doherty, 28 June 2000.
27. Interview with Micheál McDonnacha, 27 April 2000.
28. *An Phoblacht/Republican News*, 5 December 1985.
29. Ibid.
30. *An Phoblacht/Republican News*, 21 November 1985.
31. M. Ryan, *War and Peace in Ireland: Britain and the IRA in the New World Order*, London: Pluto, p. 67.
32. *An Phoblacht/Republican News*, 5 December 1985.
33. Ibid.

34. B. O'Leary and J. McGarry, *The Politics of Antagonism*, London: Athlone, 1996.
35. *An Phoblacht/Republican News*, 21 November 1985.
36. *Fortnight*, October 1986, cited in M.L.R. Smith, *Fighting for Ireland: the Military Strategy of the Irish Republican Movement*, London: Routledge, p. 190.
37. *An Phoblacht/Republican News*, 12 December 1985.
38. Martin McGuinness, Bodenstown Oration 1986, Dublin: Sinn Féin.
39. P. Taylor, *Provos: the IRA and Sinn Féin*, London: Bloomsbury, 1997.
40. See H. Patterson, *The Politics of Illusion: a Political History of the IRA*, London: Serif, 1997.
41. *Hibernia*, 25 October 1979.

Chapter 9   Republican Reappraisal: The Initiatives of Gerry Adams

1. *An Phoblacht/Republican News*, 7 April 1983.
2. *An Phoblacht/Republican News*, 3 March 1983.
3. *An Phoblacht/Republican News*, 7 July 1983.
4. *An Phoblacht/Republican News*, 4 November 1982.
5. *An Phoblacht/Republican News*, 17 November 1983.
6. *An Phoblacht/Republican News*, 17 November 1983.
7. *An Phoblacht/Republican News*, 28 April 1983.
8. *An Phoblacht/Republican News*, 17 November 1983.
9. *Magill*, June 1983.
10. *An Phoblacht/Republican News*, 12 September 1985.
11. *An Phoblacht/Republican News*, 8 August 1985.
12. *An Phoblacht/Republican News*, 25 February 1987.
13. M. Ó Muilleoir, *Belfast's Dome of Delight: city Hall Politics, 1981–2000*, Belfast: Beyond the Pale, 1999, p. 15.
14. See P. Walsh, *Irish Republicanism and Socialism: the Politics of the Republican Movement 1905 to 1994*, Belfast: Athol, 1994, p. 230.
15. *An Phoblacht/Republican News*, 21 November 1985.
16. Letter from Alex O'Connor, *An Phoblacht/Republican News*, 5 December 1985.
17. Letter from Antóin MacUaid, *An Phoblacht/Republican News*, 28 November 1985.
18. M. Ryan, *War and Peace in Ireland: Britain and the IRA in the New World Order*, London: Pluto, 1994.
19. *An Phoblacht/Republican News*, 23 June 1983.
20. *An Phoblacht/Republican News*, 17 November 1983.
21. *An Phoblacht/Republican News*, 26 February 1987.
22. *An Phoblacht/Republican News*, 17 November 1983.
23. *An Phoblacht/Republican News*, 4 April 1985.
24. *An Phoblacht/Republican News*, 18 April 1985.
25. *An Phoblacht/Republican News*, 16 October 1986.
26. *An Phoblacht/Republican News*, 16 October 1986.
27. Quoted in P. Taylor, *Provos: the IRA and Sinn Féin*, London: Bloomsbury, 1997, p. 290.
28. Letter from Thomas Cullen, *An Phoblacht/Republican News*, 16 October 1985.

29. *An Phoblacht/Republican News*, 4 November 1982.

30. *An Phoblacht/Republican News*, 30 October 1985.

31. *An Phoblacht/Republican News*, 30 October 1985.

32. P. Taylor, op. cit., p. 290.

33. Ibid. p. 291.

34. *An Phoblacht/Republican News*, 16 October 1985.

35. *An Phoblacht/Republican News*, 16 October 1985.

36. *An Phoblacht/Republican News*, 16 November 1986.

37. *An Phoblacht/Republican News*, 30 October 1986.

38. *Provos*, BBC Television, 1998.

39. E. Moloney, *A Secret History of the IRA*, London: Penguin, 2003, pp. 296–7.

40. B. O'Brien, *The Long War: the IRA and Sinn Féin*, Dublin: O'Brien, 1999.

41. E. Moloney (note 39).

42. Ibid.

43. Ibid.

44. This was acknowledged by the former Secretary of State for Northern Ireland, Peter Brooke, in a interview on the *Dispatches* programme, Channel 4, May 1996.

45. For a general discussion, see P. Dixon, *Northern Ireland: the Politics of War and Peace*, Basingstoke: Palgrave, 2001.

46. E. Moloney (note 39), p. 252.

47. Ibid. p. 253.

48. *An Phoblacht/Republican News*, 28 April 1983.

49. For an analysis of the views of SDLP members, see J. Evans, J. Tonge and G. Murray, 'Constitutional Nationalism and Socialism in Northern Ireland: the Greening of the SDLP', in P. Cowley, D. Denver, L. Harrison and A. Russell (eds), *British Elections and Parties Review* 10, London: Frank Cass, 2000, pp. 117–32.

50. BBC, *Behind the Headlines*, 31 January 1985.

51. *An Phoblacht/Republican News*, 7 February 1985.

52. *An Phoblacht/Republican News*, 7 February 1985.

53. Evans, Tonge and Murray.

54. *An Phoblacht/Republican News*, 8 August 1985.

55. Sinn Féin, *A Scenario for Peace*, Dublin: Sinn Féin, 1987, pp. 5–7.

56. *An Phoblacht/Republican News*, 12 November 1987.

57. B. Hayes and I. McAllister, 'British and Irish Public Opinion towards the Northern Ireland Problem', *Irish Political Studies*, vol. 11, 1996, pp. 61–82.

58. The *New Ireland Forum Report* was published on the 3 May 1984, Dublin: Stationery Office. The Report was a detailed analysis of the Northern Ireland problem from a constitutional nationalist perspective.

59. Sinn Féin, *The Sinn Féin/SDLP Talks*, Dublin: Sinn Féin, 1988.

60. Paragraph 3.20 of the *New Ireland Forum Report* op cit.

61. SDLP document No. 1, 17 March 1988, Linen Hall Library, Belfast (P. 3395).

62. Ibid.

63. Sinn Féin (note 59).

64. John Hume leader's address at the SDLP annual conference, 21–23 November 1986.

65. Sinn Féin (note 59) p. 7.

66. Ibid. p. 6.
67. Ibid. (SDLP final document) p. 19.
68. For a discussion of this, see M. Cunningham, 'The Political Language of John Hume', *Irish Political Studies*, vol. 12, 1997, pp. 13–22.
69. SDLP Document No. 1, 17 March 1988. Letter from John Hume to Gerry Adams, 17 March 1988 (P. 3395).
70. *News Letter*, 3 February 1989.
71. Ibid.
72. *Belfast Telegraph*, 3 February 1989.
73. Ibid.
74. *News Letter*, 6 February 1989.
75. Ibid.
76. Ibid.
77. Interview with Austin Currie, 2 August 1995.

Chapter 10   Towards Peace, Pan-Nationalism and Co-Determination

1. D. Bloomfield, *Political Dialogue in Northern Ireland: the Brooke Initiative, 1990–92*, London: Macmillan, 1998.
2. J. McGarry and B. O'Leary, *Explaining Northern Ireland*, Oxford: Blackwell, 1995.
3. *Irish News*, 28 September 1992.
4. *Irish Times*, 28 September 1992.
5. G. Murray, *John Hume and the SDLP*, Dublin: Irish Academic Press, 1998, p. 191.
6. E. Moloney, *A Secret History of the IRA*, London: Penguin, 2003.
7. Ibid.
8. Ibid.
9. See E. Mallie and D. McKittrick, *The Fight for Peace: the Secret Story behind the Irish Peace Process*, London: Heinemann, 1996.
10. Ibid.
11. E. Moloney op. cit. highlights the role of informers in this respect (note 6).
12. K. Bean, 'The New Departure', *Irish Studies Review*, No. 10, Spring 1995, p. 6.
13. E. Collins, *Killing Rage*, London: Granta, 1997.
14. Mallie and McKittrick (note 9), p. 107.
15. Sinn Féin, *Setting the Record Straight*, Dublin: Sinn Féin, 1994.
16. Quoted in H. Patterson, *The Politics of Illusion: a Political History of the IRA*, London: Serif, 1997, p. 240.
17. As one example, the former Belfast (Oldpark) Sinn Féin Councillor Bobby Lavery argued that 'for most republicans the attitude to the Free State remained the same'. Interview, 16 March 2000.
18. Interview with Mitchel McLaughlin, 28 June 2000.
19. G. Adams, *Free Ireland: Towards a Lasting Peace*, Dingle: Brandon, 1995, p. 211.
20. *Sunday Tribune*, 27 August 1995.
21. A. McIntyre, 'Modern Irish Republicanism: the Product of British State Strategies', *Irish Political Studies*, vol. 10, 1995, p. 117.
22. Sinn Féin (note 15), p. 26.
23. McIntyre (note 21).

24. T. Harnden, *Bandit Country: the IRA and South Armagh*, London: Hodder and Stoughton, 2000.

25. Sinn Féin, *Self-determination, Consent, Accommodation of Minorities and Democracy in Ireland*, Submission to the Irish Forum for Peace and Reconciliation, Dublin: Sinn Féin, 1995.

26. *Irish Reporter*, 21 February 1996, p. 46.

27. J. Bowyer-Bell, *The Secret Army*, Dublin: Poolbeg, 1998, p. 641.

28. M. Ryan, *War and Peace in Ireland: Britain and the IRA in the New World Order*, London: Pluto; L. Clarke, *Broadening the Battlefields: the H Blocks and the Rise of Sinn Féin*, Dublin: Gill and Macmillan, 1987.

29. J. Stevenson, *We Wrecked the Place: Contemplating an End to the Northern Irish Troubles*, New York: Free Press, 1995, p. 217.

30. In an otherwise sound account Peter Taylor's *Provos* (London: Bloomsbury, 1997) incorrectly states that this loss occurred in 1987. It also refers to the 1982 election; there was no general election in (Westminster) Britain in 1982.

31. M. Ó Muilleoir, *Belfast's Dome of Delight: City Hall Politics, 1981–2000*, Belfast: Beyond the Pale, 1999.

32. Patterson (note 16).

33. *Sunday Business Post*, 2 January 1994.

34. Mallie and McKittrick (note 9).

35. Patterson (note 16), p. 225.

36. See Mallie and McKittrick (note 9), p. 383.

37. Sinn Féin, *The Nature of the Problem and the Principles Underlying its Resolution*, Submission to the Irish Forum for Peace and Reconciliation, Dublin: Sinn Féin, 1994.

38. Sinn Féin, *Self-determination, Consent, Accommodation of Minorities and Democracy in Ireland: Responses and suggested amendments to paper from Dr Asbjorne Eide*, Submission to the Irish Forum for Peace and Reconciliation, Dublin: Sinn Féin, 1994.

39. See B. O'Leary and J. McGarry, *The Politics of Antagonism*, London: Athlone, 1996.

40. Sinn Féin, *Charter for Justice and Peace in Ireland*, Dublin: Sinn Féin, 1995.

41. *Starry Plough*, Autumn 1994.

42. Adams (note 19), p. 229.

43. Sinn Féin, *Initial Discussion of a New Framework for Agreement*, Submission to the Irish Forum for Peace and Reconciliation, 5 May 1995.

44. G. Murray, *John Hume and the SDLP*, Dublin: Irish Academic Press, p. 237.

45. W. Flackes and S. Elliott, *Northern Ireland: a Political Directory 1968–1999*, Belfast: Blackstaff, 1999.

46. *Sunday Tribune*, 15 February 1997.

47. Mallie and McKittrick (note 9), p. 277.

48. *Irish News*, 21 January 1998.

49. *Irish Times*, 19 January 1998.

50. For the best discussion, see Moloney (note 6).

51. *An Phoblacht/Republican News*, 23 March 1996.

52. *An Phoblact/Republican News*, 23 March 1996.

53. E. Moloney (note 6).

54. Ibid.

55. Ibid., pp. 450–54.
56. Ibid.
57. See his first speech on the subject, quoted in J. Tonge, *Northern Ireland: Conflict and Change*, London: Pearson, 2002, p. 179.
58. B. O'Brien, *The Long War: the IRA and Sinn Féin*, Dublin: O'Brien, 1999.
59. One prominent youthful member of Sinn Féin, for example, visited an 'errant' *cumann* in North Dublin to persuade it to adopt the 'right' approach.
60. Interview with Robbie Smyth, 27 April 2000.

Chapter 11   The Good Friday Agreement: SDLP Triumph?

1. See T. Hennessey, *The Northern Ireland Peace Process*, Dublin: Gill and Macmillan, 2000.
2. J. Tonge, 'From Sunningdale to the Good Friday Agreement: Creating Devolved Government In Northern Ireland', *Contemporary British History*, 14/3, 2000, pp. 39–60.
3. D. O'Hearn, S. Porter and A. Harpur, 'Turning Agreement to Process: Republican Aims and Change in Northern Ireland', *Capital and Class* 69, 1999, pp. 1–26.
4. G. Adams, Presidential address to Sinn Féin *Ard Fheis*, Dublin, 1998.
5. For a discussion, see B. Hadfield, 'The Belfast Agreement, Sovereignty and the State of the Union,' *Public Law*, 1998, Winter, p. 615.
6. W. Hazleton, 'Devolution and the Peace Process in Northern Ireland', Paper presented to the American Political Science Association Annual Conference, Boston, 1998.
7. Adams (note 4).
8. Ibid.
9. Part 11 of SDLP Commentary on Draft Policy Document on Proposals Relating to the Present Situation in Northern Ireland, prepared Sept. 1971 and presented at Special Executive Meeting, 15 Jan. 1972.
10. Anthony McIntyre, quoted in K. Bean and M. Hayes (eds), *Republican Voices*, Monaghan: Seesyu, 2001.
11. Part 11 SDLP Commentary (note 9).
12. Ibid.
13. Ibid.
14. Interview with the author, October 2001.
15. First stated by John Hume, 1964.
16. See J. Evans, J. Tonge and G. Murray, 'Constitutional Nationalism and Socialism in Northern Ireland: the Greening of the SDLP', in P. Cowley, D. Denver, A. Russell and L. Harrison, *British Elections and Parties Review* 10, London: Frank Cass, 2000.
17. B. Feeney, *Sinn Féin. A Hundred Turbulent Years*, Dublin: O'Brien, p. 368.
18. Evans, Tonge and Murray (note 16). Percentage formulated from SDLP membership data from ESRC project R000222668, led by J. Tonge.
19. Ibid.
20. Ibid.
21. Ibid.
22. Clause 2.2 of SDLP amended constitution.

23. Statement by Seán Farren, 30 Nov. 1998 in relation to public meeting of the Patten Commission held in Ballymena, Co Antrim.

24. *Northern Ireland Life and Times Survey*, 1998, www.ark.ac.uk The *Northern Ireland Life and Times Survey* is a joint project between Queen's University, Belfast and the University of Ulster. The Centre for Social Research at Queen's University, Belfast, provided these statistics for this survey as weighted figures in relation to the SDLP and Sinn Féin.

25. The SDLP Analysis of the Nature of the Problem, May 1991.

26. SDLP, 'Policing Realities and Responsibilities', policy document presented to the fourth annual conference, 1973.

27. Hennessey (note 1), pp. 152–3.

28. SDLP response to Patten Report, 6 Dec. 1999.

29. Sinn Féin, *Policing in Transition*, Ard Chomhairle Policy Paper, Dublin: Sinn Féin, 1998.

30. www.irlnet.com, 25 Nov. 2002.

31. Northern Ireland Office, *Report of the Independent Commission on Policing for Northern Ireland, Implementation Plan*, June 2000.

32. *Irish Times*, 12 Feb. 2001.

33. SDLP Policing Special—SDLP website http://www.sdlp.ie, 2001.

34. Hennessey (note 27), p. 153.

35. Alex Attwood MLA, Criminal Justice Review, SDLP Press Release, 30 March 2000.

36. *Sunday Tribune*, 10 June 2001.

37. *Belfast Telegraph*, 17 March 1997.

38. Evans, Tonge and Murray (note 16).

Chapter 12   Triumph Or Sell-Out? Sinn Féin and Constitutional Republicanism

1. Sinn Féin discussion document, 24 March 1998. For further analysis of this, see part III of T. Hennessey, *The Northern Ireland Peace Process*, Dublin: Gill & Macmillan, 2000.

2. Ibid.

3. *An Phoblacht/Republican News*, 25 November 1999, p. 9.

4. *Irish Times*, 8 January 1998.

5. B. Hadfield, 'The Belfast Agreement, Sovereignty and the State of the Union', *Public Law*, vol. 15, Winter 1998, p. 615.

6. *An Phoblacht/Republican News*, 23 April 1998, p. 6.

7. See Adams' intended address to plenary session at Stormont Castle, *An Phoblacht*, 13 June 1996.

8. *An Phoblacht/Republican News*, 23 April 1998, p. 14–15.

9. Sinn Féin Ard Chomhairle paper to 1998 Ard Fheis, Resolution Number 1.

10. Northern Ireland Human Rights Commission, *Making a Bill of Rights for Northern Ireland*, Belfast: NIHRC, 2001.

11. Sinn Féin, *A Bridge to the Future*, Dublin: Sinn Féin, 1998.

12. Sinn Féin 94th Ard Fheis; Ard Chomhairle Political Report, pp. 2–11, Dublin: Sinn Féin.

13. Gerry Adams, Presidential address to Sinn Féin Ard Fheis, 29 March 2003.

14. Speech to Sinn Féin Ard Fheis, September 2001.

15. www.irlnet.com, 26 August 2001.

16. For Sinn Féin's view of this, see G. Kelly, 'A New Beginning to Policing?' *Left Republican Review*, 2, Sept./Oct. 2000, pp. 4–7. For an academic critique of the dilution of Patten, see J. McGarry, 'Police Reform in Northern Ireland', *Irish Political Studies* 15, 2000, pp. 183–92.

17. Interview with Cllr Lyn Fleming, Derry, 29 June 2000.

18. Interview with Cllr Michael Brown, Belfast, 16 March 2000.

19. Interview with Cllr Bobby Lavery, Belfast, 16 March 2000.

20. *Fourthwrite*, no. 1, 2000, p. 7.

21. *Sunday Business Post*, 27 August 2000.

22. Sinn Féin, *A New Opportunity for Peace*, Westminster Election Manifesto 1997, Belfast: Sinn Féin.

23. E. Moloney, A *Secret History of the IRA* London: Penguin, 2003.

24. Ibid.

25. *Sovereign Nation*, vol. 1, no. 7, July/August 1999.

26. O'Brien, S. Breen, 'A New Era?', *Fortnight*, 382, January 2000, p. 7.

27. H. Patterson, 'Towards 2016', *Fourthwrite*, no. 1, Spring 2000, p. 5.

28. *Saoirse*, February 2000.

29. See transcript of RTE interview with Brendan Hughes, *Sovereign Nation*, vol. 2, issue 3, March/April 2000; interview with Bernadette McAliskey, vol. 2, issue 4, July/August 2000.

30. *Saoirse*, October 2000.

31. *Saoirse*, July 1998.

32. A. McIntyre, 'Modern Republicanism and the Belfast Agreement', in R. Wilford (ed.), *Aspects of the Belfast Agreement*, Oxford University Press, 2001, p. 204.

33. *Observer*, 22 July 2001.

34. Quoted in *Irish Post*, 28 July 2001.

35. Quoted in S. Elliott and W. Flackes (2000), *Northern Ireland: a Political Directory 1968–1999*, Belfast: Blackstaff.

36. *Financial Times*, 17 June 1998.

37. *Guardian*, 6 July 1999.

38. *Observer*, 10 October 1999.

39. www.irlnet.com, 5 June 2001.

40. Speech at Westminster Hall, 10 July 2001. www.irlnet.com, 11 July 2001.

41. Ibid.

42. www.irlnet.com. 31 October 2001.

43. Interview, *Hearts and Minds*, BBC Northern Ireland, 25 November 2001.

44. www.irlnet.com, 28 June 2001.

45. Bríd Rogers, SDLP Press Release, 31 Jan. 2000.

46. Ibid. 3 July 2001.

47. Seán Farren speaking in Ballymena on the occasion of his selection as SDLP candidate for the forthcoming general elections, SDLP press release, 21 Feb 2001.

48. *Irish Times*, 2 July 2001.
49. Ibid. 16 June 2001.
50. www.irlnet.com, 20 June 2001.
51. www.irlnet.com, 14 June 2001.
52. Interview with Mitchel McLaughlin, 28 June 2000.
53. www.irlnet.com, 20 June 2001.
54. Ibid.
55. A. Lijphart, *The Politics of Accommodation: Pluralism and Democracy in the Netherlands*, Berkeley: University of California Press, 1975; S. Wolinetz, 'The Consociational Party System' in K. Luther and K. Deschouwer (eds), *Party Elites in Divided Societies: Political Parties in Consociational Democracy*, London: Routledge, 1999.
56. M. Gallagher, 'Stability and Turmoil: Analysis of the Results', in M. Gallagher, M. Marsh and P. Mitchell (eds), *How Ireland Voted 2002*, London: Palgrave, 2003.
57. Discussion with Sinn Féin councillor, 3 March 2003.
58. Private information.
59. *Irish Independent*, 29 November 2003.
60. See Bruce Arnold, 'Who do we blame for what has happened?', *Irish Independent*, 29 November 2003.
61. See Susan McKay, 'We've got the truth down our thick gullets—the agreement is in tatters', *Sunday Tribune*, 30 November 2003.
62. www.irlnet.com, 12 May 2003.
63. www.irlnet.com, 28 April 2003.
64. Speech at the Hillgrove, Monaghan, 26 October 2002, www.irlnet.com, 28 October 2003.
65. The strategy was clearly outlined by Declan Kearney in a John Joe McGirl Commemoration Speech in August 2002: 'Beyond the road map: Preparing for power', www.irlnet.com, 3 September 2002.
66. Ibid.
67. Speech at the Hillgrove, Monaghan, 26 October 2002, www.irlnet.com, 28 October 2003.
68. Ibid.
69. See, for example, interview in *Irish News*, 30 July 1996.
70. 'Hume-Adams: The Road to Disaster?' *Sovereign Nation*, vol. 2, no. 2, Jan./Feb. 2000.
71. Quoted in www.irlnet.com, 19 July 2001.
72. Quoted in *Labour Left Briefing*, June 1996, p. 16.
73. Danny Morrison, 'Stretching republicans too far', *Guardian*, 13 July 1999.
74. See G. Boyce, 'Northern Ireland: the Nationalists', in M. Watson (ed.), *Contemporary Minority Nationalism*, London: Routledge, 1990.
75. J. Todd, 'Nationalism, Republicanism and the Good Friday Agreement' in J. Todd and J. Ruane (eds), *After the Good Friday Agreement: Analysing Political Change in Ireland*, Dublin: UCD Press, 1999.
76. M. Smith, *Fighting for Ireland: the Military Strategy of the Irish Republican Movement*, London: Routledge, 1995.
77. M. Cox, 'Northern Ireland after the Cold War' in M. Cox, A. Guelke and F. Stephen (eds), *A Farewell to Arms? From 'Long War' to Long Peace in Northern Ireland*,

Manchester University Press, 2000. For a briefer summary, see M. Cox, 'The Cold War and the IRA Ceasefire', *Fortnight*, 367, Dec. 1996/Jan. 1997, pp. 20–2.

78. Ibid.

79. F. Halliday, 'Peace Processes in the Late Twentieth Century', in Cox *et al.* (eds) (note 74), p. 284.

80. A. Guelke, 'Comparatively Peaceful': South Africa, the Middle East and Northern Ireland', in Cox *et al.* (eds) (note 74).

81. M. Ryan, *War and Peace in Ireland: Britain and the IRA in the New World Order*, London: Pluto, 1994.

82. S. Breen (2000), 'On the One Road', *Fortnight*, 388, 2000, pp. 18–19.

83. See A. McIntyre, 'Modern Irish Republicanism: the Product of British State Strategies', *Irish Political Studies*, vol. 10, 1995. A. McIntyre, 'Modern Republicanism and the Belfast Agreement: Chickens Coming Home to Roost, or Turkeys Celebrating Christmas?' in R. Wilford (ed.), *Aspects of the Belfast Agreement*, Oxford University Press, 2001.

84. Ibid.

85. Quoted in M. Mansergh, 'The Background to the Peace Process', *Irish Studies in International Affairs*, vol. 6, 1995, pp. 145–58.

86. B. O'Brien (note 26), p. 395.

87. *An Phoblacht/Republican News*, 25 November 1999.

88. McIntyre (note 32).

89. K. Bean, 'The Lava Cools: from Insurrectionary Social Movement to Bureaucratic Political Party: Irish Republicanism 1977–1998', Paper presented to the British Association of Irish Studies Bi-Annual Conference, Bath Spa University College, September 1998.

90. P. Taylor, *Provos*, London: Bloomsbury, 1997.

91. Ibid.

Chapter 13   New Agendas? Nationalist Social and Economic Policies

1. See H. Patterson, *The Politics of Illusion: a Political History of the IRA*, London: Serif, 1997.

2. *An Phoblacht/Republican News*, 13 April 2000.

3. Motion 110 from Pádraig Pearse *Cumann*, Derry; Motion 111 from Jim Murphy *cumann*, Fermanagh.

4. C. Moffat, 'Selection—the Big Test', *Fortnight*, 390, December 2000.

5. C. Moffat, 'Must Try Harder', *Fortnight*, 396, June 2001.

6. See Sinn Féin's *Westminster Election Manifesto 2001* for the party's outline of education targets.

7. Sinn Féin, *'Educate that you might be free': Sinn Féin's Proposals for an Irish Education System in the 21st Century*, Dublin: Sinn Féin, 2003.

8. Ibid.

9. Ibid.

10. Motion 36 from the Jim Murphy *Cumann*, Fermanagh.

11. Sinn Féin (note 7), p. 41.

12. The exact figures were 77.9 per cent and 52.1 per cent respectively. See J. Tonge and J. Evans, 'Party Members and the Good Friday Agreement', *Irish Political Studies*, vol. 17, no. 2, 2002, pp. 59–73.

13. Sinn Féin 1998, *Putting People First*, Dublin: Sinn Féin, 1998, p. 11.

14. Ibid.

15. See *Fortnight*, 384, April 2000.

16. *An Phoblacht/Republican News*, 13 April 2000.

17. Sinn Féin, *Health for All*, Dublin: Sinn Féin, 2001.

18. SDLP Annual Conference, 1997.

19. Interview with Seán Crowe, Dublin, 27 April 2000.

20. Interview with Michelle Gildernew MLA, Belfast, 28 June 2000.

21. Ibid.

22. *Housing: a Fundamental Human Right*, Motion 118, SDLP Annual Conference, 2000.

23. SDLP Policies on SDLP website.

24. Ibid.

25. Housing: a Fundamental Human Right, op. cit., footnote 3.

26. D. O'Hearn and C. Fisher, *Jobs or Just Promises? the IDB and West Belfast*, West Belfast Economic Forum, 1999; D. O'Hearn, S. Porter and A. Harpur, 'Turning Agreement to Process: Republicanism and Change in Northern Ireland', *Capital and Class*, 69, 1999, pp. 7–25.

27. *Innovation, Investment and Social Justice: a Framework for Economic Development*, SDLP Discussion Paper, February 1999.

28. Ibid.

29. Sinn Féin, *A New Opportunity for Peace*, Westminster election manifesto, Sinn Féin, 1997, p. 8.

30. *An Phoblacht/Republican News*, 27 November 1997, p. 6.

31. Sinn Féin, *The Private Finance Initiative*. Position Paper, Policy Review and Development Department, Dublin: Sinn Féin, 2003, p. 4.

32. Ibid.

33. Sinn Féin, *Sinn Féin and the European Union*, Ard Chomhairle draft policy discussion paper, Dublin: Sinn Féin, 1999, p. 18.

34. Sinn Féin, *Sinn Féin and the European Union*, policy discussion document, Dublin: Sinn Féin, 2003.

35. Sinn Féin (note 33), p. 18.

36. Ibid., p. 11.

37. Sinn Féin, *Sinn Féin and the European Union*, policy discussion document, Dublin: Sinn Féin, 2003.

38. Sinn Féin, *Europe and Irish Republicanism: a Discussion Document*, Dublin: Sinn Féin, 1992.

39. www.irlnet.com, 20 June 2001.

40. *SDLP European Election Manifesto, 1999*.

41. SDLP Annual Conference, 1985.

42. *Fortnight*, 387, July/August 2000, p. 11.

43. Sinn Féin, *Women in Ireland*, Dublin: Sinn Féin, 1999.

44. Ibid., p. 28.

45. Interview with Joan O'Connor, Sinn Féin HQ, Dublin, 27 April 2000.
46. Interview with Eoin O'Broin, 16 March 2000.
47. SDLP Annual Conference, motion put forward by Ormeau/Stranmillis branch, 1999.
48. Sinn Féin, *Civic Forum—Proposals*, Belfast: Sinn Féin, 1999.
49. Interview with Mary Nelis MLA, 28 June 2000.
50. SDLP Press Release, 'Women Breaking Through the Glass Ceiling', 14 May 2001.
51. Interviews with Joan O'Connor, 28 April 2000; Micheal McDonnacha, Sinn Féin, Dublin, 29 April 2000.
52. Opening address by Brid Rogers, 'Women in Public Life' Conference, Belfast, 10 May 2001.
53. D. O'Hearn, S. Porter and A. Harpur (note 26).

Chapter 14   Conclusion

1. BBC Northern Ireland *Hearts and Minds* poll, 9 May 2000. See G. Murray, 'The Good Friday Agreement: An SDLP Analysis of the Northern Ireland Conflict' in J. Neuheiser and S. Wolff (eds), *Peace at Last? The Impact of the Good Friday Agreement on Northern Ireland*, Oxford: Berghahn, 2002.
2. Micky McMullen, quoted in K. Bean and M. Hayes (ed.), *Republican Voices*, Monaghan: Seesyu, 2001, p. 122.
3. I. McAllister, *The Northern Ireland Social Democratic and Labour Party*, Basingstoke: Macmillan, 1977.
4. *An Phoblacht/Republican News*, 28 April 1983.
5. *An Phoblacht/Republican News*, 17 November 1983.
6. *An Phoblacht/Republican News*, 6 February 1998.
7. T. Hennessey, *The Northern Ireland Peace Process: Ending the Troubles?*, Dublin: Gill & Macmillan, 2000, p. 220.
8. Mitchell McLaughlin, 'Sinn Féin and the Peace Process', seminar presentation, University of Salford, November 2000.
9. K. Bean, 'Defining Republicanism: Shifting Discourses of New Nationalism and Post-Republicanism', in M. Elliott (ed.), *The Long Road to Peace*, Liverpool University Press, p. 133.
10. Interview with Peter Anderson, 29 June 2000.
11. Interviews with Mitchell McLaughlin and Michelle Gildernew, 28 June 2000.
12. As one party worker in Dublin put it: 'I've read the thing [GFA] over and over again and it will never create a united Ireland'. Interview, 28 April 2000.
13. J. Todd, 'Nationalism, Republicanism and the Good Friday Agreement' in J. Todd and J. Ruane (eds), *After the Good Friday Agreement: Analysing Political Change in Northern Ireland*, Dublin: UCD Press, 1999.
14. See K. Bean, 'Defining Republicanism: Shifting Discourses of New Nationalism and Post Republicanism', in M. Elliott (ed.), *The Long Road to Peace in Northern Ireland*, Liverpool University Press, 2002.
15. See R. English, *Armed Struggle*, London: Macmillan, 2003.

16. For an example of such a portrayal, see M. Ryan, *War and Peace in Ireland: Britain and the IRA in the New World Order*, London: Pluto, 1994.

17. *Sovereign Nation*, June/July 2001, p. 5.

18. K. Bean, 'The Lava Cools: from Insurrectionary Social Movement to Bureaucratic Political Party: Irish Republicanism 1977–1998', paper presented to the British Association of Irish Studies Annual Conference, Bath Spa University College, September 1998, p. 8.

19. See S. Breen, 'Fast Operators', *Fortnight*, 394, April 2001, p. 7.

20. See Ryan (note 16), M. Cox, A. Guelke and F. Stephen, *A Farewell to Arms? From 'Long War' to Long Peace in Northern Ireland*, Manchester: Manchester University Press, 2000, as examples of this thesis.

21. K. Bean (note 14).

22. B. Feeney, *Sinn Féin. A Hundred Turbulent Years*, p. 428.

23. Ulster Marketing Surveys poll, reported in *Belfast Telegraph*, May 2001.

24. R. MacGinty, 'A Breathing Space for Devolution. Public Attitudes to Constitutional Issues in a Devolved Northern Ireland', Birmingham: Economic and Social Research Council, 2002, p. 11.

25. G. Murray, *John Hume and the SDLP*, Dublin: Irish Academic Press, p. 221.

26. *Fourthwrite*, Summer 2001, p. 3.

27. Mark Durkan, Leadership Address to the SDLP 32nd Annual Conference, 2002.

28. See M. Kelly and J. Doyle, 'The Good Friday Agreement and Electoral Behaviour—an Analysis of Transfers under PRSTV in the Northern Ireland Assembly Elections of 1982 and 1988', paper presented to the Political Studies Association of Ireland Annual Conference, University College Cork, October 2000.

INDEX

Abortion Act 1967 250–1

Adams, Gerry and: Abstentionism 157; Anglo-Irish Agreement 149, 151; Brooke-Mayhew talks 179; Electoralism 115; Good Friday Agreement 237; Irish America 190–1; PIRA ceasefire 1974–5 77; Political strategy 102–3, 131; Prisoner releases 199; republican violence, 154; Whitelaw talks 69–70; West Belfast Constituency 123, 186, 194

African National Congress 215

Agnew, Paddy 111

Ahern, Dermot 179

Ahtisaari, Martti 225

Alliance Party xi, 43, 44, 50, 111, 171

Alliance Party of Northern Ireland (APNI) 41, 175

Anglo-Irish Agreement 93, 136–52, 258

Anglo-Irish Secretariat 143, 176–7

Anglo-Irish Treaty 2, 3

An Phoblacht-Republican News 20, 30, 36–7, 149, 159

Anti-internment demonstration 27

Assembly (1982) 121, 122

Atkins, Humphrey 63, 108, 118

Attwood, Alex 211

Barry, Peter 127, 145

Bell, Ivor 69

Biaggi, Mario 87

Blair, Tony 193–4

Bloody Friday 70

Bloody Sunday 68, 85, 90

Bradford, Roy 113

Brighton bomb 133

Brooke-Mayhew talks 177–81

Brooke, Peter 175–6

Bruton, John 193, 233

Burns Commission 242

Cahill, Joe 20–1, 40, 236

Caraher, Ben 12

Carey, Hugh 85, 86

Carron, Owen 111

Carter, Jimmy 85–6

Catholic Church 1, 30, 36, 107, 108, 111, 112

Chichester-Clark, James 39

Civic Forum 251

Civil Rights Movement 7, 10–11, 18, 19, 22, 246, 257

Clann na Poblachta 15

Clinton, Bill 85, 99, 190–1

Connolly Association 18

Constitutional Convention 50–4

Coogan, Tim Pat 16

Cooper, Ivan 10, 27

Cosgrove, Liam 81

Costello, Seamus 41

Council of Ireland 1, 9, 44, 48, 49, 51, 126–7

Craig, James 3, 5

Craig, William 48, 52–4

Crowe, Sean 130

Currie, Austin 10, 11, 12, 48, 57, 58, 62, 63, 110, 121, 172

De Bruin, Bairbre 229, 244–5

Delors, Jacques 177

Democratic Unionist Party (DUP) 171, 175, 212, 228, 230–1, 255, 266

De Valera, Eamon 2–3, 14, 83, 84, 264

Devlin 11, 26, 57

Devlin, Joe 4–5

Devlin, Paddy 10, 48, 59–60

Diplock Courts 145

Doherty, Kieran 111

Doherty, Pat 149, 228

Donlon, Sean 90–91, 143

Downing Street Declaration 183–17, 196

Drumm, Jimmy 71, 102

Drumm, Maire 71

Duffy, John 10

Duffy, Paddy 57

Dungiven Parliament 27

297

Durkan, Mark 210, 259, 266, 267

Elections: General Election 1918 1–2; General Election 1955 13–14; General Election 1959 16; Northern Ireland Assembly 1974 45–6; Constitutional Convention 1975 52; General Election 1979 62–3; Fermanagh and South Tyrone By-Elections 1981 110–11; Northern Ireland Assembly 1982 121; General Election 1983 123; 1984 European Election 154; General Election 1992 186; General Election 1997 194; Northern Ireland Assembly 1998 209; General and Local Elections 2001 210–11; Assembly Elections 2003 230–1
Éire Núa 36–9, 71, 72–3, 75, 79, 128–7

Falklands War 120
Farrell, Michael 16
Farren, Sean 121, 172, 227, 241–3, 268
Faul, Dennis 108, 112
Faulkner, Brian 26, 44
Feeley, Frank 121
Fianna Fáil 2, 5, 14, 15, 19, 30, 31, 32, 33, 57, 62, 64, 90, 107, 153, 179, 233, 264, 268
Fianna Uladh 15
Fine Gael 2, 19, 45, 62, 81, 9, 146, 161, 172, 173, 193, 233
Fitt, Gerry 10, 11, 12, 48, 56, 57, 62–4, 65, 94, 123
FitzGerald, Garret 90, 91, 119, 120, 122, 136, 141, 258
Four Horsemen 86
Framework Documents 189–90, 192, 197
Friends of Ireland 87, 92

Gallagher, Tommy 211
Gardiner Report 55
Gibney, Jim 108, 158, 181, 233
Gildernew, Michelle 211, 245–6, 262
Goodall, Sir David 137
Good Friday Agreement 196–203, 213, 215–19, 232, 267–8
Goulding, Cathal 17, 18, 19, 22
Government of Ireland Act 1920 1, 178, 214
Griffith, Arthur 2
Green Book 103

Hartley, Tom 166
Haughey, Charles 32, 91, 120, 122, 123, 128, 132, 146, 153, 172, 178
Haughey, Denis 121

Hendron, Joe 121, 186, 211
Hermon, Sir John 146
Hughes, Brendan 160
Hume-Adams Dialogue 162, 166–74, 182, 235, 259
Hume, John: convention elections, 50; decommissioning 227; Diplock Courts 145; election to Westminster 123; Europe 93–6, 154, 249, 259; Fitt's resignation 63–4; Irish America 85–90, 93; leadership of SDLP 94, 259, 266, 268; Sunningdale 48; withdrawal from Stormont, 26
Hutchinson, Billy 245

Internment 40, 68
Ireland Act 1949 6
Irish Commission for Justice and Peace 111
Irish Forum for Peace and Reconciliation 188
Irish Labour Party 31, 172, 268
Irish National Caucus 92
Irish National Liberation Army (INLA) 41, 132
Irish Independence Party 60, 105, 116
Irish Republican Army (IRA) (Pre-1969 Split) IRA: border campaign 13–16; civil rights 18–19; partition 4; Continuity IRA 221–2, 260; Official IRA: ceasefire 40–4; feud with PIRA 76; military strategy 30–2; proroguing of Stormont 67; Provisional IRA: abstentionism 30–1; Army Council 160, 193; bombing operations 104, 133–4, 185, 192, 260; ceasefires 74–7, 79, 187, 196; decommissioning 223–6, 230; formation 13; Good Friday Agreement 215–19; Libya 100; proroguing of Stormont 67–9; tactical use of Armed Struggle (TUAS) 187–8; targeting of SDLP 57–8; Whitelaw talks 69–70
Real IRA 194, 220–3, 260
Irish Republican Socialist Party 116
Irish Union Association 5

Johnston, Roy 20

Kelly, Gerry 70, 160
Kelly, Liam 15
Kennedy, Edward 85–6, 87, 191
Kennedy-Smith, Jean 191
King, Tom 176

Lemass, Sean 7, 83
Logue, Hugh 27
Lynch, Jack 30, 64, 90, 91

MacBride Principles 89, 247
MacGiolla, Tomas 21
Maghery Convention 8
Maginnis, Ken 111
Maguire, Frank 110
Maguire, Tom 30, 159
Mallon, Seamus 57, 58, 62, 63, 65, 119, 123, 133, 197, 266–7, 268
Mandelson, Peter 207
Maskey, Alex 32, 153, 230
Mason, Roy 56, 59, 60–1, 81, 106–7
Mayhew, Patrick 176
McAlisker, Bernadette 109–110
McAteer, Eddie 6–7, 8, 10
McAteer, Fergus 60
McDonnacha, Micheal 149
McFarlane, Bik 111
McGrady, Eddie 48, 49, 57, 121, 172, 210, 267, 268
McGuinness, Martin 69, 150, 152, 154, 187, 211, 228–9, 241–3
McKee, Billy 32, 40
McKevitt, Mickey 194
McLaughlin, Mitchell 149, 166, 182, 223, 262
McManus, Frank 60
McMullan, Mickey 226
McStiofáin, Seán 20, 23, 69, 78
Meehan, Martin 22
Mitchell Report 192, 220
Mitchell, Tom 14
Molyneaux, James 60, 176
Morrison, Danny 102, 149, 154, 164, 166, 228, 234
Moynihan, Daniel 86
Murray, Raymond 108

National Democratic Institute for International Affairs (NDI) 87–8
National Democratic Party 7–10, 12
Nationalist Party 4, 6–7, 11, 12
National League of the North 4–5
Neave, Airey 61, 82, 107, 132
New Ireland Forum 121–8, 132–3, 138–40
NORAID 87, 92, 99
Northern Ireland Human Rights Commission 216

Ó Brádaigh, Ruarí 37, 39, 69, 75, 109, 130, 153, 160–2
Ó Caoláin, C. 214
Ó Conaill, Dáithí 69, 79, 130
O'Dowd, Niall 190

Ó Fiaich, Tomas 107–8, 162
O'Hanlon, Feargal 14
O'Hanlon, Paddy 63, 65, 121
Ó Néill, Criostoir 14
O'Neill, Terence 7, 18, 39
O'Neill, Tip 86, 87
Orange Order 78, 130
O'Sullivan, D., 90

Paisley, Ian 18–19, 176, 266
Parades Commission 199
Patten, Chris 206, 216–17
Peace People 81
Price Sisters 70–1
Prior, James 118–20, 132, 141

Ramaphosa, Cyril 225
Reagan, Ronald 92, 143
Rees, Merlyn 55
Reid, Alec 162–3, 166, 171, 171
Republican Sinn Féin 162, 220–3
Reynolds, Albert 186, 233
Rogers, Brid 58, 210–11, 226, 253, 268

Sands, Bobby 110–11, 118
Sands-McKevitt, Bernadette 214, 220
Saor Uladh 15
Shelvyn, Myles 69
Sinn Féin: abstentionism 15, 22, 73, 151–2, 156–62, 181, 228, 234; advice centres 112; Anglo-Irish Agreement 147–152; Assembly election (2003) 266; Broadcasting Ban 147; Brooke-Mayhew talks 177; decommissioning 224–6; dialogue with SDLP, 166–70; Downing Street Declaration 184–7; education policy, 241–2; electoral competition, 208–12, 226–31; electoralism 110–17, 153–6, 227–8, 261–2; employment policy, 246–8; ETA 100, 235; European Union 248–50; extent of change, 233–9; Good Friday Agreement 213–15, 217–18, 238, 253, 255–6, 260; health policy 244–5; housing policy 245–6; hunger strikes 106–113, 116; Irish America 99; local government 244; moral agendas, 250–2; New Ireland Forum 127–8; Nice Treaty 228; policing 205–8, 216–17, 232; policy documents 19, 36–9, 71, 72–3, 75, 79, 128, 165, 166, 181–2, 233, 245; PLO 100; Republican Split 1969 20–4; socialism, 130–1, 152; Sunningdale 73–4, 198
Smyth, Martin 55

Social Democratic and Labour Party (SDLP): Anglo-Irish Agreement 138–47; Brooke-Mayhew talks 178; civil disobedience 26–7; dialogue with Sinn Fein, 166–70; Duisburg talks, 171–3; education policy, 242–3; electoral competition, 208–12; employment policy 246–8; Europe 93–6, 248–50; formation 10–13; health policy, 245; housing policy 246–7; local government, 243–4; membership 203–5; moral agendas 250–2; negotiated independence 55, 57, 59; New Ireland Forum 124–7, 257; policing 54, 146, 200, 205–8; policy documents 59, 65–6, 201–2, 204; Sunningdale 46–9; withdrawal from Stormont 26

Soderbergh, Nancy 191
South, Sean 14
Special Powers Act 4–5, 27, 39

Stalker, John 145–6
Sunningdale Agreement 44–6

Taylor, John 41
Thatcher, Margaret 62, 92, 120, 123, 143
Thirty-Two County Sovereignty Committee 220–2, 260
Trimble, David 19, 227
Troops Out Movement 105
Twomey, Seamus 40

Ulster Defence Association (UDA) 70, 171
Ulster Unionist Party (UUP) 171, 175, 224, 228–9
Ulster Volunteer Force (UVF) 78–9
United Irishman 20

Whitelaw, William 69–70
Wilson, Paddy 10
Wilson, Padraig 223
Wolfe Tone Society 18